FAMILIES IN CRISIS

The Impact of Intensive Family
Preservation Services

MODERN APPLICATIONS OF SOCIAL WORK

An *Aldine de Gruyter Series of Texts and Monographs*

SERIES EDITOR

James K. Whittaker

Ralph E. Anderson and Irl Carter, **Human Behavior in the Social Environment: A Social Systems Approach** (fourth edition)

Richard P. Barth and Marianne Berry, **Adoption and Disruption: Rates, Risks, and Responses**

Larry K. Brendtro and Arlin E. Ness, **Re-Educating Troubled Youth: Environments for Teaching and Treatment**

Kathleen Ell and Helen Northen, **Families and Health Care: Psychosocial Practice**

Marian Fatout, **Models for Change in Social Group Work**

Mark Fraser, Peter J. Pecora, and David Haapala (eds.), **Families in Crisis: The Impact of Intensive Family Preservation**

James Garbarino, **Children and Families in the Social Environment**

James Garbarino, Patrick E. Brookhouser, Karen J. Authier, and Associates, **Special Children—Special Risks: The Maltreatment of Children with Disabilities**

James Garbarino, Cynthia J. Schellenbach, Janet Sebes, and Associates, **Troubled Youth, Troubled Families: Understanding Families At-Risk for Adolescent Maltreatment**

Roberta Greene, **Social Work with the Aged and Their Families**

Roberta R. Greene and Paul H. Ephross, **Human Behavior Theory and Social Work Practice**

Jill Kinney, David Haapala, and Charlotte Booth, **Keeping Families Together: The Homebuilders Model**

Paul K. H. Kim (ed.), **Serving the Elderly: Skills for Practice**

Robert M. Moroney, **Shared Responsibility: Families and Social Policy**

Robert M. Moroney, **Social Policy and Social Work**

Peter J. Pecora and Mark Fraser, **Evaluating Family Preservation Services**

Peter J. Pecora, James K. Whittaker, Anthony N. Maluccio, Richard P. Barth, and Robert D. Plotnick, **The Child Welfare Challenge: Policy, Practice, and Research**

Steven P. Schinke (ed.), **Behavioral Methods in Social Welfare**

Albert E. Trieschman, James K. Whittaker, and Larry K. Brendtro, **The Other 23 Hours: Child-Care Work with Emotionally Disturbed Children in a Therapeutic Milieu**

Deborah Valentine and Patricia G. Conway, **Guide for Helping the Natural Healer**

Harry H. Vorrath and Larry K. Brendtro, **Positive Peer Culture** (second edition)

Betsy Vourlekis and Roberta R. Greene (eds.), **Social Work Case Management**

Heather B. Weiss and Francine H. Jacobs (eds.), **Evaluating Family Programs**

James K. Whittaker and James Garbarino, **Social Support Networks: Informal Helping in the Human Services**

James K. Whittaker, Jill Kinney, Elizabeth M. Tracy, and Charlotte Booth (eds.), **Reaching High-Risk Families: Intensive Family Preservation in Human Services**

James K. Whittaker and Elizabeth M. Tracy, **Social Treatment, 2nd Edition: An Introduction to Interpersonal Helping in Social Work Practice**

Hide Yamatani, **Applied Social Work Research: An Explanatory Framework**

FAMILIES IN CRISIS

The Impact of Intensive Family
Preservation Services

Mark W. Fraser, Peter J. Pecora,
and David A. Haapala

ALDINE DE GRUYTER

New York

About the Authors

Mark W. Fraser holds a Ph.D. in Social Welfare from the University of Washington. He is an Associate Professor at the Graduate Schoool of Social Work, University of Utah and director of the School's Ph.D. Program.

Peter J. Pecora holds a Ph.D. in Social Welfare from the University of Washington. He is the Manager of Research with The Casey Family Program, and an Associate Professor at the School of Social Work, University of Washington.

David A. Haapala holds a Ph.D. in Psychology from the Saybrook Institute. He is Executive Director of Behavioral Sciences Institute in Federal Way, Washington, where he and Dr. Jill Kinney co-founded the Homebuilders Program in 1974. BSI is a nonprofit corporation to provide, promote, and study community-based family-centered services.

ALDINE DE GRUYTER
A division of Walter de Gruyter, Inc.
200 Saw Mill River Road
Hawthorne, New York 10532

The paper used in this publication meets the minimum requirements of American National Standards for Information Sciences—Permanence of Paper for Printed Library Materials, ANSI Z39.48-1984. ∞

Library of Congress Cataloging-in-Publication Data
Families in crisis : the impact of intensive family preservation
  services / Mark W. Fraser, Peter J. Pecora, and David A. Haapala,
  authors.
     p. cm. — (Modern applications of social work)
    Includes bibliographical references and index.
    ISBN 0-202-36069-5 (cloth). — ISBN 0-202-36070-9 (paper)
    1. Family social work—United States—Case studies. 2. Family
social work—Utah—Case studies. 3. Family social work—Washington
(State)—Case studies. I. Fraser, Mark W., 1946- . II. Pecora,
Peter J. III. Haapala, David, 1949- . IV. Series.
HV699.F26 1991
362.82′0973—dc20
                         91-6430
                         CIP

Manufactured in the United States of America

10 9 8 7 6 5 4 3 2 1

Contents

Contributors to this Volume and Their Position
at the time the Project was Conducted

Jeffrey A. Bartlomé

FIT Project Coordinator
University of Utah

Robert B. Bennett

Research Assistant
FIT Project

Mark W. Fraser

Co-Principal Investigator
FIT Project

David A. Haapala

Co-Principal Investigator
FIT Project

Nance M. Kohlert

Research Assistant
FIT Project

Robert E. Lewis

FIT Project Liaison
Utah Department of Social Services

Vicky L. Magana

Research Assistant
FIT Project

Peter J. Pecora

Co-Principal Investigator
FIT Project

Wanda M. Spaid

Family Specialist
FIT Project

Connie K. Sperry

Research Assistant
FIT Project

Acknowledgments

Funding for the research described in this book was made possible by a grant from the U.S. Office of Human Development Services, Administration for Children, Youth, and Families (Grant No. 90-CW-0731). In addition, we are grateful to the Edna McConnell Clark Foundation which provided supplemental funding for much of the data analysis presented in Chapters 9, 10, and 11. To both agencies and the many dedicated people in them, we are indebted.

Special thanks to Katherine McDade, who coordinated the data collection in the *Homebuilders** Program in Washington; and to Beth Moses, Stephen Magura, and Mary Ann Jones for their advice regarding the Family Risk Scales. Cecelia Sudia, Alice Fuscillo, Soledad Sombrano, Charles Gershensen, Bonnie Lantz, and Phillip AuClaire helped us identify critical research questions. Our colleagues on the Social Work Educators Projects** at the University of Washington and Case Western Reserve University helped us identify many of the program and policy issues that research in this field must address.

We also want to thank David Olson and his associates for permission to use the FACES III, and Robert Milardo for permission to use his Social Support Inventory. Jeff Bartlomé and Ardis Gillund were instrumental in managing the data files and providing support to interviewers in Utah. Jewel Nelson, Kim Apple, Sandy Hiskey, Mary Broadbent, and Mary Hubbert provided word processing support throughout the project. We are especially indebted to Chirapat Popuang who helped us format data files and conduct the event history data analysis. Finally, the advice and encouragement of the following IFPS administrators, supervisors, and therapists is appreciated. This project could not have been accomplished without their dedication to their clients and this program model:

Utah

Administrators
Norm Angus, Judie Barrus, Jerry Callister, Joan Henninger, Tim Holm, Jean Nielsen, Ray Terry, Ed Van Sweden, Bill Ward

Homebuilders™ is the trademark of Behavioral Science Institute. Subsequent references to "Homebuilders" throughout the book should be regarded as implicitly carrying the registered trademark.

Supervisors
Adrienne Boudreaux, Bonnie Lantz, Linda Mitchell, Kathleen Smith, Grant Tolley

Therapists
Paul Brandt, Bonnie Christiansen, Stephanie Duran, Ginni Gerek, Wes Hiroaka, David Kay, Mika Leatherwood, Neal Orton, Heather Whitehead

Support Staff
Chris Robinson

Washington

The Washington State Division of Child and Family Services, Department of Social and Health Services cooperated fully with the FIT project. Regional administrators, Roy Harrington, John George, Winnie Wiatrak, and Colleen Waterhouse, made possible our research work with their field staff and client families.

BSI Administrators
Charlotte Booth, Jill Kinney, Shelley Leavitt

BSI Supervisors
Karen Bream, Mary Fischer, Brewster Johnston, Diane Knutson, Peg Marckworth, Kris Romstad

BSI Therapists
Linda Alexander, Don Bender, Melissa Brooks, Colleen Cline, Ellen Douthat, Sandy Edelstein, Nancy Wells Gladow, Juanita Gonzalez, Jan Jiles, Sue McCarthy, Peggy Mandin, Don Miner, Carole Presson, Scott Reed, Jody Regan, Lauren Fry, Debbie Winkcompleck, Barb Dubin, Elaine Sonntag Johnson, Leona DeRocco, David Bryant, Francine Caroll, Beatrix Hu, Carol Mitchell, Monica Wafstet-Solin, Susan Irwin

BSI Support Staff
Connie Davis, Kelly Dittmar, Merri Hiatt, Joyce Jensen, Lois Kutscha, Kendall Richards, Kim Apple, Anne Nearn

** *Social Work Educators Project Members* (1988–1989, 1990–1991).
Gary Anderson, Rick Barth, Betty Blythe, Charlotte Booth, Betsy Cole, Arthur Frankel, David Hawkins, Vanessa Hodges, Jill Kinney, Shelly Leavitt, Tony Maluccio, Brenda McGowan, Tina Rzepnicki, Ted Teather, Elizabeth Tracy, Jim Whittaker, and Carol Williams.

Foreword

In 1930, President Herbert Hoover's White House Conference on Child Health and Protection pledged itself to certain aims for the children of this country articulated as *The Children's Charter.* This third White House Conference on Children (the first was held in 1909 and provided the impetus for the creation of the Children's Bureau in 1912) was convened shortly after the Great Depression had had a severe impact on millions of families. The Charter states as a right for every child, "a home and that love and security which a home provides; and for that child who must receive foster care, the nearest substitute for his own home." Furthermore, the Charter continues, "For every child a dwelling place safe, sanitary, and wholesome, with reasonable provisions for privacy, free from conditions which tend to thwart his development; and a home environment harmonious and enriching." And in recognition of the impact of economics on the family, "For every child the right to grow up in a family with an adequate standard of living and the security of a stable income as the surest safeguard against social handicaps."

For two generations maternal and child health, child welfare and education programs have attempted to achieve the Charter's aims of a nurturing family environment for children. However, by 1990, at the apex of a long period of economic growth, there were 12.8 million children living in poverty; more than 500,000 children living in out-of-home placements; 2.5 million reports of alleged child abuse and neglect; one child out of four was born to a single parent; and 10 million children had one or more developmental, learning, or emotional problems.

Historically, this country has struggled about its moral commitment to families and children and the various forms of care. From the colonial period onwards, the local community and subsequently the nation have been concerned about children living in families that failed to provide their basic needs. At each historical period, the consensus favored either home care or the asylum. Indenture and binding-out in families that needed child labor during the early Colonial period gave way to the use of the asylum, the alms house. When this practice was no longer considered good for children, Charles Loring Brace placed them on trains and shipped them from the eastern cities of "vice" to the rural farm families in mid-America, where

xi

morality and hard work prevailed. Again, over time, opposition developed and large institutions were built to care for the dependent, neglected, and delinquent children at the beginning of the Progressive Era.

With the advent of scientific inquiry and the emergence of a science of child development, a series of research studies revealed the deleterious impact of institutional life on the child. This marked the early use of evaluation research to change policies and programs affecting children in placement. By the late 1940s the preference was back to the primary use of a substitute family, a foster family, no longer for purposes of child labor, but for the protection and care of the child.

As the population grew and the structure of the family became more fragile, the number of children removed from their families also increased. By 1977, 502,000 children were estimated to be under the supervision of the public child welfare foster care program. Another 1.3 million children were receiving services in the home of the family or relative. Studies during the 1960s and 1970s were documenting "foster care drift" and the "warehousing" of children.

In the early 1970s, Victor Pike demonstrated in Oregon that a focused assessment of the child and family and intensive work with the family or an adoptive family reduced the number of children in long-term foster care. This effort, packaged as "permanency planning," was codified into federal legislation in 1980 through The Adoption Assistance and Child Welfare Act, P. L. 96-272. This act primarily provided an administrative and judicial review and control mechanism to insure prescribed foster care protections. Though a requirement to make "reasonable efforts" to prevent placement was included in the legislation, this was mostly ignored for nearly the first decade of implementation. The federal and state energies were devoted to moving children out of the "warehouses" and to control "drifting" within the foster care system.

Permanency planning succeeded in reducing the number of children in foster care to 276,000 by 1985. But that was the end of the honeymoon for P. L. 96-272. Foster care population has been on the rise again. By 1989 an estimated 360,000 children were in foster care and the number is still increasing. Evidence accumulated that the increase was due to several factors, including the re-entry of children into care (approximately one out of three children entering care were previously in foster care), an increase in the number of children entering annually, and a relative decrease in the number leaving foster care. The increase is primarily in young children and minority children, reflecting the impact of the use of crack cocaine by their mothers.

About the same time that Victor Pike was developing permanency planning, David Haapala and Jill Kinney in neighboring Washington were developing a Homebuilder's Model of intensive family preservation services. This effort preceded P. L. 96-272's mandate of "reasonable effort" to prevent placement and thus, along with other family-based services, was not included in the legislation in more specific terms. Only now is Congress considering legislation to further define "reasonable effort."

The development of the Homebuilder's Model represented a shift in the out-of-home child placement paradigm, from protecting the child through removal from the family to changing the family dynamics to safely nurture the child. Focus was placed on the family dynamics with a belief that changes could occur in a relatively short period of time to modify the nurturing environment sufficiently to insure the safety of the child. The process entailed intensive work with the entire family at the place of residence through the use of crisis intervention, social learning, and Rogerian theory supplemented with concrete and advocacy services for a time-limited period of approximately four to six weeks.

The theoretical construct and operational strategy limited the program to "families in crisis" involving an "imminent risk" of a child being removed from the family. Furthermore, when the safety of the child was in jeopardy or when no parent was willing to accept services, no effort was made to provide intensive services. There was recognition that not all families faced with placement disruption could be served with this model.

Earlier, about the mid-1960s, another paradigm shift occurred—evaluative research. There had been earlier research studying the effectiveness of services, but the formal development of conceptual frameworks and methodologies of evaluation has occurred within the past 25 years. The powerful tools of behavioral and social science research in conjunction with advances in statistical theory and operations research were applied to naturalistic programs serving families and children.

Initially, the evaluative findings of the effectiveness of intensive family preservation programs were unusually high: 97 percent of the children averted placement. This attracted a great deal of attention from various groups, including the Children's Bureau. Support was provided by the Bureau for two studies to examine the conceptual framework and the outcomes of this new program.

Evaluative research theory and application have changed greatly during the past two decades, and the conjunction of an evolving Homebuilder's model and diverse conceptual frameworks for evaluation has left a trail of disparate findings. All evaluative studies are fallible. All are subject to criticism for conceptual or methodological assumptions. All, however, contribute some information to understanding complex social programs. In regard to intensive family preservation programs, all but one study is conceptualized and designed for the application of measurement and statistical theory. The conceptual framework is remarkably consistent, i.e., the use of a production framework in which the input (intensive family services) leads to a desired output (prevention of placement).

In the medical model for testing new drugs, evaluation examines in sequence: safety, dosage, effectiveness, and, ultimately, effectiveness in relation to other drugs. Paralleling this sequence, intensive family preservation services have proven their safety (primarily by refusing to accept children whose safety is at risk); dosage has changed with a reduction in time while contact hours have been held relatively constant; effectiveness is currently the issue under examination through a variety of completed and continuing studies; and two comparative assessments, one completed and one in progress, begin the final phase in the evaluative process from a clinical viewpoint. Evaluation of systems impact awaits program saturation in a local area, e.g., Wayne County, Michigan, or statewide implementation.

This book is about dosage and effectiveness. It describes in detail the blending of clinical and evaluative concepts, the process and impact of two quality programs. It makes use of measurement and statistical theory to advance our understanding of the paradigm shift in working with families under stress facing a crisis that may result in removal of a child. There is much for the reader to learn; there is much to stimulate further thought.

Charles P. Gershenson, Ph.D.
Senior Policy Analyst
Center for the Study of Social Policy

Chapter 1

Family Preservation Services to Prevent Out-of-Home Placement: The Family-Based Intensive Treatment Project

MARK W. FRASER, PETER J. PECORA, and DAVID A. HAAPALA

Introduction

A body of research and policy literature has documented what many of us have experienced firsthand or observed through the media: children are being removed unnecessarily from their families because human service programs lack both the resources and the technology to strengthen families in crisis. In many states, child placement rates are increasing. Many family advocates are concerned about the rising number of children being placed in restrictive types of correctional and psychiatric facilities.

Child welfare administrators and workers have been criticized for placing large number of children out of their homes unnecessarily. A recent Edna McConnell Clark Foundation (1985) report charged that "children are separated from their families by default. Too few alternatives are available to help them [families] stay together safely" (p. 2). In fact, many children have been placed outside their homes not once, but multiple times (e.g., Fanshel & Shinn, 1978; Rzepnicki, 1987).

To address this problem, a number of policy and program innovations were instituted by federal, state, and local authorities (see, e.g., Pine, 1986). Most notable among these were permanency planning and related program and fiscal reforms promoted by P.L. 96-272. The permanency planning reforms of the 1970s and 1980s have been supplemented recently by new programs that are designed to help children by helping families. These programs have many different names—family-based services, family-centered services, home-based services, and intensive family prevention services—and are purported to provide viable placement alternatives to out-of-home placement, significantly reducing the number of children who are placed in substitute care (e.g., Wells & Biegel, 1991; Bryce & Lloyd, 1981; Compher, 1983; Maybanks & Bryce, 1979).

1

The Homebuilders program is one of the most well-established family-centered family preservation service programs in the nation. As indicated in the following case example, Homebuilders works with multiproblem families, teaching them new skills and providing a range of services to help them stay together safely.

The Norton family was referred to Homebuilders by a public child welfare caseworker as an emergency response to increasingly violent family arguments. The caseworker, who had five years of contact with the family, said she was ready to place immediately the 14-year-old Norton boy, Bill, when Mrs. Norton requested placement because she feared for the safety of all the family members. However, when the caseworker offered Homebuilders as an alternative to placement, the parents, who had previously said that they had lost hope in keeping Bill at home, expressed interest in trying the in-home service. That was enough to send Brewster Johnston, a Homebuilders therapist, out to the Norton Home.

Brewster visited the family on the same day the referral was telephoned into Homebuilders. Arriving at the Norton home he first met Bill's parents, Arnold, an architect, and Brooke, a homemaker. Arnold and Brooke, married for 21 years, were both 43 years old.

Sitting around the kitchen table with cups of coffee, the two parents told Brewster that they felt helpless about improving their home life. They had been struggling for years to influence Bill's behavior. Adopted as an infant, Bill had been in and out of individual psychotherapy with a variety of psychiatrists, psychologists, and counselors for 11 years. He had been diagnosed as hyperactive and learning disabled. With his diagnosis had come prescriptions for Ritalin, Haldol, Thorazine, and Melleril at different times in the past. He had been placed in a residential treatment center for almost three years and returned home one and a half years prior to Homebuilders involvement. Arnold and Brooke had attended years of family therapy with Bill but had seen little positive effect. Brooke admitted that she experienced a "nervous breakdown" when Bill was three years old. She thought the breakdown was brought on by the stresses of a miscarriage and the deaths of both her mother and father. She feared that the breakdown in turn had caused Bill's problems.

Bill came into the first session late and presented Brewster with a difficult challenge. His first words to Brewster were, "Get out of here. I hate psychiatrists." Caught a bit off guard, Brewster said that he didn't always enjoy psychiatrists either and encouraged Bill to join in for awhile. Bill did sit down but said nothing more for the rest of the meeting. While Brewster thought his time with Bill seemed to be unproductive, Arnold and Brooke were amazed that Bill spent 25 minutes in the same room with Brewster.

Bill had been physically threatening his parents since he was a young boy. Brooke reported that, when angry, Bill frequently pushed her to the floor or physically blocked her exit from the house. When agitated, Bill threw things at his parents and kicked the doors. It was common for Bill to swear at Brooke. Most parental requests were met with angry defiance. Two weeks ago it was alleged that he had hit a neighbor woman in the arm with a baseball and he had recently upset another neighbor by throwing trash in his yard. Arnold and Brooke recognized that they were unable to control Bill and feared that unless something was done quickly someone in the family or neighborhood was going to be seriously hurt.

The First Week

During the first week of involvement with the Norton family, Brewster spent 11½ hours in face-to-face or telephone contact. He tried to utilize that time to learn more about the specifics of the family's problems and how they had attempted to resolve them. He also worked on ways to keep their home safe. Brewster dealt almost exclusively with Arnold and Brooke as he believed that in this case and at this time in the therapy the parents' involvement and support were crucial to a successful treatment outcome.

Brewster learned that the parents had tried various parenting ideas including parent effectiveness training and "time out" of the room for Bill when he was inappropriate. "Time out" was the major parenting technique being used now. When Bill behaved badly, Arnold or Brooke would try to get Bill to go to his room. Through observation and parent report, Brewster learned that the other main method for dealing with Bill was for Brooke to "entertain" him. She felt responsible for keeping Bill from getting bored, especially now during the summer, and as a result she spent much of the day in a state of anxiety as she tried to find things to do that would please Bill. Arnold and Brooke agreed that the current ways of managing Bill were not very effective.

Brewster recognized that Brooke's role in the family was central to the whole family. Because Arnold worked at his office downtown during the day, Brooke was the primary parent who interacted with Bill. Therefore, Brewster emphasized strategies that he hoped would address her concerns and problems. For example, Brooke seemed to get more upset about Bill's behavior than did Arnold. Brewster used that information to teach Brooke about rational emotive therapy as a method to help her gain better control over her own thoughts, feelings, and behaviors. Brewster taught her to dissect specific thoughts like, "I'm going to die from embarrassment when Bill acts inappropriately in public." In pulling apart these statements Brooke began to learn how she exaggerated some situations, felt more unhappy by placing unrealistic demands on herself and her son, and readily dismissed too many of her helpful and rational thoughts.

Brewster also began introducing Brooke and Arnold to the parenting technique of attending to a child's appropriate behavior as it occurred. He talked about the research support for reinforcing actions that parents value and had them go through an exercise that clarified the importance and positive impact of rewarding Bill's good behavior when they saw it.

The Second Week

By the second week of service Brewster had, with the help of the family, established treatment goals. During the second week the majority of his time was spent in reinforcing the notion of goals, reminding family members of the goals that had been specified, and working on techniques and strategies to achieve these goals.

The most basic goal developed for this family was to increase the parents' sense of hope so that Bill could remain at home. When Brewster made his first visit to the Nortons, Arnold and Brooke told Brewster they had no hope that Bill could live with them at home. At the end of the second week the parents reported a moderate increase (two points on a five-point scale) in their level of hope. Apparently this was due to many factors. Brewster listened empathically to the parents describe their problems with Bill. They also showed interest in a new reward system Brewster set up with them to recognize Bill's appropriate behavior. Brewster continued teaching Brooke how better to control her irrational thinking and upset feelings, and Brewster encouraged her to behave in unpredictable ways with Bill to break out of the conditioned ineffective behavioral interactions that she had established with Bill. For example, instead of struggling with Bill if he tried to keep her from leaving the room, Brewster recommended that she go limp or start to sing. Brewster believed that it was crucial that Brooke learn new and competing behaviors to those ineffective ones that she had been using with Bill.

The second goal called for Arnold and Brooke to reward Bill's acceptable behavior more frequently. According to Brewster's assessment, Bill received attention from Arnold or Brooke as they tried to get him to leave the room, when he misbehaved by swearing, arguing, etc. Bill also had come to depend on his mother to keep him amused. This expectation kept Brooke prisoner in her own home.

By using rationales related to less time having to be spent involved in Bill's disruptive behavior, Brewster was able to convince the Norton parents, especially Brooke, to try a system that rewarded Bill when he behaved according to his parents' wishes. At the end of the second week Brooke said she liked the new system for charting and rewarding Bill's behavior. While Bill only earned about half the total points possible this week, he did turn in some of his points to get a special snack on three afternoons and use of the go-cart for three 20-minute sessions.

Brooke learned that Bill could earn many points but still maintain his irritating manner. Brewster thanked her for trying the point system and agreed that adjustments needed to be made in the procedures. He told her that this was to be expected. Nonetheless, he told Brooke that he was pleased with her consistency in carrying out the reward system.

Brooke and Brewster made some changes in the way Bill could earn points, discussed these changes with Arnold and Bill, then put the modified system back into action. Brewster also encouraged Arnold and Brooke to call the police if Bill go so out of control that he began physically to hit them. Bill was told of the plan to call police if he hit his parents.

The third goal was to increase counseling sessions with Bill. Arnold and Brooke were emphatic—their sense of hope that things would work out demanded that Bill participate with Homebuilders. Bill had not attended any other therapy sessions after the initial meeting of the first week and his parents were afraid that he would continue that pattern. If they were going to work hard to make life better at home, then Bill needed to show some real effort.

To increase the chances that Bill would meet with him, Brewster worked out a plan that allowed Bill to rent a parent-approved videotape for every 45 minutes of active participation in therapy. Reluctantly, Bill agreed to the plan.

In Brewster's first meeting alone with Bill the boy told him that he did not like social workers because they all ask questions and try to counsel him when he doesn't need any help. Brewster simply expressed sympathy for Bill's plight. That session lasted 15 minutes.

Brewster made the Norton parents agree not to threaten or plead with Bill to participate in counseling. Instead, he urged them to remind Bill of the possible videotape he could earn whenever he complained that there was nothing to do. After a couple of days, Bill called Brewster at the office and politely asked if Brewster could come over to the house "to talk." Bit by bit Brewster was able to get Bill to talk about what made him angry. Brewster also was able to point out how his quick temper was letting others, especially kids at school, get the best of him by setting him up to get into trouble. Bill agreed that other kids knew how to upset him. At this point Brewster told Bill about a technique that Bill might learn if this topic could be discussed at the next meeting. By the end of the week the boy had earned a rental video.

The Third Week

Arnold and Brooke reported that their level of hope that Bill could remain home was at the same level as it was last week. Bill continued his verbal abusiveness; this was particularly noticeable early in the week. There were various times during the week when the Nortons thought of giving up. Brooke, however, did agree that she felt somewhat less frustrated when she practiced her rational emotive therapy skills. She also followed a suggestion of Brewster's to engage in at least two pleasant events during the week. She went out of the house alone for a couple of hours on one day and got herself an ice-cream cone on another day. These events helped her feel better. Fall had come and Bill was to start school in a new building next week, and Brooke told Brewster that changing schools and the start of school made her feel more hopeful.

Brooke showed Brewster the high level of points that Bill had earned for the week. Bill had received about 85 percent of the total points possible. Bill actively enjoyed the positive attention, cupcakes, and quarters for video games he was earning.

After a slow start this week Bill spent a total of one and a half hours with Brewster. Much of the time was spent discussing effective social skills. Bill had already memorized the steps of anger management that Brewster taught him. During a therapy session early in the week Bill threw some carrots and swore at Brewster. Brewster was initially shocked, but was pleased later when Bill apologized for his tantrum.

The Fourth Week

Brooke told Brewster that her sense of hope was much higher this week because Bill's behavior was better almost all week. She also said that she was becoming better every day at using rational emotive therapy as little irritations cropped up. For example, she told Brewster that she knew that Bill would misbehave again in the future—that might be expected. But if he were to misbehave that would not mean that things aren't working. Nothing works perfectly, she noted.

Bill had told his mother that he wasn't going to go to school this week unless Brooke bought him some new pants. He had bleached his pants by mistake and said he couldn't wear them now. After consulting with Brewster, Brooke agreed to tell Bill that she could not afford to buy him new pants and politely remind him that this was a problem that he could solve on his own. Brooke knew that Bill wanted to see his friends who would be at school but also steeled herself for how she would handle the situation if he did not go to school. However, to Brooke and Arnold's delight, Bill went to school every day.

The latter part of the week was spent in reviewing what had been learned and preparation for handling problems without Brewster. Brooke, Arnold, and Bill all expressed satisfaction with the final revisions of the reward system. Bill was earning almost all of his points, and Brooke said that she preferred telling Bill that he was doing things right.

Bill met with Brewster for an hour and 15 minutes this week. He worked on negotiation skills since threatening had not been working lately. Bill agreed that he was getting more of what he wanted because he was willing to do what his parents asked. He agreed to try apologizing to his mother when he did something wrong. Brewster wrote down on a sheet of paper the steps that Bill might follow when he did something his mother disapproved of and he wanted to rectify the situation.

Near the end of the fourth week Brewster made referrals to a Tough Love group for Bill's parents and an assertiveness training class for the whole family.

After a short farewell party held on Brewster's last in-home counseling visit, he terminated the Norton family from Homebuilders services. Brewster and the Nortons had worked together for just one month and two days.

One year later, Bill continued with his parents. His parents no longer discussed placing Bill in out-of-home care, and Brooke reported that while the family still had ups and downs, the relationship between Bill and his parents was much better.

Is it possible to work with families so troubled? So chaotic? Increasingly the answer is yes. The treatment model described above, called "intensive family preservation services," is one among many models emerging in innovative child welfare, family services, mental health, and youth services agencies across the nation. Intensive family preservation service programs represent a promising method of treating families so troubled that out-of-home placement for the children would have been seen in the past as the only safe solution.

Program Variation Sparks Confusion

Within the broad framework of family preservation services, there is wide variation across the nation in the kind of interventions, duration of services, size of caseloads, and components of service that characterize these programs. Perhaps this is inherent to all program innovations. It is one of the reasons why research findings on "family-based" services have been confusing and contradictory. Despite a growing body of literature on family preservation programs, it is not clear what these services are and who benefits from them.

There is enormous variation in the service characteristics of these new programs. The programs themselves are described using terms such as *family support, family-centered, home-based, placement prevention,* and *family-based* services. The term *family support* has been used as an umbrella under which to cluster a broad range of family-strengthening programs. While home-based or family preservation service programs have been cited as family support programs, these programs are relatively distinct from prenatal, early childhood education, parent education, home-school-community linkage, day-care, and other family-focused programs that tend to provide one type of service (e.g., education, housing, financial, or counseling), work with clients exclusively in an office or classroom, provide treatment over a long period of time (one year or more), or plan/monitor client services delivered by other agencies. (For examples of these types of programs, see Jones, 1985, pp. 27–34; Levine, 1988; Yale Bush Center in Child Development and Social Policy, and Family Resource Coalition, 1983.)

Recently, the Child Welfare League of America (1989) proposed a trichotomized topology of family-centered programs:

1. *Family resource, support, and education services.* Community-based services that assist and support adults in their roles as parents. These services should be equally available to all families with children and should not impose criteria for participation that might separate or stigmatize certain parents.

2. *Family-centered services.* These services encompass a range of activities for families with problems that threaten their stability such as case management, counseling/therapy, education, skill-building, advocacy, and/or provision of concrete services.

3. *Intensive family-centered crisis services.* These services are designed for families in crisis, at a time when removal of a child is imminent, or the return of a child from out-of-home care is being considered. They share the same philosophical orientation and characteristics as family-centered services, but what is different is the intensity of service (including time frame and caseload size). The caseload should range from two to six families—families should be seen an average of eight to ten hours per week. Approximately 60% of worker time should be spent in direct face-to-face contact with families, and the time period of intervention should be from 4 to 12 weeks. In addition, the emphasis is upon providing intensive counseling, education, and supportive services to families in serious crisis, with the goal of protecting the child, strengthening and preserving the family, and preventing what would be an unnecessary placement of children, or promoting the return of children in out-of-home care.

The target population is families in serious crisis, including families no longer able to cope with problems that threaten family stability, families in which a decision has been made by an authorized public social service agency to place a child outside the home, and families whose children are in temporary out-of-home care and are being reunited. Thus, the service is appropriate for families served by social service, juvenile justice, or mental health systems. Adoptive or foster families facing potential disruption are also appropriate for this service.

Unfortunately, the distinction between the latter two categories is not definitive, but the taxonomy does help clarify the program design issues faced by practitioners and administrators in the field. A general topology that we have found helpful classifies these programs into three types as shown in Figure 1.1. The first is family-based or family-centered services (FBS), which encourages a wide variety of family programs, some of which focus on placement prevention while others focus on family strengthening. These programs may be office- or home-based, short- or long-term, intensive or diffuse. The second is family-centered home-based services (HBS), which have many or all of the characteristics of the FBS programs, except that the majority of services are provided in the family's home setting. The third type is intensive family preservation services (IFPS), which is short-term, home-based, and intensive.

Currently, the Edna McConnell Clark Foundation and other program advocates are promoting the use of the term *intensive family preservation services* to designate programs that deliver both clinical and concrete services in the home setting, and provide a more intensive service than other family-centered programs (e.g., provision of a minimum of five hours of client contact per week with a service duration of about 60 days or less) (Edna McConnell Clark Foundation, 1985; Whittaker, Kinney, Tracy, &

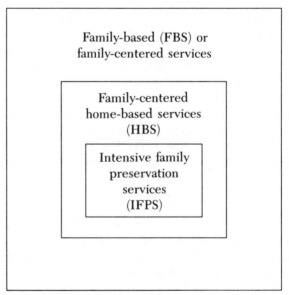

Figure 1.1.   A typology of family-based service programs.

Booth, 1990). The programs evaluated for this report meet the criteria commonly listed for IFPS programs and intensive family-centered crisis services. Throughout the remaining chapters, when reviewing the general literature on family-based or family-centered services we will use the term *family-based services* (FBS). When referring specifically to programs that are home-based, family-centered, and intensive, we will use the term *intensive family preservation services* (IFPS).

The purpose of this book is to summarize the findings from an evaluation of IFPS programs in two states, Utah and Washington. The evaluation, called the family-based intensive treatment (FIT) research project, was designed to identify families that benefit or fail to benefit from intensive family preservation services.

Intensive Family Preservation Services

IFPS have become an important alternative to out-of-home placement. IFPS therapists are distinguished from many other types of child welfare and mental health therapists in that they provide a wide range of counseling, advocacy, training, and concrete assistance to families. As indicated in the example of the Norton family, services are provided in the family's natural environment—primarily the home—and are directed towards maintaining children with their families.

Typically, IFPS therapists carry small caseloads of between two and six families, and they or one of their colleagues are on call at all times to provide 24-hour-a-day case coverage. Services are crisis-oriented, intensive, and brief. On average, they are provided for between four and eight weeks, and it is not uncommon for IFPS therapists to spend ten or more hours a week with a family during the initial stages of treatment and five to eight hours a week thereafter. The family is viewed as the fundamental service unit and most of the counseling takes place at the convenience of the family. Services are rarely, if ever, rendered in an office setting because many IFPS models draw on ecological and social learning theories (see, e.g., Bronfenbrenner, 1979). IFPS therapists argue that a more accurate understanding of family life and interaction is to be found in the family's natural environment. The provision of or advocacy for resources such as food stamps, income assistance, transportation, medical care, day care, and employment training is coordinated through the worker. IFPS staff also provide a variety of clinical services, including training in child management, effective communication (e.g., active listening), managing anger and other emotions, de-escalating crises (including working with family members who have threatened or attempted suicide), and avoiding the use of physical force or violence.

Evaluation Issues in Intensive Family Preservation Services

Recent studies indicate that the provision of IFPS prevents placement (see Chapter 2). However, lacking a definitive body of controlled studies, the literature must be viewed with caution. The IFPS programs have emerged in child welfare agencies across the country at an astonishing pace; and they appear to provide a new resource to support families and prevent or delay out-of-home placement. But many prior evaluations have been flawed by small samples, weak designs, and poor measurement.

To ensure that emerging IFPS programs maintain their promise, more specific, research-based service guidelines are needed. While state policymakers and program administrators appear reasonably certain that IFPS provide an important community-based alternative to out-of-home placement programs, they lack reliable guidelines that specify which elements of IFPS produce desirable outcomes for particular types of families.

Moreover, on the basis of research to date, the correlates of treatment success and failure are not clear, and this has at least one serious implication. Because the provision of these services leads to a situation in which children who are thought to be at risk of child neglect and other social problems are *not* removed from the home, some children may be endangered by the decision to provide IFPS rather than substitute-care services. In addition, the provision of IFPS is a gamble in the sense that the placement rate in spite of service participation appears to range between 10 and 35%. While one of the benefits often cited by program proponents is that these services result in less restrictive and shorter placements, a small proportion of the children in families that receive services may be put in jeopardy of child maltreatment or other dangers—homicide, suicide, and family violence. These risks could be reduced if it were possible to specify those families which are not likely to benefit from treatment. To date, however, little work has been done on the correlates of treatment success and failure. Consequently, there are few data to permit the development of more specific service standards, supplementary service strategies, and intake criteria.

Purpose and Methods of the Study

In an effort to contribute to an empirical base from which service guidelines might be constructed, a research project with the purpose of describing factors associated with IFPS failures and successes was designed. IFPS programs in two states—Utah and Washington—participated in the study. The central research question that provided a focal point for the investigation was, What factors are associated with IFPS failures?

Service failure was defined as the placement of a child outside the home with someone other than a relative for two weeks or more within 12 months following IFPS intake. Runaway behavior for two weeks or more was included as a failure condition. Consequently, when we use the term *placement* or *service failure*, it refers to a set of circumstances in which a child is living outside the home "on the street," with neighbors or friends, or in any number of agency-related short- and long-term out-of-home placement settings such as a foster family home, group home, residential treatment center, receiving home, juvenile detention, or a psychiatric hospital. Conversely, service success was defined as the maintenance of children with their families during the provision of IFPS and the 12-month follow-up period.

A variety of information describing parent and child functioning before and after treatment was collected. In addition, the events antecedent to placement or service failure were studied. (See Chapter 4 for a description of the research design and measures.) A number of measures of family functioning were adopted to assess the immediate impact of IFPS on family adaptability, cohesion, social support, parental functioning, and child behavior. These data were used to identify the child and family characteristics, as well as the elements of service, that appear to be associated with treatment failure/success.

Project Objectives

The FIT research project was designed to produce information for agencies that may be considering the adoption, design, or refinement of IFPS. Data were collected to identify the elements of IFPS that appear to help families to "stay together safely." In addition, one goal of the project was to specify the characteristics of children and families who benefit and fail to benefit from IFPS treatment.

The specific objectives of the FIT project were to:

1. Collect data on three different kinds of variables that may be related to the outcome of IFPS: (a) family and client characteristics; (b) service characteristics; and (c) child welfare organization and worker characteristics.
2. Obtain a sample of clients from IFPS programs operating under both public and private auspices.
3. Describe placement outcomes by specific failure conditions, (e.g., foster family care, group care).
4. Describe the effect on service outcomes of client, treatment, and worker characteristics.

Intensive Family Preservation Services in Utah and Washington

In the early 1980s, administrators from the departments of social services in Utah and Washington made major commitments to the provision of family preservation services. In Washington, these services were delivered by the Homebuilders Program, a division of the Behavioral Sciences Institute (BSI). BSI is a private, nonprofit organization, which engages in fee-for-service contracts with state and local agencies. In Utah, the services were provided by the public Department of Human Services through regional offices, which had responsibility for the delivery of a variety of social services. The Utah IFPS staff were trained extensively by staff members from the training division of the Behavioral Sciences Institute. Consequently, a similar method of treatment was used in each state, but the auspices—private versus public—differed.

Utah

Utah was selected for the study because services were delivered by a public social services agency. The Utah IFPS programs were built upon the findings of a federally funded project that began in 1982 in West Valley City, a suburban community of Salt Lake City. In this original project, intensive behaviorally oriented therapists employing a functional family therapy approach (Alexander & Parsons, 1982) and paraprofessional trackers were offered to status offenders, minor delinquents, and their families. A 30-day follow-up of families served by the project showed that the staff were successful in preventing child placement in 82% of the families served.

Upon the project's completion, the executive director of the State Department of Human Services funded two family preservation demonstration projects by continuing the program in West Valley (also known as Kearns) and beginning another program in the Ogden Community Operations Office (Callister, Mitchell, & Tolley, 1986; Lantz, 1985). Ogden is located 35 miles north of Salt Lake City. It is bordered on the west by the Great Salt Lake and on the east by the Wasatch Mountains. Whereas the Kearns community operations site served primarily urban families, the Ogden office served both urban and rural families.

Shortly after the establishment of the Kearns and Ogden demonstration projects, IFPS resources in the state expanded markedly. Although they did not participate in the FIT project, five other regional community operations offices opened small IFPS programs in 1986. Referral procedures became more explicit and funds for cross-site training were released. Within social service district boundaries, any child who was in danger of out-of-home placement or, in a small number of cases, who was currently in placement but could be reunified with her or his family was declared eligible for family preservation services. Eligibility for services also was contingent upon an assessment that the child's safety could be reasonably ensured and that the child's parents were willing to schedule an initial meeting with IFPS therapists. All referrals were screened by a IFPS supervisor or a local placement screening committee. Over a one-year period, most IFPS therapists received 30 hours of training in the Homebuilders model of treatment by BSI trainers who were sponsored by a Child Welfare Training Project at the Graduate School of Social Work, University of Utah. In addition to this formal training and individual supervision, therapists in each IFPS program met weekly as teams to review cases.

Treatment took place in the family home and consisted of 30 to 50 hours of face-to-face contact provided over a 60-day period. As discussed in Chapter 6, a number of clinical services such as skill building, resource mobilization, relationship enhancement, and issue reframing were used to increase family functioning. While treatment was behaviorally oriented, it drew from rich literatures on Rogerian intervention and ecological theory. Caseload size was controlled. Therapists were never assigned more than six families at one time. By restricting caseloads, staff were afforded more time to work with families. The extra time allowed them to coordinate community resources on behalf of families and to work with the natural helping networks of parents and children. In a few cases (less than ten), a tracker-advocate was assigned to assist a parent or child who needed extensive assistance. Team members and supervisors maintained regular contact with juvenile court judges, probation workers, school personnel, and mental health and community service agencies. In addition, training about IFPS was provided to community groups and related service providers such as youth service organizations and juvenile court intake officers (Callister et al., 1986).

Washington

Washington was selected as a site because IFPS were provided by a private not-for-profit organization, the Homebuilders program of BSI, which has an impressive history of developing and testing early models of intensive, in-home family treatment. Conceived by David Haapala and Jill Kinney, the Homebuilders model of IFPS was founded in 1974 at Catholic Community Services in Tacoma, Washington (Kinney, Madsen, Fleming, & Haapala, 1977). During 1979–1980, Homebuilders provided services as part of a special project to evaluate the effectiveness of IFPS to prevent the psychiatric hospitalization of mentally ill and severely behaviorally disturbed children and youth (Kinney & Haapala, 1984).

In 1981, BSI was formed as a new organizational base for the Homebuilders program. Through purchase of service contracts with the Washington State Department of Social and Health Services, the Homebuilders program provided services to prevent out-of-home placement. To be eligible for service, a referring agency had to determine that at least one child within a family would be immediately placed out of the home unless intensive placement prevention services were provided. Referrals came from child protective services, juvenile court, and other community agencies, based on such problems as family violence, child abuse or neglect, chronic truancy, delinquency, and parent-adolescent conflict.

To ground their service strategies, Homebuilders staff draw from Rogerian, cognitive-behavioral, crisis, territorial, and ecological theories. The family within its social-physical environment is viewed as the "client" or focus of service. Families accepted by the program were seen within one day of referral, and therapists were on call 24 hours a day, seven days a week. On average, families received four weeks of service and, during that time, therapists' caseloads were generally restricted to two families. In this sense, the Utah and Washington program models differed. Utah's caseloads were two to three times as high, but families received service for twice as long.

Staff from four BSI offices that cover countywide areas (King, Pierce, Snohomish, and Spokane) participated in the project. King, Pierce, and Snohomish counties share the Puget Sound as a common border. To the east, these same three counties buttress the Cascade mountain range. Urban and rural areas exist in each of the counties; however, King County contains the city of Seattle and has the largest urban population. Spokane County is the largest population center in eastern Washington. Bordered on the east by the state of Idaho, much of Spokane County is rich, rolling farmland. BSI provided services in each of these counties before the FIT project, and staff trained in the Homebuilders model generally lived in the counties in which they were employed.

Central Features of the Family-Based Intensive-Treatment Research Project

The FIT project was designed to be one of the most comprehensive examinations of intensive family preservation treatment undertaken to date. In particular, it was distinguished by prospective data collection on 453 IFPS families, involving more than 1500 parents and children. Data were collected from four different sources: (a) parents or child caretakers, (b) children, (c) IFPS therapists, and (d) official records. The central features of the two-year study included:

1. Comparison of IFPS across two different organizational conditions (public auspices in Utah and private auspices in Washington),
2. Use of proximal and distal definitions of treatment failure (e.g.,

changes in family functioning, conditions of home life, child problems, parental problems, treatment goal achievement as well as the living situations of targeted children during and after provisions of IFPS),

3. Examination of three different types of factors—client, treatment, and worker characteristics—that have been considered to be associated with service outcomes.

Organization of the Book

This book is divided into chapters that summarize the IFPS literature, major aspects of the research project, and key findings from the study. Because of the number of measures used in the FIT project, each chapter contains a brief methods section that summarizes the measures relevant to the findings. Each chapter also contains comments on design limitations that relate directly to the chapter's topic. In addition, many chapters contain short literature summaries relevant to analyses in the chapter. In this sense, the organization of the book is unusual. Although the chapters cannot stand alone, readers need not thumb back to the methods chapter—Chapter 4— to obtain a description of the measures and design issues related to each chapter's content.

The chapters address different topics associated with IFPS and the FIT project. Chapter 2 provides a selective review of previous family-based research with an emphasis on HBS and IFPS programs. The correlates of treatment success and failure, as identified by previous research, and the major project hypotheses are presented in Chapter 3. The research design and measures of the project are described in Chapter 4 and reviewed selectively in subsequent chapters. Chapter 4 also contains an explanation of "hazard rates" and a section on design limitations. Before citing FIT project findings, we encourage you to read the limitations section carefully. Within the constraints of these limitations, we believe the findings are important and contribute to the knowledge base regarding family-centered services. Chapters 5 and 6 summarize the characteristics of the IFPS clients and services. Worker attitudes toward services, as well as their perceptions of agency and community support, are described in Chapter 7. An assessment of child, parent, and family functioning before and after the provision of services is presented in Chapter 8. Using different definitions of treatment failure, data regarding service outcomes are discussed in Chapter 9. This chapter also contains the results of the experimental aspects of the project. A very small case overflow comparison group was formed in Utah, and comparative outcome data are presented on the comparison group and a precision-matched experimental group in this chapter. Parent, child, and family conditions that are predictive of service success and failure are described in Chapter 10. Services predictive of goal achievement are described in Chapter 11. How IFPS consumers viewed the services they received is discussed in Chapter 12. Finally, the practice and policy implications of the findings are explored in Chapter 13.

Chapter 2

Family-Based and Intensive Family Preservation Services: A Select Literature Review

PETER J. PECORA

Family- and home-based services and IFPS arose out of concern that traditional child welfare services were not meeting the needs of children and their families in the United States. The field of child welfare was criticized during the 1960s and 1970s because it was believed that children were being placed in substitute care who could have remained at home. Of special concern were the disproportionate rates of placement for ethic minority families. The case records for many white and ethnic minority children who were in substitute care lacked clearly specified case plans. As a result, "foster care drift" occurred, with long-term placements, multiple placements, and no sense of permanence for many children.

Part of the problem stemmed from the fact that parental involvement and visitation were discouraged. Termination procedures and adoption practices constrained the use of adoption as a bona fide case goal. In addition, federal funding policies encouraged foster care placement and maintenance services, rather than adequately funding preventive or restorative services. Finally, most state agencies did not have adequate management information systems in place; consequently program administrators did not know how many children were currently placed in substitute care, the average length of placement, and other essential planning information.

Exposés or studies of the quality of child welfare services, and foster care in particular, were written and widely publicized by both child welfare experts and investigative reporters (e.g., Fanshel & Shinn, 1978; Gruber, 1973; Knitzer, Allen, & McGowan, 1978; Maas & Engler, 1959; Mnookin, 1973; Wooden, 1976). In addition, the growing incidence and costs of foster care, concern about the harmful effects of substitute care, the belief that some placements could be prevented, and the trend toward deinstitutionalization all prompted the development of a variety of foster care preventive programs (Emlen, Lahti, Downs, McKay, & Downs, 1978; Magazino, 1983; Jones, 1985; Shyne, Sherman & Phillips, 1972).[1] Following a brief history of family-based services (FBS), this chapter will review selected evaluation studies of FBS programs, with an emphasis upon HBS and IFPS.

Early Child Welfare Preventive Service Programs

One could say that the first family-based or home-based service programs in the United States consisted of the "friendly visitors" of the Charity Organization Societies who worked with immigrant and low-income families in their own homes to promote self-sufficiency and assimilation into American society in the late 1800s and early 1900s (Axinn & Levin, 1982; Bremner, 1970–71; Chambers, 1962).[2] In the 1950s and 1960s, programs were developed to treat "multiproblem families" in order to improve family functioning and reduce welfare dependency (cf. Brown, 1968; Geismar & Ayers, 1958; Geismar & Krisberg, 1966; Levine, 1964; Overton, 1953). But worker caseloads remained high and client contact was limited to once a week or once a month for a one- to two-year period (Hutchinson & Nelson, 1985).

During the late 1960s and mid-1970s, new program models for preventing foster care placement began to emerge, many of which used the cognitive-behavioral and/or family therapy treatment techniques that were being developed during that time. Some of these family-centered and HBS programs are still in operation. For example, in 1969 the Home and Community Treatment Team was established at the Mendota Mental Health Institute in Madison, Wisconsin. This program worked with families with three- to ten-year old children who have emotional and behavioral problems. Both in-home (4 hours per week) and in-office (2 hours per week) services were provided for an average of 15 months (Cautley, 1979; Kaplan, 1986).

During the early 1970s, a number of child welfare agencies were also successful in preventing child placement through family-focused counseling (Hirsch, Gailey, & Schmerl, 1976) or through the use of a variety of "emergency services" such as crisis counselors, homemakers, emergency shelters or foster homes, and emergency caretakers (Burt & Balyeat, 1974; National Center for Comprehensive Emergency Services to Children, 1978). These programs recognized the importance of crisis intervention and time-limited supportive services for families as means for preventing long-term foster care placement. At the same time a multidisciplinary family-based approach to preventing child maltreatment and placement was developed in Philadelphia (the Supportive Child Adult Network, or SCAN program). This program works primarily with black single-parent families and renders services for a minimum of two to four hours each week over 9- to 15-month periods (Tatara, Morgan, & Portner, 1986). A similar long-term service was established in Detroit (the PACT program) in 1977 (Callard & Morin, 1979).

A more time-limited and intensive HBS, the Homebuilders program, was developed in 1974 at Catholic Community Services in Tacoma, Washington.

As they did then, Homebuilders therapists receive referrals from the state child welfare agency for those cases where previous counseling or other services have been provided, but the children are in "imminent danger of placement." In practice, this has been interpreted to mean that the children will be placed within one week if a more intensive service is not offered. This program model—as implemented in two different states—is the subject of the FIT research study. It is characterized by low worker caseloads, high intensity (provision of an average of 37 client contact hours in 30 days), and provision of a variety of clinical and concrete services. In a number of quasi-experimental studies, it has been shown to prevent foster care placement in a high proportion of cases (e.g., Kinney et al., 1977; Haapala & Kinney, 1979, 1988). It is perhaps one of the best examples of an IFPS program.

Other family-based programs that are not home-based and intensive have been effective in treating families where child neglect is the major problem. One of the most famous programs is the Bowen Center (Sullivan, Spasser, & Penner, 1977), which used a variety of services such as emergency shelter care, homemaker assistance, preschool day care, and laundry facilities at the Center to "reach out" to parents and strengthen families. Initially, five-person teams were used with a dual focus on helping clients meet both concrete and psychosocial service needs. More recently, the program model shifted to one that is more home-based, with caseworkers seeing families individually for an average of 8.1 months, providing clinical, educational, and concrete services designed to promote healthy child development (Giblin & Callard, 1980; Kaplan, 1986, pp. 80–82). This program has also been successful in working with low-income and ethnic minority families, and represents a successful partnership between a university-based program and a state department of social services (Cabral & Callard, 1982; Van Meter, 1986). Another less intensive approach used individual caseworkers as the primary service providers (the New York State Preventive Services Demonstration Project). This is one of the most well-researched HBS programs, involving special units set up in two county departments of child welfare in New York City (Jones, Neuman, & Shyne, 1976). These units delivered a variety of services that produced continuing beneficial effects for children and families, as documented by a follow-up study five years after services were provided (Jones, 1985).

Current Status of Family-Based, Home-Based, and Intensive Family Preservation Service Programs

More recently, a large variety of "family-based" programs have been developed by both private and public child welfare agencies (some of which use more of an office-based approach to service delivery). The National Resource Center on Family-Based Services in 1988 published an annotated bibliography of 333 programs in over 25 states, a huge increase from the 20 programs listed in 1982 (National Resource Center on Family-Based Services, 1988a). These programs are serving clients from child welfare, mental health, developmental disabilities, juvenile corrections, and other major service areas. A variety of staffing and treatment models are being employed (e.g., Bryce & Lloyd, 1981; Hinckley & Ellis, 1985; Kagan & Schlosberg, 1989; Kammerman & Kahn, 1989; Kaplan, 1986; Maybanks & Bryce, 1979; Nelson, Emlen, Landsman, & Hutchinson, 1988), including those related to supporting families whose children are returning from foster care or residential treatment, or are in danger of experiencing adoption disruption (e.g., Haapala, McDade, & Johnston, 1988b; Hodges, Guterman, Blythe, & Bronson, 1989; Whittaker & Maluccio, 1988).

The field has therefore experienced a shift from a few small-scale and isolated demonstration projects to the use of FBS, HBS, and IFPS programs on a statewide basis in a number of states such as Florida, Illinois, Maryland, Michigan, Minnesota, and Tennessee (e.g., Grohoski, 1990; Holliday & Cronin, 1990). The implementation of these programs represents a commitment on the part of state and local governments to operationalize the principle that society should be willing to invest as many resources in preserving families as might be spent for substitute family care (Lloyd, Bryce, & Schultze, 1980, p. 3). Thus these services were developed to provide alternatives to out-of-home placement by improving family functioning as well as by linking families to sustaining services and sources of support (Bryce, 1979).

Yet, as the number of these programs has grown and claims of effectiveness have increased, agency administrators and policymakers have begun to ask a variety of questions:

- What specific services are we funding?
- How effective are these services in relation to improving child/family functioning and preventing foster care placement?
- Can the use of FBS, HBS, or IFPS save child welfare program funds?

Responding to these questions has been difficult, in part because of the challenges associated with implementing rigorous evaluation designs, accurate targeting of the population of clients most likely to be placed without substantial service investment, and the problem of dissimilar programs using the same categorical title or description. For example, as discussed in the first chapter, there is tremendous variation in the service characteristics of these programs, and they are sometimes described using terms such as *family support, home-based, family-based, family-centered, family preservation,* or *placement prevention* services.

The terms *Family support* and *family-centered* have been used to describe a broad range of programs that strengthen families. Some of the programs

programs serve families for 6 months or more and focus on addressing a range of family problems in order to reduce or eliminate the family's dependency on social services altogether (e.g., Halpern, 1990; Rosenberg, McTate & Robinson, 1982). White HBS or IFPS programs have been cited as family support programs, HBS/IFPS programs are relatively distinct from the programs such as early childhood, parent education, home visitor, home-school-community linkage, and treatment day care. However, it should be noted that many of the best family support programs promoted by the High Scope Foundation (Schweinhart, Weikart, & Larner, 1986) and others (General Accounting Office, 1990; Levine, 1988; Wasik, Bryant, & Lyons, 1990a,b) use an in-home teaching or service component, and hold many of the same service values shared by the IFPS programs.

Consequently, with the exception of the family support/family-centered programs, many social service program administrators are using one of three terms to describe their programs in this area: family-based services (FBS), home-based services (HBS), or intensive family preservation services (IFPS). The FBS term is often used as a general label to describe both home-based and office-based programs. This term refers to a group of programs that may have very different goals (Frankel, 1988). Some family-based programs are short-term and intensive, providing crisis intervention services and teaching skills to help families cope with a situation necessitating child placement (e.g., Kinney et al., 1990). The two programs evaluated in this study meet the criteria commonly listed for all three terms, but are most accurately described as intensive family preservation services (see Figure 1.1). But when reviewing the broader literature or discussing these types of programs in general, we will use the term FBS. When discussing programs that deliver services primarily in the family's environment, but on a less intensive basis with less emphasis upon the provision of concrete services, the term HBS will be used. When referring specifically to programs that are home-based, intensive, and meet the other criteria discussed in Chapter 1, we will use the term IFPS.

Placement Prevention and Family-Based Services: Selected Research Findings

Early Family-Based Services

To date, research findings regarding most types of FBS placement prevention programs, including IFPS, are contradictory. A variety of FBS programs have been evaluated, but many studies have been compromised by poor research designs, limited measures of child or family functioning, inadequate analyses, and small samples.[3] In reviewing these studies it is important to recognize that the treatment models, types of client, duration of service, intensity of client contact, and types of outcome measures vary. This makes drawing broad conclusions about the relative effectiveness of these programs difficult, but side-by-side comparisons are useful if these cautions are kept in mind. For example, Mary Ann Jones (1985) compared the program models and results of 17 preventive service programs as part of her evaluation report of the New York preventive services evaluation. The services compared varied greatly, ranging from the more traditional social casework programs, to those programs providing only counseling/ psychotherapy, and to programs that only contract and monitor the delivery of needed services. Because of the importance of her comparative summary, the full table is reprinted in Appendix A with accompanying explanatory notes.

Readers may note that the failure rates for the programs compared ranged from 3 to 31% with the comprehensive social work programs experiencing slightly better results. However, Jones cautions that direct comparisons would be unwise given differences and methodological limitations in the studies (Jones, 1985, pp. 34–35). The summary table does, however, illustrate the variety of program models and relative success of the programs that characterize the continuum of "foster care prevention services," of which HBS is one particular subclass of service model.

FBS and HBS Evaluation Studies Using
Control or Comparison Groups

The small but growing body of experimental studies of FBS programs is less positive with respect to placement prevention rates (studies of IFPS program are presented in the next section). But here again differences in the treatment models and service intensity must be taken into account. Furthermore, other outcome criteria besides placement prevention rates should also be considered but are often not measured. These criteria include improvements in child/parent/family functioning, placements that are planned or desirable, and numbers of placements in less restrictive settings or for shorter periods of time.

In a recently completed study of eight home-based programs in California, workers, on average, provided a variety of clinical and concrete services on an intensive (m hours of direct client contact = 32 hours) and time-limited basis (m days of service = 37). This evaluation included both HBS and IFPS programs, but some of the individual site data were not available at the time of this report. For the total sample of families followed for eight months after case referral (n = 675), the 80% of the families avoided placement, using data collected from county placement offices as "officially recorded placements" (Yuan, McDonald, Wheeler, Struckman, Johnson, & Rivest, 1990, p. 5.11). Children who were placed but returned home before the end of the HBS service period were not counted as service failures. The families served were young, with an average of 2.4 children whose average age was 6.7 years.

Later in the study, a comparison group was formed by randomly assigning cases to either the HBS treatment group (n of children = 356) or to a comparison group (n of children = 357). There were no significant differences in placement rates between the treatment group and the comparison group at eight months after case referral: 82% of treatment group cases were not placed versus 83% of the comparison group cases (see Table 2.1). The treatment group families, however, delayed their placement episodes longer, used a higher proportion of shelter care placements, and used 1,500 fewer days of placement than the comparison group cases. (Yuan et al. 1990, p. v).

A number of factors must be considered when interpreting the findings of this important study:

1.   There is some evidence that the provision of services between the treatment and comparison groups was not much different, other than the amount of parenting skills training, food, and rent assistance provided by the treatment group (p. 6.11).

2.   Most of the programs studied were recently implemented, and direct client contact hours varied substantially across the different programs (between 17–45 hours per case). In fact, there is some evidence that service provision varied significantly among some of the programs studied, indicating a need to view the aggregate data with caution.

3.   The children served were younger on average, than those served by other HBS or IFPS programs. Child age ranged between the 5.6 to 13 years old.

4.   While cases were tracked for eight months after referral to HBS, placements were identified only through the public agency MIS payment system and case record reviews. A variety of private placements and runaway episodes were not able to be identified.

Despite the various study limitations, the California evaluation is among the most thorough of those conducted to date. While the findings of this study are mixed with respect to placement prevention rates, there is evidence of service effectiveness across a number of outcome measures. The placement prevention rates for the experimental and control groups of an evaluation study conducted in Hennepin County, Minnesota during 1980 were also not too different (49 versus 47%). However, in terms of mean available placement days used, the experimental group cases spent, on average, 49 days in placement compared to 106 days for the control group cases (Hennepin County Community Services Department, 1980, p. 16). Part of the reason for this difference was that the experimental group cases tended to be placed as part of a plan to treat intensively or stabilize a child. Placement was integral to the therapeutic strategy rather than an alternative

Table 2.1. Placement Prevention Rates of Selected FBS Evaluation Studies Using an Experimental or Quasi-Experimental Design

Site and reference	Service intensity[a] (hours per month)	Placement prevention rates[b] (%) Experimental Group	Control or Comparison Group
California Unit of analysis: Children (Yuan et al. 1990)	High[c] (26.8)	82% (n = 356)	83% (n = 357)
Hennepin County, MN[c] Unit of analysis: families (Hennepin County, 1980)	Low (3.3)	49 (n = 66)	47 (n = 72)
Unit of analysis: children (Nelson, 1984)	Low (3–6)	77 (n = 34)	55 (n = 40)
Nebraska Unit of analysis: families (Rosenberg et al., 1982)	Medium[d] (4–8)	96 (n = 80)	89 (n = 73)
New Jersey Unit of analysis: families (Willems & DeRubeis, 1981)	Low[e] (2.09)	76 (n = 45)	82 (n = 45)
New York Unit of analysis: children (Jones et al., 1976)	Low[f] (6.8 contacts)	72 (n = 662)	61*** (n = 329)
		Follow-up (5–6 months) 78	60**
		Follow-up (5 years)[g] 66 (n = 175)	54* (n = 68)
New York City Unit of analysis: children (Halper & Jones, 1981)	Low[h] (3–6 hours)	96 (n = 156)	83*** (n = 130)
Oregon Unit of analysis: children (Szykula & Fleischman, 1985)	Medium (15–25 hours per case)	Less difficult cases 92 (n = 13)	62** (n = 13)
		More difficult cases 36 (n = 11)	55 (n = 11)

(continued)

Table 2.1.   (*Continued*)

---

*p < .05.   **p < .01.   ***p < .001.

a Service intensity is defined by the number of hours of in-person and telephone/client contact per month: low, 1–7 hours per month; medium 8–12 hours per month; high, 13 or more hours per month.

b The unit of analysis (n) used for placement prevention rates is noted for each study. Data were collected at the point of case termination unless noted in the table or in a separate note.

c Placement rates based on an 18-month follow-up

d First-year project service criteria excluded families with prior foster care placement or prior CPS referrals. Families received, on average, four contacts per month, with some families receiving much more service. Placement rates are underestimated due to a variety of factors, including difficulties in system monitoring and no tracking of relative and other privately funded placements (see Rosenberg et al., 1982, Appendix A, pp. 9–11).

e The client contact statistic does not include the services provided by the therapists as part of a variety of group activities that were offered (see Magura & DeRubeis, 1980, pp. 41–42). For example, the adolescent group met weekly for approximately two hours (Willems & De-Rubeis, 1981, pp. 12–13). Thus, for those families participating in one or more group work activities, client contact was at least at the medium level and possibly higher.

f The client contact figure was calculated using unduplicated family statistics (see Jones et al., 1976, pp. 54–56). Sample included children living at home and in placement at time of intake. Children living with friends or in an adoptive home were counted as being "at home" (Jones et al., 1976, p. 81).

g Original sample was reduced from 549 families to 142 families (243 children) by including only those families in the New York sites with at least one "at-risk" child who was at home at the start of the study (Jones, 1985, pp. 46–47).

h Families were seen by workers, on average, 2.95 times per month, with 43% of the contacts lasting over one hour (see Halper & Jones, 1981, pp. 97–100).

resorted to only in the event of treatment failure (i.e., as a means for sub-stituting for parental care). This was despite the fact that services for the experimental group were not significantly more intensive (40 hours versus 32 hours over a 12-month period).

A separate study of 74 families conducted between October 1981 and July 1982 in the Hennepin County public child welfare office found a substantive (but statistically nonsignificant, $p = .092$) difference in placement preven-tion rates between the treatment (77%) and control groups (55%) (Nelson, 1984, p. 88). Part of this difference could be due to the fact that the HBS clients were seen three times per month on average, compared to once a month for the control group cases. The HBS therapist caseloads averaged eight cases per worker compared to 21 cases for the child protective services (CPS) workers. Because the HBS cases were teamed, the HBS therapists actually carried 15 cases; but the caseload was 29% lower than those of the CPS staff (Nelson, 1984, pp. 69–70).

The study conducted by Nelson in Hennepin County is one of the earliest HBS evaluation studies to use an experimental design, and one of the few limitations of the study centered on eligibility criteria. One of the eligibility criteria was "no evidence that long-term placement was immediately pend-ing" (Nelson, 1984, p. 39). Because no measures of family functioning were employed, it was not possible to document differential improvements in family functioning between the two groups. This was a problem in that prevention of child placement of children who are judged to be appropriate only for short- or medium-term placement may artificially limit the ability to identify differences in treatment outcome between the two groups. Despite these limitations, there was a significant difference in the mean days of placement used for the HBS cases ($x = 15.7$) compared to the control group cases ($x = 53.6$).

In contrast, some research studies have found that placement rates were *greater* for the experimental group cases. For example, in a study in New Jersey where families were randomly assigned to experimental and control conditions, Willems and DeRubeis (1981, p. 16) reported that 14 placements occurred in 11 of 45 treatment families, while 15 placements occurred in 8 of 45 control families (see Table 2.1). It should be noted that these were families whose children were assessed to be at risk of placement within two *years*, and the children had not been placed previously in foster care. The families eligible for service were assigned to an experimental, control, or blind control (cases served by workers who were not aware that the case outcomes were being monitored by project staff). An unspecified follow-up period was also used.

At first glance the findings do not support the use of HBS with these types of families. But the authors reported a number of findings that indicate that the families receiving HBS experienced greater success:

1. The HBS group had higher child- and parent-related goal achievement scores; and workers rated the HBS group families at six-month intervals and found improvements in 11 of the 13 areas included on Geismar's Family Functioning Scale.
2. Control group families experienced more overall placements and more placements in restrictive settings.
3. There were more placements with relatives for the HBS families (seven), compared to the control families (three).
4. After placement, although more children were returned to their families in the control group, all of the returns were unplanned and unsuccessful, with the children returning to a family environment that had not changed (Willems & DeRubeis, 1981, pp. 16–18, 23–25).

The outcomes of this research project illustrate the complexity and problems associated with measuring "treatment success" only in terms of placement prevention rates. A similar pattern of findings was obtained by Rosenberg, McTate, and Robinson (1982, p. 10) in that while a small difference was found regarding placement prevention rates, control group cases spent, on average, over twice as many days in placement (46) compared to the experimental group (20). The treatment cases also showed improvement when assessed using the Bayley Scales of Infant Development and the Polansky Childhood Level of Living Scale (pp. 13–15).

In a landmark study published in 1976, Jones, Neuman, and Shyne examined the effects of family-based preventive services that were delivered in nine different sites in New York City and two counties outside the city. Delivering a more intensive and comprehensive service to families was one of the central goals of these pilot programs. While service intensity did vary widely for both experimental and control group cases, the program reduced foster care placements (see Table 2.1), and the differences between the experimental and control groups were even more apparent at follow-up (five or six months depending upon the site).

Furthermore, for those families where the children were at home at the time of service intake, 93% of the experimental group children were at home at the end of treatment compared to 82% of the control group children (Jones et al., 1976, p. 82). A follow-up of a subset of these children from the New York City sites five years later determined that 66% of the experimental group children did not enter care, compared to 54% of the control group children (Jones, 1985, p. 86). In addition, a survival analysis indicated that a higher proportion of the treated children did not enter substitute care for longer periods of time. When worker ratings of family improvement were compared, 59% of the treated families were rated as improved, compared to 28% of the control group families (Jones, 1985, pp. 86–94).

Another study conducted only in New York City over a two-year period found that even with a relatively low level of client contact, a higher proportion of children from an experimental group never entered foster care (96 versus 83%), when measured at case closing or at the end of the evaluation period (Halper & Jones, 1981, p. 111). In addition, positive improvements were noted in 29 areas of the Caretaking Environment of Children Scale (a revision of the original Polansky Childhood Level of Living scale) for 25% or more of the experimental group families.

Szykula and Fleischman (1985) compared randomly assigned groups of families who had children aged 3 to 12 who were considered to be at risk of having one or more children removed from the home because of child abuse and neglect. The treatment model employed was based on social learning theory, and the researchers found significant differences in placement rates between experimental and control group cases for "low-difficulty" families (92 versus 62%). But there were no significant differences for "high-difficulty" families. (Family difficulty was rated by a clinical team based on a review of the family's social history and case file.)

In a related study using an A-B-A design (baseline, intervention, withdrawal of intervention and monitoring), a two-caseworker HBS program in Oregon was first implemented and then terminated because of statewide budget reductions. Out-of-home placements dropped approximately 83 percent following the program's inception and later rebounded to prior levels following the program's termination. Placement rates of other types of non-CPS cases did not change during this time (see Szykula & Fleischman, 1985,

p. 280). In contrast, a pilot study of an HBS services unit in a CPS program in Kentucky found greater involvement of workers with the families and lower worker turnover in the experimental group, but "minimal differences" in the proportion of children removed and length of time in placement (Crumpler & Casper, 1986).

HBS Evaluation Studies Using Quasi-Experimental or Reflexive Designs

Only a few studies have used a "case overflow" control or comparison group, where the comparison group is formed by families that are referred for FBS meet the criteria for service, but cannot be served because worker caseloads are full. Hayes and Joseph (1985) conducted such a study in Columbus, Ohio. Fewer experimental group families (4/13 or 31%) experienced child placement compared to comparison group families (9/16 or 56%). Children and parents in the treatment group also made a number of small but significant improvements in a number of areas of functioning as measured by Michigan Screening Profile of Parents and the Devereaux Elementary School Behavior Rating Scale.

Another study that found mixed results used a quasi-experimental design of two groups of children. The comparison group was composed of 125 children aged 8 to 17 who entered foster care service during a one-year period (September 1977–December 1978). This group was compared to an experimental group composed of similar children who received two types of service two years later: 43 children who were served in traditional placement settings and 72 children who were served by one or more alternative programs (family-based treatment, day treatment, therapeutic foster care, or independent living arrangements). A number of methodological limitations preclude direct comparison of the relative effectiveness of the FBS with the other services, but it was interesting that a much smaller proportion of experimental group children were in placement during the first few months of service (Rosenthal & Glass, 1986, p. 313).

Another study involved the Families First program of Davis, California (Wood, Barton, & Schroeder, 1988). HBS were given to 26 families assigned from a pool of 50 families in which at least one abused or neglected child was in danger of being removed from the home. The remaining 24 families received traditional services and served as a comparison group. At the end of a year, 74% of children in the treatment group but only 45% of children in the comparison group were able to stay at home. These differences were statistically significant ($p < .01$) (Wood et al., 1988, p. 411).

HBS are just now being recognized as a strategy to help reunify families with children in substitute care (Hodges et al., 1989; Turner, 1984). One recent study found that in 55% of the 42 families served, either the families were reunified successfully (20) or the older adolescents (3) were emancipated (Bribitzer & Verdieck, 1988). This application of HBS is relatively new and little empirical research has been conducted yet, although an increasing number of HBS evaluation studies are now beginning to track reunification cases. For example, Beltrami County, Minnesota, recorded the case outcomes at case termination of 278 children in 129 cases over an eight-year period and found that placement prevention was achieved for 226 children, reunification achieved for 33 children, and 30 children were placed. Thus, reunification cases were counted as part of an 87% overall success rate for the program (Ellingson, 1990, p. 18).

The Stanford Study

Mixed findings were found by Wald, Carlsmith, & Leiderman (1988, pp. 24–28) in a two-year study that compared the physical, emotional, academic, and social development of 36 abused or neglected children aged five to ten who were treated under an experimental program in their own homes, 29 who were placed with relatives or in foster family care, and 81 who were not abused or neglected. This study was conducted by an interdisciplinary team from Stanford but was hampered by small sample sizes, differences in subsample characteristics, subject mortality, limited amount of in-home service, and other problems.

Approximately 85% of the children and their families receiving a modest amount of in-home treatment were able to remain at home without family functioning declining to a point where removal was necessary, compared to 70% of the children placed in foster care, who remained in a "permanent placement." The children who received home-based service also reported higher self-esteem scores and better peer relations (Wald et al., 1988, pp. 95–98, 183–184). The findings regarding the ability of HBS to improve parental functioning to a point where children were not reabused or neglected were less positive. Some of the children remaining at home were subjected to active psychological maltreatment and/or neglect, and two were sexually abused by relatives (pp. 95–96). The null hypothesis of no difference between the two groups was generally supported, and relatively little progress was made by both groups of children in relation to a broad range of measures such as school attendance and parental relations (p. 184).

The Stanford study is important as it attempted to address one of the most difficult and complex questions facing the field today: Compared to placing children in foster care, under what conditions is it preferable to leave them at home with special services? HBS or IFPS advocates will need to document through evaluation studies and interviews with children (the ultimate consumers in this area) a different picture than the one painted by Wald, Carlsmith, and Leiderman if these programs are going to continue to engender the support provided thus far:

> Overall, we sensed a very mixed picture for most of the home children. Many were often afraid, insecure, and depressed. They longed for better relations with their mothers. Yet most derived some sustenance from the relationships; few if any of the children would have chosen to live elsewhere. Perhaps this is not a meaningful test. Few children are in such bad situations that they will openly accept separation and rejection. Except in the worst of circumstances, children prefer the known to the unknown. To abandon one's parents and be abandoned by them is not accepted as an option by children as young as the ones we studied. Thus, we must ask who were worse off—the foster children who longed to return to their original homes, or the home children who longed for a loving relationship, free of pain, fear, and insecurity (Wald et al., 1988, p. 144)

Ironically, most of the problems described above would also apply to children in foster care, too many of whom are experiencing severe emotional trauma and are being victimized again. With more intensive HBS and better follow-up services it is likely that many of the "at-home" children would have been better adjusted and protected.

Additional Family-Based Services Research

Four additional evaluation studies of FBS that did not use control groups or comparison groups are summarized in Table 2.2. Both the placement prevention rates and other measures of family improvement are encouraging, in spite of the various methodological limitations common in these types of agency-based research studies.

One recent study is not included in Table 2.2 but has added substantially to the knowledge base in the field. Nelson, Emlen, Landsman, and Hutchinson (1988) analyzed 533 sample cases of families served by 11 FBS programs in six states (Colorado, Iowa, Minnesota, Ohio, Oregon, and Pennsylvania). The programs studied included those that were public and private, with some delivering services primarily in the office and some using more of a home-based approach. The primary purpose of the study was to identify service and client characteristics associated with success and failure of FBS; but a wide variety of information was also gathered from the social workers and program administrators. "Over 80 percent of the families showed positive change over the course of services, achieving a significant portion of their case objectives and demonstrating substantial cooperation with services" (National Resource Center on Family Based Services, 1988b, p. 1).

Placement prevention data were also gathered; program success was re-

Table 2.2. Selected Studies of HBS and IFPS Using Multiple Outcome Measures

Research study	Intensity of service[a]	Duration of service	Control or comparison group	Placement rates (families where one or more children entered placement)	Other outcome measures and selected findings
Cautley & Plane (Home & Community Treatment as described in Cautley & Plane, 1983; Jones, 1985)	High ($M = 3.6$ hours/week)	Long ($M = 11$ months)	None	12%	Parent changes scores (composite of five areas of parenting), child behavior change scores (home school), parent treatment goal attainment, and child treatment goal attainment, positive changes using all measures for certain families were noted
Leeds (1984)	High (2.6 hours of client in-person or telephone contact per week by worker; 2.9 hours per week by other staff, primarily homemakers)	Medium ($M = 5$ months)	None	4 of 28 (14%) families had placement at time of closing; 6 of 34 families (17%) had placement at any time during the service period	Problem severity scores: workers rated problem severity on a 4-point scale at initial and case closure with a reduction in problem severity averaging about 50% in relation to social, parental, child, and family functioning when items were aggregated by type

(continued)

Table 2.2. (Continued)

Research study	Intensity of service[a]	Duration of service	Control or comparison group	Placement rates (families where one or more children entered placement)	Other outcome measures and selected findings
Tanvantzis et al. (1985)	High (5 hours of in-person or telephone contact with family each week for first six weeks)	Medium (M = 3.75 months)	None	7 of 57 (12%) youth placed at exit, with this percentage continued at 6 and 12 month follow-up.	Problem reoccurrence: 50% of families had one or more of the original presenting problems occur; Bryce Family Functioning scale: scale items for 13 bipolar dimensions were rated by workers at beginning, middle, and end of treatment, with scale scores associated with case outcomes; referring caseworker telephone survey: the cases of over 44% of youth were rated as "successfully treated"
Kinney & Haapala (1984)	High (9.2 hours of in-person and telephone	Short (M = 8.5 weeks)	All comparison cases	6 of 25 (24%) children placed (1 for	Global Assessment Scale ratings of therapists: M at initial = 29.1, M at closure =

32

	contact per week)	were placed— see Home-builders Mental Health Report	one week, 1 for two months)	57.6; Child Behavior Checklist ratings by therapists: M at initial = 81.7, M at closure = 43.9; parent and therapist ratings of 34 problem areas: 81.5% of the problem areas were rated as having improved; this was a study of a special population—children with mental health impairments so severe that psychiatric hospitalization was clearly the next casework action without IFPS
Lawder et al. (1984)	Medium (31 completed visits per case)	Long (M = 13.1 months but 23 (22.8%) cases were closed within 6 months	None	28 of 233 children (12%) at the end of the study were in non-relative placements	Problem profile ratings by researchers using case records: 48 families (47.5%) made partial progress and resolved their problems; client agreement with caseworker goals: 28 (32.6%) of families "acknowledged and accepted social worker's treatment goals"

[a] Mean average number of client contact hours.

33

ported to range between 75 and 96%. But these findings should be viewed cautiously. The placement prevention rates may be misleadingly high because the data were gathered from agency records at case termination, and temporary placement cases were excluded from the calculations. Case records may also not reflect the range of negative outcomes—privately funded placements and runaway episodes in particular—that may be viewed as failure or endanger children. Conversely, even if these adjustments were made, the effectiveness of the programs studies would be satisfactory. And one would likely find that these services had an effect that extended beyond the service period, even if the research design employed did not allow for gathering information on the sequelae of treatment (see Nelson et al., 1988, pp. xxix, 18–19, 24). The researchers also conducted extensive analyses to identify factors associated with success and failure, adding new findings to this area of inquiry. Some of these findings will be summarized in Chapter 3.

In a related study of home-based services in Virginia, the researchers explored the factors associated with treatment outcome (see Chapter 3), while noting that for 20 of the 42 cases served thus far, that legal custody of the identified children was returned to the parents or original caretaker, and three of the children were emancipated successfully; resulting in a 55% "success rate." The authors urge caution in the use of the term "successful;" for some families, placement was the best outcome for the child at the time. "In some cases, intensive in-home intervention helps both social service agencies and parents to reach the decision that out-of-home placement is appropriate" (Bribitzer & Vedieck, 1988, p. 259).

Finally, Maryland's Intensive Family Services program has been using teams of a social worker and a paraprofessional parent aide to provide services to families on a flexible basis in terms of intensity and service duration. One study of 80 cases referred to the program found that the placement rate was 7.5%, compared to 18% for families referred to traditional child protective services ($n = 148$). After one year, the difference remained, with 3% of the families still in placement, compared to 8% of the comparison group cases (Center for the Study of Social Policy, 1988, pp. 51–52).

Studies of IFPS Programs

Selected Program Outcomes of the Homebuilders Model of IFPS

The first published study of the Homebuilders program examined the results of serving 80 families with 134 members who were judged to be at risk of imminent out-of home placement. As discussed in Chapter 1, a short-term and intensive service was provided that consisted of both clinical and concrete services. Using a three month follow-up consisting of interviews with the child's primary caretakers, the administrators found that 97% (117/121) of the clients avoided placement (Kinney, Madsen, Fleming, & Haapala, 1977, p. 671)[4] In a later study, the administrators reported serving 207 families involving 311 potential placements in foster or psychiatric care from October 1974 to 1978. A high proportion of the families (96%) were still together at the end of the precipitating crisis, and 86–87% were still together one year after IFPS intake (Haapala & Kinney, 1979, p. 248; Kinney, 1978).

From 1976–1977, the program served a group of status offenders that were referred from the Pierce County Juvenile Court. "In this group, 73% of the clients who were seen by Homebuilders were not placed. Of the clients who were not served by Homebuilders [because caseloads were full], 72% were placed" (Kinney, Haapala, Booth, & Leavitt, 1990, p. 54).

In another project the Homebuilders program served 25 children from Pierce County, Washington who were assessed by the County Office of Involuntary Commitment as needing inpatient psychiatric hospitalization. A comparison group was formed with the cases that could not be served due to full Homebuilder caseloads at the time of the referral. The average length of service was 8.5 weeks, with 9.2 hours of in-person and phone contact per week. Only six of the 25 children were placed. Of the six children placed one spent one week at Madigan Psychiatric hospital and then went home, and one spent one month in a psychiatric unit, one month in a group home and then went home. Thus two months after IFPS treatment, 84% (21/25) of the children were at home with their families (Kinney & Haapala, 1984; Kinney et al. 1990). This study also found that the Global Assessment Ratings for the children went up after IFPS treatment (X at intake was 29.1, after treatment it was 57.6), and Child Behavior Checklist scores decreased (81.7 to 43.9). Parent and therapist ratings of 34 problem areas found that the child's behavior had improved to some degree in a high proportion of the cases (Kinney & Haapala, 1984, p. 4). In contrast, all of the comparison group cases were placed (Kinney, Haapala, Booth, & Leavitt, 1990, p. 54).

A study conducted by David Haapala in 1983 used both qualitative and quantitative approaches to examine the services provided to 41 families served by the Homebuilders program. A number of interesting findings were found. Within 25 hours of each session with the family, the clients and therapists were interviewed regarding what they saw as "critical incidents" that had occurred during the session. A total of 1,200 critical incidents from the therapy sessions were reported, including moments of family conflict, joy, insight, interruptions by neighbors or friends, behavioral charting, and practice of new skills.

Eight dimensions of treatment emerged from the content analysis, with two dimensions significantly associated with prevention of out-of home placement: (1) provision of concrete services by therapists; and (2) interruptions in the treatment session (which may have provided the therapist with opportunities to teach and demonstrate problem-solving and other skills) (Fraser & Haapala, 1987–88; Haapala, 1983; Haapala & Fraser, 1987).

Over the years the Homebuilders program has been reported to be helpful to adoptive families who are experiencing difficulty in raising one or more of their adopted children. Working with adoptive families presents some special clinical challenges that are frequently not acknowledged by the larger practice community. In a recent partnership with Medina Children's Services of Seattle, IFPS treatment was provided to 22 special needs adoptive children living in 20 adoptive family homes. The children had to meet one or more of the following criteria: intellectual, physical, or emotional disability; adopted after 6 years of age; be a member of an ethnic minority group; or were adopted as part of a sibling group.

The majority of primary caretakers and therapists reported progress on various types of treatment goals. At three months after the IFPS treatment, 18 or 82% were with their families. The majority of children (17 or 77%) had never spent any time out of the home. Of the children spending time away from home, two children were in foster care, two had run away, and one was living with her boyfriend) (Haapala, McDade & Johnston, 1988, p. 2).

One of the largest groups of children served by the Homebuilders program are those who commit status offenses (e.g., running away, truancy, delinquency). A recent analysis examined the placement prevention rates of 678 of these children served by the program from September 1, 1982 to December 31, 1985. Of the 678 youth served, 592 (87%) avoided out-of-the home placement in state funded foster, group or institutional care for 12 months following treatment (Haapala & Kinney, 1988, p. 345). Placement was determined by regularly checking the state computer printouts for placement expenditures, as well as through contact with referring caseworkers.

Finally, from 1987 to 1990, the Behavioral Sciences Institute began and ran a program to deliver IFPS treatment to families living in the Bronx neighborhood of New York City. (The administration of the program was recently transferred to a local agency and a number of similar IFPS programs were started in other sections of New York City.) Despite the difficulties involved in beginning a new program, a study of the 43 first-time families served by the Bronx IFPS program found that 34 of 43 (79.1%) of the families had avoided placement of their child in a government-authorized setting for more than 2 weeks for 3 months following the intervention, and 74% had avoided placement for 12 months after IFPS (Mitchell, Tovar & Knitzer, 1989, p. 12a). Families made significant progress in a number of areas as measured by worker ratings on the CWLA Child Well-Being Scales, and a high proportion of primary caretakers valued the services provided. A comparison group was formed in another agency that experienced similar placement prevention rates, but the small number of cases, problems in the referral procedures, and various methodological limitations prevent valid comparisons being made between the two programs.

In summary, evaluation data have consistently indicated that the IFPS treatment provided by the Homebuilders program has helped families to improve child and parent functioning in order to prevent child placement across a number of client populations (see Kinney, Haapala, Booth, & Leavitt, 1990, p. 55). Because of the lack of more studies using an experimental design and other issues discussed later in this chapter, these data should be viewed with cautious optimism. But they are similar to some of the results obtained by other IFPS programs around the country, some of which are discussed in the next section.

Evaluation Results From Other IFPS Programs

One of the first rigorous studies of an early IFPS program was conducted in Hennepin County Minnesota by Philip AuClaire and Ira Schwartz. The Hennepin County study used a form of a case overflow design and found that between August 1985 and December 1986, the experimental group used 1,435 fewer available placement days and experienced shorter lengths of stays compared to the control group (AuClaire & Schwartz, 1985, p. 41). The services delivered as part of this program were less intensive than other IFPS programs, but were short-term (an average of 13.9 in-person and phone client contact hours in 37 days of service). In this study, 5 of the 58 (8.6%) comparison group children remained with their families, compared to 24 of 55 (43.6%) of the children in the treatment group (P. AuClaire, personal communication, November 1, 1990). If the first placement of the comparison group is not counted (cf. AuClaire & Schwartz, 1986, pp. 39–40), then the differences between the two groups is decreased, but the lower number of days in placement utilization achieved by the HBS therapists is significant if the maintenance of families and program costs are both considered to be important, in addition to simple placement rates.

A recent evaluation completed in New Jersey produced an equally interesting set of findings. This study tested the efficacy of the IFPS program to prevent placement, measured changes in family functioning, and evaluated the long-term effects of the service through a one year follow-up (see Feldman, 1990, p. 5). This study is noteworthy in a number of areas, including that each IFPS referral was assessed by a designated screening committee regarding the appropriateness of the referral on the same day it was received. If the case met study criteria (which fit most other IFPS programs and was broadened slightly over time), the case was randomly assigned to either a treatment or control group.

Placement prevention rate for the 96 families in the treatment group was 92.7% at case termination compared to 85.1% for the 87 families in the control group. This difference in placement prevention, although not statistically significant at case termination, was significant at 30 days, 60 days, 90 days, 3 months, and 9 months post-termination. This statistical difference or "net effect" of IFPS, however, appeared to dissipate between 9 months and 1 year after treatment (Feldman, 1990, pp. 28–29). Thus the IFPS intervention appeared to only delay placement for some of the treatment group children. Both the control and treatment groups made similar gains on two of the measures of family functioning (Family Environment Scale; Interpersonal Support Evaluation List), but the IFPS families scored significantly higher on a number of the Child Well-Being Scales (pp. 30–33).

Feldman and his colleagues note that while the IFPS staff provided more intensive services to the treatment group families, it was not possible to determine exactly what level of services were received by the control group families. And only 8.8% of the treatment group families received concrete services, a proportion much lower than other IFPS programs. Among other things, the researchers recommended that closer comparisons be made between treatment and comparison groups, and that follow-up visits by the IFPS workers be used as a possible strategy of helping families maintain the gains made in IFPS treatment (Feldman, 1990, p. 37).

A similar state-led IFPS initiative in Florida begun in 1981 with therapist training by the Behavioral Sciences Institute had grown to FPS projects in 10 of 11 state districts by 1988. Placement prevention data for the period from July 1, 1985 to March 30, 1987 indicated that 87.3 of the 1,166 families served during this period were intact at the termination of IFPS. While placement prevention rates decrease with time, 61.8% of the families surveyed 12 months later were still together (The Center for the Study of Social Policy, 1988, p. 31).

Finally, two home-based treatment programs in Canada that build upon the treatment technology of the Teaching Family Model group homes and the Homebuilders program are showing early signs of success using standardized measures of child and family functioning, as well as placement prevention data. The first, Alberta Family Support Services, has found that the proportion of 87 children served who were with their families increased from 84% at 6 months post-treatment to 95% at 11 months post-treatment (Fixen et al. 1988; Olivier et al. 1990, p. 18). The second, Community Support Services, found that with the first 27 families served, the proportion of children scoring in the clinical range of the Child Behavior Checklist dropped from 69% to 39%; parent-child communication problems, as measured by the Conflict Behavior Questionnaire, had decreased; and worker ratings of family functioning had improved (Bernfeld et al. 1990).

Cost-Effectiveness of Home-Based and Intensive Family Preservation Services

One of the major driving forces behind the popularity of HBS and IFPS programs with state legislators and administrators is the perception that this service is more cost-effective than traditional child welfare, juvenile justice, or mental health services. The cost-benefit research conducted thus far for HBS and IFPS has produced a mixed set of findings.[5] Some evaluations have documented significant cost savings (e.g., Halper & Jones, 1981; Kinney et al., 1977; Olivier et al. 1990). More specifically, a Florida study found that by providing HBS, foster care placement was prevented in 80% of the cases as measured by a six-month follow-up. The researchers estimated that $619,290 was saved when a time horizon of one year was used as the basis for the calculations (Florida Department of Health and Rehabilitative Services, 1982, pp. iv–v). In the Halper and Jones study (1981, p. 142) agency savings were reported to be $61,625, with a time horizon of two years.

In contrast, other research studies have found that a high-quality HBS or IFPS program may cost as much or more than traditional services. Using experimental or quasi-experimental designs, some studies have reported that HBS were effective in preventing child placements, but appeared to cost more than traditional services (Hayes & Joseph, 1985, pp. 27–28; Hennepin County Community Services, 1980, pp. 18–19; Rosenberg et al., 1982, pp. 44–45). One of the most recent studies, however, found that costs for providing a relatively intensive home-based service were approximately $2,000 per child or an average per day rate of $39.73. "This compares favorably with many types of out-of-home care" (Yuan et al., 1990, p. vi).[6]

One of the limitations of many analyses is that the benefits of HBS and IFPS programs in terms of quality of life or prevention of future child dysfunction are often not fully measured. Quantifying the benefits that are produced by these services beyond comparing the savings in substitute care funds is difficult. For example, how does one begin to quantify the financial value of improvements in parent self-esteem, child school attendance, or cessation of child maltreatment?

Some of these benefits can be assigned market values, while other "intangible" benefits must be estimated using the amount that analysts think people would be willing to pay for that benefit (e.g., the ability to use nonabusive discipline techniques, anger management skills). As one might imagine, there are a host of problems associated with implementing this in practice, including the difference between personal/societal willingness to pay versus the actual ability to pay (Buxbaum, 1981). Furthermore, the issue of sorting out the relative importance of pecuniary benefits (personal versus societal benefits) needs to be addressed as well.

Conversely, the costs associated with HBS or IFPS therapist, supervisor, and administrator salaries and fringe benefits need to be incorporated into the analyses, along with other agency overhead costs. Community service costs incurred while the family is participating in HBS or IFPS treatment (and possibly for a certain period of time thereafter) should also be tracked. Child placement costs must be calculated as well, involving an analysis of the various types of placements (not just the most expensive), average cost of care per day, and the average length of stay for various types of clients.

From a more technical perspective, determining a suitable time horizon and discount rate are additional challenges. The time horizon is generally concerned with when the benefits are expected to take effect, and the length of time that the various benefits of the service will last. Calculating time horizons for IFPS client outcomes is dependent in part upon the availability of research data that specify client outcomes based on rigorous follow-up studies. Most HBS and IFPS evaluation studies have used follow-up periods of six months or less. In addition, because some benefits will occur in the future, the value of these benefits must be discounted because dollars saved later are worth less than dollars spent or saved immediately (i.e., the "net present value" of the funds must be calculated). While the concept of discounting is relatively straightforward, the choice of a discount rate and the implications that it has for the cost-benefit ratio are complex (Buxbaum, 1981; Sherraden, 1986).

In terms of cost-effectiveness, the findings to date are encouraging but limited, given that most HBS and IFPS cost-effectiveness or benefit-cost analyses have not taken into account an adequate assessment of the benefits accrued from the service, and a wide range of cost centers such as supervisory, administrative, overhead, and ancillary service costs. These analyses might be best carried out with experimental or quasi-experimental designs with at least a 12- to 24-month follow-up period.

Methodological and Other Issues Raised by the Literature Review

In reviewing past evaluative research, it is clear that there is a substantial basis for supporting the continued study of HBS and IFPS. One of the major limitations in this body of evaluative research is the lack of comparability across research studies. Both treatment models and outcome variables are defined and measured in different ways. Because of these problems, it is difficult to determine if the differences in outcomes across programs are related to the service itself, client selection criteria, or methods of evaluation (Frankel, 1988, p. 145; Jones 1985, pp. 35–37). A useful approach to this dilemma would be to develop a typology of family-based program models, which could then be tested and compared using a small set of standard outcome variables and measures. In addition, control or comparison groups should be employed. This would allow administrators, policymakers, and practitioners to compare the differential effectiveness of various HBS or IFPS programs (Pecora, Haapala, & Fraser, 1991a). A variety of more specific methodological and other issues arising from the literature review will be discussed in the sections below.

Addressing Contradictory Research Findings

Although research on family-based programs has been promising, findings relating to effectiveness and benefit-cost have been contradictory. The studies cited span almost two decades, and while program technology has improved, social conditions generally have declined. The highest rates of success and cost savings have been reported in nonexperimental studies in which there were no comparison groups. For many experimental studies, the placement prevention rates are lower, yet other measures of treatment effectiveness are very positive. Part of the problem relates to when the evaluation is conducted. Many research studies are conducted during the first few years of a program—during a period of time when the program staff are "settling in," the treatment model is being refined, and critical organizational and community relationships are just being established. Naturally, treatment effectiveness will often be lower at this point in time, despite the initial enthusiasm of the FBS staff. Yet few research consumers such as administrators and policymakers take this into account. Thus the more cautious researchers are focusing on HBS and IFPS programs that have been "up and running" in a stable fashion for at least two years in order to avoid these problems.

Expanding Measures of Program Effectiveness

The field has not yet sufficiently addressed the issue of what criteria should be used to document treatment success. One of the concerns of many FBS practitioners and researchers has been the overemphasis of the field upon placement prevention, rather than considering additional types of outcomes, such as the following:

- improvement in child functioning (e.g., behavior, school attendance, school performance, self-esteem)
- positive changes in parental functioning (e.g., depression, employment, substance abuse, anger management, self-esteem, or parenting skills such as the use of appropriate discipline techniques and child care)
- improvements in family functioning (e.g., family conflict, communication, cohesion, adaptability, or social support)

• use of child placement as a stabilizing influence and means for family reunification, or use of HBS or IFPS to stabilize a foster home as a "permanent placement" for children who should not return home

The use of placement prevention as the sole criterion is problematic, especially since many adolescents experience one or more short placements before stabilizing at home (Rzepnicki, 1987). FBS practitioners and researchers would also benefit by developing more specific criteria for judging the suitability of various placements in order to determine degrees of case success (e.g., Bernstein, Snider, & Meezan, 1975; Janchill, 1975, 1981). Furthermore, as mentioned earlier, treatment success can depend on the family situation. In one study in Israel of home-based marital therapy for families with multiple needs, independence from public assistance payments and social service agency support (two important forms of "self-sufficiency") were the major treatment objectives that were achieved for 36 of the 39 families (Rabin, Rosenbaum, & Sens, 1982).

The broader evaluation literature suggests that FBS research studies would benefit by using a common "core" of outcome criteria and measures that assess the major aspects of child, parent, and family functioning expected to change as a result of the intervention. This need for commonality, however, must be balanced by the advantages of testing the use of multiple types of outcome criteria and instruments. In addition, even in the most rigorous studies, what is being compared are two forms of service—FBS versus another type. Comparison of FBS treatment with a no-treatment condition would likely produce more dramatic differences between the two groups, but this design is rarely feasible, and of course studies that propose no treatment comparison groups are more likely to receive greater scrutiny due to ethical concerns.

Defining Eligibility and Screening Criteria for Intake

A growing number of HBS and IFPS programs state that they will serve only families where the children or adolescents are in danger of being placed at some point in the future (e.g., immediately, within one week, within one year). The validity and reliability of the processes that workers in child welfare use to make decisions about the need for placement are not very high (Stein & Rzepnicki, 1984); and a number of problems regarding adherence to HBS intake criteria have been discussed by Feldman (1990a), Jones (1985, pp. 35–36), Tracy (1991), and others. For example, some HBS or IFPS programs attempt to screen in cases that other similarly identified programs would avoid. In other cases, referring workers are not receiving sufficient training and supervision to ensure consistency in the referral process.

Determining what criteria and screening process to use is complex. For many cases, the process might involve assessing the risk of future child maltreatment. For other cases it may be determining how much risk this child poses to herself or others through substance abuse, delinquency or other behaviors. In addition, appropriate families might be identified as those where a referring worker, with prior approval from a juvenile court judge, plans to place a child outside the home in a non-shelter care type of placement within five days. Developing decision-making protocols has been hampered by the lack of valid conceptual frameworks for decision-making and assessment instruments (Pecora, 1990; Stein & Rzepnicki, 1983; Wald & Woolverton, 1990), although a number of groups have been developing resources in this area (e.g., Haapala, Kinney, & McDade, 1988a; Holder & Corey, 1986).

Articulating a More Unified Theoretical Framework for HBS and IFPS Programs

Part of defining a model of home-based or intensive family preservation treatment involves clearly specifying a theoretical framework that explains why these programs are successful, this remains an unfulfilled challenge. Geismer (1979) has criticized family-based treatment for its lack of a theoretical foundation. Jones (1985) also considered the field of HBS to be atheoretical and concluded that a theoretical framework for intervention could only be built through slowly accumulating research findings.

In fact, most research studies of HBS and IFPS services have not addressed this issue; not many of these intervention models and the theories underlying them have been explicated or tested. But this situation is to be expected, for theory-based treatment models require time to develop and to describe. Many HBS programs serve small numbers of clients within a turbulent organizational climate. Under such conditions, merely maintaining funding and serving clients are major challenges, let alone defining tenets of theory.

Nevertheless, it is clear that HBS and IFPS practitioners have been creatively blending clinical techniques from a variety of theoretical paradigms to serve multiproblem families. Major treatment theories utilized by HBS and IFPS practitioners include social learning theory (including cognitive-behavioral theory), ecological theory, various forms of family systems theory, crisis intervention theory, and communications theory (e.g., Barth, 1989; Bryce & Lloyd, 1981; Kaplan, 1986; Lewis, 1990; Spaid, 1988).[7] Therapists in many programs are using concepts from social learning and cognitive-behavioral theory to teach client skills in such areas as anger management, parenting, stress reduction, conflict resolution, and household management. In addition, a variety of clinical techniques are being used, including rational emotive therapy; functional, structural, and strategic family therapy; guided imagery; Gestalt therapy; family sculpting; ecomapping; and genogram analysis.

While concepts borrowed from other forms of clinical practice may be easily used in IFPS, they may need to be modified for the different treatment contexts and services needed by families who are served in their natural environment. That is, these intervention theories might benefit from careful reconceptualization of descriptive and explanatory principles, based on an emphasis on the ecology of in-home services. One of the challenges to this field is the need to test operationally defined treatment models empirically.

Overcoming Implementation Problems in Control Group Studies

In rigorous experiments, random assignment can sometimes operate to place an agency at risk of failure to meet contractual obligations. Referrals may decline because the referral agencies are discouraged by the possibility that their clients have a 50% chance of not receiving the special services. It has been reported that occasionally referring workers spend extra time treating control group cases in an effort to "compete" against the new treatment service. It is also not unheard of for a study site to terminate prematurely their participation in an experiment because low referral rates are brought about by referring workers discouraged because not all of the clients they refer will receive IFPS. When this occurs, new FBS programs may find it impossible to serve the number of cases called for in a service contract. Withdrawal from the evaluation study becomes necessary in these cases. These problems must be overcome if studies using experimental designs are to provide valid results (Pecora, Fraser, and Haapala, in press).

Strengthening Procedures for Tracking Families and Assessing Program Effectiveness

Wide variation exists among the extant HBS and IFPS evaluation studies regarding how carefully families are followed regarding posttreatment functioning. "Greater attention should be paid to the posttreatment period to understand the dynamics of the family's living situation, interaction with community services, the nature of subsequent crises, and the family's response" (Gershenson, 1990, p. 7). With more information, it would be possible to more carefully specify what situations constitute IFPS treatment failure as opposed to problems in the larger child welfare system or community.

Definitions of what constitutes "placement" and follow-up periods differ among the studies. In addition, some evaluators rely only on one or two assessment methods (e.g., case records, caseworker interviews, agency MIS data) for determining how well a family is functioning and if the child has been placed. Methodological differences among these studies are important because, depending on the length of follow-up and the definition of placement, placement prevention rates will vary widely. The limitations of using only case records and MIS data are serious, because after caseworkers have closed or transferred the case, they are frequently not aware of what happens to children. Agency MIS systems only track publicly funded placements and this is adequate only when avoidance of publicly funded placements is the major criterion for effectiveness. Many state agencies are resisting the "dumping" of clients into their system by private psychiatric programs when the family's insurance coverage has been exhausted. For these agencies avoidance of both private and public placements is important. Finally, child runaway behavior places most children at risk of exploitation of maltreatment, so some programs consider this outcome to be important for assessing treatment effectiveness. Yet after treatment has ended, this is usually determined only by contacting the child's caretakers. Researchers need to interview primary caretakers for follow-up data, in addition to monitoring other sources of information.

Examining Factors Associated with Treatment Success and Failure

The single or combined service, system, and/or client characteristics that are associated with treatment success need to be identified in more detail so that more specific treatment models and client intake criteria can be developed. Little information regarding the factors empirically associated with success is available; and factors associated with client outcome are difficult to compare across studies because of the methodological limitations identified above. However, some of the research findings regarding factors associated with treatment success and failure are discussed in the next chapter, along with the major hypotheses of the FIT study.

Implementing Ongoing Performance Tracking Systems. FBS programs need to develop tracking systems that provide the agency with ongoing feedback about program effectiveness with different types of families, rather than waiting for long periods of time for "after-the-fact" types of evaluations. To ensure timely feedback at various points in time, program evaluation should therefore take various forms including the following: (1) structured reviews of cases with the best and worst outcomes—the "Professional Review Action Group," (2) experimental studies using large samples of at least 350 families in each group to ensure adequate statistical power, (3) ethnographic research to examine placement decisions in great detail, and (4) "system analyses" types of studies (McCaffrey, Anderson, McCold, & Kim, 1985) that attempt to model the complexity of placement decision-making and program effects within the larger ecology of the community (Gershenson, 1990; Personal communication C. Gershenson, September 1989).

Summary of the Literature Review

This chapter has summarized a cross-section of research studies for various types of FBS, HBS and IFPS programs. The existing research data suggest that certain HBS and IFPS programs have been effective in improving child and parent functioning. Research in this field, however, is hindered by the lack of a typology to categorize program models, few controlled studies, nonspecific intake criteria, poor specification of outcome measures beyond placement prevention rates, nonstandardized outcome measures, and scarce use of multivariate statistics to determine the relative effects of various factors on treatment success or failure. Designing and conducting field-based evaluation studies with some form of control condition is exceedingly difficult. Yet rigorously designed studies are necessary before HBS and IFPS advocates will be able to respond to child welfare experts who, earlier in the development of this service, cautioned the field that these services may be less costly, but marginal substitutes for traditional child welfare services (Magazino, 1983; Magura, 1981; Stein, 1985; Wald, 1988).

In examining the number and breadth of studies of these services, it is impressive that so many evaluations have been undertaken in an era when program funds were reduced drastically. To some extent, state administrators and local child welfare agency directors have been stretching scarce program dollars in an effort to support the evaluation of FBS programs. With the exception of a few occasional foundation grants and limited federal funding through discretionary research awards, relatively little financial support external to agencies and universities has been earmarked for evaluating these programs despite the importance attributed to them by federal and state authorities. Much more federal and state investment in research that is longitudinal in design and methodologically sophisticated is necessary if the field is going to be able to document the effectiveness of various types of FBS programs.

In summary, the studies conducted thus far provide a foundation to support cautious optimism that some HBS and IFPS are able to improve child, parent, and family functioning to the extent that child placement is prevented for at least a short (six month) period of time. Which specific client, service, or worker factors are most responsible for treatment success is not clear. The next chapter summarizes factors associated with treatment success in various FBS programs and describes the major hypotheses that were established for the FIT research project.

Notes

1.   One of the principal assumptions underlying foster care prevention and permanency planning efforts is that in most cases a child's development and emotional

well-being is best ensured through efforts to maintain the child in the home of her or his biological or "blended" family (providing that at least minimal standards of parenting are maintained). Most child welfare practitioners and researchers would agree with this assumption. In addition, permanency planning has been praised for providing children with more permanent family relationships. However, the research literature comparing the benefits of, for example, leaving children with their birth families under marginal conditions versus placing children in foster care is inconclusive because of a number of methodological factors such as the oversimplification of independent and dependent variables, and a lack of longitudinal research. See, for example, Barth & Berry (1987), Fanshel, Finch, and Grundy (1989a,b), Fanshel & Shinn (1978), Festinger (1983), Maluccio, Fein, & Olmstead (1986), Maluccio & Fein (1987), and Seltzer & Bloksberg (1987).

2.   The current FBS and IFPS treatment philosophy differs from the beliefs of many Charity Organization Society workers. These workers tended to believe that social problems were the result of character flaws, and that such flaws differentiated the worthy from the unworthy poor. In contrast, most modern IFPS programs shared much of their philosophy with another early program that was more focused on community organization and was not necessarily home-based—the Settlement House movement. Settlement Houses were established in poor or immigrant-filled neighborhoods by "socially concerned middle-class and upper-class university students and others, who . . . shared their lives with the poor—a kind of Peace Corps of the time" (Wood & Geismar, 1989, p. 47). Settlement Houses were begun about the same time as the Charity Organization Societies but their philosophical approaches were significantly different (Leiby, 1978). Thus it is ironic that some of the intervention components of family preservation services stem from two related but significantly different programs.

3.   For critical reviews of selected evaluation studies of FBS or IFPS programs, see Frankel (1988), Jones (1985), Magura (1981), and Stein (1985).

4.   Only 121 clients were served early enough in the study to be included in the three-month follow-up.

5.   This section is adapted from Pecora (1989, pp. 139–140). Cost benefit analyses can be used to examine whether the outcomes of a particular FBS or IFPS program are worth more in pecuniary terms than the costs of the program. Generally, a program is compared to itself, in contrast to cost-effectiveness studies where two or more programs, such as family preservation services and foster care, are compared (White, 1988, pp. 430–431). Most FBS or IFPS evaluations of this type are actually cost-effectiveness studies.

6.   For more information about cost-benefit analysis and examples of studies conducted for human service programs, see Armstrong (1982), Buxbaum (1981), Haugard, Hokanson, and National Resource Center on Family-Based Services (1983), Kugajevsky (1979), Levin (1983, 1985), Magura (1981), Orr and Bell (1987), Settles, Culley, & Van Name (1976), Sherraden (1986), Wald, Carlsmith, & Leiderman (1988), and Young and Allen (1977).

7.   For more information regarding the theoretical base underlying the HOME-BUILDERS and other IFPS programs, see Kinney et al. 1991 and chapters in Tracy, Kinney, Haapala, & Pecora (1991).

Chapter 3

Factors Associated with Success and Failure in Family-Based and Intensive Family Preservation Services

WANDA M. SPAID, ROBERT E. LEWIS, and PETER J. PECORA

Chapter Overview

In this chapter, the correlates of treatment success and failure as documented by previous research for various FBS and IFPS programs are summarized. Factors that may be important, as suggested by practitioners and related research studies, are discussed. The major study hypotheses and supportive research findings are also presented.

Variables Associated with Treatment Success and Failure

In attempting to address the issue of differential effectiveness, FBS and IFPS practitioners and researchers are beginning to ask the classic question: "*Which* methods work with *which* clients in *which* settings to produce *which* outcomes?" (Videka-Sherman, 1985, p. 11).

While a growing set of evaluative studies increased confidence in the overall effectiveness of various forms of FBS, program models and intake criteria need to be specified using knowledge based on the factors associated with treatment success. In the next section, a summary of the factors associated with treatment success and/or failure will be presented for the following areas:

- client demographics
- child's location and status of the problem at intake
- nature and locus of dysfunction
- service and program variables

The summary should be viewed with caution because of differences in the various program models and methodological limitations of the FBS and IFPS literature. As discussed in Chapter 2, these limitations include the use of few control groups, poor definitions of client problems, the use of incommensurable outcome measures, and overreliance upon bivariate analyses.

Client Demographic Characteristics

In attempting to summarize client or other factors associated with child placement from selected FBS research studies, reviewers commonly find many contradictions. In some studies no differences are found (e.g., Willems and DeRubeis, 1981, p. 32), while in other studies certain client characteristics are significantly associated with either treatment success or failure.

Low income was correlated with child placement in five of the ten program sites in one recent study (Nelson et al., 1988, p. xxxvi). This factor has not been extensively researched in FBS, probably because most practitioners believe in the importance of adequate family income for facilitating successful treatment.

Marital status, race, and education have been reported both to be correlated with outcome and to be independent of outcome. The marital status of primary caretakers (unmarried or divorced) was correlated with negative case outcomes in some studies (AuClaire & Schwartz, 1986, p. 52; Bribitzer & Verdieck, 1988, p. 261; Halper & Jones, 1981, p. 156; Jones, 1985, p. 97; Leeds, 1984, p. 33). But it was independent of outcome in others (PACT study, as cited in Hayes & Joseph, 1985, p. 13; Sherman, Phillips, Haring, & Shyne, 1973, p. 103; Tavantzis et al., 1985, p. 84). Feldman (1990, p. 34), in a study of 96 families participating in an IFPS program, reported placement was more likely if children were living with their father or other relative rather than with their mother or both parents. Leeds (1984, p. 33) and Cautley and Plane (1983, p. 2) found that the less educated the mother, the more negative the outcome. Jones (1985, p. 113) reported a similar result, as a mother's lack of a high school diploma was a weak but significant factor emerging from a multivariate analysis of the factors predicting foster care placement in her total sample of treatment and control group cases.

Contradictory findings have also emerged regarding client race and ethnicity. Feldman (1990, p. 34) reported that minority families were more likely to experience placement than were white, non-hispanic families, but he did not identify a specific minority group. His treatment sample contained 51% white (non-hispanic origin), 33.3% Black, and 14.6% Hispanic families (Feldman, 1990, p. 21). AuClaire and Schwartz (1986, p. 52) found that placement occurred significantly more often in black families, whereas Phillips and his associates (Phillips, Shyne, and Haring, 1971, pp. 27–28), Bribitzer & Verdieck (1988, p. 260), and Yuan & associates (1990, p. 5.18) found no correlation between race and placement outcomes. Such findings must be viewed with caution because, in many studies, racial distributions are skewed. For example, all of the children placed in the Halper and Jones (1971, p. 156) study were black or Hispanic, but 88% of the sample was black or Hispanic. Simple comparisons by ethnicity may be misleading if the study sample contains only a small number of children from a particular ethnic group. Tests of proportions across subsamples are necessary to determine whether race and ethnicity are factors correlated with service outcomes. To accomplish these analyses, adequate subsample sizes are required.

Child's Location and Status of the Problem Situation at Intake

The location of the children at the time of intake to FBS programs is a factor that has been consistently associated with placement outcome. Jones et al. (1976, p. 82) reported lower success rates for children who were not at home initially. In more recent studies, a lower proportion of children who were in placement at the time of intake had positive outcomes (AuClaire & Schwartz, 1986, p. 52; Leeds, 1984, p. 33). The correlation was not statistically significant in the AuClaire and Schwartz study, but this was attributed to the small sample size. In a related study, children who were provided FBS as part of an after-care program following day or residential treatment had higher placement rates (Heying, 1985, p. 525).

In a recent study in California, children who were not at home at the time of referral, or who had been previously placed were more likely to be placed (Yuan et al., 1990, p. 5.29). Yet in contrast to these studies of child location, Tavantzis and his associates (1985, p. 86) did not find a correlation between a child being in placement at intake and negative outcomes. Furthermore, Bribitzer and Verdieck (1988, p. 260) and Feldman (1990, p. 34) found no significant association between placement and history of previous placement.

A number of studies have found that placement was also more likely if the case situation involved an intensification of a long-term problem, compared to an unchanging chronic or a more recent problem (Halper & Jones, 1971, p. 156; Phillips et al., 1971, p. 26). This pattern was also true for the control group cases in a more recent study, although problems of a more recent nature were found to be associated with placement for the experimental group cases in this study (Jones, 1985, p. 121).

Nature and Locus of Dysfunction

Few studies have measured such factors as parent mental illness, emotional problems, supervision of children, and commitment to keeping the children at home. Using global definitions and measures, at least three studies have found that parental impairment due to mental illness (and related problems) was associated with child placement or poor outcomes (Halper & Jones, 1981, p. 156; Leeds, 1984, p. 30; Phillips et al., 1971,

p. 50). In a recent national study of various types of in-home and office-based FBS, low functioning on the Child Well-Being Scales related to child care-taker functioning was correlated with child placement for five of the ten programs studied (Nelson et al., 1988, p. xxxvi). Parent mental health, how-ever, was not a significant correlate of outcome in the PACT study (cited in Hayes & Joseph, 1985, p. 13).

In contrast, child-related problems have been found often to be predictive of service outcomes. Perceived child-related problems rather than physical abuse or neglect were associated with placement at the trend level in the Bribitzer and Verdieck study (1988, p. 261). Poor school and home behavior were associated with child placement in studies by Jones (1985, pp. 108, 122), Nelson et al. (1988, p. xxxvi), and Phillips et al. (1971, pp. 46–50). In a recent study of placement prevention and family reunification services, "the children who were eventually placed had more behavior problems and prob-ably as a result were more likely to have been adjudicated as delinquent or as persons in need of supervision and to have been placed on probation" (Reid, Kagan, & Schlosberg, 1988, p. 29). While parenting skills and disposition, availability of resources, parental ability and motivation to solve problems, and the availability of a habitable residence were found to be highly related to placement outcomes in the California study, such child characteristics as number of previous placements, disabilities, and school performance were also linked with placement (Yuan, McDonald, Wheeler, & Struckman-John-son, 1988, p. 5.11). In a similar vein, Feldman (1990, p. 34) reported that families referred because of a combined problem of poor parenting and emotional or behavioral problems in the child were more likely to experi-ence placement.

As indicated above, most studies have found that both child and parent problems or "level of difficulty" are associated with placement (including Cautley & Plane, 1983, p. 2; Reid et al., 1988, pp. 33–35). Unfortunately, because of the limited use of operationally defined variables and multivariate analyses, the differential effects of various problems across parents and chil-dren have not been adequately addressed.

Program Variables Associated with Service Effectiveness

The characteristics of FBS and IFPS, including types of clinical and con-crete services, intensity and duration of treatment, and use of ancillary community services, are factors that might logically be associated with treat-ment success. On balance, the FBS research literature is relatively uninfor-mative regarding the role of these factors. For example, Feldman (1990, pp. 24–29) describes the IFPS in his study in detail, but only reports that the treatment families made significant gains as compared with the comparison group. He does not report analyses of individual treatment components in relation to treatment outcomes. But some service and program variables have been associated with treatment success and/or the prevention of child placement.

Amount or Intensity of Service

Amount of client contact has been associated with treatment success in at least one study (Sherman et al., 1973, pp. 106–109). However, Yuan and her associates (1990, p. 5.26) reported that the number of direct service hours were not significantly associated with placement outcomes, although the intensity of services was significantly associated with placement. That is, families receiving more intensive services, but for a shorter period of time, were less likely to experience placement. This is an important variable because it has major implications for program design. It relates directly to service guidelines for caseloads and the number of hours of client contact that should be provided per case. This is a variable that is misleading if examined solely through bivariate analyses, because certain cases may require an especially large or small amount of client contact. And treatment success may be determined by other factors. In addition, there may be a "threshold effect" occurring for certain types of cases where certain levels of client contact within a certain period of time are essential, while unusually large amounts of client contact may indicate an inappropriate referral or unusually difficult case.

Duration of Service

An early study of services to children in their own homes found that longer periods of service were associated with treatment success (Sherman et al., 1973, p. 106). But this study focused on a service model that was not intensive. In contrast, the Homebuilders program has not found any differences in placement prevention rates when the duration of treatment was systematically varied between four, six, and eight weeks (D. A. Haapala, personal communication, February 11, 1988). A study currently being conducted by the National Resource Center on Family-Based Services is comparing the effectiveness of service when treatment length is systematically varied across programs.

Provision of Concrete or "Hard" Services

Transportation, employment, recreation, housecleaning, and other services are widely recognized in the child welfare field as ancillary services that support working effectively with multiproblem families (e.g., Kaplan, 1986; Levine, 1964; Polansky, Chalmers, Buttenweiser, & Williams, 1981). However, only a few studies have examined the effects of concrete services within the context of FBS. Bryce (1982, as cited in Frankel, 1988, p. 150) found that clients rated the provision of practical help (i.e., concrete services), providing services in the home, and therapist availability through flexible hours as more helpful than the use of specific therapeutic techniques (teaching communication skills, help with expressing feelings, help with understanding behavior). The PACT program also reported provision of concrete services as essential for treatment effectiveness (Van Meter, 1986, pp. 80–81).

Haapala's (1983) study is one of the few to test, through bivariate or multivariate analyses, whether the provision of concrete services was significantly associated with treatment success. He identified critical incidents occurring in the treatment of 41 single-parent families. Once a week, mothers, children, and therapists were asked to identify and rate events that occurred during targeted sessions involving the therapist and one or more family member. Using qualitative methodology, the events were categorized and then coded for statistical analysis. A discriminant analysis of the mothers' and target children's data sets indicated that when the Homebuilders therapist supported the client in obtaining "concrete services," or when "hard services" were provided by the Homebuilders therapist, then treatment success was more likely to occur. The more times the counselor did something or encouraged family members to obtain something concrete and tangible for the family and child, the more likely the child was to stay at home.

Haapala (1983), in interpreting these findings, suggested that, although offering and providing hard services to clients was helpful to parents and children in a tangible way, perhaps the message—"what was important to the client was something that the therapist would try to resolve"—communicated by the therapist in offering concrete assistance was a powerful and unusual one. The therapist did not compartmentalize client needs into those appropriate for counseling and those inappropriate for counseling—all requests were considered to be important. All of these studies underscore the importance of concrete services for effective treatment. And this service component is one that distinguishes HBS or IFPS programs from mental health or office-based family therapy programs where clinical treatment is the dominant mode of service.

What Else May Affect the Outcome of Family-Based and Intensive Family Preservation Services?

Although we have little data on them, there are a number of other factors that are conceptually related to service success and failure. Treatment *process* variables are among the most difficult to measure and yet are most clearly associated with service outcomes. Haapala (1983) and Fraser and

Haapala (1988) found that three factors discriminated treatment success from treatment failure (based upon the analysis of the data obtained from mothers receiving IFPS services). One was related to client characteristics (younger children were more likely to be placed) and two were related to events that occurred during the process of providing service. The child respondents, the offering of concrete "hard services" by the therapist was significantly associated with positive outcomes, as was "interruptions and disruptions," such as crying babies, impromptu visits by neighbors, and telephone calls, that occurred during the counseling sessions. The more frequently mothers identified disruptive treatment events, the more likely it was that the child was at home at the time of the three-month follow-up point.

Thus a higher proportion of children remained in the home of those families who experienced more interruptions and disruption while therapists were in the home. Why? Hypothetically, this finding makes sense if these disruptive activities indicate that the family has lost its ability to maintain household routines and stability. Such families may be less resistive to service and more receptive to learning new ways of interacting. Thus, interruptions during therapy sessions gave the skilled therapists opportunities to demonstrate in vivo problem-solving (what some have termed "teachable moments"). Another possible explanation is that these families, while chaotic, had some sources of social support that assisted them in making the changes necessary to prevent child placement.

Categorizing the Correlates of Service Outcomes

Clearly many factors affect service outcomes. These can be clustered under client, problem, service, or program variables. Examples of each category are listed below:

1. *client variables:* child and parent demographic characteristics; length or number of episodes of previous outpatient counseling, length or number of episodes of previous inpatient placements, and child's adoptive status
2. *problem variables:* mother or father supervision of younger (or older) children, use of corporal punishment, psychological maltreatment (e.g., style of verbal discipline), knowledge of child care and development, substance abuse; type and nature of child problems such as truancy, substance abuse, promiscuity, depression, anxiety
3. *service variables:* types of service (e.g., parenting skills training, services to improve school performance); major service goals; types of concrete services (e.g., transportation, financial assistance); time spent providing concrete services; types of clinical services; intensity

of the provision of various clinical services; and use of combinations of concrete and clinical services

4. *program variables:* overall length of treatment, amount of time elapsing between referral and family contact, amount of time spent during the initial weeks of service and over the course of treatment in face-to-face contact with the family, telephone contact time, and indirect service time.

Summary of the Literature Review: Research Hypotheses

In summary, the research studies conducted thus far provide a foundation to support cautious optimism that home-based and intensive family services improve child, parent, and family functioning. Which specific client, service, and therapist factors are responsible for treatment success is not clear. The lack of reliable information about the correlates of service success and failure was the motivating force behind the FIT project. Based on the need for information in this area, the project sought to test the following hypotheses:

1. Prior placement in foster, group, or institutional care will be positively associated with treatment failure.
2. Greater attainment of specific treatment goals during IFPS will be positively associated with treatment success.
3. Greater provision of concrete services, such as housing, transportation, and employment, by the IFPS therapist will be associated with treatment success.
4. Lack of social support will be positively associated with treatment failure.
5. The amount of time elapsing between the family crisis/agency referral and IFPS therapist response will be positively correlated with treatment failure.

The final sections of this chapter will present selected research studies or practice literature that support each of the five major hypotheses.

1. Prior placement in foster family, group, or institutional care will be positively associated with treatment failure.   Findings from recent studies have indicated that treatment success rates for families with children who have had prior placements are generally lower (AuClaire & Schwartz, 1986; Leeds, 1984; Nelson et al., 1988). Unpublished research conducted by the Behavioral Sciences Institute found that prior long-term placements were significantly correlated with subsequent child placement after IFPS treatment. In addition, Heying (1985, p. 525) found lower treatment success rates with families served after a child had completed a period of residential or day treatment services.

2. *Greater attainment of treatment goals will be associated with successful treatment.* Willems and DeRubeis (1981, pp. 21–22) found that treatment group cases had higher child and parent goal achievement scores than control group families, and a smaller proportion of treatment group cases experienced placement. The Hennepin County Community Services study (AuClaire & Schwartz, 1986, pp. 14–15) also provides some support for this hypothesis in that nonplaced families from the treatment group had higher goal attainment ratings at six months compared to the other groups.

3. *Greater provision of concrete services will be associated with successful treatment.* Haapala, in a qualitative and quantitative study of IFPS, found that the provision of concrete services was one of the few variables that predicted the avoidance of out-of-home placement (Haapala, 1983; Haapala & Fraser, 1986, pp. 10–11; Fraser & Haapala, 1988).

4. *Lack of social support will be positively associated with treatment failure.* As a correlate of outcome across families that participate in family preservation services, social support has rarely been studied. Social support was reported by Phillips et al. (1971, p. 27) and Jones (1985, p. 99) to be associated with reductions in placement rates. But Jones's findings were not statistically significant. In a third study, Hayes and Joseph (PACT, 1985, p. 13) failed to find any evidence for the hypothesis that social support affects the outcome of service. Bribitzer and Verdieck (1988, pp. 261–263) reported that families receiving more supportive services were significantly less likely to experience placement. However, "supportive" services were not clearly defined. However, Robert Wahler's recent research strongly supports the hypothesis. In his development of the concept of "insularity," he postulates that treatment failures are less likely to occur in families that are embedded in informal kinship and friendship networks. His research found that families were more likely to experience treatment failure when their social contacts were characterized by unsolicited, aversive interactions (Dumas & Wahler, 1983; Wahler, 1980; Wahler, Leske, & Rogers, 1979).

5. *The amount of time elapsing between the family crisis/agency referral and in-home therapist response will be positively correlated with treatment failure.* Crisis intervention theory and child welfare studies by Shapiro (1976) and others emphasize the importance of timely response to families in crisis. Evaluation results regarding the efficacy of crisis intervention services, however, are mixed (see Barth, 1990, pp. 98–99). But in terms of IFPS, individuals and families appear to be more amenable to change while they are in a state of crisis and when "normal" coping mechanisms for dysfunctional situations are not working (e.g., Smith, 1986). Thus, an immediate

response by the IFPS therapist should result in better case outcomes as compared to those cases where immediate response was not made.

Conclusion

This chapter has reviewed the major factors associated with success and failure in various placement prevention programs, with an emphasis upon HBS and IFPS. Additional exploratory hypotheses and research questions will be discussed and tested in the chapters that present the project findings. The next chapter will describe the study design and measures.

Chapter 4

Project Methodology

MARK W. FRASER, PETER J. PECORA, and DAVID A. HAAPALA

As indicated by the project objectives, the purpose of this study was to explore factors associated with IFPS failures. To do so, it was necessary to distinguish between families with successful and unsuccessful outcomes. Because it is impossible to consider failures without concomitantly considering successes, we will focus on factors associated with both success and failure in IFPS.

Hypothetically, IFPS might be successful or unsuccessful for a variety of reasons. Clients who are referred to an IFPS program may have such severe problems that they are not prepared to participate in treatment. They may fail early on. Some clients may be trapped in relationships so aversive that the learning opportunities afforded by in-home treatment cannot be used to full effect. Therapists may differ in training, and their differential knowledge, skills, and attitudes may affect outcomes. Certain elements of treatment—for example, parenting training, communication skills, or problem-solving—may be differentially effective; and some elements of service may be more used than others. The management and administration of programs may significantly affect the effectiveness of service impact through policies and supports for IFPS workers. In addition, environment-related factors such as the availability of community services or the view of the local juvenile court regarding the out-of-home placement of children may affect failure rates. In sum, a variety of client, treatment, management, and environmental factors probably affect the outcome of IFPS and, indeed, all social services.

In order to investigate the relationship between client, treatment, or therapist/system characteristics, and service outcomes, a descriptive study incorporating measures for each of these domains was developed. The study was designed so that a variety of information on recipients of IFPS and the nature of the services that they received could be examined. As shown in Figure 4.1, three broad classifications of variables—client, treatment, and therapist/system characteristics—were hypothesized to be associated with service failures. This conceptual framework guided the adoption and devel-

59

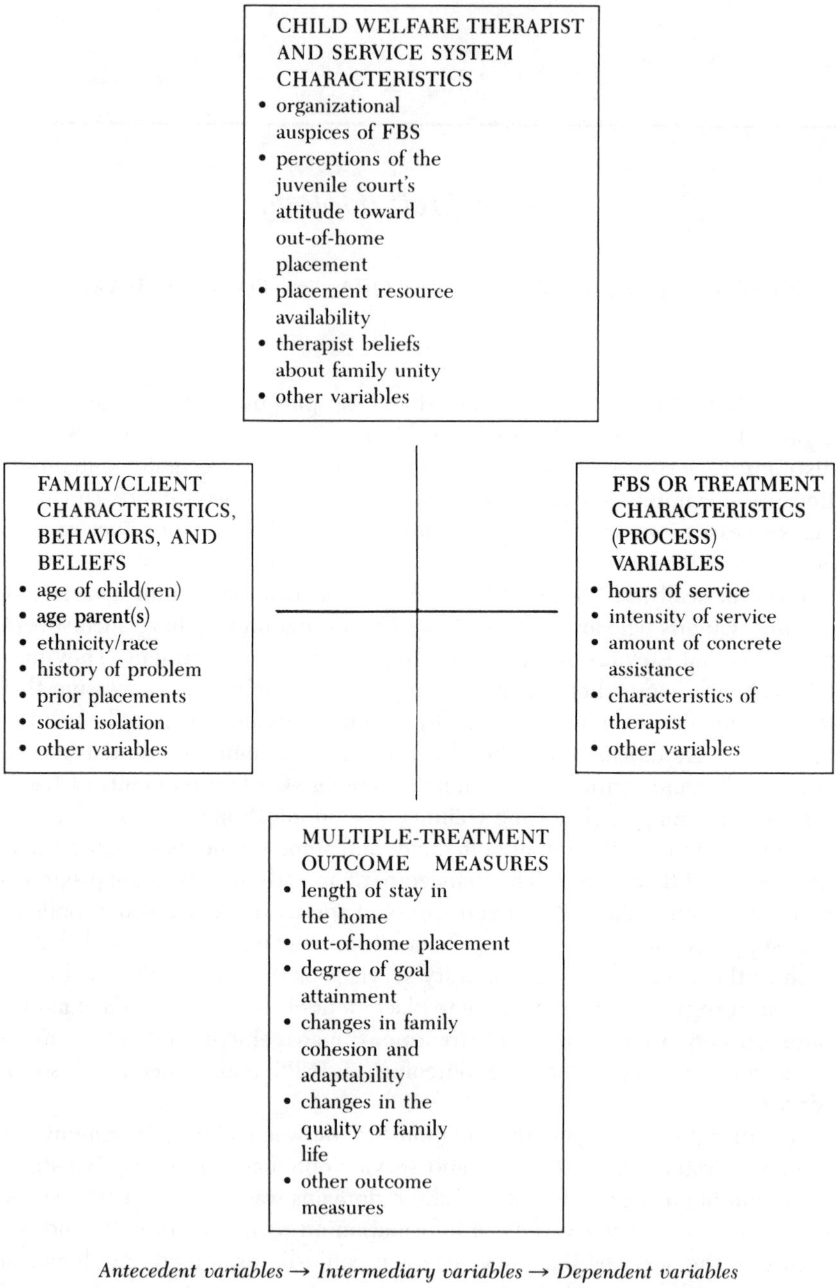

CHILD WELFARE THERAPIST
AND SERVICE SYSTEM
CHARACTERISTICS
• organizational
auspices of FBS
• perceptions of the
juvenile court's
attitude toward
out-of-home
placement
• placement resource
availability
• therapist beliefs
about family unity
• other variables

FAMILY/CLIENT
CHARACTERISTICS,
BEHAVIORS, AND
BELIEFS
• age of child(ren)
• age parent(s)
• ethnicity/race
• history of problem
• prior placements
• social isolation
• other variables

FBS OR TREATMENT
CHARACTERISTICS
(PROCESS)
VARIABLES
• hours of service
• intensity of service
• amount of concrete
assistance
• characteristics of
therapist
• other variables

MULTIPLE-TREATMENT
OUTCOME   MEASURES
• length of stay in
the home
• out-of-home placement
• degree of goal
attainment
• changes in family
cohesion and
adaptability
• changes in the
quality of family
life
• other outcome
measures

Antecedent variables → Intermediary variables → Dependent variables

Figure 4.1. Antecedent and intermediary factors influencing outcomes of family-based child welfare services.

opment of instruments for the study. On the basis of the existing literature, multiple measures of factors thought to be associated with outcomes in each category were sought.[1]

As a whole, this chapter will describe the research strategy and the measurement model developed to answer the research question, What factors are associated with IFPS failures? Subsequent chapters of the book are organized around the conceptual framework introduced above. There are chapters on service characteristics, family functioning, and placement outcomes. Here we will review the sampling method, process and outcome measures, data collection instruments, and data analysis strategies.

Research Design

To identify factors associated with treatment success and failure, a quasi-experimental design ("one-group pretest-posttest") with a partial 12-month follow-up period was employed (Cook & Campbell, 1979, p. 99). This design is also known as a "reflexive control" design because it used the pretreatment observations of the clients as a "control" or comparison for the posttreatment observations (Rossi & Freeman, 1989, pp. 310–314). It is diagrammed as follows with O representing observations, X the provision of IFPS, and O_{FU} the follow-up 12 months after IFPS intake:

$$O \ X \ O \cdots O_{FU}$$

In addition, a small case overflow comparison group was created in Utah to estimate failure rates in the absence of IFPS. The design in Utah is depicted below, with T signifying the IFPS treatment groups and C the case overflow comparison group:

$$T: \ O \ X \ O \ . \ . \ . \ O_{FU}$$
$$C: \ O \ . \ . \ . \ O_{FU}$$

Between August 14, 1985, and August 13, 1987, pre- and posttreatment data on 453 families that received IFPS in one of six program sites in the states of Utah and Washington were collected. Data were collected from 263 families that had entered treatment sufficiently early in the course of the study to be eligible for inclusion in 12-month follow-up sample (Table 4.1).

In 446 (98.5%) of the 453 families that participated in treatment, there were 581 first-, second-, or third-born children (Utah, 172; Washington, 409) who were designated as at risk of placement. In seven families there were no at-risk children who were first-, second-, or third-born. These families were exceptionally large, and fourth-, fifth-, or sixth-born children were identified as at risk. For individual-level analyses, they were removed from the data set. Although we will report the characteristics of service for 453 families,

Table 4.1.   Sample Sizes for Various Subgroups of the FIT Study

	Utah	*Washington*	*Total*
Families			
Participating in the study	141	312	453
With first, second, and third eldest children at risk of imminent placement[a]	139	307	446
Entering treatment early enough to be part of the 12-month follow-up sample	76	187	263
Children at risk of placement			
First, second and third eldest children in the total study sample	172	409	581
First, second, and third eldest children in the 12-month follow-up sample	97	245	342

[a] Seven families had only fourth, fifth, and sixth eldest children at risk of imminent placement.

the 581 children from 446 families that received the service are the major focus of the study. In an earlier report, data for primary and secondary caretakers plus each child from first- through sixth-born were analyzed separately (see Fraser, Pecora, & Haapala, 1989).

In the 263 families that participated in the 12-month follow-up, there were 342 first-, second-, or third-born children (Utah, 97; Washington, 245) who were designated as at risk of placement. These children are the focus of the follow-up sample. Families that entered treatment in the second year of the project were ineligible for follow-up because 12 months had not elapsed between the date of entry into treatment and the termination of the project's data collection activities. Consequently, the follow-up sample consisted only of families that received IFPS between August 1985 and August 1986. However, even though project timelines limited the size of the 12-month follow-up sample, all families—regardless of the date of intake—were tracked through August 13, 1987. Thus, information from all sources except the follow-up interview was available on all 581 children.

Intensive tracking or monitoring of each participating family was made possible by the computerized management information systems in the public child welfare agencies of both states. Arrangements were made such that project staff were notified when a state-funded, out-of-home placement occurred. In other cases, IFPS therapists learned of short-term detentions, privately funded placements, and runaways through posttermination contacts with family members and referring child welfare workers. In a small percentage of cases, contact with the family at the 12-month follow-up enabled the project staff to determine when and where a placement had occurred when it had not been detected by the other methods.

If at any time during the monitoring period of the study, a child from a participating family was placed out of the home, primary and secondary caretakers, the IFPS therapist, and her/his supervisor were interviewed to determine the causes of placement. These interviews produced unusually descriptive qualitative and quantitative data on family members' and therapists' views of the reasons for treatment failure and placement.

Sampling and Data Collection Procedures

Overview

Data were collected at two IFPS treatment program sites in Utah and four sites in Washington. The two states were selected because they represented two different organizational auspices for the delivery of a similar model of IFPS, the Homebuilders model. Utah's services were provided directly by public child welfare employees of the Department of Human Services; while in Washington, the Department of Social and Health Services contracted with the Behavioral Sciences Institute—a private agency—for the provision of IFPS.

The selection of Utah and Washington permitted a crude test of the influence of organizational auspices on staff attitudes, family functioning, service delivery, and placement outcome while holding treatment philosophy and methods relatively constant. Readers are cautioned, however, that the two states differ in marked ways and observed differences cannot be causally related to agency auspices.

Intake Criteria and Human Subjects Safeguards

In both states, families were eligible for service if one or more of their children were at "risk of imminent placement." The operational definition of "imminence" was that a referring agency must have been planning to place a child within one week, if IFPS were not provided. In Utah more than half of the cases were referred by CPS, and about 25% of the cases came directly from a juvenile court judge or screening committee, which had determined that the child was to be placed immediately if IFPS were not offered. In about 5% of the cases, a child was currently in placement but the referral source believed that the child could be reunified with her/his family through the provision of IFPS. In Washington, all referrals came from two units within the Division of Child and Family Services, Department of Social and Health Services. Workers from CPS (serving child abuse and neglect families) and family reconciliation services (serving ungovernable children and families in conflict) referred families to Homebuilders.

In both states, eligibility was contingent upon reasonable assurances that a child's safety could be ensured and that at least one parent was willing to schedule an initial meeting with the IFPS therapist. According to the criteria outlined above, all referrals were screened by an IFPS supervisor, intake coordinator, or a local placement screening committee.

At the six sites, all adults in families referred for family treatment services and all IFPS therapists were invited to participate in the study. Families were assured verbally and in writing that their participation in the research project was completely voluntary, and that refusal to participate in the study would not result in service provision penalties. Both IFPS therapists and clients were afforded the opportunity to decline participation. If families chose to participate, they were reimbursed modestly for the time required to fill out surveys and participate in interviews.

Prior to the start of data collection, all instruments and data collection procedures were reviewed and approved by the University of Utah Institutional Review Board, the Human Subjects Review Committee of the Utah Department of Human Services, and the Human Subjects Review Section of the Washington State Department of Social and Health Services.

Data Collection Procedures

All consenting IFPS clients in the Utah and Washington program sites were interviewed at intake to gather referral and demographic data. Family members completed assessment instruments to measure family functioning and social support during these interviews. In addition, during the first few days of service, the IFPS therapist filled out an instrument designed to assess parental functioning, child problems, and characteristics of home life. With the exception of demographic information, the same instruments and surveys were completed at the close of treatment. (See Tables 4.2 and 4.3 for data collection summaries.)

During and after treatment, IFPS therapists used a form to record case goals and the degree of goal attainment. In addition, clinical and concrete service checklists were used to record the nature and amount of services provided to families. At the termination of treatment, these checklists were reviewed by the therapists, and a case termination worksheet was completed. This worksheet summarized the total hours of face-to-face and telephone contact with family members and other service response information. At approximately the same time, the primary caretaker in each family was interviewed by a member of the research staff. These interviews

Table 4.2.   Data Collection Points

Instrument	Intake	Service termination	Service "failure"	12 months after service intake
FACES III	X	X	X	X
CWLA Family Risk Scales	X	X		
Social Support Inventory	X	X		
Case and service characteristics		X		
Consumer satisfaction		X		X
Placement causes			X	
Services follow-up				X

focused on consumer satisfaction, client perceptions of the key elements of service, changes in child, parent, or family problems, and treatment outcome.

If at any time within 12 months of IFPS intake a family experienced a treatment failure, research staff interviewed family members, the IFPS therapist, and the IFPS supervisor to assess the circumstances leading to "placement." (At this point, data collection for that family ceased.) Those families that avoided treatment failure—based on our definition of placement—were interviewed 12 months following intake. Families that started treatment after August 14, 1986, were not eligible for the 12-month follow-up interview due to the termination of data collection on August 13, 1987.

Utah Case Overflow Comparison Group

For the Utah IFPS sites, a comparison group was formed of families that were referred but not served by the IFPS program. For the period August 14, 1985, to April 22, 1987, any family that was referred for IFPS and met the criteria for acceptance but could not be served due to full therapist caseloads was identified and tracked until a child was placed or for 12 months, whichever occurred first.[2] A total of 26 families were identified. Selected child and family demographic data, and information about the placement location(s) of children during this follow-up period were gathered for each family.

Program administrators in Utah estimated that approximately 38 families were actually referred, met the criteria for IFPS, but were not served during this period. Consequently, the comparison group sample represents 68% of the population of families who were referred for IFPS treatment in Utah, met the criteria for service, and were not able to be accepted due to full therapist caseloads.

Table 4.3. Data Collection Summary

Type of data collected	Research participants involved	When data were collected	Staff person collecting data
1. Family adaptability and cohesion (FACES III)	Mothers, fathers, and children	Intake, termination, and follow-up (12-month)	Research assistant
2. Child, parent, and family functioning (CWLA Family Risk Scale)	Family-based therapists	Intake and termination	Family-based therapist
3. Social support (Milardo Social Support Inventory)	Mothers and fathers	Intake and termination	Research assistant
4. Family-based therapist characteristics and perceptions of client	Family-based therapists	First year of project	Research assistant
5. Child welfare and juvenile court system variables	Family-based therapists, CPS therapists, juvenile court and probation staff	First year of project	Research assistant
6. Goal attainment	Family-based therapists	Case termination	Family-based therapist
7. Case and service characteristics	Famly-based therapists	Case termination	Family-based therapist
8. Consumer satisfaction ratings	Primary caretaker	Case termination	Research assistant
9. Placement causes survey	Primary and secondary caretakers of family with placement, family-based therapists, and supervisors	Whenever placement occurs during the project	Research assistant
10. Services effectiveness follow-up	Families in the first-year sample	12 months after IFPS intake	Research assistant

Demographic and Service Measures

Family and Child Demographic Characteristics

As indicated in Figure 4.1, three broad sets of variables were hypothesized to relate to the differential service outcome measures discussed in the previous section. Client and family characteristics, process data (describing the services delivered), and child welfare therapist and system information were collected as explanatory variables.

At intake, IFPS therapists collected descriptive information from both primary and secondary child caretakers living at home. These data included age, gender, years of education, employment, marital status, and ethnicity. In addition, a range of data was collected on the characteristics of the families: family structure, religion, religious involvement, mobility, home ownership, income, and number of children living/not living at home. At the same time, data were collected on the children considered as potential removals (PRs), that is, the children at risk of placement. These data included adoption/birth status, age, number of prior placements, length of last placement, current placement, projected placement, school attendance, drug/alcohol involvement, handicaps, previous use of outpatient counseling services, and previous psychiatric hospitalizations (see Fraser et al., 1989, Volume II, for copies of the data collection instruments).

Clinical Services

A checklist of 74 clinical techniques or services that are commonly used by IFPS therapists was developed through a review of the IFPS literature and Homebuilders training materials. A panel comprised of IFPS therapists and supervisors from Utah and Washington reviewed and revised the items. Services that were listed on the Clinical Services Checklist included such variables as anger management, use of reinforcement in parenting, use of crisis cards, reframing, and a variety of other clinical techniques. The IFPS therapists were asked to record, through the use of a check mark, clinical techniques that they used with family members. In addition, the therapists identified those techniques that were a "major emphasis" of treatment.

Clinical services were measured on a three-point scale (1, not used; 2, provided; 3, provided as a major emphasis). Two approaches to the scoring of clinical items were tested in this process. The first involved the use of three point scales per se. The second involved the creation of two different binary indices: (1) one based upon a service either being given at any level or not (i.e., 2 and 3 versus 1), and (2) the other representing whether major use of the specific service had been specified (i.e., 3 versus 1 and 2).

Factor analysis and multidimensional scaling were applied to these measures using all cases in the sample, and the Washington cases only (the number of subjects was too small for Utah, given the number of service variables). These approaches to scaling resulted in substantially similar, computed scales that measured such clinical techniques as problem-solving, treatment relationship building, depression management, making referrals, parenting training, child behavior modification, assertiveness training, rational-emotive treatment, and crisis intervention. Internal reliability of the scales ranged from .33 to .89, with most alpha coefficient or bivariate correlations above .67 (see Fraser et al., 1989, Table 3.1).

Concrete Services

A variety of concrete services are commonly provided by IFPS therapists who subscribe to the Homebuilders model. These services include such activities as providing transportation, household goods, and clothing, or arranging for families to receive financial assistance. A list of 25 concrete services was developed using a process similar to that used to develop the Clinical Services Checklist.

IFPS therapists were asked to record the number of hours they spent providing specific concrete services. To develop summated concrete service scales, factor analysis with varimax rotation was used. However, no substantive dimensions were derived. Following the failure of factor analysis to produce acceptable scales, four summated scales were created on theoretical grounds. These measures consisted of summations of (1) all concrete service variables, (2) all concrete services except for providing transportation, (3) all concrete services involving IFPS therapists doing or directly providing the services, and (4) all concrete services in which the therapist enabled or empowered family members to meet a need by taking action on their own behalf. "Enabling" concrete services focused on showing family members how to procure a resource, how to fill out an application, how to request low-income assistance for a utility bill, etc.

Treatment Goals

In conjunction with the IFPS therapists and supervisors in the two states, a checklist of commonly used treatment goals was also developed by the evaluation staff. The Goal Checklist contained 16 goals along with behaviorally specific examples of each goal. Goals focused on both parent- and child-related objectives. They included those relating to increasing parenting, anger management, conflict resolution, and communication skills. And they also focused on such child-related goals as decreasing delinquent behavior, running away, and alcohol/drug abuse.

Therapists were requested to indicate all goals that were part of each family's case plan, and they were asked to designate the two goals that were most important. For all of the goals that were identified, therapists rated the level of goal achievement using a five-point scale with three anchors: no program, about half achieved, totally achieved. Across all goals specified for each family, "mean goal achievement" was computed.

Service Characteristics

In order more fully to describe the elements of IFPS and to assess the relative influence of each element in producing different outcomes, data describing the response time and the amount of service provided to each family were recorded. Using a Case Termination Therapist Survey, IFPS therapists reported these and other summative data at the close of family preservation services.

The Case Termination Therapist Survey contained items on elapsed time between referral and case assignment, elapsed time between case assignment and first contact with the family, hours of face-to-face and phone contact in the first week, hours of face-to-face and telephone contact in first two weeks, total contact hours (face-to-face and telephone), hours of advocacy on behalf of client, reason for termination, and length of service in days.

Distal Outcomes: Placement

As indicated in the previous chapters, the literature on family-based child welfare services contains remarkable assertions regarding the effectiveness of family-centered, HBS, and IFPS care. Studies suggest that many programs have been successful in preventing out-of-home placement. Some program proponents claim to prevent placement in over 85% of the cases that complete treatment.

However, the measures of success and failure used in most evaluations have been quite limited (Yuan & Rivest, 1990). In particular, no common measures other than child placement have been used, and child placement itself has been defined many different ways. The follow-up periods across which families have been monitored have varied significantly and, in some cases, placement of a child with a relative has been defined as failure and in other cases as success (see Chapter 2). In many studies, placement of a child in a foster family or group home has been the sole determinant of service failure, with children who were placed in shelter care or who ran away from home excluded from analyses. The lack of clear, consistent, and comparable outcome measures has seriously compromised the literature on family-centered services.

In this study, multiple measures of the outcome of treatment were used. The number of children who were placed outside the home in public foster or residential care during or subsequent to treatment was supplemented by a variety of other placement-related measures. They are defined in the next section.

In addition, treatment outcome was assessed by a series of "intermediate" outcome measures that were designed to describe changes in family functioning and the conditions in the home. These latter measures are more proximal to treatment and may be more sensitive to changes in parenting practices and child behavior. For example, data on family cohesion and adaptability were collected from all family members (including children) prior to treatment and at the termination of treatment. The use of these proximal outcomes, described in the following section, permitted us to assess the relationship between family functioning and the likelihood of placement.

Service Success and Failure: Using Multiple Perspectives

Out-of-Home Placement.   Multiple measures of "treatment failure" were developed. Failure was defined as any placement of two-weeks duration or longer in foster family, group, or institutional care. Treatment was also declared to have failed if a child was absent from the home for more than two weeks due to running away from home, temporary "placement" with friends or neighbors, or in juvenile detention or shelter care. These latter "placements" usually did not require formal court action but resulted in the child residing outside the home. From the perspective of family preservation, service may be thought of as having failed. Based on this definition of service failure, families were divided into two groups—successes and failures—and comparisons of the two groups across the three domains of variables (Figure 4.1) were undertaken.

In addition to the dichotomous measure of success/failure that is discussed above, other measures of placement were developed. Dichotomous measures are limited in important ways. First, they are fairly crude measures of treatment failure. Families that drop out of treatment or experience placement within two to three weeks of intake are classified in the same way as families that experience placement many months after successfully completing treatment. Consider the case of the child who is placed in foster care 11 months after participating with her/his family in IFPS. Relatively speaking, such families might be considered successful for ten months, but, because a child is placed in the eleventh month after IFPS intake, the family's treatment is declared a failure when a dichotomous measure is used. By aggregating families that fail early in the treatment evaluation period with those that stay together for extended periods, important information is lost.

Second, most definitions of placement do not take into account the type of placement. In 1979, the Homebuilders program began a project to work with families containing children who were severely emotionally disturbed. These children were about to be placed in a psychiatric inpatient facility.

Using a dichotomous outcome measure, 6 of the 25 cases (children) were classified as placements or "failures." However, 3 of the 6 children were placed in group homes, and 1 of these 3 children quickly returned home (Kinney & Haapala, 1984). From the perspective of the restrictiveness of placement, these three cases might be viewed as partial successes, for IFPS resulted in the use of a nonpsychiatric, less restrictive, and less expensive placement resource. Outcome studies that focus solely on the proportion of children placed cannot make fine-grained analyses of the relative merit and desirability of different placement outcomes.

An alternative approach to the measurement of failure and success in IFPS involves the adoption of measurement strategies that permit the specification of success in varying degrees. One such measure is time-to-placement or the "hazard rate for placement."

Time-to-Placement and "Hazard Rates" for Treatment Failure. Treatment success may be represented as the amount of time that has elapsed between intake and service failure or, in the event that no placement or runaway episode has occurred, between intake and the end of a follow-up period. The use of such a measure permits the calculation of a "hazard rate" as an outcome measure. The hazard rate is the probability that a child will be placed (or run) at time t, given that the child was at risk at time t. At any point during a follow-up period, the risk of placement or runaway behavior for each child may be expressed as the odds of service failure. For example, if out of a sample of 200 children, 20 are placed or run away in the first week of treatment, the odds of treatment failure are 20/200 or 1/10. In the second week, if 18 children are placed or run away, then the odds of failure are 18/180 (or still 1/10) because the sample at risk was reduced by 20, the number of children who experienced a placement or ran away in the first week.

A hazard rate may be computed by plotting the log-odds of service failure for each child for every day of risk. Hazard rates may change as a function of time. One might posit, for example, that the risk of service failure would be higher just after intake and treatment termination than during the course of treatment and during the months following treatment. The former are points in time when families are making major changes. The hazard rate also might be different for families with different social or demographic characteristics. For example, the hazard rate may be higher for families with children who have had prior placements as opposed to families with children who have never been placed out of the home. In sum, the hazard rate may change as a function of time and explanatory variables (for a discussion of issues related to hazard rates, see Fraser, Pecora, Popuang, & Haapala, 1992).

Type of Placement. Data were collected on the type of placement, and treatment outcomes are reported in Chapter 9 by various out-of-home conditions. Type of placement categories included (1) in home, (2) with relatives,

(3) with friends, (4) shelter care, receiving home, crisis residential center, (5) foster family home, (6) group home, (7) residential treatment, (8) inpatient psychiatric facility, (9) state hospital, (10) runaway, and (11) other (secure correctional facility, boarding school, etc.).

Proximal Outcomes: Parent and Child Functioning

The Family Risk Scales

In order to help measure change across a number of areas of child, parent, and household functioning, the Family Risk Scales (FRS) were used in the study. Developed as a part of a study of child placement preventive services in New York State, these scales were constructed to assess a child's risk of entry into foster care (Magura & Moses, 1986). Scale items are fully anchored and were selected because they were designed to be predictive of out-of-home placement (Magura, Moses, & Jones, 1987).

The FRS focus on parenting capacity, individual (both parent and child) functioning, and environmental situations that have been shown to be associated with out-of-home placement *and* that may be changed or manipulated in treatment. Personal and family characteristics that are not potentially goals in treatment are not included. For example, the FRS contain items on supervision of children and knowledge of child care, but no items on family size and the age or gender of the primary caretaker.

In all, the FRS contain 26 items, each of which has four to six response categories. All response categories are based on a continuum of functioning from adequate to inadequate performance. Each level is fully defined in relatively clear and behaviorally specific language.

Each of the scale items is designed to measure a different parent-related, child-related, or economic risk factor. Items cover habitability of the family residence, suitability of living conditions, financial problems, social support, parental health, parental mental health, parental substance abuse, parenting skill, use of physical punishment, use of verbal discipline, sexual abuse of child, child's physical health, child's mental health, child's school adjustment, delinquency, child's home-related behavior, and other risk indicators. Because of copyright restrictions, the FRS are not appended but can be purchased from the Child Welfare League of America.[3]

The breadth of the FRS is both an advantage and a disadvantage. On the one hand, many behaviors and conditions are rated. On the other hand, many of the risk factors such as "parent's substance abuse" and "child's delinquent behavior" are complex, multidimensional phenomena that should properly be assessed by a series of items. However, the scales do provide a useful range of indicators of child and family functioning and therapists found them easy to use. After initial training and practice, they required about 20 minutes to complete.

Scale norms for primary caretakers at intake have been published by the League (see Magura et al., 1987, pp. 9–11). These scores are based on a survey of 1158 families (with 2287 children) that participated in child preventive service programs in New York City in 1983. When these scores were compared with the primary caretaker intake scores for the FIT project families, caretakers differed on seven measures. The New York families lived in somewhat more inadequate housing but were more strongly motivated to prevent out-of-home placement. They were less cooperative with case planning, and less committed and prepared for parenthood. Yet in comparison to the families participating in the FIT Project, New York families also had children who were less delinquent and more compliant in the home. On average, too, the New York children were reported to have had fewer identifiable mental health problems.

The Family Adaptability and Cohesion Scales

The Family Adaptability and Cohesion Scale (FACES III) was designed to measure flexibility in problem-solving and family togetherness. It is a self-report inventory and family members over 12 years of age completed the scale at intake and at the termination of services. In addition, caretakers filled out the FACES at the point of placement, if one occurred, and 12 months following IFPS intake.

Based on the circumplex model of marital and family systems in which families may be classified into one of sixteen different types (Olson & Killorin, 1985), the FACES III contains ten items that measure family adaptability and ten items that measure family cohesion. Adaptability refers to the capacity of a family to adjust to new conditions. Adaptability includes such concepts as nature of family leadership (authoritarian, equalitarian, erratic), discipline (strict, democratic, laissez-faire), use of negotiation, role sharing, and consistency of rules. Similarly, cohesion refers to the closeness—emotional bonding, family involvement, marital unity, parent-child coalitions, and boundaries—in a family.

Adaptability is scored from low to high on a continuum with four anchors: rigid, structured, flexible, and chaotic. Cohesion is scored from low to high and has four different anchors: disengaged, separated, connected, and enmeshed. Sixteen family types are defined by cross-classifying adaptability and cohesion. Olson, Portner, and Lavee (1985) have computed norms for each type of family and have conducted extensive analyses using FACES-derived measures.

The internal consistency of the adaptability and cohesion indices was assessed using Cronbach's alpha. The alpha reliability at IFPS intake for cohesion was acceptable (.80), and it was moderately acceptable for adaptability (.64). The reliabilities of the cohesion and adaptability subscales at case termination (exit) were similar, .86 and .69, respectively.

Parental Social Support: Empathy, Aversion, and Coaching

In the past decade, the findings from numerous animal studies, analog experiments, and prospective surveys have suggested that social support is causally related to health maintenance, psychological well-being, and treatment prognosis (for reviews, see Cohen & Wills, 1985; Tracy & Whittaker, 1987; Whittaker & Garbarino, 1985). In particular, Wahler and his colleagues have found that failures in parenting training are correlated with "parental insularity," or a lack of social support (Wahler, 1980; Wahler et al., 1979). Furthermore, social support networks that place heavy demands upon families or are the source of criticism have been linked to higher family stress and difficulty in becoming self-sufficient (e.g., Stack, 1974; Whittaker, Tracy, & Marckworth, 1989).

Recently, Dumas, Wahler, and others have reported that socially isolated families are doubly at risk of treatment failure because they are not just isolated: they are embedded in coercive interactions with bill collectors, landlords, protective services caseworkers, food stamp clerks, counselors, police, and other social-control agents (Dumas, 1984; Dumas & Albin, 1986; Dumas & Whaler, 1983; Wahler & Dumas, 1989). The lack of social support is thought to affect both the psychological and material resources that insular families may bring to bear in solving financial, housing, health, child care, and other problems. Thus insular families are hypothesized to be more likely to fail to respond to treatment.

To measure social support, a Social Support Inventory based in part on Barrera, Sandler, and Ramsay's (1981) Inventory of Socially Supportive Behaviors (ISSB) was used. The ISSB contains 40 items and instructions call for respondents to rate each item's frequency of occurrence (Tardy, 1985). In 1983, Robert Milardo revised the ISSB for use with distressed families and added items to measure aversive social interactions.

At the same time, Milardo reduced the total number of items to 25 and expanded the response scale from five to seven categories: 1, once a day or more; 2, about every other day; 3, about twice a week; 4, about once a week; 5, about once every two weeks; 6, about once a month; and 7, about once every two months (Milardo, 1983). This revised instrument was used in the FIT project.

From primary and secondary caretakers, information about two general types of social support was gathered: (1) spousal (or cohabitant) social support, and (2) extended family/nonkin (including neighbors, friends, and acquaintances through organizations). At intake and termination, caretakers filled out one Social Support Inventory for spousal (or cohabitant) support and one for extended family/nonkin support. On the extended family instrument, respondents were asked to exclude activities that occurred with spouses, live-in companions, children, or professional agency personnel such as mental health therapists, social service workers, or homemakers.

Readers are cautioned that the social support scales did not measure the extent to which respondents felt that the amount or type of their social support was adequate. In the same vein, social network data per se were not collected.

Factor analysis with varimax rotation was used to extract three common factors that describe the underlying dimensions of social support among IFPS clients. Factor analyses of intake and exit reports from both primary and secondary caretakers produced remarkably similar structures across spouse and nonfamily/kin relationships (see Fraser et al., 1989). The factor scales were comparable to those developed by Barrera and Ainlay (1983) and Milardo (1983). The first factor was labeled "empathetic friendship" and incorporates elements of nondirective social support and positive social interaction. This factor contains expressions of intimacy, unconditional acceptance, respect, and trust. It appears to describe the central elements of a confidant relationship—physical affection, listening, and comforting. The second factor was defined by high loadings that describe aversive relationships of the sort described by Wahler and Dumas. Coercion and intrusion characterize this dimension of social relations for IFPS clients. Parents who score in the high range on this factor are likely to be embedded in relationships where they are frequently criticized and blamed. The third factor is equivalent to the factor that Barrera called "directive guidance." It has been labeled "coaching." It was defined by loadings that describe guidance and feedback activities such as giving information, teaching, and directive advising.

Based on the intake factor solutions, additive scales representing empathetic friendship, aversive contacts, and coaching relationships were created. To ensure that each scale was defined by variables that loaded on one and only one dimension, an inclusion criterion level of .600 was used. The scales were created by summing scores from items with loadings of .600 or higher and dividing the resulting sum by the number of variables included in the scale. The internal consistency of each scale was assessed using Cronbach's alpha. For the empathetic friendship (.93), aversion (.85), and coaching (.81) subscales reported in spousal relationships, the reliabilities were acceptable. Similarly, for the empathetic friendship (.93), aversive contact (.88), and coaching (.75) subscales for nonfamily relationships, the reliabilities were also acceptable.

Consumer Satisfaction

A Consumer Satisfaction Survey (CSS), based on an instrument developed by the Behavioral Sciences Institute staff, was used to cross-validate therapists' reports of the kinds of services delivered and to assess clients' perceptions of the relative value of key elements of IFPS. Items on the satisfaction survey included importance of in-home provision of services, importance of skill-building, and frequency of therapist behaviors (e.g., scheduling convenient appointments, explaining procedures, being available, being reliable, avoiding the taking of sides in arguments). Qualitative data were collected regarding what parents thought were the most and least helpful activities, as well as the current location of children who had been identified as being at risk of out-of-home placement.

In addition, clients were asked to rate various problems and areas of child, parent, and family functioning on a five-point severity scale (1, not a problem; 2, 3, 4, no anchors; 5, extreme problem) before and after treatment. These items were behaviorally specific and included the following items drawn from an outcome survey developed by Magura and Moses (1986, pp. 203–226): lack of appliances and/or furniture, being evicted, lack of income for rent, inability to provide food or clothing for children, losing temper with children, children fighting among themselves, children stealing, children using drugs or drinking, children wetting bed, parental substance abuse, marital fighting, and parental poor health.

Therapists' Characteristics and System Influences

There is a growing amount of evidence that the beliefs and attitudes of human services professionals affect their performance (e.g., Churchill, Carlson, & Nybell, 1979; Horejsi, 1982). While individual-level factors affect a therapist's performance, work climate, supervisor support, and other ecological factors also are acknowledged to affect workers' performance. To measure these factors and to assess their influence, an IFPS therapist survey was constructed.

The survey was designed to describe the social and demographic characteristics of IFPS therapists who provided services to families that participated in the FIT project. Data were collected on years of experience in child welfare; months of experience in FBS; formal education; continuing education; hours of supervision received from peers, supervisors, and outside consultants; and demographic characteristics such as age and sex. In addition, data were collected on therapists' perceptions of the availability of resources to help families, elements of IFPS thought to be particularly important, and the significance of family preservation as a public policy principle that should underpin the goals of child welfare services. Therapists were also asked to assess their agency's, supervisor's, and juvenile court's support of their IFPS program and prevention efforts to avoid out-of-home placements.

The instrument contained a section on service techniques that was developed by the staff of a research project at the National Resource Center on Family Based Services (Nelson et al., 1988). Similar to the FIT project, this project was designed to describe factors contributing to the failure of family-based child welfare services. Primarily retrospective in nature, the National Resource Center project included case record analyses and staff surveys at 11 family-based service agencies in six states. By including similar items on both the FIT and National Resource Center surveys, comparison of Utah and Washington therapists with IFPS therapists from 11 other programs was made possible. These comparisons, however, are not included in this report.[4]

Statistical Significance

Throughout the report, we will use the two-tailed $p < .05$ level of statistical significance.[5] However, we will report also statistical trends at the $.05 < p < .10$ level. We believe that, given the sample size, the trend level findings shed important information on the correlates of IFPS treatment outcomes, and thus trends are indicated in most tables.

Study Limitations

Causal Attribution. Despite the use of a small case overflow comparison group, the evaluation design is primarily correlational and does not permit identification of the causes of service outcomes. Placement outcomes cannot be considered to be causally related to IFPS.

Generalization. Data were gathered from families served by IFPS programs at six sites in two states. Both urban and rural families were served. The participating families were, by and large, reflective of the families served by the larger child welfare delivery system. But because probability sampling was not used, it is not possible to generalize to other sites in either state, to Utah and Washington child welfare populations at-large, or to child welfare populations in other states.

Definition of "Imminence." While the intake criteria were explicit (the child had to be at "risk of imminent placement" as measured by a child welfare worker's intention to place a child in one week or less), not all sites reviewed referrals with a placement screening committee or juvenile court judge. Thus it is possible that a small number of cases may not have met the intake criteria strictly. In particular, the appropriate court screening committee or judge may not have established "jurisdiction" and the "intent to place" for every child identified as a "potential removal" (PR).

Measurement: The Problem of Limited Variation. Some data collection instruments were used that contained items with nominal and three-point response scales (e.g., Clinical Services Checklist, Goal Checklist). These scales were adopted because IFPS therapists, supervisors, and the evaluators were concerned about research paperwork. Response categories were restricted to shorten the length of time required to fill out forms on participating families. The use of a "checklist," short-response format, however, hindered the construction of factor-based scales because of "floor and ceiling" effects.

To a limited degree, nonmetric factoring procedures are useful in identifying structure in correlational matrices containing nominal and ordinal data, but nonmetric procedures are less sensitive than parametric procedures and cannot rescue data from lack of variation. Compromises made in the name of parsimony may have limited the descriptive nature of the services provided. In part, variation was also constrained *perforce* because only one method of treatment, the Homebuilders model, was evaluated. In studies of several different models of FBS, there is likely to be much greater variation.

Sibling Dependency in Statistical Analyses. Of the 581 children, 135 were siblings of older children at risk. The inclusion of these children in the child-focused analyses makes it somewhat more likely that the family characteristics of families with at least two at-risk children will be identified as correlates of service outcomes. This is a potential limitation.

On the other hand, approximately 77% (446/581) of the children were singled out as being at risk, and no other children in their families were identified. Only 23% of the children were siblings of other at-risk children, and it is well known that children within the same families may have quite different dispositions and behaviors. Parents may react differently to different children within their families. The loss of variation as a result of ignoring siblings at risk and eliminating them from the analysis is potentially great. By excluding at-risk siblings substantial variation in child-level characteristics might be sacrificed. Thus for the child-level analyses in this report (see, especially, Chapter 8 and 10), siblings were included. In other reports, we have analyzed the sibling data by birth order (see Fraser et al., 1989b). Here, however, we made the decision, like Jones (1985), that the cost of leaving out siblings was greater than the cost of sibling dependency in statistical analyses.

Limitations of Change Scores. Measures of child, parent, and family functioning were taken before and after treatment. Then for some analyses, "change" scores were calculated to assess pre- and posttreatment gains or losses across all measures. Change scores are a valuable tool in evaluating the way people respond over time to a service, but they are subject to regression-to-the-mean effects. It is commonly recognized that extreme scores tend to be less extreme at a later point in time (Cook & Campbell, 1979, p. 100). In other words, people cannot stay in crisis for long. They get better (i.e., score toward the mean). As discussed in Chapter 8, posttreatment scores were, on average, less extreme than pretreatment scores. We call this "treatment response," but because of the design, regression effects cannot be separated from true treatment response effects. Although pre- and posttreatment standard deviations tended to be similar for similar variables (suggesting that regression may not be a confound), the change scores may contain an error component due to regression.

Differing Exposure Periods. Not all subjects entered and completed treatment at the same point in time, yet follow-up data collection was terminated at the same point in time. Thus, with the exception of the families in the 12-month follow-up study, families had different exposure periods for risk of treatment failure. Families that completed treatment in 1985 and early 1986 had a full year of exposure, whereas families that completed treatment after mid-1986 had less than one year of exposure. This is why data from the 12-month follow-up sample are used extensively in the various subanalyses, and why event history analysis is used to estimate the correlates of treatment outcome.[6]

Differential Participation in Washington. In Utah, virtually all eligible families elected to participate in the study, but in Washington, only 46% of the families referred to Homebuilders during the study period participated. Of the families that did not participate, half (51%) were not asked to participate by their therapists. About a quarter (24%) refused to participate, and 20% were not afforded the opportunity to participate because of research administration problems. Five percent were in such crisis at intake that they were excluded for treatment reasons from the study. It is possible, therefore, that the research sample from Washington did not represent the true Homebuilders client population on measures of problem severity. However, a comparison of client demographics and other characteristics between those Homebuilders families that participated and those that did not revealed no significant differences (Fraser, McDade, Haapala, and Pecora, 1990).

Reactivity and Limitations in Caretaker Recall. Although interviewers were carefully trained and confidentiality was guaranteed, it is possible that parents and therapists responded in socially desirable ways to questions regarding child placement. In addition, during the 12-month follow-up interviews, caretakers were asked to recall "informal" placements of their children with neighbors, friends, relatives, and others who may have helped families after termination of IFPS. Respondents' recall with regard to such events may have poor reliability.

Restrictive Measure of Treatment Success. The primary outcome measure was placement. Success was declared only when a family remained intact or utilized a relative—an extended family member—to help care for a child (i.e., informally to place a child). Conversely, failure was declared when a family experienced a nonrelative placement of two weeks duration or greater. This measure of success may have elevated "failure" or "placement rates" by the inclusion of children who ran away from home and who went to live with neighbors or friends. In addition, although multiple outcome measures were used to assess the effects of IFPS, the dependent measure related to child placement did not examine the stability of the child's living situation. Both the quality and stability of placement are important outcome variables, as discussed by Fanshel and others (see, for example, Fanshel et al., 1989a,b). Readers are cautioned that the definition of "placement" and treatment "success" may make placement rates observed in different IFPS studies incommensurable.

Placements of two-weeks duration or more involving any form of substitute care, including shelter care, inpatient psychiatric treatment, and juvenile corrections-related dispositions were counted as service failures. Some of the children in the study returned to their families three to six weeks after removal. Thus, the placement outcomes reported in this article do not differentiate between short- versus long-term placements, and by including shorter term placements may be inflated. The social desirability of placements was also not assessed. Consequently, it was not possible to distinguish between those placements that should have been prevented and those that may have been in the best interest of the child and his/her family.

Limitations of the Comparison Group Design and Sample. The comparison group employed for this study was based on tracking 26 of the 38 families (68%) that were referred but not served by the Utah IFPS units. It is possible that the 12 families that were not successfully tracked avoided child placement. Thus, the observed placement rate for the comparison group many have been lower had all the comparison group cases been tracked successfully. Counterbalancing this potential bias is the fact that only the referring therapists, and not the comparison group families, were interviewed for the comparison group follow-up. Some privately arranged placements or runaway episodes, therefore, may not have been identified. The placement rate of the comparison group should be interpreted with caution, for the sample size is small, the follow-up interview method differed from that of the treatment condition, and the findings describe only the public agency (Utah) sites.

Conclusion

This chapter has reviewed the research design and instruments used in the FIT study. While a number of study limitations are presented, the use of multiple measures and multiple sources of data strengthen the design and the confidence that may be placed in the findings. In subsequent chapters, brief methods sections will review in detail the measures and limitations particularly relevant to each chapter's focus. The most detailed description of the methods may be found in Fraser et al. (1989).

Notes

1. Although there is little IFPS "theory" in a formal sense, we attempted to draw on prior research and theory from related fields as we selected measures. In each chapter, we will review the research and theory that influenced our choice of measures. For more information on theory-driven evaluation, see Berk and Rossi (1990), Chen (1990), and Rossi and Freeman (1989).

2. Each comparison group case that was categorized as a success was tracked for 12 months.

3. The reliability of the FRS was assessed using Cronbach's alpha for each of three factor-based scales: an economic, a parent-centered, and a child-centered risk scale. The Alpha coefficients were .78, .88, and .83 respectively. See Magura et al., (1987, pp. 3–5) for information on the content and factorial validity of the scales. Copies of the FRS may be ordered from the Child Welfare League of America, c/o CSSC, 300 Raritan Center Parkway, Edison, NJ 08818 (Stock No. 2759).

4. Readers may obtain the Iowa family-centered worker survey data for comparison by contacting the National Resource Center on Family Based Services, School of Social Work, University of Iowa, Iowa City, Iowa 52242.

5. This means that approximately 1 of every 20 statistical tests may be significant by chance alone.

6. Event history analysis is useful when a data set contains partial or "censored" follow-up observations. See Allison (1984) and Fraser et al. (1992).

Chapter 5

Family and Child Characteristics: Who Received Intensive Family Preservation Services?

MARK W. FRASER and PETER J. PECORA

Who were the families that participated in the IFPS offered by the programs in Utah and Washington? The purpose of this chapter is to describe these families in terms of their major social and demographic characteristics. In addition, differences in family characteristics between the two states will be discussed. These data suggest the degree to which the states are comparable, and they provide a base for comparing FIT findings with those of other research projects that focus on FBS, HBS, or IFPS (for information on differences by site, see Fraser et al., 1989).

Method

Data Collection Procedures

At intake, data were collected on a variety of family characteristics for each of the 453 families that participated in the project (Utah, 141; Washington, 312). An IFPS therapist completed a Family Intake and Demographics Questionnaire for each family. This questionnaire contained items on child caretaker characteristics (e.g., age, gender, and education), family size, ethnocultural background, family structure, referral source, religious affiliation, religious involvement, home ownership, gross family income, and income source. In addition, information was gathered for each child in the home (for up to six children). These data included age, number of prior placements, length of last placement (if one), and whether the child was identified as being at risk of placement (not all children were targeted for out-of-home placement in every family). For the children who were identified as being at risk of placement, additional information about placement location at time of referral, placement location at time of intake, projected placement (assuming family preservation services were not able to be offered), school attendance, drug/alcohol involvement, physical/mental disabilities, and previous

83

mental health treatment were collected. For most of the analyses in this chapter, data on children will be presented by birth order (e.g., oldest child or second oldest child in the home).

Study Limitations

In general, intake data were recorded when therapists first began working with the family. In about one-third of the Washington cases, an intake coordinator for Homebuilders interviewed parents and case therapists to gather the information. In most cases, demographic data were based on the first and second interviews with families and supplemented by case record information. It is possible that some prior placements and other information may have not been mentioned by parents or listed in the case record. In addition, some socially sensitive problems such as substance abuse and truancy may have been underreported or not identified until later in the service period.

Findings

The Parents

As indicated in Table 5.1, parenting functions were carried out by birthparents, stepparents, relatives, and/or caretaking adults who were unrelated to the children identified as being at risk of placement. Approximately 41% of the homes were headed by single parents (single parents by divorce or separation, or single, never-married parents), while 19% of the homes were headed by both birthparents. The proportion of single-parent households was higher in Washington (43%) than in Utah (38%). On average, Utah families were slightly larger than Washington families (4.7 vs. 4.3 members) and they were less mobile, having changed addresses significantly fewer times than Washington families (see Table 5.1).

The child caretakers in Utah and Washington were qualitatively different with respect to certain characteristics. In Washington, more than 93% of the primary caretakers were women, whereas in Utah 86% were women. Washington primary caretakers were significantly younger and better educated. Compared to their Utah counterparts, they were more likely to be renting their homes. There were no differences in the age or education of the secondary child caretakers between the states. Although not statistically significant, caretaker ethnicity in the two states differed. A higher percentage of ethnic minority clients was seen in Washington (18.3%) than in Utah (13.5%). This reflects state demographic differences.

The Families

Reflecting state economic and cultural differences, the families in Utah and Washington differed on measures of income, participation in public

Table 5.1. Caretaker and Family Characteristics at Intake by State

General characteristics[c]	Utah	Washington	Total
Primary caretaker			
Age (years)			
M	38.2	35.0[a]	36.0
(SD)	(7.47)	(6.75)	(7.13)
Female (%)	86.5	93.2	91.1
Education (years)			
M	11.9	12.4[a]	12.3
(SD)	(1.79)	(2.13)	(2.04)
Secondary caretaker			
Age (years)			
M	39.4	37.5	38.1
(SD)	(9.00)	(10.00)	(9.70)
Female (%)	9.2	3.5[a]	5.3
Education (years)			
M	12.6	13.0	12.9
(SD)	(2.29)	(2.27)	(2.25)
Household size			
M	4.7	4.3[a]	4.5
(SD)	(1.85)	(1.55)	(1.66)
Asian, black, Hispanic, and Other			
minorities served (%)	13.5	18.3	16.8
Family structure (%)			
Birthparents together	22.0	17.7[b]	19.0
Single parent, divorce or			
separation	36.9	36.7	36.7
Birthparent with stepparent	27.7	19.3	21.9
Birthparent living with other			
adult	8.5	12.5	11.3
Single, never married	1.4	5.8	4.4
Other	3.5	8.0	6.6
Case referral source (%)			
Child protective services (CPS)			
Family reconciliation services	59.0	45.5[b]	49.3
(FRS)	.0	54.5	39.1
Youth services	15.6	.0	4.4
Juvenile court	24.6	.0	6.9
Self-referred	.8	.0	.2
Religious affiliation (%)			
Catholic	9.4	14.1[b]	12.6
LDS (Mormon)	62.6	4.6	22.7
Protestant	2.9	36.6	26.1
None	15.8	31.7	26.7
Other	9.4	13.1	11.9

(*continued*)

Table 5.1.   (Continued)

General characteristics[c]	Utah	Washington	Total
Degree of religious involvement (5-point scale from *great* to *none*)			
M	3.84	3.90	3.88
(SD)	(1.29)	(1.38)	(1.35)
Number of address changes in last five years			
M	1.8	2.4[a]	2.2
(SD)	(2.05)	(2.25)	(2.20)
Primary caretaker renting home (%)	43.0	61.2[b]	55.8
Caretaker structure (%)			
Living together, married	51.1	39.9[b]	43.4
Living together, unmarried	8.5	11.6	10.6
Not living together	15.6	11.6	12.8
Single caretaker	23.4	35.7	31.9
Other	1.4	1.3	1.3
Family gross income (%)[d]			
5,000 and under	8.8	10.1[b]	9.7
5,001–10,000	23.5	33.2	30.2
10,001–15,000	19.9	16.9	17.8
15,001–20,000	12.5	15.0	14.2
20,001–25,000	16.9	6.8	9.9
25,001–30,000	10.3	6.5	7.7
Over 30,000	8.1	11.4	10.4
Major source of family income (%)			
Job	73.0	62.8	66.0
Social Security	5.0	3.2	3.8
Income assistance (e.g., GA, AFDC)	16.3	29.1	25.1
Retirement	.7	.0	.2
Unemployment	1.4	1.3	1.3
None	.0	.3	.2
Other	3.5	3.2	3.3

[a] Indicates that the two states differ significantly at the $p < .05$ level using ANOVA F-test.
[b] Indicates that the two states differ significantly at the $p < .05$ level using χ^2-test.
[c] M, mean; SD, standard deviation.
[d] Cost of living statistics for the major data collection sites indicate that cost of living in the Utah sites (Salt Lake City and Ogden, 95.6) was lower than for most of the Washington sites (Spokane, 91.6; Tacoma, 102.5; and Seattle, 108.5). These scores are the percentage of the average score for all metropolitan areas participating in the national Chamber of Commerce survey, anchored at a "midmanagement" style of living and including the following cost categories: grocery items, housing, utilities, transportation, health care, and miscellaneous goods and services (American Chamber of Commerce Researchers Association, 1989).

assistance programs, child caretaking responsibility, home ownership, and religious affiliation. In Utah, 32.3% of the families reported incomes of less than $10,000, while in Washington, 43.3% had incomes less than $10,000. Similarly, more than 35% of the Utah families reported gross incomes that exceeded $20,000, whereas less than 25% of the Washington families had incomes above that level. Roughly 29% of the Washington sample reported receiving some form of public assistance, whereas in Utah, 16% of the sample reported receiving public assistance (usually AFDC) as an income source.

The lower unemployment rates and less generous public assistance programs in Utah, as well as the fact that the Washington caretakers were slightly younger, may account for these differences in income and participation in public assistance. In addition, these differences may reflect the work ethic of the Mormon church (the Church of Jesus Christ of Latter Day Saints), for close to 63% of the Utah sample was Mormon.

However, caretakers from the two states did not differ on their extent of religious involvement, a variable that has been shown to be more important in predicting behavior than religious affiliation (e.g., Burkett & White, 1974; Higgins & Albrecht, 1977; Jensen and Rojek, 1980). Religious affiliation in this study was generally not associated with outcome, but cultural differences that are rooted in the traditions of the Mormon church may be manifest in state public assistance policies that place great emphasis on self-reliance. In addition, the Mormon church administers for church members a small public assistance program, largely consisting of the provision of food and short-term financial assistance. In sum, Utah's lower unemployment rates, cultural emphasis upon self-sufficiency, lack of pockets of urban decay, and less generous public assistance programs may operate to create a more economically self-sufficient IFPS clientele.

Referral Sources

In Utah, 59% of referrals for family preservation services came from CPS, and 24.6% came directly from the juvenile court. For close to 84% of the cases, state agencies had established jurisdiction and placement was considered imminent for virtually all of the cases at the time of referral. A small proportion of these cases were characterized by situations in which a child was in danger of being placed after being reunified with her/his parents (less than 5%). The Utah IFPS programs also received referrals from youth services programs: 15.6% of the IFPS families were referred by youth-serving agencies to the two family preservation projects (Kearns and Ogden) as a last alternative to court referral for such child-related problems as noncompliance, truancy, and delinquency.

All of the referrals to the Homebuilders program in Washington came from CPS (45.5%) or FRS (54.5%), both units within the Washington Department of Social and Health Services. Historically, FRS was developed to provide services to incorrigible youths whose families were in conflict. Today, the Family Reconciliation program provides services to older youths who are truant, on the run, or in conflict with their families. Often caretakers and children in FRS-referred families have requested out-of-home placement, parent-child conflict is severe, and workers believe that the child is a danger to her/himself or others. Homebuilders is requested to help prevent that placement. Youths under the age of 11 who have been abused or neglected are referred directly to the Homebuilders program from CPS. When such a referral is made, it is viewed as the last alternative to out-of-home placement.

The Children at Risk

At intake, the risk of placement for each child in the participating families was assessed. Of the 1164 children whose families received IFPS treatment, 608 (52.2%) children were identified as being "at risk." In some families, all children were designated as "at risk," but in the majority of families only one child was assessed as in danger of placement. Of the 608 children at risk, 581 (95.6%) were first-, second-, or third-born. They came from 446 of the 453 families. Because fourth-, fifth-, and sixth-born children accounted for less than 5% of the at risk sample (few families were large enough to have a fourth-, fifth-, or sixth-eldest child at risk of placement) and because they tended to be very young, child-related analyses in subsequent chapters focus on first-, second-, and third-oldest at-risk children.

As indicated in Table 5.2, the average age of oldest children with the potential of removal (PR) was 12.5 years. There were significant differences across the states. In Utah, the oldest, second-oldest, and third-oldest children were 14.0, 12.7, and 11.7 years of age, respectively. In contrast, the Washington children were 11.9, 9.5, and 7.7 years of age, respectively. Reflecting their older age, children at risk in the Utah sample had significantly more prior placements than children in the Washington sample. But when a prior placement had occurred in either Utah or Washington, there were no significant differences in its length.

Oldest Children At Risk. Of the 317 eldest children at risk, approximately one of four was truant, attending school no more than half of the time. About 40% were reported to be involved with drugs or alcohol. Seventy percent had been involved in previous outpatient mental health counseling, and 16.1% had been placed at some point in inpatient mental health facilities.

Second-Oldest Children At Risk. The average age of the 195 second-oldest children at risk was 10.6 years, but as indicated in Table 5.2, there was significant variation across the states. Approximately one in five of the second oldest PRs was truant, and less than 10% were reported to be involved with psychoactive substances. Close to two-thirds had been involved in outpatient counseling and one in five had been in an inpatient mental health unit.

Third-Oldest Children At Risk. The 69 third oldest children at risk constituted 11.2% of the PR sample. The average age of third-oldest child was 9.0 years, but there was significant variation across sites. In Utah, third-oldest children averaged 11.7 years of age, while in Washington they averaged 7.7 years of age. Approximately 10% of third-oldest children were reported to have substance abuse–related problems and about 25% were truant.

Fourth-Oldest Children at Risk. Across fourth-oldest children identified as at-risk of placement, there were no significant differences. The average age of fourth-oldest children was 6.2 years. Most of these children were too young to be attending school and none were reported to have any drug involvement. Approximately 40% of their families had been involved in outpatient counseling services.

Fifth- and Sixth-Oldest Children At Risk. The percentages describing these children were highly unstable, influenced by missing data and low cell counts. Fifth- and sixth-oldest children ranged in age from 3 to 8 years of age. They were, for the most part, passive participants in IFPS treatment and were usually identified as at risk because all children in the home had been assessed as endangered by parent-related factors.

Summary and Discussion

The differences between the two states with respect to a number of family, parent, and child factors indicate that the aggregate findings should be viewed cautiously. The Utah and Washington IFPS programs may have served slightly different client populations and, for that reason, state by state analyses may be as informative as the aggregated findings.

In particular, it appears that Utah served an older (preadolescent or adolescent) population, while younger children were more frequently found in the Washington population. Moreover, Utah families appear to have had more fiscal resources, and possibly more parenting resources (because of a higher percentage of two-parent households). Readers are cautioned, however, regarding the comparative strengths of the Utah families. The pres-

Table 5.2. Characteristics of Children at Risk of Out-of-Home, Nonrelative Placement[a] at Intake by State[b]

General characteristics[c]	Utah	Washington	Total
Children at risk who were adopted (%)	4.3	3.5	3.8
Age of children at risk			
Oldest child			
M	14.0	11.9[d]	12.5
(SD)	(2.64)	(4.25)	(4.00)
Second oldest			
M	12.7	9.5[d]	10.6
(SD)	(3.21)	(4.89)	(4.63)
Third oldest			
M	11.7	7.7[d]	9.0
(SD)	(3.64)	(4.53)	(4.64)
Prior placements of children at risk			
Oldest child			
M	1.05	.43[d]	.60
(SD)	(1.40)	(.84)	(1.05)
Second oldest			
M	.97	.38[d]	.58
(SD)	(1.18)	(.91)	(1.05)
Third oldest			
M	.81	.33[d]	.49
(SD)	(1.12)	(.74)	(.90)
Length of time (months) of prior placements (if one) of children at risk			
Oldest child			
M	4.1	4.9	4.6
(SD)	(5.2)	(6.7)	(6.2)
Second oldest			
M	3.5	4.9	4.1
(SD)	(3.3)	(5.8)	(4.6)
Third oldest			
M	5.8	4.2	5.1
(SD)	(9.2)	(4.0)	(7.1)
Oldest child at risk			
Placed at time of referral (% not at home)	29.1	18.5	21.4
Placed at time of intake (% not at home)	12.6	12.1	12.3
Projected placement (% out of home)	89.4	93.5	92.4
School attendance (% attending half or less of time)[a]	33.8	24.6[e]	27.2
Proportion of children with no drug/alcohol involvement[b]	32.5	69.3[e]	59.6
Major handicapping conditions			
Learning problems	20.5	10.8	13.4

(*continued*)

Table 5.2. (Continued)

General characteristics[c]	Utah	Washington	Total
Psychiatric problems	10.8	0.4	3.2
Previous outpatient counseling services (% involved)[b]	74.7	68.8[e]	70.4
Previous inpatient counseling services (% involved)[b]	33.3	10.0	16.1
Second child at risk			
Placed at time of referral (% not at home)	30.9	10.0	17.2
Placed at time of intake (% not at home)	20.9	7.7	12.2
Projected placement (% out of home)	85.3	93.8	90.9
School attendance (% attending half or less of the time)	29.0	17.2	21.6
Proportion of children with no drug/alcohol involvements[b]	79.5	97.3	92.4
Major handicapping conditions			
Learning problems	15.4	8.5	10.8
Psychiatric problems	9.2	0.0	3.1
Previous outpatient counseling services (% involved)[b]	81.0	56.7[e]	64.7
Previous inpatient counseling services (% involved)[b]	41.3	9.4	19.9
Third child at risk			
Placed at time of referral (% not at home)	29.2	10.4[e]	16.7
Placed at time of intake (% not at home)	16.7	6.4	9.9
Projected placement (% out of home)	83.3	87.8	86.3
School attendance (% attending half or less of the time)	30.4	21.3	25.5
Proportion of children with no drug/alcohol involvement	81.0	93.8	89.9
Major handicapping conditions			
Learning problems	23.1	8.3	13.5
Psychiatric problems	7.7	0.0	2.7
Previous outpatient counseling services (% involved)[b]	75.0	51.0[e]	58.9
Previous inpatient counseling services (% involved)[b]	28.0	8.2[e]	14.9

[a] Including runaway, detention, living with neighbor/friend, or other out-of-home living arrangement of two-weeks duration or more.

[b] The client intake coordinator in Washington recorded much of the client demographic data at intake, while in Utah these data were recorded by the IFPS therapists. Thus the differences between the two states should be viewed with caution.

[c] M, mean; SD, standard deviation.

[d] Indicates that the two states differ significantly at the $p < .05$ level using ANOVA F-test.

[e] Indicates that the two states differ significantly at the $p < .05$ level using χ^2-test.

ence of a second child caretaker cannot be assumed always to be a benefit. IFPS therapists report that some secondary caretakers are less motivated to participate in treatment and attempt to subvert treatment goals.

Despite the demographic differences between the two states, the parents and children in the study appear to be quite similar to other IFPS or family-based care study populations, although some studies have involved a higher proportion of minorities (e.g., Jones, 1985) or only served families with adolescents (e.g., AuClaire & Schwartz, 1986). Based on the social and demographic characteristics of the participants in the two states, the aggregate findings from the FIT project would appear to describe the risk of failure in IFPS for a broad population of families with both young and adolescent children. Conversely, state by state analyses would tend to describe results for families with older children, in the case of Utah, and younger children, in the case of Washington. (Remember, however, that each program served families across the full range of child ages.)

Chapter 6

What Are the Characteristics of Intensive Family Preservation Services?

ROBERT E. LEWIS

In the previous chapter, characteristics of IFPS recipients were reported. This chapter provides descriptions of the service interventions utilized by IFPS therapists to treat these children and their families. More specifically, data will be reported regarding the provision of concrete and clinical services, case response, treatment goals, and degree of goal attainment. These data are based upon an analysis of the services provided to 453 families served under the FIT project. The data for analysis were drawn from four instruments completed by the IFPS therapists at the conclusion of services: Concrete Services Checklist, the Clinical Services Checklist, the Goal Checklist, and the Case Termination Survey (see Chapter 4).

Findings

Concrete Services

An important component of many IFPS programs is the supplying of "hard" or concrete services, such as the provision of public assistance funds, household goods, transportation, or food (Frankel, 1988; Jones, 1985). Concrete services are given a particularly central role in the Homebuilders IFPS model (Haapala & Kinney, 1979; Kinney et al., 1991), and a wide variety of concrete services were provided to the IFPS families in this study. Approximately three-fourths (74.2%) of all study families were given some type of concrete service. However, only one service, providing transportation, was provided in the majority of cases, which indicates the diversity of concrete services needed by families (see Table 6.1). Transportation was provided in more than 50% of all cases in the study, while the next most utilized concrete service, providing recreational activities, occurred in only approximately 20% of the cases.

In addition to the specific services, three summated scales of concrete

Table 6.1.   Concrete Service Provision (*N* = 453)

Concrete service	Cases served		Hours per case served	
	Number	Percent	Mean	SD
Provide transportation	244	53.9	3.46	3.36
Provide recreation activities	89	19.6	4.02	3.43
Help client get a job	62	13.7	2.15	1.49
Do housework with client	58	12.8	3.74	5.25
Arrange recreation activities	58	13.0	1.97	1.76
Help secure financial assistance	57	12.0	1.98	1.29
Provide child-care	55	12.1	3.95	3.57
Give financial assistance	50	11.0	1.30	0.76
Provide food	45	10.2	1.69	1.22
Help get food	45	9.9	1.82	1.15
Help with transportation	44	9.7	1.46	1.00
Help obtain medical/dental services	41	9.1	2.93	4.22
Provide toys or recreation equipment	39	8.8	1.46	0.82
Help obtain utility benefits	36	7.9	2.36	4.83
Help secure child-care	36	7.9	2.36	1.76
Arrange life-skill classes	32	7.3	2.31	2.68
Help obtain housing	25	5.5	3.48	4.26
Help secure clothing	25	5.5	2.08	2.81
Provide household goods	20	4.6	1.90	1.21
Help obtain household goods	17	3.8	2.00	1.60
Help obtain legal aid	16	3.8	2.38	2.66
Provide clothing	15	3.3	1.20	0.41
Move client to new location	9	2.0	4.11	2.21
Provide a job	9	2.0	2.56	1.13
Help arrange cleaning services	6	1.3	2.00	2.00
All "doing" services[a]	203	44.8	5.45	5.75
All "enabling" services	199	43.9	4.55	6.22
All concrete services	336	74.2	9.47	10.64

[a] The concrete service of providing transportation is not included in this summated scale.

services were created and analyzed, based upon theoretical distinctions in the Homebuilders IFPS model. These scales are "all 'doing' services," "all 'enabling' services," and "all concrete services."

An average of 2.54 concrete services were provided to each family for the total study sample. The average time spent in providing concrete services across the entire sample ranged from 1.19 hours for providing clothing to a high of 4.12 hours to move a client to a new location (see Table 6.1).

For those cases where concrete services were delivered, therapists provided an average of 9.47 hours per case over the course of IFPS treatment.

Concrete services accounted for 25.6% of direct service time for those cases where concrete services were delivered and about one-fifth of all direct service time overall. These figures emphasize the relative importance given to concrete services in the Homebuilders IFPS model.

Clinical Services

A total of 75 clinical service activities were examined (see Table 6.2). Of the nine most widely utilized service interventions—all being used in more than 70% of cases—four involved activities that tended to be used to establish and facilitate therapeutic relationships (listening, offering support, relationship building, encouraging) and three others were related to providing structure for treatment (clarifying problems, setting treatment goals, reframing). In addition, two problem- or technique-specific activities associated with behavioral treatment were among this group of most widely used services (use of reinforcements, identification and use of natural or logical consequences). Other specific treatment techniques, which might be applied differentially depending upon the presence of various family problems and needs, were also used widely but in a smaller proportion of cases.

In general, therapists reported high levels of provision for the entire range of clinical services or techniques. The median usage for the 75 clinical services was with 43% of the cases. The IFPS therapists reported an average of 31.8 different clinical service activities per case, suggesting the eclectic nature of IFPS. In spite of the short-term nature of IFPS, therapists appear to use a broad range of clinical techniques.

The clinical aspects of the Homebuilders IFPS model have been characterized as "psychoeducational," meaning that a combination of both psychotherapeutic and social learning approaches are utilized (Haapala & Kinney, 1979; Kinney et al., 1991). The former are focused upon managing personal problems of clients, while the latter emphasize the teaching of new life skills. The entire range of clinical services provided in this study was classified as to whether each intervention was primarily educational, the direct application of a psychotherapeutic technique, or a combination of the two. (Detailed descriptions of the clinical services are provided in Appendix B.) Approaches classified as educational constituted 33.5% of total reported services, direct application techniques 54.6%, and services combining both approaches 11.7%. Both psychotherapeutic and educational approaches appear to have been heavily used by the IFPS therapists.

Several composite scales and indices were developed from the specific clinical measures.[1] These included developing treatment relationships, solve problems/reduce conflict, parent effectiveness training, manage depression/stress, behavior modification, and make referrals/advocacy. Two-variable indices were assertiveness training, rational-emotive therapy, crisis

Table 6.2. Clinical Service Provision (*N* = 453)

Clinical service	Cases served		Cases served (major emphasis)	
	Number	Percent	Number	Percent
Listening to client	432	95.4	292	64.5
Encouraging	397	87.6	223	49.2
Offer support/understanding	374	82.6	184	40.6
Relationship building	369	81.5	195	43.0
Use of reinforcement	365	80.6	206	45.5
Setting treatment goals	351	77.5	107	23.6
Reframing	343	75.7	119	26.3
Natural/logical consequences	331	73.1	157	34.7
Clarify problem behaviors	324	71.5	138	30.5
Child development	305	67.3	103	22.7
Provide literature	304	67.1	82	18.1
Rational-emotive therapy concepts	303	66.9	176	38.9
Building hope	297	65.6	125	27.6
"I" statements	290	64.0	169	37.3
Anger management	285	62.9	197	43.5
Monitoring clients	273	60.3	85	18.8
Consultation with other service agencies	270	59.6	102	22.5
Clarify family rules	269	59.4	101	22.3
Improve compliance	267	58.9	163	36.0
Active listening skill	263	58.1	140	30.9
Defusing crisis	262	57.8	129	28.5
Providing reinforcers	262	57.8	94	20.8
Make treatment plans	261	57.6	75	16.6
Rational-emotive therapy techniques	256	56.5	165	36.4
Tracking behaviors	237	52.3	105	23.2
Build self-esteem	236	52.1	95	21.0
Track/chart behaviors	226	49.9	99	21.9
Clarify family roles	225	49.7	85	18.8
Handle frustration	224	49.4	84	18.5
Process of change	224	49.4	64	14.1
Refer to other counseling	217	47.9	53	11.7
Problem ownership	216	47.7	96	21.2
Build structure/routine	214	47.2	84	18.5
Negotiation skills	206	45.5	107	23.6
Timeout	204	45.0	82	18.1
Problem-solving	202	44.6	115	25.4
Environmental controls	196	43.3	62	13.7
De-escalating	195	43.0	92	20.3
Behavior rehearsal/role play	185	40.8	58	12.8
Use of crisis card	179	39.5	77	17.0
Refer to other counseling	174	38.4	43	9.5

(*continued*)

Table 6.2. *(Continued)*

Clinical service	Cases served		Cases served (major emphasis)	
	Number	Percent	Number	Percent
No-lose problem-solving	172	38.0	88	19.4
Meet with other providers	164	36.2	80	17.7
Accepting "no"	163	36.0	72	15.9
Self-criticism reduction	154	34.0	53	11.7
Depression management	153	33.8	73	16.1
Pleasant events	153	33.8	40	8.8
Impulse management	150	33.1	66	14.6
Advocacy with schools	145	32.0	66	14.6
Refer to social service	145	32.0	41	9.1
Give and accept feedback	139	30.7	52	11.5
Teach use of leisure	119	26.3	39	8.6
Social skills	117	25.8	23	5.1
Assertiveness	115	25.4	47	10.4
Anxiety management	113	24.9	50	11.0
Values clarification	113	24.9	22	4.9
Relaxation	107	23.6	22	4.9
Conversational skills	104	23.0	26	5.7
Family council	102	22.5	39	8.6
Provide paper/pencil tests	101	22.3	15	3.3
Track emotion	91	20.1	30	6.6
Develop informal supports	77	17.0	24	5.3
Fair fighting	69	15.2	20	4.4
Money management	69	15.2	16	3.5
Appropriate sexual behavior	68	15.0	18	4.0
Recognize suicide potential	67	14.8	23	5.1
Time management	66	14.6	18	4.0
Attend/testify at court	61	13.5	29	6.4
Teach job hunting	48	10.6	14	3.1
Academic skills	47	10.4	11	2.4
Territoriality concepts	43	9.5	9	2.0
Protect from sexual abuse	37	8.2	14	3.1
How to use journal	33	7.3	7	1.5
Advocacy with utilities	22	4.9	7	1.5
Multiple-impact therapy	10	2.2	4	.9

intervention, time/money management, and alleviate inappropriate sexual behavior/abuse. The final summated scales with their alpha scores and the two-variable indices with interitem correlations are presented in Table 6.3.

How extensively the service clusters described by these scales are used is summarized in Table 6.4. Consistent with the figures for highest usage of individual services, 97.6% of the IFPS cases were reported with scores on

Table 6.3. Clinical Service Summated Scales and Indices

Scale or index name Clinical services	Alpha reliability	Scale or index name Clinical services	Alpha reliability
Solve problems/reduce conflict	.887	Modify problem behaviors	.768
Problem ownership		Tracking behaviors	
Anger management		Environmental conrols	
Handle frustration		Improve compliance	
Impulse management		Providing reinforcers	
Problem solving		Build structure/routine	
Negotiation skills		Track/chart behaviors	
Give and accept feedback			
Accepting "no"		Improve parent effectiveness	.762
Fair fighting		Use of reinforcement	
Family council		Natural/logical consequences	
Clarify family roles		Active listening skill	
Process of change		"I" statements	
Attend/testify at court		No-lose problem-solving	
		Rational-emotive therapy	
Develop treatment	.865	concepts	
relationship		Rational-emotive therapy	
Listening to client		techniques	
Encouraging		Territoriality concepts	
Building hope		Assertiveness	
Relationship building			

98

Clarify problem behaviors	
Defusing crisis	
Reframing	
Setting treatment goals	
Make treatment plans	
De-escalating	
Offer support/understanding	
Clarify family rules	
Manage depression/stress	.793
Depression management	
Anxiety management	
Self-criticism reduction	
Build self-esteem	
Use of crisis card	
Pleasant events	
Relaxation	
Track emotion	
Conversational skills	
How to use journal	
Refer to other counseling	
Values clarification	
Teach use of leisure	
Develop informal supports	
Provide literature	
Make referrals/advocacy	.634
Refer to other counseling	
Refer to social service	
Consultation with other service providers	
Advocacy with schools	
Meet with other providers	
Apply rational-emotive therapy	.807*
Concepts	
Techniques	
Teach assertiveness	.377*
Territoriality concepts	
Assertiveness	
Teach time/money management	.353*
Money management	
Time management	
Alleviate crisis	.667*
Defusing crisis	
De-escalating	
Alleviate sexual abuse/dysfunction	.333*
Appropriate sexual behavior	
Protect from sexual abuse	

a Bivariate correlation.

Table 6.4. Clinical Service Utilization for Summated Scales and Indices
(N = 453)

| | Cases served | | Mean | |
Clinical service	Number	Percent	score[a]	SD
Summated scales				
Solve problems/reduce conflict	434	95.8	10.50	7.66
Develop treatment relationship	442	97.6	14.33	6.22
Manage depression/stress	403	89.0	5.91	4.85
Behavior modification	403	89.0	6.77	3.89
Improve parent effectiveness	433	95.6	7.13	3.97
Make referrals/advocacy	352	77.7	2.72	2.31
Two-variable indices:				
Rational-emotive therapy	314	69.3	1.99	1.65
Assertiveness	125	27.6	.47	.88
Time/money management	105	23.2	.37	.78
Crisis intervention	279	61.6	1.50	1.49
Sexual behavior/abuse	85	18.8	.30	.73

[a] The mean score was derived by summing the individual usage scores for the specific variables that make up the particular scale or index. High scores indicate greater utilization of that set of clinical services or techniques.

the develop treatment relationships scale. This scale also had the largest mean summated score for usage, which indicates that this set of techniques was used, on average, as a treatment method across all cases. A very high proportion of cases also had scores on the solve problems/reduce conflict (95.8%) and improve parent effectiveness (95.6%) scales. In addition, substantial proportions (89%) of the IFPS families were provided services related to manage depression/stress and behavior modification. Referral/advocacy services were reported for 77.7% of the cases.

For the two-variable indices, rational-emotive therapy approaches and crisis intervention techniques were reported as being used in approximately two-thirds of the IFPS cases. The other indices were utilized in a smaller proportion of cases.

In summary, study findings about the clinical nature of services provided considerable evidence of the wide-ranging and eclectic base of family preservation treatment. While relationship-building activities were present in nearly every case, a broad mix of other intervention techniques was also almost always utilized.

Case Response and Service Time

Variations in case response and service time have been the focus of considerable concern in the FBS literature. One major issue in the design of such services is the amount or intensity of service (Bryce & Lloyd, 1981; Edna McConnell Clark Foundation, 1985; Nelson et al., 1988; Sherman et al., 1973). The Homebuilders IFPS model emphasizes providing a particularly large number of hours in direct client service in a relatively short period of time. A second area of concern is the speed of response to referrals. The crisis intervention concept that quick response to referrals makes clients more susceptible to change (Butcher and Koss, 1978) has been incorporated into the Homebuilders model. A third issue that has been the focus of spirited debate has been the duration of FBS. Conflicting reports exist about the relative effectiveness of FBS of differing lengths (see Chapter 3 of this book, D. A. Haapala, personal communication, February 11, 1988; Nelson et al., 1988; Sherman et al., 1973). Findings that bear upon differences in time and response are reported in later chapters; while this chapter provides a descriptive base for understanding the time and response data.

Time is an important characteristic of IFPS treatment (see Table 6.5.). Therapists averaged over 37 hours of direct client contact per case. For the entire sample of cases from both the Washington and Utah programs, 95.1% of the cases were assigned to therapists within two days of the receipt of the referral. Over two-thirds of the families were contacted within 24 hours after therapists received case assignments, while 93.5% of the families were seen within 48 hours and 98.1% within 72 hours. Thus, the picture across the entire sample is one of a relatively rapid response to referrals, few delays in initiating services, and the provision of service on an intensive basis.

Somewhat greater disparity was present between the states in the timing of case response and in patterns of time spent in service delivery than for comparisons of concrete and clinical services provided.[2] Some differences were expected because of the 30-day time limit for service in the Washington programs, where workers had a caseload size of two to three families, as opposed to a 60-day time limit for the Utah IFPS programs with a four- to six-family caseload. Significant differences in other areas were not expected, but some were found. For example, the time associated with processing referrals was somewhat different for the two states. The average length of time from agency receipt of cases to delivery to the assigned IFPS therapist was considerably shorter for Washington (.05 days as compared to 2.40 days). In 95.2% of the cases, the Washington therapists were given a case the same day that it was received by the agency. In Utah, only 16% of the cases were assigned to therapists on the same day that they were received by the program. The majority of the Utah cases (47.1%) were assigned to therapists the day following receipt, and 17.6% of the cases were assigned two days or more after referral.

Patterns somewhat similar to those for the timing of case assignment were also reported for the average number of hours required for therapists to achieve face-to-face contact with clients after receiving the case. Washington

Table 6.5.   Case Response and Hours of Service Provided[a]

	Utah (N = 141)		Washington (N = 312)		Total (N = 453)	
Variable	Mean	(SD)	Mean	(SD)	Mean	(SD)
Days elapsed from referral to therapist receipt of case	2.40	(4.08)	.05	(.24)	.71	(2.40)***
Hours elapsed from therapist receipt of case to first in-person contact	27.42	(26.87)	18.59	(15.37)	21.25	(19.94)***
Hours of face-to-face contact first week	5.46	(2.82)	8.94	(4.26)	7.89	(4.20)***
Hours of telephone contact first week	1.04	(1.18)	.65	(.69)	.76	(0.88)***
Hours of face-to-face contact first two weeks	10.08	(4.90)	16.82	(6.73)	14.80	(6.95)***
Hours of telephone contact first two weeks	2.05	(2.47)	1.27	(1.26)	1.50	(1.74)**
Total direct client contact hours per case	38.56	(20.09)	36.35	(15.96)	37.01	(17.29)
Total indirect hours per case	17.79	(11.75)	17.10	(9.86)	17.30	(10.45)
Elapsed days from receipt of case to termination	62.82	(12.62)	30.16	(6.28)	40.10	(17.37)***
Percent direct hours first quarter	.34	(.15)	.29	(.11)	.30	(.13)
Total direct hours, last three quarters	26.83	(16.63)	26.78	(13.95)	26.79	(14.75)
Average direct hours per quarter, last three quarters	7.66	(4.37)	8.17	(3.83)	8.03	(3.99)

[a] Indications of significance refer to significant differences between the states based on the
t-test. Service length standards affect the case response and hours of service between the
states.
*$p < .05.$ **$p < .01.$ ***$p < .001.$

therapists contacted new clients within an average of 18.6 hours, while Utah
therapists averaged 27.4 hours.

Differences in standard operating procedure for service length between
the Utah and Washington programs were reflected in the total days that the
case was open in the IFPS program (exclusive of child protection or other

services). Washington therapists averaged 30.2 calendar days per case, while the Utah average was 62.8 days. Yet in spite of the differences in the length of service time, the hours spent per case over the course of the intervention were remarkably similar. Utah therapists averaged slightly more hours of both direct (in-person and telephone contact with clients) and indirect (e.g., collateral contacts, case staffings) client contact than did their Washington counterparts (Utah mean = 38.56 hours, Washington mean = 36.35). But the difference was not statistically significant.

In summary, IFPS service time and case response figures indicate that services were delivered quickly and intensively. The number of days that the case was open in each state was influenced by different standards for length of service—30 days for Washington and 60 days for Utah. While Washington IFPS therapists contacted clients somewhat more rapidly than their Utah counterparts, almost all families served in both states were contacted in less than three days from the time a therapist was assigned to the case.

Service Goals: What Were the Objectives of Treatment?

The setting and achievement of service goals have been a matter of consideration in several studies of FBS (AuClaire & Schwartz, 1986; Nelson et al., 1988; Willems & DeRubeis, 1981). IFPS therapists set specific treatment goals with clients as a routine part of treatment planning. Therapists supplied goal-related information on their cases in three ways: identification of all goals established for each case, identification of the two most important goals, and ratings of the extent of goal attainment for each of the established goals.

Given the brief-duration term of service, IFPS therapists appear to have tried to achieve a substantial number of goals per case. Therapists averaged 4.6 goals per IFPS case. Washington therapists averaged slightly more goals (5.1) per case than Utah staff (3.6). The frequencies with which the various goals were used are showed in Table 6.6. Eleven of the 16 goals were set with more frequency by the Washington sites compared to the Utah sites. Within the two states, goal setting was quite comparable.

Six goals were set much more commonly than other goals: increase parenting skills (77.7% of all cases), increase anger management (60.9%), increase communication (54.3%), increase compliance with house rules (51.9%), establish trust (44.2%), and improve school performance (34.2%). Other goals were established for 8–22% of cases. The first six goals accounted for 71.3% of all goals established in IFPS cases.

Table 6.6 also compares goal attainment across the various service goals and the average across all goals set, i.e., mean goal achievement. Goal attainment was measured on a five-point scale: 1, not achieved; 3, half achieved; 5, fully achieved (2 and 4 were not anchored). The goal of establish-

Table 6.6.   Service Goal Usage and Attainment (*N* = 453)

	Goal usage		Goal attainment[a]	
Service goal	Number	Percent	Mean	SD
Establish trust	200	44.15	3.84	1.04
Increase communication	246	54.30	3.11	.91
Increase parenting skills	352	77.70	3.28	.93
Increase anger management	276	60.93	3.17	.92
Improve school performance	155	34.22	3.16	1.29
Increase self-esteem	89	19.65	3.07	.85
Decrease anxiety/worry/fear	97	21.41	3.22	.81
Decrease depression	79	17.44	3.33	.85
Increase compliance with house rules	235	51.88	3.34	.93
Decrease running away	60	13.25	3.55	1.56
Improve home physical conditions	38	8.39	2.97	1.10
Increase social support	58	12.80	3.00	1.06
Increase use of community resources	66	14.57	3.44	.99
Decrease delinquent behavior	38	8.39	3.11	1.03
Decrease drug/alcohol use	30	6.62	2.53	1.28
Increase appropriate sexual behavior	34	7.51	3.15	1.21
Mean goal achievement			3.30	.77

[a] Goal attainment was measured on a five-point scale where 1 = not attained and 5 = fully attained.

ing trust was reported nearly or fully achieved (rating of 4.0 or above) in 66% of cases where this goal was identified (i.e., parents and therapists mutually identified goals to be accomplished during treatment) and had the highest mean level of attainment (3.8). Two of the goals that were established less often but had high achievement ratings were decrease running away and increase use of community resources. These goals were reported as achieved in over half of the instances where the goal had been identified, as compared to other goals, where achievement rates ranged from 24 to 47%. Goals with the lowest mean attainment scores were decrease drug/alcohol use (2.5) and improve the physical condition of the home (3.0). This suggests that drug/alcohol problems and problems related to the physical conditions of homes many be relatively more intractable and less able to be achieved through a brief intervention. IFPS therapists may instead be focusing on beginning the change process and referring clients to less intensive follow-up services.

Goal attainment appeared to be relatively more difficult for affective problems as well. Goals such as decrease depression, increase self-esteem, increase anger management, and decrease anxiety/worry/fear showed moderate responsiveness to IFPS interventions.

The achievement level for goals relating to the management of behavioral problems was positive but mixed—therapists reported relatively high rates of achievement when dealing with runaways, inappropriate sexual behaviors, and house rule compliance. For a small number of cases with the goals of decreasing delinquent behavior or drug/alcohol problems, the degree of attainment was lower.[3] The average across all 16 goals for goal achievement was 3.3.

Discussion

Findings reported in this chapter confirm the wide-ranging, eclectic, and intensive nature of IFPS. First, the provision of concrete services was shown to be a significant aspect of IFPS, accounting for approximately a quarter of the service time. About three-fourths of the IFPS families were supplied some kind of concrete services as a part of treatment. Transportation was the most common concrete service given and was utilized in more than half of all the IFPS cases.[4]

Second, therapists reported a high level of utilization of the entire range of clinical services. The median case usage rate for the 75 clinical services was 43%. IFPS therapists reported an average of 31.8 different clinical service activities per case. These findings suggest that in spite of the brief nature of this model of IFPS, therapists provided a complex array of clinical and concrete services. Clinical services provided included not only a heavy concentration of psychotherapeutic techniques, but also a substantial number of educational or social learning approaches. Over 45% of clinical services were educational in nature.

IFPS therapists gave high priority to working directly with clients. Cases averaged more than 37 hours of direct client contact over the course of treatment, and this figure does *not* include time spent in paperwork, staffing, and other indirect aspects of casework. This amount of direct service time is equivalent to that provided in nine months of traditional, once-a-week, mental health treatment. A rapid response and a substantial investment of therapist time in a brief period are salient components of this treatment model.

Six of the goals for family preservation services were used much more commonly than the remaining goals. These six accounted for over 70% of all goals established. They were increase parenting skills, increase anger management, increase communication, increase child compliance with house rules, establish trust, and improve school performance. Such goals reflect the client situations that bring many families to the child welfare system: child neglect, physical child abuse, and parent-adolescent conflict.

Service goals varied considerably in terms of attainment. The goal establish trust had the highest level of attainment (a score of 4.0 or greater in 66% of cases where this goal was set). The goals of decrease running away and increase use of community resources, although used sparingly, were reported as achieved in over half of the cases where the goal had been identified. The remaining goals were achieved in less than half of cases set. Goals with the lowest level of attainment were decrease drug/alcohol use and improve physical condition of the home.

For most goals, a partial level of achievement was reported in many cases. But the relatively low level of attainment for these goals may be related to the complexity of these social problems and their amenability to brief treatment. The attainment of goals focusing on behavioral problems was mixed—relatively high for dealing with runaway incidents, inappropriate sexual behaviors, and rule compliance problems, but lower with delinquent behavior or drug/alcohol problems.

Summary

IFPS therapists in both states provided a substantial amount of direct contact to families, distinguishing these IFPS programs from many others. Concrete services were provided to about 75% of the families in the study. In addition, a wide variety of clinical services or techniques were used in serving IFPS families, with major emphasis given both to psychotherapeutic and educational approaches. Some differences were found in state patterns, but the differences were not sufficient to suggest that Utah and Washington provided fundamentally different services.

In comparing the amount of direct client contact, the two states were remarkably similar. Washington therapists provided a more intensive service because they employed a shorter service period (30 versus 60 days) and smaller caseloads (2-3 families versus 4-6 families). Washington therapists made contact with new referrals somewhat more quickly than Utah staff, but both programs made relatively rapid responses to client referrals. When rated by importance, the most commonly selected goals focused on increasing parenting skill, anger management, communication skills, child compliance with house rules, and school performance. Attainment levels were highest for the goals establish trust, decrease running away, and increase use of community resources.

Notes

1.   Groupings of similar variables were identified using multidimensional scaling; then additive scales were evaluated using standard reliability techniques. Several

approaches to the scoring of clinical items were tested in this process, including the use of three-point scales and two different binary scales. The binary scales included one that was based upon the service either being given at any level or not (0, 1). It categorized clinical services into those that therapists indicated were used in a "major way" versus those not used or used in a minor way.

2. Site differences within the two states for service and time/response variables were described extensively in Lewis (1989, 1990). Many similarities and some differences were found. For example, the usage of concrete services was similar. In the application of clinical services, Washington therapists tended to have a somewhat more relationship-building and crisis intervention emphasis, while Utah therapists were somewhat more problem and technique oriented. Goal usage and particularly, rates of goal attainment, were similar between the two states. Compelling evidence was not present to argue that different IFPS models were being used by the two states or the various sites within the states. Rather, the differences found probably represent normal variation that might be expected within any service delivery system. They reflect variations in client needs, program setting, therapist treatment performances, and therapist experience levels. The different standards for length of service may also have allowed for, or perhaps even dictated, some differences in service approaches. While the programs appear similar, some caution in interpreting findings should be employed, for several characteristics of services (e.g., supervision and training) were not measured. For this reason, the findings are presented in aggregate and by state in this and the following chapters.

3. Since the completion of this research project, Behavioral Sciences Institute (Homebuilders) staff have begun working on new approaches to deal with families affected by drugs and alcohol.

4. It is important to remember that many families had the monetary resources to secure concrete services. These services should not be thought of as predominantly for the poor. Rather, concrete services appear to be provided to augment a global treatment strategy including giving support, enhancing relationships, and communicating to clients that no type of task is "below" the IFPS worker (Haapala, 1983).

Chapter 7

Therapist Perceptions of Organizational Support and Job Satisfaction

NANCE M. KOHLERT, and PETER J. PECORA

In Chapters 1–4, we proposed that three categories of variables influence the outcome of IFPS: (1) attributes of the children at risk of placement and their families; (2) type and amount of services provided; and (3) attributes of the IFPS therapists, their organizational climate and supports, community resources, and political pressures. Of the three categories, therapist-related factors and their effect upon the provision of intensive HBS has been the least investigated.

The impact that therapist demographics, attitudes, abilities, resources, skills, and job satisfaction have on the successful treatment of families is only beginning to be understood. In comparison to therapists' characteristics, family demographics and service characteristics have been more thoroughly researched. This chapter will review briefly some of the practice literature related to this topic. Then we will present FIT research findings on their characteristics, attitudes, and perceptions of organization and community support.

Training Characteristics of Family-Based Service Therapists

In the HBS literature, there is scant information on the influence of such therapist characteristics as gender, age, and experience on service outcomes. What findings exist must be examined with extreme caution because of methodological limitations, including the limited use of multivariate analyses. In addition, research studies have focused on FBS programs with widely divergent treatment approaches and target populations. It is not clear that findings of these studies are comparable.

Previous studies, however, do provide some information that may help in identifying therapist characteristics that may be associated with family-centered treatment effectiveness. For example, Jones, Neuman, and Shyne

(1976) reported that therapists with more years of experience in the field of child welfare had a higher proportion of cases where placement was avoided.

Compared to work experiences, a little more attention has been given to the impact that level of therapist education may have on service outcomes. While many FBS agencies employ staff with MSWs or another type of master's degree (Haapala & Kinney, 1979; Maybanks & Bryce, 1979), it is not at all clear that therapists with a MSW degree or another type of clinically oriented degree provide superior services. In a study of nonintensive, long-term FBS, Jones (1985, pp. 125–134) found, for example, that families served by MSW-level therapists had higher out-of-home placement rates. In contrast, informal research conducted by the Behavioral Sciences Institute on the Homebuilders program has found no differences in placement rates among IFPS therapists with different educational levels (D. A. Haapala, personal communication, 1987).

Furthermore, a few family-centered programs are staffed by a high proportion of paraprofessionals or workers with baccalaureate degrees (Levine & McDaid, 1979; Stephens, 1979). Yet other issues are raised regarding the strategy of using paraprofessionals. It is not clear that employing paraprofessionals offers advantages over employing professionals who provide the full spectrum of clinical and concrete services. Some researchers, in fact, are concerned that paraprofessionals may more easily get "overinvolved" in a case, lose perspective regarding the treatment process, and need more supervision (Kaplan, 1986, p. 50). In addition, a number of studies suggest that social work training, whether at the BSW or MSW level, has a significant and positive impact on job performance:

1. Teare (1987, p. 12) found that the curriculum of one MSW program provided graduates with knowledge and skills that were highly job-related for practice in public social service and mental health positions.
2. In an analysis of the educational background of the therapists in the 1977 National Study of Social Services to Children and Their Families, researchers found that therapists with a BSW were more successful in actually providing or obtaining the services that were recommended as part of the service plan (Olsen & Holmes, 1982, p. 98). MSWs were more successful in delivering or obtaining adoption and group home services.
3. Compared to persons with other educational degrees, BSW and MSW staff were found to have had more educational and practicum preparation in many of the knowledge/skill areas necessary for child welfare practice (Lieberman, Hornby, & Russell, 1988; Bureau of Children's Services Advisory Committee, 1982).
4. A recent evaluation of the job performance of child welfare staff mem-

bers found that staff with a MSW performed significantly better than therapists without a MSW (Booz-Allen and Hamilton, 1987).

5. Finally, Bailey found that BSW-trained social welfare staff, compared to staff with undifferentiated BA degrees, had more job-related knowledge and received higher performance ratings (Baily, 1978; National Association of Social Workers, 1980).

While these studies are salutary with regard to professional social work training, they must be viewed with caution because they were not conducted on a national basis, the findings are not uniformly clear, and each has methodological limitations. Nevertheless, they provide some evidence that educational preparation is important for practice in public social services, and therefore possibly in FBS (Pecora, Briar, & Zlotnick, 1989).

Therapists' Perceived Support from Supervisors, Administrators, and Allied Professionals

Many people wonder how therapists generate the physical and emotional energy necessary to provide the intensive and demanding services that characterize IFPS (i.e., what are *therapist* sources of help and support?). Some attention has been given to this issue. Stephens (1979) argued that agency support for therapists is imperative. He recommended that therapists receive at least two hours of supervision per week. Kaplan (1986) regards high-quality supervision as a way to retain staff, provide support, increase motivation, inspire creativity, and decrease burnout.

Homebuilders administrators also emphasize the importance of organizational and supervisory support. Supervisors in their agency are on call to their staff 24 hours a day, participate in case planning, and provide staff with support during critical periods in the case, including accompanying therapists on home visits as necessary. Because of supervisory involvement in cases, extensive therapist training regarding crisis intervention, and use of techniques for helping families cope with problems between therapist visits, the IFPS therapists (and supervisors) find that late-night calls and visits are infrequent. Consequently, Homebuilders administrators have found that "concerns about staff burnout and rapid turnover have not been supported" (Haapala & Kinney, 1979, p. 248).

There is very little literature concerning the extent to which IFPS therapists are receiving the administrative and allied professional support necessary for consistent service delivery. Indeed, anecdotal reports from IFPS therapists in many states indicate that support for new programs has been mixed, with administrators in some agencies feeling uneasy about the lower caseloads, unusual work schedules, risks to children, and other aspects of the program. In addition, juvenile court judges in some areas do not appear to understand the purpose and function of family preservation services; these judges may be reluctant to refer children to the program or, conversely, may refer a large number of inappropriate cases to the program as a "cure-all." Fortunately, the National Council of Juvenile Court Judges and a number of judges, such as Judge Fitzpatrick in Kentucky, view IFPS as a necessary component for meeting the placement prevention service requirements mandated by P.L. 96-272. These advocates of children are working to ensure that the proper state and federal legislation is passed to support these services.

These efforts are important as most IFPS program specialists believe that judicial, legislative, supervisory, administrative, and allied professional support is essential for program success. Yet the importance of this support (or therapist perceptions of it) for treatment effectiveness has not been well-documented. And the degree to which IFPS therapists feel that they are supported by supervisors, administrators, and allied professionals is not well-known.

Availability of Community Resources

A few researchers have tried to examine how the availability of community social service resources affects the provision of FBS. These resources comprise the tools that therapists use to give assistance and to bring about change in families. Goldstein (1981) listed the following resources that were typically least available to family-based therapists: mental health services, low-cost housing, low-cost day care, entry level jobs with low skills requirements, transportation, legal services, and religious programs.

Even if services are available, gaining access to them may be difficult or time-consuming. IFPS therapists from private agencies may be less able to gain access to a variety of resources, particularly types of public assistance. The extent to which certain services are less available or less accessible and the effect that other system level variables have on treatment outcome have not been well-researched.

Therapist Attitudes Regarding the Use of Certain Clinical Techniques and Concrete Services

The IFPS practice technology is nascent and IFPS therapists are only beginning to identify therapeutic techniques and practice theories that underlie IFPS treatment. Little empirical research has been conducted that carefully specifies various components of treatment and links these components with specific theories. In addition, few studies have identified, in specific ways, the interventions or techniques that IFPS therapists use or value. What complicates this line of inquiry, among other things, is that researchers are just beginning systematically to investigate specific clinical and concrete services that are associated with successful treatment.

One technique that has drawn a great deal of comment, but limited scientific testing, is that of providing concrete services. Numerous researchers regard "hard services" or practical help as useful (e.g., Dumas & Wahler, 1983; Jones et al., 1976). Jones et al. (1976) found concrete assistance (such as help with housing, health, and financial assistance) to be positively correlated with successful outcome. Furthermore, in a qualitative research study distinguished by the analysis of 1200 "critical incidents" occurring during IFPS therapy sessions, concrete-service assistance was reported at a significantly higher rate by mothers whose children remained in the home, in comparison to those mothers whose children experienced less successful treatment outcomes (see Chapter 6 in this book; Haapala, 1983; Fraser & Haapala, 1988).

Another technique widely cited and valued is the clinical and social support provided by the IFPS therapist (Goldstein, 1981; Haapala & Kinney, 1979; Sherman et al., 1973). Clinical support is usually composed of those client-centered, relationship-building activities such as listening, encouragement, establishing client-therapist rapport, and building hope. However, when tested empirically by Fraser and Haapala (1988), no significant differences were found between families with successful and unsuccessful outcomes regarding degree of therapist clinical support.

Fraser and Haapala (1988), however, draw a link between concrete-service provision and client-therapist relationships by theorizing that trust and client rapport are increased by the provision of concrete services. This may be an important link as Jones et al. (1976) believe that "trust" is one of the most significant service components. It may be that the mixed research findings regarding these clinical components are due to limitations in the ability of researchers clearly to operationalize and measure both the components of clinical support and client outcomes.

A variety of important clinical techniques have been identified by FBS of IFPS studies, including client advocacy (Goldstein, 1981; Haapala & Fraser, 1987; Nelson et al., 1988) and problem-solving (e.g., Goldstein, 1981). Teaching clients skills in such areas as anger management, assertion, and problem-solving are also emphasized by many HBS or IFPS programs (Haapala & Kinney, 1979; Lewis, 1990).

As indicated by the above discussion, a variety of research studies are beginning to identify some of the services and therapist characteristics that may contribute to the success of IFPS. It is useful to cross-check this data by determining the extent to which IFPS therapists actually believe various services and clinical techniques are important. This will not only help identify the practice techniques that should be examined more closely, but may highlight differences between the two sets of findings.

In one recent study, changes in child welfare worker and IFPS therapist attitudes toward various aspects of IFPS treatment and services were documented as part of an evaluation of training effectiveness. In this study, concrete services, client participation in goal-setting, 24-hour service coverage, delivering services in the home, time-limited treatment, and minimizing service barriers were some of the treatment or service components valued highly by the child welfare staff members (Pecora, Delewski, Booth, Haapala, & Kinney, 1985, pp. 534–535). Most of the same items of the attitude scale used in the 1985 Utah study were also employed to study the attitudes of FBS therapists in Hennepin County, Minnesota. Similar attitudes were found on 68% (17/25) of the items, with the notable exception that a large proportion of the Hennepin County therapists reported that FBS therapists should not directly provide concrete services (AuClaire & Schwartz, 1986, pp. 87–100).[1]

Research Questions Examined by the FIT Study

While these studies provide some initial findings regarding the attitudes of child welfare and IFPS therapists toward clinical techniques and services, we were unable to locate any FBS research that used a design that allowed for a rigorous assessment of the differential effects of therapist attitudes, education, training, organizational support, or allied professional support upon treatment effectiveness. To examine this area in more detail, several research questions were addressed in the FIT study:

- What are the demographic characteristics of IFPS therapists in Utah and Washington?
- How available are various ancillary services and resources, according to IFPS therapists in Utah and Washington?
- What differences exist or are perceived to exist between therapists, supervisors, agency administrators, and juvenile court judges regarding their attitudes toward HBS and child placement?
- How much pressure did the IFPS staff feel was placed on them to achieve positive results? What are the sources of this pressure?
- According to IFPS staff, what are the most important factors that contribute to staff turnover?
- What is the therapist level of job satisfaction and program morale across the two states?

Method

Subjects and Data Collection Procedures

All of the IFPS therapists in Utah ($N = 8$) and Washington ($N = 37$) who participated in the FIT project answered a therapist attitude survey that required 30 minutes to complete. The therapists filled out the survey instrument individually.

Instrument

Items for the survey instrument were either developed by project staff, adapted from previous IFPS attitude surveys (Pecora et al., 1985), or selected from a concurrent study of family-centered programs conducted by the Iowa National Resource Center on Family Based Services (Nelson et al., 1988). The survey instrument was divided into sections addressing the following topics: therapist demographics and general information; availability of services; agency, supervisor, juvenile court, and therapist attitudes about certain aspects of IFPS; sources of support and pressure; job satisfaction and program morale; reasons why staff left the IFPS program; and the importance of various clinical techniques or services for achieving case goals.[2]

Study Limitations

Case outcomes by individual therapist are not analyzed. Consequently, individual therapist characteristics and case outcomes are not directly compared. A direct test of whether therapist education affects the outcome of IFPS was also not conducted.

In addition, therapists were surveyed regarding their perceptions of the views held by IFPS and public child welfare agency administrators, as well as by juvenile court judges. The attitudes of IFPS and public child welfare agency administrators and juvenile court judges were not solicited directly. Some researchers (especially those in the social support field) would argue that the *perception* of support may be as important a factor in affecting behavior as the actual degree of support (Tracy, 1990). Finally, because the number of Utah IFPS therapists is so small, compared to the Washington therapists, state comparisons must be viewed cautiously.

Findings

Therapist Characteristics

The IFPS therapists who participated in this study had worked in the IFPS program for an average of 25.2 months (SD = 22.7); with a total of 6.4

years of child welfare experience (SD = 9.1). They had attended an average of 5.5 (SD = 14.4) IFPS-related workshops in the past year. Average number of years of education was 18 years with 4.4 years since their last degree. The educational profile of respondents is summarized below:

- MSW: 23 (51.1%)
- MA/MS in social science: 14 (31.1%)
- bachelor degree: 4 (8.8%)
- MA/MS in another field: 2 (4.4%)
- PhD/DSW: 2 (4.4%)

The majority of the IFPS staff were female (71.1%). Average age was 33.5 years old (SD = 6). The average caseload size was 3.1 families, but this finding should be viewed with caution, as Washington staff usually carry two families at a time, while Utah staff were assigned between four and six families. Cases served were from rural, suburban, and urban areas with the majority of cases from medium-sized cities (100,000–500,000 people).

Therapist versus Agency Attitudes toward the IFPS Model

IFPS therapists were asked to rate their views of IFPS service and then to report other perceptions of their agency's administrators. As a group, the therapists rated favorably the following aspects of IFPS: use of concrete services, client-determined goals, referring families to counseling, providing services in the home, setting appointments at the convenience of the family, providing intensive services, and children are better off in their own homes (see Table 7.1).

Therapists believed that their agencies supported, as a whole, many of these same program principles or techniques. There were, however, four areas of disagreement, where the therapists perceived differences between themselves and their agencies. The therapists believed that their agencies valued the following program characteristics significantly more highly then they did: 24-hour therapist availability, whether it was necessary to make contact in 24 hours, use of a brief-service model (less than 90 days), and focus on goal-oriented case plans.

Many of these differences reflect the attitudes of child welfare staff in different program areas, as some therapists prefer not to be called or paged at home, and feel that families could often benefit from a service that is longer in duration. Differences regarding the use of goal-oriented case plans may reflect the difficulties inherent in developing behaviorally specific and time-limited case plans with many child welfare clients. Workers valued more highly the idea the families can assume greater responsibility and self-determination, compared to their perceptions of their agencies.

Table 7.1. IFPS Therapist Attitudes toward IFPS and Their Perception of Agency Attitudes (N = 42)

	Therapist attitude		Agency attitude[b]	
Scale items[a]	*M*	*(SD)*	*M*	*(SD)*
a. Delivery of concrete services like moving, cleaning, grocery shopping with clients	4.3	(.89)	4.4	(.87)
b. Asking clients to identify/determine and prioritize their own treatment	4.5	(.59)	4.4	(.76)
c. Workers are available 24 hours a day for emergency visits or calls	4.3	(.78)	4.8	(.60)***
d. Referring family to other counseling services (if warranted or needed)	4.3	(.75)	4.3	(.79)
e. Services are routinely provided in the home	4.7	(.56)	4.7	(.73)
f. Services are routinely provided at night or on weekends	4.2	(1.04)	4.4	(1.05)
g. Client appointments are at the convenience of the families	4.6	(.62)	4.7	(.91)
h. Initial contact with clients is made within 24 hours of the referral	4.2	(.86)	4.7	(.77)**
i. Services are brief in duration, not lasting for more than 90 days	3.9	(1.10)	4.5	(.70)**
j. Services are intense, provided two or three times a week for one to four hours per time	4.5	(.89)	4.4	(1.04)
k. "Nonmotivated" clients are accepted for service	4.3	(1.03)	4.6	(.82)
l. The philosophy of service providers is that most kids are better off in their own homes	4.7	(.49)	4.8	(.49)
m. Service providers encourage families to assume greater responsibility and self-determination over their own lives (family empowerment)	4.8	(.37)	4.6	(.72)
n. Services are focused on goal-oriented case plans	4.5	(.70)	4.8	(.59)*

[a] Scale items were rated on a 5-point scale with the following scale anchors: (1) not at all important, (2) slightly important, (3) moderately important, (4) quite important, (5) extremely important. Anchors for "doesn't apply" and "don't know" were also listed but rarely selected.
[b] Differences between therapists and agency attitudes were tested using the Wilcoxon Matched Pairs Signed Ranks test.
*$p < .05$.   **$p < .01$.   ***$p < .001$.

In terms of state differences, there was more consonance between the personal views of Washington therapists and the values promoted by their agency compared to the Utah therapists. Utah IFPS therapists, in comparing their views with those of their agency, rated themselves as significantly more skeptical of the brief-intervention model, more in favor of 24-hour initial contact, more willing to work nights and weekends, more willing to have 24-hour service, more willing to work with poorly motivated clients, and more in favor of goal-oriented planning. In addition, compared to the position of their agency, they saw themselves as more in favor of family self-determination.

In contrast, Washington therapists valued concrete services more than their agency. In general, the Homebuilders agency was rated significantly higher on emphasizing 24-hour emergency services, having client appointments in the family home, providing intensive service, and accepting nonmotivated clients. Utah therapists, however, saw their agency as valuing more highly the philosophy that "kids are better off in their own homes."

Differences in Therapist, Attributed Supervisor, and Attributed Judicial Attitudes toward IFPS Program Principles and Procedures

Therapists were asked to rate the importance of certain policies and procedures common to IFPS programs. Then, on the same scales, they were asked to rate the views of their supervisors and the local juvenile court judges as a group. There was considerable agreement between therapist and attributed supervisor ratings regarding IFPS policies and procedures. Those items with the most agreement were (1) backing up a therapist who had made an honest and justifiable mistake in leaving a child who was subsequently injured in a home; and (2) not placing a child due to pressure from school personnel to do so (see Table 7.2).

Two areas of disagreement between therapists and therapists' attributions of supervisors emerged. In comparison to their supervisors, IFPS therapists tended to agree more strongly with the positions that (1) acting-out adolescents belong in foster or group care; and (2) there are limitations in what IFPS therapists can accomplish in one to three months.

In contrast, there was surprisingly little agreement between therapists and their perceptions of juvenile court judge attitudes. Therapists rated judges significantly differently on six out of nine policy and practice items. The biggest difference between therapists and judges was that judges were rated as being more skeptical of what short-term IFPS programs can accomplish. Other differences emerged regarding the perceived level of support for a therapist who makes an honest mistake. Therapists agreed that judges would back therapists most of the time; yet only a few therapists believed judges would always back therapists who had made an honest mistake.

Table 7.2. Worker Ratings of Therapist, Supervisor, and Juvenile Court Judge Attitudes toward the IFPS Program and Child Placement

Scale items[a]	Supervisor		Therapist		Juvenile court judge	
	M	(SD)	M	(SD)	M	(SD)
a. Believes that keeping children and families together sometimes means that while home-based treatment services are being provided, a child may be at some risk of injury	3.8	(1.70)	4.3	(1.70)	4.0	(1.40)[b]
b. Always reviews out-of-home placement recommendations (for therapists, makes instead of reviews)	5.3	(1.40)	1.7	(1.20)	5.1	(1.40)[c]
c. Reviews out-of-home placement recommendations carefully, and often with skepticism	4.5	(1.40)	4.9	(1.60)	3.7***	(1.30)
d. Reviews out-of-home placement more critically (and is less likely to recommend such action) as a result of recent controversial child welfare cases that have come to the attention of the public through the media	3.9	(1.40)	3.6	(1.50)	4.2*	(1.10)
e. Believes that acting-out adolescents (e.g., truants, runaways) belong in foster or group care	1.2	(.37)	1.5**	(.59)	3.6***	(1.30)
f. Has a critical and skeptical view of what can be accomplished by HBS programs that have only a one- to three-month intervention	1.4	(1.10)	2.0*	(1.20)	4.3***	(1.50)
g. Believes that younger children are more likely than older children to be placed outside the home,						

(continued)

Table 7.2.   (Continued)

	Supervisor		Therapist		Juvenile court judge	
Scale items[a]	M	*(SD)*	M	*(SD)*	M	*(SD)*
situations being equally severe	3.7	(1.80)	4.1	(1.70)	4.6	(1.40)
h. Would back up a worker who made an honest and justifiable mistake in leaving a child, who was subsequently injured, in a home	5.6	(.69)	5.5	(1.00)	3.7***	(1.20)
i. Generally recommends that a child be placed if school personnel pressure for an out-of-home placement	1.4	(.50)	1.5	(.70)	3.9***	(1.40)

[a] Scale items were rated on a 7-point scale with the following scale anchors: (1) strongly disagree, (2) disagree, (3) slightly disagree, (4) neither disagree or agree, (5) slightly agree, (6) agree, (7) strongly agree.

[b] Pairwise comparisons for attitude differences between therapists and supervisors, and therapists versus judges were tested using t-tests.

[c] Group comparisons can only be made between the ratings of supervisors and juvenile court judges because the therapist question was dissimilar.

*$p < .05$.   **$p < .01$.   ***$p < .001$.

In terms of specific state differences, Washington therapist ratings of supervisor and judicial attitudes were similar to those reported for the total sample. Utah therapists rated court attitudes similar to those of the total sample, but, compared to Washington, they reported greater agreement with supervisors regarding the placement of acting-out adolescents, the limitations of brief interventions, and the placement of younger children.

Sources of Therapist Support and Pressure

Those sources from which IFPS therapists felt they received the most overall support were their own supervisor, the IFPS program administrators, other supervisors, and top-level administrators.[3] Therapists as a group felt that they experienced the least support from local (county-city) government, juvenile court judges, and public child welfare agency district office administrators.

Therapists were surveyed to assess the external pressure that they felt to reduce out-of-home placements, and an interesting pattern emerged. Those sources from which therapists felt the most pressure were the same sources from which they garnered the most support: IFPS administrators, their

IFPS supervisor, child protective or other child welfare therapists, and top administrators. In contrast, therapists reported that they experienced little pressure from juvenile court judges. In addition, little or no pressure was reported from news media, advocacy groups, county social services agency, ad hoc committees/task forces, and juvenile probation.

Job Satisfaction

One section of the IFPS therapist survey focused on IFPS therapist job satisfaction, morale, and staff retention. Therapist job satisfaction was very high, averaging 1.5 (SD = .66) when measured on a 4-point scale (1, very satisfied; 4, not at all satisfied). Therapists in the total sample rated the morale of their IFPS programs as above average with a mean rating of 3.6 (SD = .88), when measured on a five-point scale (1, very low; 5, very high).

The pattern of responses on these two questions confirms common perceptions in the field that most IFPS therapists are satisfied with their positions and perceive their peers to be satisfied. Nelson et al. (1988), for example, found that morale in the 11 agencies that they studied was perceived as average to high by approximately 70% of the therapists. A troubling finding was that "a considerably larger proportion believed that morale was declining rather than increasing during the study period" (Nelson et al., 1988, p. 52).

Therapists were also asked to project reasons why an IFPS staff person might leave the program. For the total sample, the reasons most frequently cited were the following: stress related to the demands of FBS, personal or family reasons unrelated to the job, low pay, need for a change, and opportunities for advancement in another program or agency. Those reasons rated as least important were layoffs or reductions in staff, lack of supervision, personality conflicts, reassignment by agency, and lack of administrative support.

Here again, there were similarities and differences with a recent national study. FBS worker members reported that financial rewards, job security, working conditions, opportunities for promotion, and job clarity were less than adequate. They also reported that workloads were too heavy and some role conflict existed (Nelson et al., 1988, p. 53). These findings are similar to the FIT data, as discussed above, with the exception that the Utah and Washington staff did not report their workload as being too heavy, probably because these programs use lower caseloads and are more intensive than the programs examined in the Nelson et al. report.

Availability of Resources to Help Families

The resources that were rated by IFPS therapists as most available were ranked by accessibility as child or parent support groups (e.g., Parents Anonymous, AA), day care, counseling services, mental health outpatient services, food stamps, secure care facility for juvenile offenders, crisis nursery or protective day care, financial aid (public assistance), and crisis residential or detention services (less than 72 hours). Those services that therapists rated as most difficult to access included emergency housing, homemaker services, group homes, parent aid services, inpatient drug and alcohol treatment, and respite care.

Importance of Treatment Techniques

The degree of importance that therapists assigned to various treatment techniques for achieving case goals was the final focus of the survey. For the total sample, the treatment techniques most valued by the therapists were the following: listening with understanding and acceptance, encouragement, discussing alternative solutions and consequences, helping clients to recognize patterns of behavior, role modeling and role playing to teach parenting skills, continuing help despite client "resistance," and setting mutually agreed-upon treatment goals (see Table 7.3). The techniques listed above were ranked by mean scores as well as by the percentage of respondents rating it as "extremely important." The rank order was similar, so the items were ranked by their mean rating of importance.

Treatment techniques least valued included discussion of early life experiences, use of authority to make suggestions, helping clients understand early life experiences, use of coercion such as courts, helping clients understand the connections between early life events and present behavior, helping clients to understand reactions to treatment process in light of clients' own developmental history, and exploring clients' reactions to the treatment relationship. In summary, therapists from the total sample preferred relationship-building and client-centered problem-solving techniques, with little or no emphasis on use of therapist authority and interpretation of current life events on the basis of past experiences.

Therapist attitudes in the FIT study regarding the importance of treatment techniques were similar to those found by Nelson et al. (1988), but there were a small number of exceptions. For example, three areas were rated lower in importance by respondents in the Nelson et al. study: brief services (90 days or less), concrete services, and provision of services routinely at night or on weekends (Nelson et al., 1988, p. 54). These differences were expected because a variety of different programs were represented in the Nelson et al. study; and even within that study, individual program ratings varied widely.

Therapists ratings in the FIT study were also compared to the 1985 Hennepin County evaluation. While some of the items were different, the Hennepin County therapists ratings were quite similar to those found in the FIT survey. There were some exceptions, in that the eight staff surveyed

Table 7.3. Degree of Importance of Treatment Techniques for Achieving Case Goals

Treatment techniques[a]	Total sample (N = 45)		Utah (N = 8)		Washington[b] (N = 37)	
	M	(SD)	M	(SD)	M	(SD)
a. Sympathetic listening, expression of concern, understanding and acceptance, helping clients ventilate	3.9	(.25)	3.7	(.46)	4.0	(.16)*
b. General encouragement (expressions of confidence in client's abilities, recognition of client's achievements, etc.)	3.8	(.37)	3.7	(.46)	3.9	(.35)
c. Reassurance in relation to feelings of anxiety and/or guilt	3.4	(.58)	3.2	(.70)	3.4	(.56)
d. Outreach (continuing to help despite client resistance)	3.6	(.58)	3.3	(.74)	3.7	(.53)
e. Escorting clients to appointments to provide support and encouragement (not advocacy only) and to teach clients to negotiate with system	3.4	(.62)	2.9	(.64)	3.5**	(.56)
f. Promoting/discouraging certain behavior by suggestions or advice	3.3	(.71)	3.2	(.70)	3.4	(.72)
g. Educating by giving information, reading material, etc.	3.5	(.55)	3.6	(.52)	3.5	(.56)
h. Role modeling or role playing to teach parenting or other skills	3.6	(.58)	3.5	(.76)	3.6	(.54)
i. Setting mutually agreed-upon goals	3.6	(.54)	3.7	(.46)	3.6	(.55)
j. Discuss alternative solutions/consequences to identified problems	3.8	(.39)	3.7	(.46)	3.8	(.37)
k. Using authority to make suggestions or recommendations about client's decisions or behavior	1.9	(.74)	1.9	(.64)	1.9	(.77)
l. Intervention in or coercion to affect client's behavior (use of court, police, etc.)	1.9	(.74)	2.2	(.74)	1.8	(.74)
m. Encouraging examination of current behavior and its effect on self and others	3.4	(.54)	3.2	(.70)	3.5	(.50)

(continued)

Table 7.3. (Continued)

Treatment techniques[a]	Total sample (N = 45)		Utah (N = 8)		Washington[b] (N = 37)	
	M	(SD)	M	(SD)	M	(SD)
n. Encouraging exploration of current feelings and how they are affecting current behavior	3.5	(.55)	3.6	(.52)	3.5	(.56)
o. Helping clients recognize patterns of behavior and how these help or hinder achievement or expressed goals	3.7	(.47)	3.7	(.46)	3.7	(.47)
p. Exploring client's reactions to the treatment relationship	2.7	(.85)	3.1	(.90)	2.7	(.83)
q. Giving information about available resources	3.5	(.59)	3.2	(.71)	3.6	(.55)
r. Making referrals to agencies for other needed services	3.3	(.70)	3.0	(.53)	3.4	(.72)
s. Advocating for clients with other agencies or persons through mail or telephone	3.4	(.62)	3.2	(.46)	3.4	(.65)
t. Accompanying clients to other agencies or persons to advocate for the clients or to make certain clients receive needed services and assistance	3.4	(.65)	3.1	(.64)	3.4	(.65)
u. Encouraging discussion of early life experiences of clients	2.0	(.64)	2.0	(.76)	2.0	(.62)
v. Helping clients understand connections between early life events or reactions and present behavior, reactions, feelings, etc.	2.1	(.84)	2.4	(.92)	2.0	(.83)
w. Helping clients understand responses to treatment process in light of client's own developmental history and similar response patterns outside the treatment relationship	2.1	(.93)	2.4	(1.30)	2.0	(.86)
x. Shopping with or for client for furniture, food, etc.	2.9	(.85)	2.5	(.76)	3.0	(.84)
y. Providing other concrete services	3.4	(.69)	2.9	(.64)	3.6**	(.65)

[a] Scale items were rated on a 4-point scale with the following scale anchors: (1) extremely unimportant, (2) relatively unimportant, (3) relatively important, and (4) extremely important. Anchors for "doesn't apply" and "don't know" were listed but rarely selected.
[b] Differences between Utah and Washington were tested using the Mann-Whitney U-Wilcoxon Rank Sum W test.
$*p < .05.$ $**p < .01.$ $***p < .001.$

did not agree as strongly with the FIT study ratings in the following areas: seeing clients face-to-face within 24 hours of the referral, provision of concrete services, avoiding client confrontation, never insisting that all family members participate in treatment sessions, and placing less value on the meaning of the term *family therapy* in a case plan (AuClaire & Schwartz, 1986, pp. 97–100).

These differences are reflective of the variation in program models and therapist philosophy across the country. More importantly, they represent critical program design issues that remain to be addressed by the field, namely, which treatment approaches are more effective for which clients.

Selected State Differences

The Utah and Washington therapist survey data were compared to identify areas where the therapists in both states differed. As mentioned earlier, the Utah IFPS therapists worked in a public social service setting where public assistance offices are co-located in the same building complex. The Washington IFPS staff were part of a private nonprofit social service agency that contracts with the Washington Department of Social and Health Services.

Utah versus Washington Demographics

Therapist demographic and other characteristics between the two states were compared. There was much similarity between the two states with the following exceptions. The Washington therapists were more likely to be female and to have more experience (78% female and a mean of 27.8 months in HBS). The Utah IFPS therapists were 62.5% male with an average of 13 months of IFPS experience.

Utah therapists carried large caseloads, with a state average of approximately five as compared to a caseload size averaging between two and three families in Washington. Utah therapists received more individual supervision per month, with a mean average of 5.0 hours (median = 3), and Washington averaging 4.1 hours per month (median = 3). Washington staff, however, spent an average of 10.4 hours per month (median = 10) in group supervision (staffing cases) while Utah staff spent an average of 9.5 hours per month (median = 8) in group supervision.

Utah versus Washington Resource Availability

There were a number of services that were either less or more difficult to access depending upon the state and individual program site. These services are listed in Table 7.4. Caution, however, must be exercised in examining

Table 7.4.   Differences in Availability of Resources by State and Site

	Less difficult than norm	*More difficult than norm*
Utah		
Kearns	Respite care Residential drug and alcohol Homemaker service	Secure care: Juveniles Mental health outpatient Foster home
Ogden	Homemaker service Outpatient drug and alcohol	Parent classes
Washington		
Pierce	Respite care School support Residential treatment or inpatient	Crisis nursery
King	None	Crisis nursery Financial aid Crisis residential
Snohomish	Respite care Residential drug and alcohol	Counseling—Youth services
Spokane	None	Food stamps Secure care juvenile Crisis nursery

these data because some site responses were based on small numbers of therapists.

Utah and Washington Ratings of Pressure and Support

Compared to Washington therapists, Utah IFPS therapists rated themselves as receiving less support from district administrators ($p < .01$), other supervisors ($p < .001$), and other child welfare program units or therapists ($p < .001$). Utah therapists also reported experiencing more pressure from Department of Social Services administrators, district office administrators ($p < .017$) and supervisors ($p < .001$).

Utah and Washington Differences in Job Satisfaction and Program Morale

Utah therapists ($M = 1.8$, SD = .92) tended to be slightly less satisfied with their work than Washington therapists ($M = 1.4$, SD = .71). Morale, however, differed significantly (Wilcoxon Rank Sum $z = -3.35$, $p < .001$). Utah therapists rated the overall morale of their IFPS program as slightly "below average" ($M = 2.6$, SD = .92), while Washington therapists rated their program morale as "above average" ($M = 3.9$, SD = .71).

The Washington IFPS staff rated low pay as an important reason why they thought therapists might leave the Homebuilders program. Utah staff rated stress related to the demands of IFPS, lack of administrative support, reassignment by the agency, and stress due to the structure and policies of the agency as likely reasons for leaving.

Treatment Techniques and Frequency of Court Hearings

There were few differences between the two states regarding how much IFPS therapists thought certain treatment techniques were important for achieving case goals. Utah therapists valued significantly more the technique of "exploring client reactions to treatment." Compared to the Washington staff, they valued three practical applications less: concrete services, shopping with clients, and escorting clients to appointments. During the most recent year, Utah therapists $(M = 6.6)$ had been required to participate in court hearings for more cases than Washington therapists $(M = .6)$. These findings suggest that, compared to the Utah therapists, Washington therapists may have been somewhat more removed from formal decision-making in child welfare.

Discussion

Resources and Support

As a group, Washington therapists reported much greater difficulty in obtaining allied services than Utah therapists. Eight out of 22 of the resources listed in the survey were rated as significantly more difficult to obtain. Three other resources were also more difficult for Washington therapists to obtain but the differences were at a trend level. At least two factors may explain this finding. First, the IFPS therapists in Washington, because of their private-agency auspice, may have more difficulty in accessing certain resources for their client families. That is, there may be inherent disadvantages in private auspices. But alternatively, the differences may reflect the amount and variety of ancillary services that are available in each state. Given the design, it is not possible to disaggregate the influence of private auspices and state environmental factors.

Both the public and private therapists in this study reported receiving a considerable amount of supervision and other support. Utah therapists received slightly more hours of individual supervision per month, but Washington therapists received slightly more group supervision. Moreover, Washington therapists indicated that they received significantly more support from district administrators, other supervisors, and other therapists.

Because of limitations in the research design, the differential effects of agency or supervisor support on treatment effectiveness, therapist morale, and therapist turnover cannot be determined, except to raise the issue that the successful program outcomes of both states could be due, in part, to this support. In fact, it is noteworthy that in examining the reasons rated least important for why IFPS staff might leave (layoffs, lack of supervision, personality conflicts, and lack of administrative support) most IFPS staff, at least those in this study, seem unaffected by the kinds of concerns that many child welfare staff experience.

Valued Services and Therapist Morale

Those helping interventions that are often clustered under relationship building and promoting client hope were highly valued by the IFPS therapists in this study, specifically, listening and encouragement. One of the other components of service that is discussed in the HBS literature is that of concrete services (see for example, Dumas & Wahler, 1983; Jones et al., 1976). The findings provided further evidence that many IFPS therapists place high value on the importance of concrete services for both establishing important therapeutic relationships and improving family functioning.

Therapist morale differed by state, with therapists in Utah rating morale significantly lower than Washington. An important area that needs to be addressed by future research relates to determining which factors affect IFPS therapist morale. This is especially important if therapist morale is identified as one of the correlates of treatment success. How important is the amount and quality of supervision versus other types or sources of agency or therapist support? Pay may not be a key factor; while Washington therapists expressed concerns about salary, they also had high job satisfaction and high overall program morale. Difficulty obtaining ancillary resources also was not associated with low morale. But because successful treatment outcomes may be associated with higher morale (see Chapter 11), identifying which factors affect morale would be useful for program design and administration.

Conclusion

Responses to the therapist survey data indicate the most IFPS therapists in both states support the basic tenets of the IFPS model as it is evolving. They support, for example, providing intensive services in the home, client contact within the first 24 hours, and providing 24-hour case coverage. Differences in perspective, especially between therapist ratings and therapist perceptions of juvenile court judges were found. Yet along with IFPS supervisors and administrators, juvenile court judges were perceived as important sources of therapist support.

While these analyses have provided some intriguing findings, additional research is needed to examine the relationship between therapist attitudes, use of specific clinical techniques and concrete services, and attainment of specific treatment goals in a more detailed and controlled manner than was possible in this project.

Notes

1.   Since the completion of the study, Hennepin County child welfare administrators changed their program policy so that IFPS therapists rather than case aides are expected to provide the majority of concrete services.

2.   For a copy of the IFPS Therapist Survey, see Fraser et al. (1989, Appendix J).

3.   For more information regarding therapist sources of support or pressure and morale, see Kohlert and Pecora (1989, pp. 165–173).

Chapter 8

Changes in Family Functioning: Is Participation in Intensive Family Preservation Services Correlated with Changes in Attitudes or Behaviors?

WANDA M. SPAID, MARK W. FRASER, and ROBERT E. LEWIS

How do IFPS affect families? One of the purposes of the FIT project was to describe the changes that occur in children and parents as they participate in IFPS. In this chapter, we focus on those parent and child behaviors—plus home conditions—that often lead to placement decisions and may be considered the most proximal outcomes of treatment. These include parents' child management skills, parent and child health-related factors, family problem-solving capacity (adaptability and cohesion), social support, and a variety of problem conditions. In the scheme of outcome measures for IFPS, such variables reflect the immediate changes that occur in families during the treatment process. If changes in attitudes and behaviors were to be found, they would help to explain the reasons why Homebuilders-based services have achieved the promising results described elsewhere in this book.

Reviewed in Chapter 4, four instruments were used to assess child, parent, and family functioning: (1) the Family Risk Scales (FRS), (2) the Family Adaptability and Cohesion Scales (FACES III), (3) the Milardo Social Support Inventory, and (4) parent problem ratings from the Consumer Outcome Survey. Parent and child functioning across a variety of areas was rated by therapists using the FRS at intake and at the close of services. Also at intake and at the close of services, parents filled out the FACES III, Social Support, and the Consumer Outcome inventories. That is, they assessed and reported on their own functioning. In addition, children over the age of 12 completed the FACES. The data collection at the end of treatment was conducted by a research assistant who visited families' homes. Thus the data used in this chapter are based on parent and child self-reports as well as therapists' ratings.

Rationale for the Use of the Instruments

Family Risk Scales

The CWLA FRS were developed to assess a child's risk of entering foster care. The scales were designed to improve a worker's ability to identify situations predictive of "near-term" child placement (Magura et al., 1987). They contain items that tap well-known risk factors for out-of-home placement. These include a variety of fully anchored measures of parent and child functioning in the home and community. Although the scales were not published until 1987, permission was obtained from the publishers to use a' prepublication version. The recently published "cousin" to the FRS—the Child Well-Being Scales (Magura and Moses, 1986)—has been criticized as trying to measure a global conception of "child-well-being" when there is insufficient consensus regarding the meaning of this term. There is concern that such scales will be applied in ways that ignore societal factors contributing to parental inadequacy, local community differences, changing standards, and a "minimum-standards" approach to case decision-making in child welfare (Seaberg, 1988, 1990).

Arguments supporting and refuting Seaberg's criticisms can be made, but readers should note that the FIT project did not attempt to use the FRS to derive a summated score of child or family functioning. Instead, individual scale information was collected at IFPS intake and exit, and then compared by scale. In the FIT project, we were interested in using scales with relatively clear anchor points, and that measured discrete areas of child, parent, and family functioning. While some of the scales need to be revised to be more unidimensional or more sensitive to change, at the time of the initiation of the study (1985), these scales represented a good balance of clarity, breadth, and practicality for evaluation of IFPS programs.

FACES III

The FACES instrument is based on Olson's circumplex model of family functioning (Olson, Russell, & Sprenkle, 1989). In the circumplex model, family cohesion and adaptability are posited to be primary dimensions of family functioning. Cohesion is defined as the emotional bonding of family members, whereas adaptability is defined as the ability of a family system to change, to encounter and resolve situational as well as developmental problems.

The FACES was developed in 1978 (Olson et al., 1985), and has been shown to distinguish a variety of "problem" children and families from children and families without problems (e.g., Rodick, Henggeler, & Hanson, 1986; Garbarino, Sebes, & Schellenbach, 1984; Olson, McCubbin, Barnes,

Larsen, Muxen, & Wilson, 1983, p. 79; Olson, 1986). The basic tenet of the circumplex perspective of family functioning is that the more dysfunctional a family, the more extreme its scores on cohesion and adaptability. The model posits a curvilinear relationship with family functioning in the sense that extremely low and extremely high scores are thought to predict problem behavior.

Each dimension has four anchor points or levels. Across the cohesion dimension, "disengaged" is defined as the polar opposite of "enmeshed," while "separated" and "connected" are posited as balanced levels of functioning. As indicated in Figure 8.1, the scale runs from left to right: disengaged→separated→connected→enmeshed. Extreme scores in the disengaged or enmeshed ranges are viewed as placing family members at greater risk of delinquency, child maltreatment, and other problems. For the adaptability measure, "rigid" is defined as the polar opposite of "chaotic," while "structured" and "flexible" are considered normative or balanced levels. Like cohesion, it runs from rigid to structured to flexible to chaotic. Theoretically, better functioning families are predicted to have midrange or balanced scores.

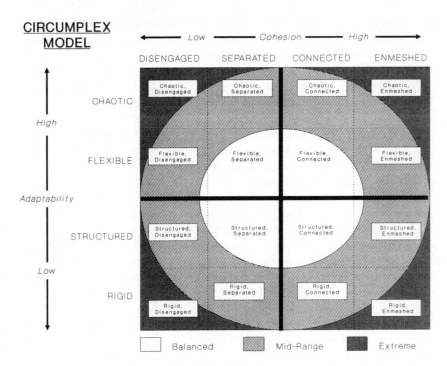

Figure 8.1. Circumplex model. Source: Olson et al. (1985, p. 7).

Social Support Inventory

Measures of social support were included because a growing body of literature suggests that behavior is affected strongly by social and environmental conditions (Whittaker & Garbarino, 1985). Epidemiological research has shown that noncompliant and delinquent children often come from homes characterized by poverty, family violence, crowding, and poor education (e.g., Loeber & Stouthamer-Loeber, 1986). And recent research indicates that such families are more likely to fail in treatment or to drop out. In Patterson's work, for example, lower-social-class and father-absent families showed fewer treatment gains at 12-month follow-up than middle-class, two-parent families (for a summary, see Patterson, 1985). Four months after the conclusion of parenting training, Wahler and Afton (1980) found that low-income "insular" mothers—women who had few primary social contacts and whose contacts were largely aversive in nature—were less successful in implementing child management strategies than middle-class mothers, who on average reported fewer coercive relationships and more supportive social ties.

The importance of the social environment in family treatment has been underscored in experiments by Dumas and Wahler (1983). Socioeconomic disadvantage (a summated scale of family income, family size, family composition, maternal education, neighborhood crime rate, and treatment referral source) and maternal insularity (an index of daily social contacts weighted by the relative helpfulness of each contact) accounted for 49% of the variance between successful and unsuccessful parenting training outcomes one year following treatment. Such findings appear to indicate that socially and economically disadvantaged families that lack positive, supportive social networks and who may be trapped in aversive relationships with CPS, other social agencies, the police, neighbors, and relatives are less likely to respond successfully to parenting training.

In a recent report, Wahler and Dumas (1989) concluded, "[The] evidence suggests clearly that a mother's ability to fulfill her caretaking responsibilities and, if necessary, to benefit from standardized treatment procedures is related to her level of social support and socioeconomic background" (p. 118). In light of this work (which includes in-home parenting training interventions), the outcomes of IFPS were hypothesized to be related to social and environmental conditions. An explicit attempt was made to measure the characteristics of caretakers' social support networks. Although the term *support* connotes positive aspects of social interaction, Milardo purposefully incorporated items in his Social Support Inventory that measure negative or aversive aspects of social support. Thus, for the purposes of this study, social support was conceptualized as having both supportive and aversive elements.

Perhaps one of the more potentially useful and theoretically relevant findings from the FIT study is the discovery of three apparently reliable and stable dimensions of social support in families that received IFPS. At intake and at exit, across independent reports from both primary and secondary caretakers, the central features of clients' social support networks were remarkably alike. These networks afforded caretakers solace in the form of *empathetic friendships*, helpful advice/guidance in the form of *coaching*, and, in a negative sense, coercive or stressful influences in the form of *aversive social ties*. These three elements of social support characterized caretakers' spousal relationships and extended family/nonkin relationships— measured separately—in IFPS.

Parent Self-Report of Family Problems

At the conclusion of service, primary caretakers were asked to rate the severity of various child, parent, and family problems before and after the provision of IFPS. This assessment was patterned after parent outcome interviewing methods developed by Magura and Moses (1986). Obtaining the client's perspective in assessing service effectiveness has recently been reemphasized by a number of program evaluation experts in child welfare and other fields (see e.g., Ellsworth, 1975; Hargreaves & Attkisson, 1978; Magura & Moses, 1984; Maluccio, 1979a,b; Millar & Millar, 1981). The use of client self-reports in evaluation, a practice much maligned as "reactive" and biased in the past, provides valuable information. There is strong evidence that self-reports can be valid indicators of a host of problems ranging from parent-child interaction to delinquency (see, e.g., Hindelang, Hirschi, & Weis, 1981).

Methodology

Data Collection Procedures

Using the instruments described above, data were collected at the start and completion of services. Parents and children were assured that their responses were confidential and would not affect their eligibility for services or other aspects of their involvement with IFPS.

Limitations of the Study

Interpretations based on the findings are limited by the pre-post design. Because families were not randomly assigned to a treatment group or a control group, it cannot be concluded that observed differences in child, parent, or family functioning are due, in a causal sense, to participation in

IFPS. Thus in this chapter, we focus only on *changes that are correlated* with participation in treatment.

Only children over the age of 12 were invited to complete the FACES instrument. Thus the sample sizes for children are small and represent only the perspectives of older children at risk.

With regard to social support, information was not collected on individual network members. Consequently, it was not possible to assess network size, multiplexity, or density. It also was not possible to determine changes in the composition of caretakers' networks. The inventory was designed to measure the perception of social support—defined broadly to include supportive and aversive social ties—and not network characteristics.

Family Adaptability and Cohesion

Families in Both States

Based on norms developed by Olson and his associates, cohesion scores of less than 34 are thought to indicate severe family disengagement and adaptability scores of 20–29 to indicate a "normal" level of functioning (Olson et al., 1985, p. 27). As shown in Tables 8.1 and 8.2, families across both states scored in the extreme range on cohesion and in the mid-range on adaptability.

Families in Utah

In terms of cohesion, the IFPS families in Utah scored within the "disengaged" range at the beginning and at the end of IFPS. While the family and individual scores moved toward the less extreme range at case termination, no score fell outside the disengaged range. Scores on adaptability at intake and exit were within Olson's normal or "balanced" range (20–29) for well-functioning families. The parents and children served in Utah appear to have come from disengaged families that have normative adaptive capacities.

Families in Washington

As with the Utah families, Washington family members' scores on the FACES III fell within the extreme range on the cohesion measure. The family mean at intake for the Washington families on cohesion, as seen in Table 8.1, was within the disengaged range. At exit, the families continued to be disengaged. Scores on the adaptability dimension were within the balanced range. Both parent and child ratings of family functioning suggest that FIT project families were disengaged but capable of adaptive problem-solving.

Table 8.1. FACES III Intake Cohesion and Adaptability Scores[a]

Family unit	Utah			Washington			Total sample		
	N	Cohesion	Adaptability	N	Cohesion	Adaptability	N	Cohesion	Adaptability
Primary caretaker	134	31.410[a] (7.227)	25.903 (5.515)	308	33.114 (6.921)	25.445 (5.619)	442	32.597 (7.051)	25.584 (5.586)
Secondary caretaker	74	32.662 (7.325)	26.541 (5.460)	134	33.433 (7.398)	23.955 (5.434)	208	33.159 (7.363)	24.875 (5.570)
Child 1 (oldest)	90	28.333 (7.115)	25.467 (6.761)	174	27.891 (7.709)	23.868 (5.925)	264	28.042 (7.501)	24.413 (6.652)
Child 2	67	29.194 (7.678)	26.731 (6.333)	93	27.538 (7.673)	24.742 (6.784)	160	28.231 (7.695)	25.575 (6.652)
Child 3	26	28.538 (8.594)	26.038 (5.909)	28	28.821 (8.037)	23.786 (6.779)	54	28.685 (8.232)	24.870 (6.417)
Family means	136	30.648 (5.872)	25.918 (4.634)	311	31.764 (6.299)	24.725 (4.559)	447	31.424 (6.187)	25.088 (4.610)

[a] Mean; SD in parentheses.

Table 8.2. FACES III Exit Cohesion and Adaptability Scores

Family unit	Utah			Washington			Total sample		
	N	Cohesion	Adaptability	N	Cohesion	Adaptability	N	Cohesion	Adaptability
Primary caretaker	102	33.431	25.392	267	34.749	25.861	369	34.385	25.732
		(8.022)	(4.881)		(7.266)	(5.875)		(7.494)	(5.615)
Secondary caretaker	49	34.245	25.286	101	34.416	26.604	150	34.360	26.173
		(4.944)	(4.743)		(7.549)	(4.819)		(6.792)	(4.819)
Child 1 (oldest)	59	30.339	25.407	135	29.259	24.126	194	29.588	24.515
		(7.480)	(6.254)		(8.755)	(6.416)		(8.384)	(6.379)
Child 2	46	30.109	26.391	68	29.426	25.000	114	29.702	25.561
		(8.266)	(6.705)		(7.774)	(6.633)		(7.947)	(6.668)
Child 3	18	32.611	28.778	22	30.636	24.909	40	31.525	26.650
		(6.409)	(6.264)		(7.162)	(5.291)		(6.820)	(5.998)
Family means	104	32.817	25.623	270	33.272	25.337	374	33.145	25.416
		(6.539)	(4.276)		(6.556)	(4.899)		(6.546)	(4.731)

[a] Mean; SD in parentheses.

Risk Factors for Placement

Families in Both States

As shown in Table 8.3, children, parents, and the family environment appear to have changed significantly during the course of treatment. Therapists rated families as significantly improved on 23 of 25 measures in the aggregate sample. The same 23 measures were significant in the follow-up cohort (not shown), which suggests that the subsample of families that was tracked for 12 months represents the aggregate sample in terms of family change. Only caretaker's health and cooperation in treatment and child's cooperation in treatment failed to show improvement.

Families in Utah

As shown also in Table 8.3, Utah children and parents appear to have changed significantly during the course of treatment. Therapist ratings at intake indicate that children frequently engaged in minor delinquencies, such as shoplifting and vandalism. At home, children were generally argumentative and uncooperative. Many children appear to have been performing poorly in school and were frequently truant. The pre-post changes suggest that treatment was effective in promoting changes in these and a wide range of other behaviors. Therapists rated families as significantly improved on 22 of 25 items. In the follow-up sample (not shown), families who were part of the follow-up cohort were rated as improved on 15 of 25 items from IFPS intake to case closure, the difference due probably to the smaller number of children ($N = 97$) in the follow-up survey from Utah.

Families in Washington

The pre-post changes observed in families in Washington were similar to those observed by workers in Utah. Significant differences were found on 21 of 25 measures. The major differences between the two states were on the variable assessing changes in home suitability, caretaker's cooperation in treatment, and child's cooperation in treatment. The suitability of homes in the Homebuilders families in Washington appears to have improved more than that of the suitability of homes in Utah. But in contrast, Utah families appear to have become more cooperative during the course of treatment, while Washington families began treatment with a slightly more cooperative profile and stayed reasonably cooperative during the course of services. Like Utah children, Washington children were performing poorly in school at intake. They tended to be argumentative and uncooperative at home. But by the close of services, significant changes were observed on all of these variables. The findings suggest that participation in IFPS is correlated with significant reductions in child, parent, and family problems.

Table 8.3. Pre-Post Mean Scores on FRS: Workers Ratings by Child[a]

Item	Aggregate (N = 581)		Utah (N = 172)		Washington (N = 409)	
	Pre	Post	Pre	Post	Pre	Post
Habitability	1.24	1.14***	1.35	1.17***	1.19	1.13**
Suitability	1.35	1.25***	1.29	1.24	1.37	1.25***
Financial problems	1.94	1.86***	1.88	1.77*	1.96	1.90*
Adult relationships	2.00	1.86***	2.00	1.70***	2.00	1.93
Social support	1.91	1.79***	1.99	1.87*	1.88	1.76***
Caretaker's mental health	1.74	1.58***	1.85	1.65**	1.70	1.55***
Caretaker's physical health	1.54	1.55	1.46	1.50	1.57	1.57
Caretaker's child supervision	1.62	1.32***	1.68	1.36***	1.59	1.30***
Caretaker's parenting skill	2.46	2.02***	2.60	2.05***	2.39	2.00***
Caretaker's use of physical punishment	1.78	1.50***	1.75	1.46***	1.79	1.51***
Caretaker's skill in verbal discipline	2.14	1.79***	2.29	1.82***	2.08	1.78***
Caretaker's motivation to solve family problem	1.98	1.71***	2.06	1.67***	1.96	1.73***

Caretaker's interest in preventing placement	1.67	1.45***	1.64	1.41***	1.68	1.46***
Caretaker's knowledge of child care	2.31	1.96***	2.37	2.05***	2.29	1.93***
Caretaker's cooperation in treatment	1.47	1.40*	1.62	1.45**	1.40	1.39
Caretaker's use/abuse of alcohol and drugs	1.32	1.19***	1.29	1.18*	1.33	1.20***
Child's mental health	1.89	1.63***	2.18	1.81***	1.80	1.57***
Child's physical health	1.34	1.28**	1.33	1.25*	1.35	1.28*
Child's physical needs	1.31	1.24***	1.32	1.20***	1.31	1.25*
Child's school adjustment	2.45	1.98***	2.90	2.07***	2.23	1.94***
Child's emotional care	2.16	1.92***	2.32	1.99***	2.09	1.90***
Child's oppositional or delinquent behavior	1.95	1.52***	2.27	1.72***	1.83	1.44***
Child's oppositional behavior in home	2.21	1.72***	2.38	1.88***	2.14	1.66***
Child's cooperation in treatment	1.73	1.70	1.94	1.79*	1.63	1.66
Child's risk of sexual abuse	1.33	1.23**	1.38	1.22	1.32	1.23**

[a] Pre-post differences were tested using the paired t-test and Wilcoxon Matched-Pairs test. High mean scores indicate greater dysfunction. Lower scores indicate less dysfunction.

Parent Ratings of Social Support

Families in Both States

As shown in Table 8.4, changes in social support between treatment intake and exit indicate that IFPS reduced aversive social interactions between spouses (including cohabitants, where caretakers were not married but living together). Also, it appears to have increased empathic friendships with extended kin and network members. Both findings may be due to the attention placed on informal support systems by the IFPS therapist during the intervention period.

Families in Utah

Primary and secondary caretakers in Utah reported significant reductions in aversive relations within their families (with spouses). As suggested above, the frequency of empathic interaction between primary caretakers and others in their extended network increased significantly.

Families in Washington

In Washington, primary caretakers reported significant reductions in aversive social contacts with spouses and with extended family/nonkin. This suggests that IFPS programs may be successful in affecting environmental stressors. However, it is also possible that aversive interactions are reduced in clients' social networks because all network members are relieved that the family is seeking and participating in treatment. Both primary and secondary caretakers reported small, but significant increases in empathic support from their nonkin, extended network.

Parent Ratings of Family Problems

Families in Both States

On average, parents rated family problems as much reduced at the close of treatment. Across both states, parents reported significant decreases on 26 of 28 problem scales (see Table 8.5). Although ratings such as these are affected by social desirability (because of attachments to workers, parents may have felt obliged to report changes in a positive direction), the direction and degree of change support and extend findings from other sources.

Table 8.4. Mean Scores on Social Support Dimensions before and after Treatment: Dependent t-Tests by State[a]

	Utah			Washington			Total sample		
	N	Before	After	N	Before	After	N	Before	After
Primary child caretakers									
Spouse/cohabitant									
Empathic friendship	75	3.400	3.573	184	3.527	3.429	259	3.490	3.471
Aversive relation	75	5.357	6.227***	184	4.973	5.505***	259	5.081	5.714***
Coaching relation	70	4.486	4.929*	181	4.807	4.762	251	4.717	4.809
Extended family/nonkin									
Empathic friendship	130	4.685	4.131**	379	4.335	4.195*	509	4.424	4.179**
Aversive relations	130	6.962	7.000	377	6.443	6.722***	501	6.576	6.793***
Coaching relations	129	5.450	5.457	371	4.992	4.992	500	5.110	5.112
Secondary child caretakers									
Spouse/cohabitant									
Empathic friendship	58	3.207	3.293	136	3.176	3.132	194	3.186	3.180
Aversive relation	58	5.466	5.914*	136	5.360	5.757**	194	5.392	5.804***
Coaching relation	58	4.672	4.448	136	4.654	4.507	194	4.660	4.490
Extended family/nonkin									
Empathic friendship	59	5.458	5.186	136	5.596	5.154**	195	5.554	5.164**
Aversive relations	59	6.814	6.966	135	7.015	7.052	194	6.954	7.026
Coaching relations	56	5.429	5.304	129	5.457	5.310	185	5.449	5.308

[a] Scale: 1, once a day or more; 2, about every other day; 3, about twice a week; 4, about once a week; 5, about once every two weeks; 6, about once a month; 7, about once every two months; 8, not at all.
*p < .05.   **p < .01.   ***p < .001.

Table 8.5. Primary Caretaker Ratings of Problem Severity^a before and after IFPS

Problems	Utah^b (N = 108) Before M (SD)	After M (SD)	Washington^b (N = 242) Before M (SD)	After M (SD)	Total (N = 350) Before M (SD)	After M (SD)
Inadequate housing conditions						
a. Lack of appliances and/or furniture?	1.3 (.9)	1.2 (.6)*	1.4 (1.0)	1.2 (.7)***	1.4 (1.0)	1.2 (.7)****
b. Unsafe conditions in the house?	1.2 (.7)	1.0 (.3)**	1.4 (1.0)	1.2 (.7)****	1.3 (.9)	1.2 (.6)****
c. Being evicted?	1.3 (.9)	1.2 (.8)	1.2 (.8)	1.2 (.6)	1.2 (.9)	1.2 (.7)
Inadequate finances						
d. For rent, utilities, food, health care, and clothing?	2.3 (1.5)	2.2 (1.5)	2.2 (1.4)	2.1 (1.3)****	2.3 (1.5)	2.1 (1.4)****
Inability to provide the level of physical care for your children that you would like						
e. For food or clothing:	2.0 (1.4)	1.9 (1.2)*	1.8 (1.2)	1.7 (1.2)	1.8 (1.3)	1.8 (1.2)*
f. Children playing where they shouldn't or playing with dangerous things?	1.8 (1.3)	1.5 (.9)****	1.6 (1.2)	1.4 (.9)****	1.7 (1.2)	1.4 (.9)****
Problems with discipline or the emotional care of your children						
g. Losing your temper?	3.0 (1.4)	2.1 (1.1)****	3.1 (1.4)	2.0 (.9)****	3.1 (1.4)	2.0 (1.0)****
h. Inappropriate punishment?	2.2 (1.3)	1.6 (.9)****	2.5 (1.4)	1.6 (.9)****	2.4 (1.4)	1.6 (.9)****
i. Unrealistic expectations for children like sometimes blaming them for things that weren't their fault?	2.4 (1.2)	1.7 (.9)****	2.3 (1.3)	1.6 (.8)****	2.4 (1.3)	1.6 (.8)****
Problems with your child(ren)'s behavior						
j. Fighting?	3.5 (1.4)	1.6 (1.3)****	3.5 (1.5)	2.5 (1.1)****	3.5 (1.5)	2.5 (1.2)****

k. Children lying?	3.6 (1.4)	2.6 (1.3)****	3.4 (1.6)	2.5 (1.3)****	3.5 (1.5)	2.6 (1.3)****
l. Children stealing?	3.1 (1.6)	2.1 (1.3)****	2.6 (1.7)	2.0 (1.3)****	2.8 (1.7)	2.0 (1.3)****
m. Children not attending school?	3.6 (1.7)	2.5 (1.7)****	2.6 (1.8)	2.0 (1.5)****	3.0 (1.8)	2.2 (1.6)****
n. Drinking or using drugs?	2.6 (1.6)	1.9 (1.3)****	1.8 (1.4)	1.5 (1.1)****	2.0 (1.5)	1.6 (1.2)****
o. Running away?	2.9 (1.7)	1.6 (1.2)****	2.4 (1.7)	1.6 (1.1)****	2.6 (1.7)	1.6 (1.2)****
p. Being sexually promiscuous or having sex and sleeping around?	1.8 (1.4)	1.6 (1.3)	1.7 (1.3)	1.4 (1.0)****	1.7 (1.3)	1.5 (1.1)****
Emotional problems of children						
q. Being anxious, afraid, or tense?	3.0 (1.5)	2.4 (1.3)****	3.0 (1.5)	2.2 (1.2)****	3.0 (1.5)	2.3 (1.2)****
r. Being sad, depressed, or suicidal?	2.9 (1.5)	2.2 (1.3)****	2.7 (1.6)	1.9 (1.2)****	2.8 (1.6)	2.0 (1.2)****
s. Being moody?	3.5 (1.4)	2.8 (1.4)****	3.3 (1.5)	2.4 (1.2)****	3.4 (1.5)	2.6 (1.3)****
t. Wetting or soiling the bed?	1.6 (1.3)	1.4 (1.0)**	1.6 (1.3)	1.4 (1.1)****	1.6 (1.3)	1.4 (1.1)****
Have you						
u. Been having poor health?	2.2 (1.4)	1.9 (1.3)****	2.0 (1.4)	1.8 (1.2)****	2.1 (1.4)	1.8 (1.2)****
v. Been having trouble with drinking too much or using drugs?	1.2 (.7)	1.0 (.6)	1.2 (.8)	1.1 (.5)****	1.2 (.7)	1.1 (.5)****
w. Been feeling sad or depressed?	3.4 (1.4)	2.6 (1.3)****	3.1 (1.5)	2.1 (1.1)****	3.2 (1.5)	2.3 (1.2)****
x. Been feeling overwhelmed and that there is no one to help you?	3.2 (1.6)	2.2 (1.3)****	3.5 (1.5)	2.2 (1.2)****	3.4 (1.5)	2.2 (1.2)****
y. Been fighting?	2.5 (1.5)	1.8 (1.1)****	2.4 (1.6)	1.6 (.9)****	2.4 (1.6)	1.7 (1.0)****
z. Been tense or nervous?	3.4 (1.4)	2.4 (1.2)****	3.3 (1.4)	2.3 (1.1)****	3.3 (1.4)	2.3 (1.2)****
aa. Been hating yourself or feeling worthless?	2.6 (1.7)	1.9 (1.2)****	2.6 (1.6)	1.8 (1.1)****	2.6 (1.6)	1.8 (1.1)****
bb. Been feeling lonely?	2.7 (1.5)	2.3 (1.4)****	2.8 (1.6)	2.1 (1.3)****	2.8 (1.6)	2.2 (1.3)****

a Problem severity was rated using a five-point scale with the following scale anchors: (1) not a problem and (5) extreme problem.
b Sample sizes for each state on individual items may vary by 15% due to missing data.
*p < .10.   **p < .05.   ***p < .01.   ****p < .001.

145

Families in Utah

As indicated in Table 8.5, Utah parents reported significant changes on 23 of the 28 items. The largest child-focused improvements were reported for noncompliant behaviors: fighting, lying, school attendance, and runaway behavior. Significant reductions were reported in each of these areas. The largest parent-focused improvements were reported for loss of temper, sadness or depression, feeling overwhelmed, and tension or nervousness. The findings suggest that caretakers feel in greater control of themselves and their family's circumstances.

Families in Washington

Similar patterns of change as those observed in the Utah sample were observed in the Washington sample. As shown in Table 8.5, Washington parents reported significant decreases on 26 of the 28 parent-rated family problems.

Comparisons between Utah and Washington

Family Adaptability and Cohesion

Because the relationship between cohesion and adaptability was posited to be curvilinear—that is, both high and low scores are thought to be dysfunctional—cross-plotting was used to place family members' scores in the context of the circumplex model. Families did not differ by state on cohesion and adaptability scores, and so their scores were combined for these cross-plots. No significant differences were found.

Risk Factors for Placement at Intake

Utah and Washington therapist ratings of families differed on several measures. The client populations in the two states may have been different with respect to certain areas of social functioning. Utah and Washington workers rated parents significantly different on three items: (1) use of verbal discipline, (2) cooperation with the agency, and (3) the emotional care and stimulation of their children. While Utah parents were more dysfunctional on all three items, the differences between the means were relatively small. Children in the two states were rated differently on four items: (1) mental health, (2) school adjustment, (3) delinquent behavior, and (4) home-related behavior. In a pattern that replicates the differences between therapist ratings of parents, Utah children were rated as more dysfunctional than Washington children on each variable. The differences between the means were generally larger than the differences in means on the parent-related measures. In addition, the differences in the means frequently placed children from the two states within different problem levels, such as within level one as opposed to level two. Although interrater reliability among the therapists from both states was not assessed, the clarity of the scale anchors should have provided a framework for improving consistency among staff members. Given these assumptions, these comparisons imply that the Utah IFPS units may have served a slightly more troubled population of families, with children that were somewhat more noncompliant in the home and the school.

Parent Ratings of Social Support

Participants in the Utah and Washington IFPS programs differed significantly on only 1 of 12 dimensions of social support at intake. The primary caretakers in Washington families reported somewhat more frequent aversive interactions with extended family and nonkin network members. In Utah, aversive contacts were reported to occur about once every two months, while in Washington, they occurred once every four to six weeks.

By the end of treatment, this difference washed out; however, other differences emerged. Primary caretakers in Washington reported significantly more advisement and assistance (i.e., coaching) from extended family members/nonkin than primary caretakers in Utah. The Homebuilders staff in Washington may have been somewhat more effective in converting aversive relationships with relatives and friends into supportive, coaching relationships. But such an interpretation is tentative at best, for spousal relationships at the close of service in Washington appear to have been more aversive than spousal relationships in Utah.

Parent Ratings of Family Problems

Parent ratings of family problems reflected differences in the ages and behaviors of children served by the two states. Children in Utah were more likely to be reported as oppositional—stealing, being truant, drinking or using drugs, and running away. Although Washington parents tended to feel more overwhelmed (that there was no one to help with family problems) than Utah parents, other parent ratings of housing, financial, and personal problems did not differ.

Global Family Ratings by Parents

In addition to the therapist and parent ratings of specific home and family conditions, parents were asked to rate their family situation at the close of treatment on a five-point scale (1, a lot worse now; 2, a little worse now; 3, about the same now; 4, a little better now; 5, a lot better now). As compared to when they first began working with the IFPS therapist, primary care-takers in Utah ($M = 4.1$, SD = 0.9) and Washington ($M = 4.4$, SD = 0.8) rated their overall family situation as "a little better now." In aggregate, parents appear to have found service helpful ($M = 4.3$, SD = 0.9), while families in Washington rated their situations significantly more improved than families in Utah ($p < .01$).

Although such global ratings of the impact of a service must be viewed with caution, parents' global ratings are consistent with other findings. They contribute to a preliminary conclusion that participation in IFPS is associ-ated with substantial improvements in the quality of home life.

Discussion

The FACES III scores for the families and older children did not improve as much as expected, but a comparison of the individual items of the FACES III and the major treatment goals set by the families indicated that less than three quarters of the items were the focus of service. In addition, some of the items on the FACES III represented more enduring types of family traits that would be difficult to change as part of a 30–60 day intervention. When the change scores of the other measures were examined, however, it was clear that participation in IFPS was highly correlated with improvements in the behavior of children, the parenting repertoire of parents, and conditions in the home. On the basis of reports from workers and parents, these ser-vices appear to promote a variety of child and parent changes in families. To be sure, our design does not permit attributing these changes to the service per se, but the pattern of change that emerges from parent, child, and worker reports makes it difficult to argue that the observed pre-post dif-ferences are due entirely to social desirability, regression, maturation, and other research design confounds.

In summary, IFPS appear to strengthen families. Additional research studies using experimental designs and independent observers are needed to determine whether the observed changes are due in a causal sense to the home-based intervention, but the evidence is strongly suggestive of a cause-and-effect relationship. Tentatively, one might hypothesize that IFPS pro-grams using the Homebuilders treatment model create changes in parents' child management skills, and that these changes reduce child-related problems.

Chapter 9

Placement Rates of Children and Families Served by Intensive Family Preservation Services Programs

PETER J. PECORA, MARK W. FRASER, ROBERT B. BENNETT, and DAVID A. HAAPALA

In previous chapters, we have shown that IFPS appear to produce significant changes in child-related problems, parenting skills, social support, and family environmental conditions. These changes are important because they suggest that IFPS reduce functional deficits in families with children at risk of out-of-home placement. If placements are made in a rational way such that children in poorly functioning families are more likely to be placed, then services that improve family functioning should operate to prevent placement. The purpose of this chapter is to describe the outcomes of IFPS in terms of placement rates. In addition, placement locations and rates for a small case overflow comparison group comprised of families referred but not served by IFPS in Utah will be presented.

Out-of-home child placement is a complex event. It involves the transfer of certain parental rights to the state, the removal of a child or children from the home, and a disposition decision about type of placement (e.g., foster family care, group home, psychiatric facility, correctional center). If a placement occurs, it is usually the culminating event in a series of unsuccessful (or only partially successful) efforts to strengthen the home and protect the child(ren). In this sense, it can be used to denote the failure of family preservation efforts. But as discussed in earlier chapters, the criteria used to define service failure are indeed relative, if not controversial. They include the location, appropriateness, and desirability of a specific placement. The social desirability of placement has been examined by only a few studies (see for example, Nelson et al., 1988, pp. 67–72). In some cases, placement may be a desirable alternative for a child and her/his family, but the appropriateness of alternative placements varies in relation to the family, child situation, community norms, and agency resources (such as foster homes available). There is no general consensus on what constitutes an appropriate and socially desirable placement. This represents a major challenge to the field and a major problem to evaluators who elect to use placement as an outcome measure.

Both the perceived causes—in the form of antecedent events and problems—and the desirability of placement will also be discussed in this chapter. Contrasting opinions about the events that led to placement will be examined from the perspectives of the parents whose children were placed during the course of the study, the IFPS therapists who served families that experienced a placement, and the supervisors of the IFPS therapists who served families that experienced a placement. Moreover, data on caretakers' views of services or actions that might have prevented placement will be presented and discussed.

Competing Definitions of Placement

Placement must be assessed in the context of competing definitions of those out-of-home conditions that are negative. In most studies, foster family, group, and institutional care are considered negative outcomes. But because few studies have interviewed clients as part of a service follow-up, few studies have reported the placement of children with relatives, neighbors, and friends. As an indicator of the success or failure of treatment, how should such placements be evaluated? Are they negative or positive for children and their parents? In one sense, these "informal" placements connote the failure of treatment in that a child's birth family may not remain the central socializing unit in her/his life.

Yet in a different sense, the use of a family's social network, such as relatives or friends, by IFPS therapists or CPS caseworkers to prevent placements at public expense may have significant benefits. Children are often able to remain in contact with their parents. They may continue to live in the same neighborhood and to attend the same school. Compared to foster care, this kind of placement may be less disruptive and may not strain important attachments to peers and adults who act as role models (Lewis & Fraser, 1987). Generally, relative placements are also less costly to the child welfare system.

As indicated earlier, informal placements with relatives were defined as successful outcomes in this study. Informal placements with neighbors and friends, and cases where a child ran away from home, were defined as negative outcomes. These criteria for success and failure are debatable. Some might say that they are too inclusive; others might say they are too exclusive. The decision to use such criteria was made because there is no clear consensus in the field regarding desirable and appropriate placement. In addition, we wanted to maximize the number of service failures for examination, while acknowledging the important role that extended family members can play in the lives of children. And we wanted to use a conservative definition of treatment success so as to include and measure as many of the clearly negative outcomes for children as possible, given the constraints of time and funding.

In the following analyses, different definitions of child placement/treatment failure will be used to illustrate how success rates vary according to the definition that is used. Success and failure rates in this study appear to be moderately influenced by the conditions that are defined as failure outcomes, like living with friends or on the street. Such outcomes are not commonly tracked or counted as failures. While this topic will be explored in a later section of this chapter, it implies that placement rates are complex and potentially misleading, given the current lack of uniform definitions. And as different units of analysis (e.g., children vs. family,) are being used across the field, it is important to note that, although a focus on individual children may be a more accurate measure of placement avoidance, the removal of even one child from a family constitutes a major disruption and is traumatizing to many families.

Organizational and Environmental Influences on Placement Rates

Placement is subject to many influences, and variation in placement rates across states may represent differences in state policies and resources as much as differences in the effectiveness of placement prevention services. It is one thing to reduce placements in a state where placements rates are declining overall, and it is quite another thing to reduce placements in states where placement rates are stable or increasing. The organizational and environmental context of IFPS programs must be assessed, and placement rates should be viewed within the "social ecology" of changing public policies and practices (Feldman, 1990; Pecora, 1990b; Tracy, 1990).

As shown in Figures 9.1 and 9.2, placement rates in Utah and Washington appear to have been relatively stable during the study period (August 1985 to August 1987). The figures for Utah, however, are based upon foster care placements, while the figures for Washington are based upon total out-of-home care rates. In actuality, there would be little difference in *trends* if the total out-of-home placement rates for Utah were used, with the exception of a slight increase in the number of inpatient psychiatric placements in late 1986 and 1987.

Placement incidence statistics, however, are more revealing as they provide a more accurate picture of the extent to which communities use child placement as a service option. Foster family care incidence rates in 1985 (at the start of the project) did vary by state with placement rates over 5 times

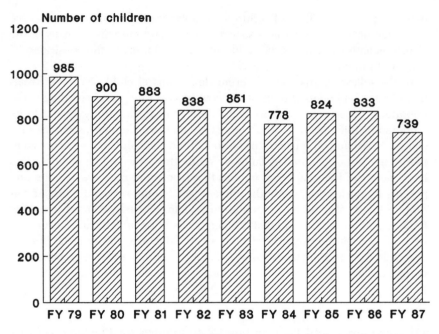

Figure 9.1. Average monthly foster care caseload in Utah

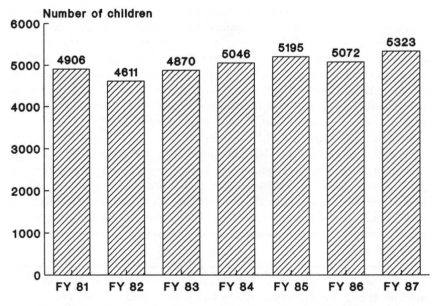

Figure 9.2. Average monthly out-of-home care caseload in Washington

higher for Washington compared to Utah during that year (Maximus, 1985). On the basis of these data, it may have been more difficult for children to be placed in foster care in Utah than in Washington.

Public Policies in Utah

The child welfare system in Utah adopted a permanency planning approach in the mid-1970s. In each CPS district office, one or more therapists were assigned permanency planning functions and received special training and consultation. While the child population rose substantially between 1970 and 1990 in Utah, foster care placement rates did not increase proportionally and instead decreased steadily until 1989, when rates began to increase slowly. This overall decrease was due largely to the emphasis upon preserving families through restricting certain types of placement services and expanding various forms of protective supervision and placement prevention services.

In addition, between 1978 and 1982, Utah embarked on a systematic attempt to deinstitutionalize youth correctional services. The state training school for juvenile offenders was closed and the state's capacity to hold youths in secure confinement was reduced from approximately 500 beds to 70 beds. Furthermore, beginning in 1983, greater emphasis was placed on licensing foster homes with relatives or family friends for the placement of especially difficult youths. The number of these "specific" foster home placements grew disproportionately to other types of placements, and probably accounts for the slight increase in the use of substitute care between 1982 and 1983.

Public Policies in Washington

The state of Washington also adopted permanency planning in the 1970s, but compared to Utah, it was implemented with less intensive training and supervision of child welfare staff. To implement practice reforms in child welfare further, the Family Reconciliation Services program was organized in 1977 to provide community-based alternatives to foster care for families with older children. With this and other service initiatives, the number of children in out-of-home care, although declining slightly between 1981 and 1982, rose slowly between 1979 and 1987. At the same time, the child population also rose steadily. With the possible exception of the years 1982–1984 and 1986–1987, the increases in child placement appear to be proportional to population growth.

There was a dramatic increase, however, in the number of placements in 1986–1987. Due to tragic case situations such as the death in 1986 of Eli Creekmore, a child who was under state supervision, high CPS caseloads and a lack of preventive services in many regions became the focus of much public outcry. Out-of-home placements rose during this period. Thus, for the last few months of the data collection period, the Homebuilders program was providing services to prevent foster care placement at a time when state CPS case workers were very concerned about child injuries and were sensitive to the criticism being directed at the Department of Social and Health Services by citizen groups and the media.

Comparing Environmental Influences in Utah and Washington

Placement rates in the two states should be assessed in the context of these different public policy environments. In Utah, there was a concerted attempt to provide services to families such that children and youths might be maintained in their own homes. In Washington, while the child welfare system had implemented a range of preventive services for at least part of the study period, CPS workers were especially concerned about child safety and the public social service system was under intense public scrutiny. In addition, there was decided skepticism in the juvenile justice system about the capacity of service providers to help families and delinquent youth. Juvenile justice legislation focused on public protection and established judicial sentencing guidelines for youth. These guidelines strongly encouraged juvenile court judges to make dispositional decisions that were proportional to a youth's age, prior record, and offense(s) (for more information about Washington's juvenile justice system, see Schram, McKelvy, Schneider, & Griswold, 1981).

Overall, it appears that environmental influences operated to minimize placement in Utah more than in Washington. From one perspective, this means that it should have been easier to prevent child placement in Washington because so many more children were being placed. However, maintaining long-term treatment success in such an environment might be more difficult. In any event, given these differences and the influence that other environmental factors may exert, comparisons of placement prevention rates between the two states must be viewed with caution.

Method

The methodology for the analysis of the outcome data for both the entire study sample, a 12-month follow-up group, and a special set of families comprising a case overflow comparison group in Utah will be described in this section.

Subjects

As mentioned in Chapter 4, a total of 453 families participated in the study. Of these 453 families, a slightly smaller group were used as the basis for placement rate analyses because only the first-, second-, and third-oldest children who were at risk of imminent placement were monitored. Thus while consumer satisfaction and service data are based on all 453 families served, placement rate data are based on 446 families with 581 children who were at risk. In addition, subsamples were formed based on whether or not the family was served early enough to be included in a 12-month follow-up group. While 446 families were served and tracked for placement data, only 263 families were included in the 12-month follow-up group. All families that completed treatment by August 13, 1986, were selected for inclusion in a 12-month follow-up study. Across the two states, the primary caretakers in these 263 families (Utah, 76; Washington, 187) were interviewed by telephone or in person. In Utah, 95% of the families that completed treatment in time to be part of the 12-month follow-up were interviewed, and in Washington 70% were interviewed.[1]

To gather information regarding the causes of child placements across the two-year period of the study, parents from all 136 families from which a child was placed were contacted. If they consented, they were interviewed at the time of placement (or when the child ran away, chose to live with friends, was admitted to a residential treatment program, etc.). These families were identified by interviews with parents at the termination of service and at 12-month follow-up (if the family was served early enough in the project to be part of the follow-up), as well as by regular examination of state computer reports regarding placement purchase of service records. (In Utah and Washington, any placement reimbursed by the public child welfare agency is tracked by computer.) This information was supplemented by anecdotal reports from IFPS and other child welfare therapists regarding detention placements, runaways, and other circumstances in which children were living out of the home with neighbors, family friends, or older siblings. When it was discovered that a child have been out of the home for at least two weeks, parents were called to verify that "placement" had occurred. Upon confirmation, interviews were scheduled.

In addition, in Utah, for the period August 14, 1985, to April 22, 1987, any family that was referred for IFPS and met the criteria for acceptance but that could not be served due to full therapist caseloads was tracked for 12 months or until the child was placed (see note 2 in Chapter 4). A total of 26 families were identified, and information about the placement location(s) of children in these families was gathered during the follow-up period. Thus, these families were used to form a comparison group for the project.

Program administrators in Utah estimated that approximately 38 families were actually referred, met the criteria for IFPS, but were not served during this period. Consequently, the sample for the case overflow comparison group represents 68% of the population of families that was referred for IFPS, met the criteria for service, and were not able to be accepted because therapists' caseloads were full.

Defining Success and Failure from Family Preservation and Child-at-Risk Perspectives

For many outcome analyses in this report, success and failure were defined from a family preservation perspective. If a family had multiple children at risk, when even one child was placed the family's service was declared to have failed. From this perspective, the preservation of the family unit is paramount and is not achieved when even one child in a family is placed. As suggested by the name *family preservation services*, a common goal of family treatment is to preserve the family as a complete supportive system. Thus is some chapters, comparisons of parent functioning, social support, and child problems are used with the sample divided into success and failure categories based on this family-oriented definition of failure.

However, placement data for each child who was identified as being at risk of placement were collected also, and will be reported to illustrate differences in success rates. In some situations, the avoidance of placements for *individual children* targeted for placement may be the best definition of success. This shift from a family- to a child-focused perspective represents the reality of agency resource consumption faced by public child welfare agencies when treatment failures occur. That is, public agencies place children—not families—in out-of-home care. Sometimes, failure families have more than one child who needs placement.[2] Multiple out-of-home placements of children translates into additional foster or group care costs for public agencies. Calculations made using families as the unit of measurement miss this dimension.

In addition, the utilization of a child-focused outcome measure allows for the consideration of partial success in those families where some but not all children were placed. From the perspectives of some families, placing some children but not others is often considered a major triumph. As discussed earlier, it is important to note that these definitions of treatment failure do not acknowledge that some child placements may have been in the best interests of both the child and the family at that time. The desirability or appropriateness of the placements was not assessed specifically, although some data addressing agency and primary caretaker views of desirability will be presented in this chapter.

Data Collection and Instruments

Child placements were identified through a variety of means including IFPS therapist reports and agency MIS data (which record agency payments for substitute care). Probably the best method of identifying any type of child placement or runaway behavior is to interview the primary caretaker. This was done by phone or in person at case termination and 12 months after the case was referred for service (IFPS intake).

Case Termination and Follow-up Interviews. The case termination and 12-month follow-up interviews focused on current family problems, the location of all target children (i.e., whether any child had been placed during the year), the length of all placements, use of relatives, neighbors, or friends as "informal" placements, episodes of running away or temporary detention, and consumer satisfaction with IFPS.[3] The collection of such a broad range of information on the living situations of children who were deemed at risk permitted the construction of placement location tables and, by altering the types of placements considered as negative outcomes, allowed the estimation of different definitions of placement.

In comparison to placement rates based on the aggregate sample, the rates from the 12-month sample may be more accurate estimates of treatment failure because, in contrast to families that completed intensive family preservation services in the second year of the study, families that completed treatment in the first year of the study were tracked for a full year. Aggregate placement rates in the entire sample of 453 families are likely to be biased downward by the lack of a full year follow-up for families that completed services after August 13, 1986.

Placement Interviews. The purpose of interviewing the caretakers of all families in which a placement occurred was to elicit views on the causes of placement and to find out whether family members affected by the placement decision thought that the provision of additional services might have prevented placement. Interviewers were trained to conduct probing discussions of events and problems that led to placement, and they recorded caretakers' descriptions using checklists of common "causes" of placement. These checklists were developed by IFPS staff and tested over time. Only when caretakers mentioned an item was it recorded. The interviews were open-ended and interviewers did not suggest causes. When a cause was identified by a caretaker—for example, "my child was not going to school"— they were asked to estimate how often it occurred and the degree to which it was a problem.[4]

Interviewers also invited caretakers to assess the desirability of the placement that was made and the services that were provided to prevent placement. They asked such questions as, Is your child's current placement better for you and the family? At the conclusion of the interview, caretakers were asked a series of questions about the degree to which IFPS had been helpful, and they were asked to identify actions that might have been undertaken to prevent the placement of their child(ren).

A similar interview was conducted with IFPS therapists who worked with families where a placement was made and interviews were conducted with therapists' supervisors as well. The therapists and supervisors was not asked about the desirability of placement, but they were asked about the causes of placement. They were also asked whether anything might have prevented the placement and, based on agency norms, whether their caseloads at the time of service to the subject family were normal, high, or low. For each "unsuccessful" family, therapists and supervisors were invited to identify unusual factors that may have precluded family members from benefiting from IFPS. Finally, data for the comparison group sample were collected through reviews of the agency computer records of placement payments and from interviews with the caseworkers who had served comparison families during the follow-up period.

Limitations of the Study

Reactivity. Although interviewers were carefully trained and confidentiality was guaranteed, some of the data collection methods may have been reactive. Placement is an emotional event for children, caretakers, and therapists. It is possible that caretakers and therapists responded in socially desirable ways to sensitive questions.

Limitations in Caretaker Recall. During the 12-month follow-up interviews, caretakers were asked to recall "informal" placements of their children with neighbors, friends, relatives, and others who may have helped the family after the termination of IFPS. While such events per se are likely to stand out in parents' minds, their recall with regard to the actual length or dates of placement may have poor reliability. Length of placement findings are likely to be more accurate for formal placements because they are usually based on state purchase of service agreements. In contrast, data regarding length of placement with neighbors, relatives, and private psychiatric institutions who did not receive reimbursement from public social services offices were more subject to estimation.

Limited Dependent Measure. For this chapter, the outcome measure has been defined dichotomously. For most analyses, success was declared when families remained intact or utilized a relative—an extended family member—to place a child informally. These "relative" placements generally did not involve state support or formal agency intervention. Failure was declared when, at any time up to 12 months after service intake, a family experienced a non relative placement of two-weeks duration or greater. This definition of failure includes cases that would be counted as successes by other major evaluation studies (see, for example, Jones et al., 1976, p. 81; Nelson et al., 1988, p. 70). For instance, a case was counted as a failure even if a child spent 16 days in shelter care during treatment, but returned home before the close of treatment. Other evaluations have counted children as treatment failures only if they were out of the home at the time of case termination.

Overall placement rates in the FIT study will therefore be comparatively higher than other FBS evaluation studies because of differences in the way that failure was defined and differences in the methods used for case tracking. In many other studies, interviews with FBS therapists, case record reviews, and use of MIS system data are the only sources of placement data. These approaches underestimate placement rates as therapists typically lose touch with families after case termination, and agency MIS systems track only publicly funded placements. Conducting interviews with primary caretakers at case termination and 12 months after intake allowed the FIT project more accurately to identify a range of placement outcomes.

Limitations of the Comparison Group Design and Sample. The comparison group employed for this study was based on tracking 26 of the 38 families (68%) that were referred to but not served by the Utah IFPS units. It is possible that the 12 families that were not tracked avoided child placement. No information about these families is available. Thus, the observed placement rate for the comparison group might have been lower had all the comparison group cases been tracked. While possible, this does not seem likely. Counterbalancing this potential bias also is the fact that only the referring therapists, and not the comparison group families, were interviewed at follow-up. Some privately arranged placements or runaway episodes therefore may not have been identified. Given these limitations, comparison group placement rates should be interpreted with caution, for the sample size is small, the follow-up interview method differed from that of the treatment condition, and the findings describe only public agency (Utah) sites.

Results

Placement Outcomes for All Project Families (N = 453)

Shown in Table 9.1, 136 (30.5%) of the 453 families participating in the FIT project experienced at least one nonrelative placement or runaway episode of two-weeks duration or more (as we have done throughout this book, we use *placement rate* to refer to a broad set of negative outcomes). The placement rate was slightly higher in Utah (36.5%) than in Washington (27.7%), and the difference has a low probability of occurrence by chance alone $(p = .055)$.

The proportion of families that did not experience service failure during the project period was computed as a "placement prevention rate." Placement prevention rates, while indicating the relative success of the two IFPS programs, must be viewed with caution, as a number of control or comparison group studies (ours included) have found that not all children desig-

Table 9.1. IFPS Treatment Outcome: Entire Sample
(August 14, 1985–August 31, 1987)

		Utah	Washington	Total sample
A.	Families as the unit of analysis			
	1. Families experiencing treatment	139	307	446
	2. Families experiencing at least one out-of-home placement at any time during the study[a]	51 (36.5%)	85 (27.7%)	136 (30.5%)
	3. Placement prevention rate at case termination[b]	89.2%	92.2%	91.3%
B.	Children as the unit of analysis[c]			
	1. Number of children identified as being at risk of placement (PR)	172	409	581
	2. Number of children experiencing at least one out-of-home placement at any time during the study	55 (32.0%)	92 (22.5%)	147 (25.3%)
	3. Mean days in the home of children who were placed (SD)	145.7 (92.6)	121.2 (95.5)	130.3 (94.8)
	4. Placement prevention rate at case termination[b]	90.7%	93.9%	92.9%

[a] Placement is defined here as child placement with a nonrelative or continuous runaway behavior for two weeks or more.
[b] Case termination occurred, on average, 30.2 days after intake in Washington and 62.8 days after intake in Utah. But these statistics reflect placements that occurred at case termination irrespective of the length of service.
[c] Includes only the three oldest children, 17 and under, living at home, which represents 95.5% of the children identified as PRs.

nated "at risk of placement" are actually placed in the absence of IFPS. Using families as the unit of analysis, the placement prevention rate at case termination was 91.3% (Utah, 89.2%; Washington, 92.2%).

When children who were designated as PRs were used as the unit of analysis, placement rates significantly differed between the two states (Utah, 32.0%; Washington, 22.5%; $p = .016$). The placement prevention rate at case termination for the total sample of children served by the FIT project was 92.9%. For Utah, it was 90.7% and for Washington, it was 93.9%.

These data suggest that the Utah children experienced relatively more placements during the project period than Washington children. The Home-builders program in Washington appears to have been slightly more successful in keeping families together. Yet the number of days that the children who were eventually placed spent living at home during the project period was slightly greater for the Utah families. Placed children from the Utah families spent approximately 24 days longer in the home compared to Washington families (see Table 9.1).

Prevention Rates Adjusted for Placement with Relatives

Some recent studies have declared placements with relatives as treatment failure. We believe that caring for children using extended family members is a positive outcome for many children. Moreover, it is a tradition adhered to by many ethnic groups. But some relative placements are state-supported, and to allow comparisons between this study and other studies, a special analysis was conducted and a treatment success rate that included placements with relatives as case failure was calculated.

Only four children were placed with relatives (on a paid or unpaid basis) at or before case termination (two children were placed in Utah and two in Washington). For the total sample of children ($N = 581$), the treatment success rate at case termination, adjusted by including relative placements in the failure definition, was 92.3%. For the Utah cases, it was 89.5%; for the Washington cases, it was 93.4%.

Placement Rates Based on the 12-Month Follow-Up Sample (N = 263)

"Family Preservation" Failure Rates. In all likelihood, the placement rates for the 12-month follow-up sample are the most accurate estimates of placement after service. In the 12-month follow-up sample, each family was tracked for an equivalent time period and had therefore an equivalent opportunity to experience placement. These data are unaffected by differing periods of follow-up. In the aggregate sample, this was not true, for families that completed treatment in the second year of the project were tracked only until August 1987. Thus some families had as little as one month of follow-up before the follow-up phase of the study was terminated. For these reasons, the sample of families and children in the follow-up groups are used as the basis of many analyses in this and other chapters.

At this point, one might wax philosophical and ask, Is it realistic to hold a brief intervention responsible for outcomes many months after therapists have ceased to see family members? When IFPS therapists do not have control over the quality of follow-up services or case decisions that are made after IFPS have been completed, should we hold them responsible for long-term family functioning? Our view is that an effective IFPS program should prevent placement after the termination of services, but it may be unreasonable to expect a brief service to have an impact on families that lasts in perpetuity. Using long-term placement prevention rates as a major criterion for success may be especially inappropriate when an IFPS program is operating in a larger organizational or community environment that uses a more aggressive approach to placing children, has fewer supportive services, or places little emphasis on maximizing family strengths and resources.

In total, 263 families were served early enough during the research project to participate in a 12-month follow-up, perhaps the outer limit to which brief programs should be held responsible for outcomes. Of those, 76 (29%) were from Utah and 187 (71%) were from Washington. As a result, the two-state family preservation failure rate of 38.8% is disproportionately influenced by Washington participants and should be interpreted cautiously. State data are more illuminating. The Utah failure rate was 47.4% and the Washington rate was 35.3%, with a higher proportion of Utah families experiencing treatment failure when followed for a full 12 months after intake. This pattern of superior results in Washington is consistent with the aggregate findings.

Child-Based Failure Rates. Because data were collected on individual children, an analysis of individual child treatment failure was conducted. In the Utah follow-up sample, 97 oldest, second-oldest, and third-oldest children had been designated at intake as being at risk of placement, and in Washington 245 children had been designated as at risk (see Table 9.2). In Utah the base failure rate was 41.2%, while in Washington it was markedly lower, 29.8%. Similar to other comparisons, the pattern of lower placement rates for Washington was sustained. Across the two states, the child-based placement prevention rate was 67.0%.

Table 9.2.   IFPS Treatment Outcomes: 12-Month Follow-Up Sample
(August 14, 1985–August 13, 1986)[a]

Children as the unit of analysis[b]	Utah	Washington	Total sample
1. Number of children identified as being at risk of placement (PR)	97	245	342
2. Number of children experiencing at least one out-of-home placement[c]	40	73	113
a. Percentage of children placed	41.2%	29.8%	33.0%
3. Mean days in the home (SD)	150.7	141.5	144.7
	(93.5)	(95.5)	(94.5)
4. Placement prevention rate 12 months after intake	58.8%	70.2%	67.0%

[a] Families that began service as part of the project during this period were part of the 12-month follow-up sample.

[b] Includes only the three oldest children, 17 and under, living at home, which represents 95.5% of the children identified as PRs in the study.

[c] Placement is defined here as child placement with a nonrelative or continuous runaway behavior for two weeks or more.

Child-based treatment failures occurring over time in the study are illustrated in Figures 9.3, 9.4, and 9.5. These figures indicate that, compared to Washington, a higher proportion of Utah case failures occurred early in the treatment process.

The child-based placement prevention rate at 12 months after IFPS intake for Washington of 70.2% is very similar to the rates reported in some of the previous research studies that used comparison groups and/or careful follow-up interviews (see Chapter 2). However, the definition of treatment success

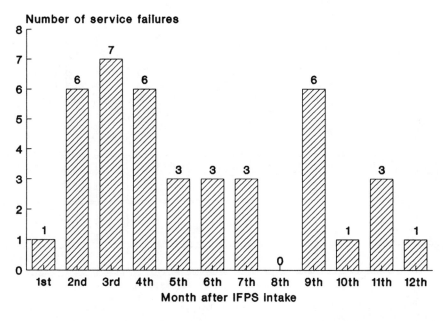

Month after IFPS intake[a]	1st	2nd	3rd	4th	5th	6th	7th	8th	9th	10th	11th	12th
Number surviving at end of month	96	90	83	77	74	71	68	68	62	61	58	57
Percent surviving	99.0	92.8	85.6	79.4	76.3	73.2	70.2	70.2	63.9	62.9	59.8	58.8

[a]Month after IFPS intake: 1st month–30 days or less, 2nd month–31-60 days, 3rd month–61-90 days, 4th month–91-120 days, 5th month–121-150 days, 6th month–151-180 days, 7th month–181-210 days, 8th month–211-240 days, 9th month–241-270 days, 10th month–271-300 days, 11th month–301-330 days, 12th month–321-365 days.

Figure 9.3. Number of child service failures by month in the 12-month follow-up sample in Utah ($n = 97$)

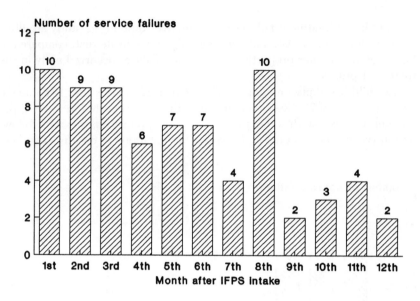

Number of service failures

Month after IFPS intake[a]	1st	2nd	3rd	4th	5th	6th	7th	8th	9th	10th	11th	12th
Number surviving at end of month	235	226	217	211	204	197	193	183	181	178	174	172
Percent surviving	95.9	92.2	88.6	86.1	83.3	80.4	78.8	74.7	73.9	72.7	71.0	70.2

[a]Month after IFPS intake: 1st month–30 days or less, 2nd month–31-60 days, 3rd month–61-90 days, 4th month–91-120 days, 5th month–121-150 days, 6th month–151-180 days, 7th month–181-210 days, 8th month–211-240 days, 9th month–241-270 days, 10th month–271-300 days, 11th month–301-330 days, 12th month–321-365 days.

Figure 9.4. Number of child service failures by month in the 12-month follow-up sample in Washington (*n* = 245)

used in the FIT project is one of the most conservative employed in studies to date, where more short-term out-of-home living situations are defined as placements. Furthermore, the placement rates reported in Tables 9.1 and 9.2 are more sensitive than most because shelter care, residential treatment (private and public), inpatient psychiatric (private and public), and other out-of-home conditions (e.g., youth corrections placements) are included in calculations. A substantial proportion of private agency placements do not appear on child welfare purchase of service agreements because they are paid

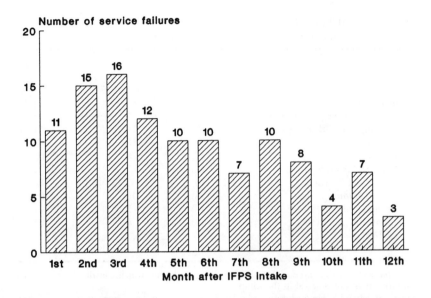

Table:

Month after IFPS intake[a]	1st	2nd	3rd	4th	5th	6th	7th	8th	9th	10th	11th	12th
Number surviving at end of month	331	316	300	288	278	268	261	251	243	239	232	229
Percent surviving	96.7	92.4	87.8	84.2	81.3	78.4	76.3	73.4	71.1	69.9	67.8	67.0

[a]Month after IFPS intake: 1st month–30 days or less, 2nd month–31-60 days, 3rd month–61-90 days, 4th month–91-120 days, 5th month–121-150 days, 6th month–151-180 days, 7th month–181-210 days, 8th month–211-240 days, 9th month–241-270 days, 10th month–271-300 days, 11th month–301-330 days, 12th month–321-365 days.

Figure 9.5. Number of child service failures by month in the aggregate 12-month follow-up sample (*n* = 342)

for by a family's insurance or directly by parents. Runaway episodes are also typically underreported in public records. Information regarding these types of placements can be collected only by interviewing former clients and asking such questions as, In the course of the last year since you and your family participated in IFPS, did [child's name] run away from home? Was she/he placed in a public or private residential treatment center? Was she/he sent to a secure youth facility for breaking the law?

The data in Table 9.3 indicate the relative dependency of placement rates

Table 9.3.   Most Restrictive Placement Locations of Children at Risk of
Placement in the 12-Month Follow-Up Sample[a]

Placement location[b]	Utah (N = 97) N (%)		Washington (N = 245) N (%)[c]		Total sample (N = 342) N (%)[c]	
A. In home or with relatives	57	(59)	172	(70)	229	(67)
B. Friends	2	(2)	3	(1)	5	(2)
C. Runaway	7	(7)	9	(4)	16	(5)
D. Shelter care/detention	2	(2)	7	(3)	9	(3)
E. Foster family care	15	(16)	32	(13)	47	(14)
F. Group home	3	(3)	13	(5)	16	(5)
G. Residential treatment	7	(7)	2	(1)	9	(3)
H. Inpatient psychiatric facility	4	(4)	6	(3)	10	(3)
I. Other[d]			1	(1)	1	(1)

[a] Data based upon the three oldest children living at home, which constitutes 95.5% of the children at risk of removal in the sample.

[b] Most restrictive placement location of each child for two weeks or more at any time during a 12-month period following IFPS intake.

[c] Percentages do not sum to 100 due to rounding error.

[d] Includes one child who was placed in juvenile corrections facility that was not a community-based group home.

on the kinds of out-of-home conditions that are defined as failure. If, as in many studies, placements with relatives, friends, in shelter care, or episodes of running away are not considered in the calculation of a failure rate, the placement prevention rates rise substantially. Under this definition, even when a 12-month follow-up period is used, Utah IFPS therapists prevented substitute care placements in 70.1% of the children they served and Washington IFPS therapists prevented substitute care placements in 78.0% of the children they served.

Differences in success rates become especially evident when the most restrictive placement locations of the children are arranged in hierarchical order. As shown in Figure 9.6, the large majority of children in the 12-month follow-up sample (69%) remained with their families, friends, or relatives for the entire follow-up period.

Data Regarding the Case Overflow Comparison Group

A total of 27 children from 26 families were included in the case overflow comparison group. Selected family and child demographic information was collected by the IFPS supervisor of the unit or one of her/his staff, along with information regarding child placement location (if any) during any time of the follow-up period.

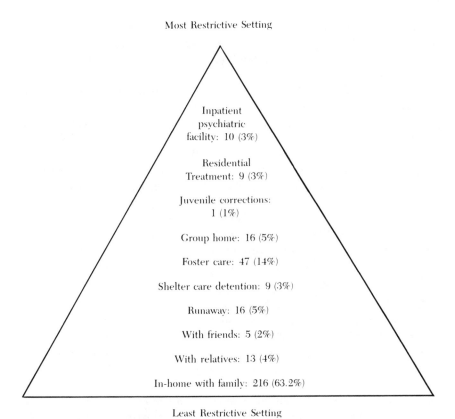

Most Restrictive Setting

Inpatient
psychiatric
facility: 10 (3%)

Residential
Treatment: 9 (3%)

Juvenile corrections:
1 (1%)

Group home: 16 (5%)

Foster care: 47 (14%)

Shelter care detention: 9 (3%)

Runaway: 16 (5%)

With friends: 5 (2%)

With relatives: 13 (4%)

In-home with family: 216 (63.2%)

Least Restrictive Setting

Figure 9.6. Placement outcomes for children included in the 12-month follow-up sample for Utah and Washington (*N* = 342). Data based upon the three oldest children living at home and identified as being at risk of placement, which constitutes 95.5% of children at risk of removal in the study. Most restrictive placement location for each child was recorded.

Demographic Characteristics. In all but one of the 26 comparison families, one child was designated as being at risk (one family had two children at risk). The families averaged 4.2 members, and all but two were of white, not of Hispanic origin. Family structure varied with 12 (46%) of the families characterized as single-parent homes (divorced or separated) and six (23%) with both birthparents married and living together. Five (19%) of the families were composed of a birthparent and a stepparent.

At the time of referral to IFPS, ten (37%) of the children were suspected of drug and/or alcohol use while 12 additional children (44%) had substantiated drug and/or alcohol usage. Five children (18%) had no drug or alcohol involvement. The majority of children in the comparison group were having school attendance problems. More specifically, 14 (52%) were rated as attending school about half or less of the time at the point of referral to the service. Six (22%) were not attending at all, had been expelled, or had dropped out.

More than half (15; 56%) of the comparison group children had some kind of physical or mental handicapping condition at the time of referral to IFPS. The most commonly identified condition was an officially diagnosed psychiatric condition identified for six (22%) of the children. Four (15%) of the children had some type of learning disability. A majority of the children (16; 59%) had not received any inpatient psychiatric services prior to their referral to IFPS. Some of the children (8; 30%) were previously placed in an inpatient psychiatric hospital, a substance abuse inpatient treatment center, or other institution. Three (11%) had been placed previously in a residential treatment center. With the exception of substance abuse and school attendance, the comparison group children did not differ significantly from the experimental group children, at least with respect to the variables measured in the study.

Placement Rate. Twenty-three (85.2%) of the 27 children identified as being at risk of placement were actually placed sometime during the follow-up period.[5] When the most restrictive placement locations were identified for each child, nine (33%) of 27 children were in inpatient psychiatric or residential treatment facilities. Surprisingly, only four (15%) of the children identified as being at risk avoided placement for the total follow-up period (including one child who left home to enroll in a Job Corps program). Thus, compared to the Utah experimental group, the comparison group cases had a significantly higher placement rate (85.2 versus 41.2%). In addition, a significantly higher proportion of the comparison group children were placed in restrictive placement settings. Seven (26%) of the comparison group children were placed in inpatient psychiatric facilities, while four (4%) of the experimental group children were treated in inpatient psychiatric settings.

Precision Matching and Analysis. A more rigorous comparison of the comparison group and experimental group cases was conducted by matching comparison group and experimental group cases on the following case characteristics: child race, child gender, previous child placement for inpatient treatment, child suspected or substantiated substance abuse, child degree of school attendance, family income, child handicap status, family structure, and household size. For each comparison group case, cases from the Utah follow-up sample that could be matched on as many of these characteristics as possible were identified. Then one case was randomly selected for use as a matched comparison case (see Table 9.4). The placement rate for the subset of matched IFPS treatment cases was 44.4%, which was still significantly lower than the placement rate for the comparison group cases (85.2%).

Why Were the Children Placed?

For families that received IFPS and participated in the FIT study, placement interviews were conducted when a child was placed out of the home. Primary caretakers, secondary caretakers, IFPS therapists, and their supervisors were interviewed for all "failure" cases. The next sections of this chapter will report the data gathered from the above four groups with regard to the following: (1) reasons for child placement, (2) services and factors that might have prevented placement, (3) degree of helpfulness of IFPS, and (4) recommendations for the improvement of IFPS.

Primary and secondary caretakers were asked to list the single most important reason underlying the placement of their child(ren). IFPS therapists and supervisors were asked to list the three most important reasons why the child was placed. These data were content-analyzed by project staff and the categories reviewed by the co-principal investigators. Because caretakers were asked to report one major reason for placement, and therapists and supervisors reported three major reasons, these data must be interpreted with caution.

Caretakers' Reasons for Child Placement. A high percentage of the reasons mentioned by primary caretakers (76.6%) and secondary caretakers (87.5%) were related to the child's behavior (see Table 9.5). The most often cited reason was child would not listen or obey. Other child-related reasons, listed in order of frequency were child wanted to be placed/did not want to live at home, committed a crime or delinquent act, drug/alcohol abuse, and child was physically violent or out of control.

Primary and secondary caretakers listed relatively few parent-related reasons for placement. Only 13.3% of reasons mentioned by primary caretakers and 5.0% of the reasons cited by secondary caretakers were parent-related. The most frequent responses of the primary caretakers were fear of hurting child/can't control my temper, need a break from parenting/exhausted/stressed out, and feel my child needs more intensive treatment.

Therapists' Reasons for Placement. IFPS therapists also identified child-related reasons as the primary reasons for child placement. The child-related reasons, in order of frequency, were the following: (1) child wouldn't listen/obey, (2) child ran away, (3) child wanted to be placed/did not want to live at home, (4) school-related problems, and (5) child committed crime/was delinquent (see Table 9.5).

Although 51.4% of the reasons mentioned by IFPS therapists were child-related, 47.3% of the primary reasons mentioned were parent-related issues. The parent-related reasons cited by IFPS therapists included the following: (1) can't control child/lack of parenting skills, (2) parent believes the child needs more intensive treatment, (3) low tolerance for child's behav-

Table 9.4. Comparison of Treatment Success of the Utah Comparison Group Cases and a Matched Set of Cases That Received IFPS ($N = 27$)

Comparison group case ID number	Matching criteria used for each case									Cases where treatment failure (F) occurred within 12 months after intake		
	Race[a]	Gender	Previous child inpatient treatment[b]	Child substance abuse[c]	Degree of school attendance[d]	Family income[e]	Child handicap status[f]	Family structure[g]	Household size[h]	Comparison group	Treatment group	(Number of matching cases)
1	X	X	X	X	X	M[i]	X	X		F		(1)
2	X	X	X	X	X	M[i]	X	X	X	F	F	(1)
3	X	X	X	X	X	X	X			F		(2)
4	X	X	X	X	X	X	X			F		(1)
5	X	X	X	X	X	M				F		(2)
6	X	X	X	X	X					F		(3)
7	X	X	X	X	X	X	X			F	F	(2)
8	X	X	X	X	X	X				F	F	(1)
9	X	X	X	X	X	X	X			F	F	(1)
10	X	X	X	X	X					F	F	(1)
11	X	X	X	X	X	X				F		(2)
12	X	X	X	X	X	X	X	X	X	F	F	(1)
20	X	X	X	X	X	X	X	X		F	F	(2)
21	X	X	X	X	X	X	X	X	X	F	F	(1)
22	X	X	X	X	X	X	X			F	F	(0)

170

23	X	X	X	X	X	X		F			(10)
24	X	X	X	X	X	X	X	X	F	F	(2)
25	X	X	X	X	X	X	X	X	X	F	(1)
26	X	X	X	X	X	X					(8)
27	X	X	X	X	X	X			F	F	(8)
28	X	X	X	X	X				F	F	(5)
29	X	X	X	X	X	X	X				(2)
30	X	X	X	X	X	X	X	M[i]		F	(2)
31	X	X	X	X	X	X			F		(3)
32	X	X	X	X	X	X	X	X	F	F	(5)
33	X	X	X	X	X	X			F		(7)
34	X	X	X	X	X	X					(1)

Percentage of cases classified as treatment failure:	85.2	44.4
Corrected chi square, p = .004:	23/27	(12/27)

[a] Race for each child was coded either as caucasian or ethnic minority

[b] This variable measured whether or not the child was placed previous to IFPS treatment. Some form of inpatient treatment facility such as residential treatment center, alcohol or drug abuse inpatient treatment, state or private psychiatric hospital was noted.

[c] Drug or alcohol usage was coded as (1) none, (2) suspected, or (3) substantiated.

[d] Degree of school attendance was coded as (1) attending all or the majority of the time, (2) attending less than half of the time, (3) not attending or formally "dropped out," or (4) not attending because of summer vcacation during the time of treatment or too young for school.

[e] Family income was coded as (1) $10,000 or less or (2) $10,0001 and over.

[f] Child handicap status included (1) none, (2) any physical or intellectual handicap, or (3) officially diagnosed psychiatric problem.

[g] Family structure was coded as (1) two-parent family (including parent living with another adult, (2) single-parent family (including never-married parents, single parent divorced or separated, and grandmother caring for children alone) or (3) other family structure.

[h] Household size was coded as (1) 1–4 persons or (2) 5 or more persons.

[i] M: data missing for a particular comparison group case.

Table 9.5.   Primary Caretaker, Secondary Caretaker, IFPS Therapist, and IFPS
Supervisor Reasons for Child Placement

	Number of reasons identified by respondents[a]			
Reasons	*Primary caretaker*	*Secondary caretaker*	*IFPS therapist*	*IFPS supervisor*
Child-related				
A. Child wouldn't listen/obey	31	17	37	25
B. Ran away	4	1	13	9
C. School-related	3	0	11	2
D. Committed crime/ delinquent	5	1	10	8
E. Drug/alcohol abuse	5	1	8	6
F. Associates with wrong friends	1	3	5	3
G. Physically violent/out of control	5	3	7	3
H. Child is pregnant or a parent	2	0	1	0
I. Sex offense	1	0	1	2
J. Emotional/self-esteem problems	2	1	4	6
K. Child is suicidal	1	2	2	2
L. Child wanted to be placed/ did not want to live at home	7	5	12	6
M. Child set fires	2	1	1	0
N. Other	0	0	13	5
Total	69	35	125	77
Percentage of reasons	(76.6%)	(87.5%)	(51.4%)	(35.0%)
Parent-related				
A. Can't control child/lack of parenting skills	0	0	24	22
B. Fear of hurting child/can't control temper	2	0	7	7
C. Emotionally abusive	0	1	3	3
D. Physical neglect	0	0	0	4
E. Needs a break from parenting/exhausted/ stressed out	2	0	7	6
F. Drug/alcohol abuse	0	0	1	1
G. Sexual abuse	1	0	6	8
H. Insufficient interest in providing adequate parenting	0	0	5	8
I. Parent believes child needs more intensive treatment	2	0	14	11
J. Low tolerance for child's behavior/expectations too high	1	0	11	7
K. Parent had to leave (medical problems, jail, etc.)	0	0	1	2

(continued)

Table 9.5. (*Continued*)

Reasons	Primary caretaker	Secondary caretaker	IFPS therapist	IFPS supervisor
	Number of reasons identified by respondents[a]			
L. Unable to provide for basic needs	1	0	6	2
M. Parent has emotional problems	0	0	7	6
N. Stepparent or live-in boyfriend problems	0	1	3	3
O. Marital problems	0	0	4	3
P. Custody issues	0	0	2	3
Q. Parent failed to learn or utilize skill from HBS	0	0	5	4
R. Other	3	0	9	9
Total	12	2	115	110
Percentage of reasons	(13.3%)	(5.0%)	(47.3%)	(50.0%)
Parent/child conflict or disagreement	3	0	9	10
Total	3	0	9	10
Percentage of reasons	(3.3%)		(3.5%)	(4.5%)
Social/institutional factors				
A. Juvenile court judge demanded placement	1	0	0	3
B. School demanded placement	1	2	1	1
C. Community/neighborhood pressures	1	0	0	1
D. CPS, agency pressured	1	0	2	4
E. Other experts pressured	1	0	0	0
F. HBS failed to stabilize child's behavior/prevent placement	0	0	1	6
G. Other services failed to stabilize child's behavior	0	0	1	0
H. Lack of access to outside supports	0	0	1	2
I. Termination of HBS	1	1	0	2
J. Factors related to family living in a shelter/group home	0	0	2	1
K. Other	0	0	0	3
Total	6	3	8	23
Percentage or reasons	(6.6%)	(1.2%)	(3.1%)	(10.4%)
Total number of reasons	90	40	257	220

[a] Primary and secondary caretakers identified the single most important reason why the child was placed. IFPS therapists and supervisors listed the three most important reasons for why the child was placed.

ior/expectations too high, (4) fear of hurting child/can't control temper, (5) needs break from parenting, and (6) parent has emotional problems.

Supervisors' Reasons for Placement. A higher proportion of the reasons for child placement identified by IFPS supervisors were parent-related (50.0%) compared to child-related (35.0%). The parent-related reasons included the following: (1) can't control child/lack of parenting skills, (2) parent believes child needs more intensive treatment, (3) stepparent or live-in boyfriend problem, (4) sexual abuse, and (5) insufficient interest in providing adequate parenting. The major child-related factors identified by supervisors were (1) child wouldn't listen/obey, (2) ran away, and (3) committed crime/delinquent.

Caretakers' versus Staff Reasons for Placement. Suggesting a research confound in studies that use only one source of information about placements, parents, therapists, and supervisors had different views of the causes of placements. The findings imply that primary and secondary caretakers, relative to therapists and supervisors, are more likely to identify child-related reasons for placement. A substantial number of child-related reasons, however, were cited by both IFPS therapists and supervisors (see Table 9.5).

Across all three sources, the two most frequent placement factors identified were the child-related problem of not listening/obeying and the parent-related problem of not being able to control the child. These responses are, in a sense, "mirror images" of parenting skills deficits. The findings suggest that IFPS should include treatment components that emphasize child management, and they support the treatment and goal attainment data that indicate program emphasis in this area is essential for treatment success, as reported in Chapter 6.

Why a higher proportion of the reasons for placement identified by supervisors were parent-related factors compared to therapists and caretakers is not clear. The difference may be explained through therapists' "hands-on" contact with the entire family system. Therapists may develop relationships with both parents and children, and come to a more systemic view of family problems, whereas supervisors, in relying on therapist-reported information, seem to interpret problems as primarily parent in origin.

In summary, participants in IFPS, both clients and staff, tended to identify child- and parent-related factors when asked to describe the reasons why IFPS fail. IFPS supervisors were prone to identify parental deficits when explaining the reasons for service failure. Caretakers and IFPS therapists were more apt to describe child-focused reasons. With the exception of duration of service, service elements were rarely identified as a reason for placement.

Such findings are worrisome in that IFPS staff members, in considering the services that they provided, did not identify many service-related factors associated with treatment failure. Although a variety of child and parent characteristics are associated with success/failure (see Chapter 10), it is likely that a study in which there was wider variation in services would find that services account for as much or more of the variance in outcome as client characteristics. In future studies, a variety of services should be rigorously tested using "dismantling" or similar designs that permit careful assessment of the effectiveness of competing elements of service. Such information might allow IFPS therapists and supervisors to fine-tune the IFPS programs that have proliferated across the country.

Services or Factors That Might Have Prevented Placement

Primary and secondary caretakers, IFPS therapists, and supervisors were asked what one service or factor might have prevented the child's placement out of the home. Over half of the primary caretakers (50.1%) and a larger proportion of the secondary caretakers (60%) felt "nothing" would have prevented placement (see Table 9.6).

Those primary caretakers who reported services or factors that might have prevented placement identified more intensive involvement from outside counseling services and more cooperation and commitment from the child to change behavior as important factors. Secondary caretakers rated more cooperation and commitment from the child to change behavior (17.5%) as the primary factor that might have prevented placement.

Approximately one in four IFPS therapists (24.0%) and supervisors (21.2%) also indicated "nothing" could have been done to prevent placement. However, IFPS therapists rated more family commitment to keep child home (24.0%) as a primary preventive factor, along with more cooperation from the child to change her/his behavior (17.5%). IFPS therapists also felt more services were needed for some cases. IFPS supervisors responses were similar to the therapists, with 34.4% of the supervisors indicating more family commitment and 11.1% preferring more services as placement preventive factors (see Table 9.6).

The pattern of services of factors that might have prevented placement reflects the differences in perception between caretakers and IFPS staff regarding responsibility for the child's behavior. Parents generally felt nothing could have prevented placement. However, of those placement prevention factors that they identified, the primary reasons mentioned were the need for outside counseling and more commitment from the child. Only 1.1% of the caretakers felt more family commitment was indicated. This is in direct contrast to the IFPS staff members. They felt most strongly that more family commitment was a primary preventive factor. The therapist and supervisor responses regarding lack of parental commitment have important ramifications for the design of treatment. Corroborating the FRS findings

Table 9.6.   Services or Factors That Might Have Prevented Placement

Service or factor	Number and percentage of respondents identifying service or factor			
	Primary caretaker (N = 90)	Secondary caretaker (N = 40)	IFPS worker (N = 100)	IFPS supervisor (N = 99)
Nothing	46	24	24	21
	(50.1%)	(60.0%)	(24.0%)	(21.2%)
More intensive	11	1	5	3
involvement from	(12.2%)	(2.5%)	(5.0%)	(3.0%)
outside counseling				
School cooperation	1	1	1	1
	(1.1%)	(2.5%)	(1.0%)	(1.0%)
More family	1	0	24	34
commitment to keep	(1.1%)		(24.0%)	(34.3%)
child home				
More services	4	3	10	11
	(4.4%)	(7.5%)	(10.0%)	(11.1%)
Better aftercare services	2	1	7	7
(ongoing)	(2.2%)	(2.5%)	(7.0%)	(7.0%)
Better transitional care	2	0	2	1
services	(2.2%)		(2.0%)	(1.0%)
More cooperation and	9	7	4	4
commitment from	(10.0%)	(17.5%)	(4.0%)	(4.0%)
child to change				
his/her behavior				
Other	14	3	23	17
	(15.6%)	(7.5%)	(23.0%)	(17.2%)

(see Chapter 8), their perceptions indicate that parental attitudes toward the child and commitment to family preservation may be central predictors of the outcome of IFPS.

IFPS Worker Actions That Might Have Prevented Placement

Primary caretakers, secondary caretakers, IFPS therapists, and supervisors were asked if there was anything the IFPS therapist could have done differently to prevent the child's placement (the most important recommendation according to the respondent was recorded). The most frequently identified factor in each respondent category was that there was "nothing the IFPS therapist could have done to prevent placement." However, a much higher proportion of primary caretakers (78.9%) and secondary caretakers (78.0%) felt this was the case, compared to therapists (52.5%) and supervisors (55.6%).

Only a few recommendations were identified by primary or secondary caretakers, including spending more time with the family, spending less time with the family, to have been more available, and better engagement with child. Primary and secondary caretakers appear to be generally satisfied with services of the IFPS therapists. The most frequently identified responses of the IFPS therapists in relation to themselves were that better engagement of child, more services, and spending more time with the family might have prevented placement of the child. Supervisors mentioned similar actions, but in a different order. They felt better engagement of parent, spend more time with the family, and more services were actions IFPS therapists could have taken to prevent placement.

Supervisors therefore appear to believe that more effective relationship building with the parent may improve service effectiveness. In contrast, the therapists thought that developing a better relationship with the child would have helped to prevent out-of-home placement.

From another perspective, in order to identify services that child caretakers, therapists, and supervisors thought were helpful for delaying placement in those situations where the child(ren) were eventually placed or ran away, study participants were asked to identify and rate the degree of helpfulness of any service they received or delivered using a five-point scale with the following scale anchors: (1) not at all, (3) somewhat, (5) a great deal. This question was treated in an open-ended manner, with services rated only if they were identified as being helpful by the respondent for a particular case. Family counseling, individual counseling, and crisis counseling were identified and rated highly (see Table 9.7).

While 42% of primary and 17.0% of secondary caretakers responded with "nothing" being helpful, only 1.4% of IFPS therapists and 2.3% of supervisors shared that impression. Caretakers in some of these families appear to believe that no particular service would have made a difference in preventing the child from being placed. A variety of factors may be operating in these families: (1) the families were not at a point where they felt they could benefit from any of the services or counseling being offered, (2) primary and secondary caretakers actually believed the services were not effective in meeting their needs, and/or (3) caretakers may be "rationalizing" the appropriateness of the placement decision by stating that nothing could have prevented the child from running away from home or being removed.

From the perspective of the therapists and supervisors, concrete services, school-related services, and advocacy services were rated high in degree of helpfulness, but they were identified for only a small proportion of cases. This was contrary to the ratings of primary caretakers, who rated school-related services and advocacy services as the least helpful for a number of cases. In fact, a discrepancy exists as to the degree of helpfulness of school-related and advocacy services. IFPS therapists and supervisors placed high value in these areas. This may be explained by the value IFPS staff place upon the added support gained through work with the school and other

Table 9.7.   Degree to Which Certain Services Were Helpful in Preventing Placement

	Mean rating of helpfulness and number of cases			
Service	Primary caretaker (N = 50) M^a (no. of cases)^b	Secondary caretaker (N = 53) M (no. of cases)	IFPS therapist (N = 209) M (no. of cases)	IFPS supervisor (N = 220) M (no. of cases)
Nothing	(21)	(9)	(3)	(5)
Family counseling	3.8 (42)	3.9 (16)	3.5 (38)	3.3 (35)
Individual counseling	3.7 (36)	3.9 (13)	3.6 (57)	3.8 (57)
Crisis counseling	3.5 (13)	4.0 (3)	3.9 (22)	3.7 (29)
Concrete services	3.0 (7)	.0 (0)	4.2 (12)	3.7 (17)
School-related	1.3 (6)	.0 (0)	4.0 (7)	3.6 (13)
Meeting with client often	3.2 (5)	3.3 (4)	3.9 (15)	N/A^d
Advocacy services	1.7 (3)	.0 (0)	4.6 (7)	3.9 (8)
Other^c	4.8 (17)	3.7 (11)	3.9 (39)	3.4 (48)

^{a} Degree of helpfulness of only those services identified by respondents for each case were rated on a five-point scale with the following scale anchors: (1) not all, (3) somewhat, (5) a great deal.
^{b} Number of cases where the service was identified as being helpful.
^{c} Other services identified by an open-ended response category.
^{d} This item was omitted from the supervisor interview schedule.

agencies for the benefit of the client system, some of which is "behind the scenes" instead of directly involving parents. Caretakers, however, may be more aware of and sensitive to direct face-to-face services, which allow them more instant feedback and input. Parents may also have an adversarial relationship with the school system. In contrast, the degree of effectiveness of family, individual, and crisis counseling was rated high by each of the respondent groups. Finally, with the exception of supervisors, meeting with the client often was mentioned by each group as helpful for preventing placement.

Summary

Did IFPS reduce the placement rates of the children served? Provisionally, it appears that the services were relatively successful. The child-based placement prevention rate at case termination was 92.9% (Utah, 90.7%; Washington, 93.9%). Twelve months after intake, the child-based placement prevention rate eroded to 67.0%, with the Homebuilders placement prevention rate higher (70.2%) than Utah's (58.8%). On the basis of comparisons between a small case overflow comparison group and the IFPS treatment group in Utah, IFPS appear to be effective in preventing out-of-home placements, including such informal placements as running away from home or living with friends and neighbors. The placement prevention rate in Utah for the case overflow comparison group of children was 14.8%. In the referred-and-served groups, it was 58.8% for the follow-up sample and 55.6% for a matched set of treatment cases. Because of the small sample and the lack of random assignment, caution is warranted in interpreting these findings. The evidence is not conclusive, but it is promising.

In terms of why services failed, both clients and staff tended to identify child- and parent-related factors. IFPS supervisors were prone to identify parental deficits when explaining the reasons for service failure. Caretakers and therapists were more apt to describe child-focused reasons. With the exception of the duration of service, service elements were rarely identified as a reason for placement, but the use of more intensive counseling, more services (in general), and better after-care services were identified as being needed by families where treatment failure occurred.

In summary, this chapter has presented data that add to the evidence base that home-based IFPS can be helpful in preventing the placement of children. Interviews with primary caretakers, IFPS therapists, and IFPS supervisors provided preliminary and useful information regarding those aspects of service that were helpful and those that were problematic in preventing child placement. In the next chapter, we examine, in more detail, the relationship between a variety of child, parent, and service characteristics and placement.

Notes

1. Placement information for the remaining 30% of Washington families was obtained by examining the Washington Department of Social Services computerized placement tracking system, and interviews with the referring caseworkers and the Homebuilders therapists. A comparison of the demographic and referral characteristics of the Washington families contacted successfully during the 12-month follow-up versus those that were not revealed no significant demographic differences.

2. The FIT project sample, however, did not contain large numbers of families with multiple child placements. Only nine families had more than one child placed, resulting in an additional 11 children being added to the placement statistics when children were used as the unit of analysis (see Table 9.1).

3. See Fraser et al. (1989, Appendix K) for more information regarding questions used for the 12-month follow-up interview.

4. See Fraser et al. (1989, Appendix L) for a copy of the instruments.

5. Using families as the unit of analysis, 22 of the 26 (84.6%) families in the comparison group had a child placed in some form of substitute care or ran away during the project period.

Chapter 10

The Correlates of Treatment Success and Failure for Intensive Family Preservation Services

MARK W. FRASER, PETER J. PECORA, and ROBERT E. LEWIS

In the previous chapter, we reviewed placement rates for IFPS participants and for a small case overflow comparison condition. In chapters before that, we described findings that suggest that IFPS produce significant changes in child-related problems, parenting skills, some aspects of social support, and family environmental conditions. This chapter examines the linkages between these two bodies of findings. Here, we investigate the relationship between service outcomes and the characteristics of the children at risk, their parents, and their homes.

Method

Research Design

To identify factors associated with treatment success and failure, a prospective quasi-experimental design with a partial 12-month follow-up period, as described earlier, was employed. Case information was collected at service intake and closure on 446 families including 581 high-risk children who received IFPS. As reviewed in Chapters 4 and 5, a wide variety of social and demographic data describing children and parents was collected. In addition, data regarding family functioning and child placement were collected 12 months after IFPS intake from 263 families (including 342 at-risk children) that had entered treatment sufficiently early in the course of the study to be eligible for inclusion in a one-year follow-up. The remaining 190 families (with 239 children) were tracked until the follow-up study period ended in August 1987, and thus had follow-up times of less than 12 months.

Definition of Placement or Service Failure/Success

Service failure was declared at any point in the treatment and follow-up period when a child was found to have resided outside her/his home in a nonrelative setting for two weeks or more. These settings included group homes, foster family care, institutional placements, detention or shelter care, and residential treatment. In addition, conditions that may endanger children such as living with friends or on the street (as is the case with many runaway children) for two weeks or more were declared to constitute service failure. Conversely, *service success* was defined as living in the home or the home of relatives, i.e., family preservation during the service and the follow-up period.

Measures of Child, Parent, and Family Functioning

Based on self-reports from child caretakers, IFPS therapists, and children, family functioning and case outcomes were assessed through the application of number of different instruments. The CWLA Family Risk Scales (FRS) were used to measure changes in various aspects of child, parent, and family functioning. Scale items were fully anchored by three- to five-sentence descriptions, and focused on parenting capacity, individual (both parent and child) functioning, and environmental conditions that have shown to be predictive of out-of-home placement. The scale is distinguished by the inclusion of variables that may potentially be altered through treatment (Magura & Moses, 1986; Magura et al., 1987).

To measure social support, a Social Support Inventory (SSI) based in part on Barrera, Sandler, and Ramsay's Inventory of Socially Supportive Behaviors (1981) was used. This instrument was used to assess spousal relationships (where there was a spouse or live-in secondary caretaker) and, separately, to assess family social support beyond the spousal dyad. Family social support was defined as significant interactions and activities with neighbors, friends, extended kin, and others. Only primary and secondary child caretakers completed the instrument, and they were asked to exclude from consideration interactions that occurred with professional agency personnel such as IFPS therapists, mental health workers, and homemakers. Social support data were collected before and after treatment.

Family functioning was measured by the third edition of the Family Adaptability and Cohesion Scales (FACES III) (Olson & Killorin, 1985). The FACES III contained ten items that measure family adaptability and ten items that measured family cohesion. Adaptability refers to the capacity of a family to adjust to new conditions. Adaptability was scored from low to high on a continuum with four anchors: rigid, structured, flexible, and chaotic. Cohesion was scored from low to high and has four different anchors: disengaged, separated, connected, and enmeshed. Extreme scores on the adaptability scale (rigid or chaotic) and extreme scores on the cohesion scale (disengaged or enmeshed) are considered dysfunctional (Olson et al., 1985).

Service Characteristics

Data were collected also on the type and amount of clinical and concrete services provided, as well as the amount of in-person and telephone contact with clients. Concrete services were partitioned into those services that were designed to "enable" or to help family members locate a resource by themselves, versus those services that were directly provided or coordinated by the IFPS therapist.

As discussed in Chapter 6, the clinical goals of service were carefully monitored. From 16 possible goals, the treatment goals for each family were specified in advance of treatment by therapists in conjunction with family members. At the close of treatment, IFPS therapists rated families on the degree to which each specified goal was achieved. A five-point scale was used with a rating of 1 equivalent to no progress or no goal achievement at all, and a rating of 5 equivalent to complete or total goal achievement. The value 3 was anchored as about half achieved, and values 2 and 4 were unanchored but implied 25 and 75% levels of achievement, respectively. Across all identified goals, mean goal achievement was computed for each family. For some analyses, goal achievement was dichotomized such that low goal achievers were defined as having scores of 2.0 or less; and modest to high goal achievers as having goal achievement scores greater than 2.0. Conceptually, goal achievement is used to describe both the main purpose or purposes of treatment at the family level and, in a proximal sense, to describe the degree to which treatment may have been successful.

Scaling Risk Factors

Demographic, FRS, SSI, and FACES III measures were dichotomized by examining frequency distributions and service failure rates. Dichotomies were created to maximize the odds of service failure across each variable, while preserving an adequate number of children in each of the categories of the independent measures. This approach sacrifices some information but it greatly promotes interpretation. For example, cohesion scores were dichotomized by collapsing participants' responses in the separated and connected categories, and then comparing them to collapsed responses from the disengaged and enmeshed categories. This produced a measure of "dysfunction" on the cohesion scale. After testing different combinations of cohesion scores (disengagement plus enmeshment, disengagement only, and enmeshment only), disengagement only was found to discriminate maximally between success and failure cases, i.e., it produced the largest relative risk of service failure for any possible combination of the four cohesion categories. This measure is used in this report and other measures in the report were scaled in a similar fashion.

Data Analysis: Event History Analysis

Event history analysis (EHA), also known as survival analysis and time-to-failure analysis, was used to examine relationships between various client and service characteristics and treatment success/failure. EHA was developed to identify the correlates of specific events—deaths, crimes, bankruptcies, illnesses, hospitalizations, divorces, and so on—that occur over time. In this study, EHA is used to identify the correlates of out-of-home placement. Because data from cases with incomplete follow-up information must be dropped from most statistical analyses, traditional approaches such as ordinary least-squares (OLS) multiple regression produce severe bias and loss of information when event data are analyzed (Allison, 1984). EHA does not. It is thus a tool of great practicality in conducting IFPS research (for a more detailed report, see Fraser et al., 1992).

There are many different EHA models, and the one used in this study was developed by David Cox, a British statistician (Cox, 1972). Formally, it takes the form (Slonim-Nevo & Clark, 1989, p. 11):

$$h_i(t) = h_o(t) \exp(B_1 x_{1i} + \cdots + B_p x_{pi})$$

where i represents the ith child in the sample ($1 \leq i \leq n$); $h_i(t)$ is a hazard function of the ith child in the sample at time t; $x_{1i}, \ldots, x_{pi}$ are the explanatory variables of the ith child in the sample; $h_o(t)$ is the hazard function when all the explanatory variables equal zero; and $B_1, B_2, \ldots, B_p$ are regression coefficients for variables 1 to p (the last explanatory variable).

Called the Cox regression or proportional hazards model, this approach is based on estimating the correlates of the odds—actually, the natural logarithm of the odds—for an event. Across time, the log-odds for the occurrence of an event may be aggregated into a "hazard" function. The hazard function represents the time to failure for each child because it is based on the odds of placement for each child for each day of participation in the study. It is used computationally as an outcome measure for treatment, and variables that explain or alter the hazard can be identified using Cox regression procedures.

Interpreting EHA Coefficients. The Cox model is often described as semiparametric because it employs a partial likelihood estimation procedure that makes use of the order in which events (placements) occur and the timing of events. It produces asymptotically unbiased and normally distributed regression coefficients for explanatory variables (Allison, 1984; Blossfeld, Hamerle, & Mayer, 1989). These coefficients may be interpreted in the same way that OLS coefficients are interpreted. That is, if the coefficient of a variable such as *age* were to be positive, then one could argue that as age increases, the risk of service failure increases. Because many of the explanatory variables in this study were dichotomized, a special interpretation is possible. The exponentiated value of the coefficient is equivalent to the relative risk or change in the log-odds of placement for a unit change in an explanatory variable. Thus, if *age* were to be dichotomized at 12 years and the exponentiated value of the coefficient were to be 2.0, one could say that children between 13 and 17 years of age are twice as likely to be placed as children 12 or less years of age. To estimate the relative risk as a percentage, the value 1.0 is subtracted from the exponentiated coefficient and the remainder is multiplied by 100. In this case, one could say that the risk of placement is 100% greater, or twice as great, for adolescents.

Inclusion of Censored Data. The most important advantage of EHA is that it incorporates time to placement in the analysis and permits the use of all data regardless of the length of follow-up. The characteristics for every child that participated in the study are included in computations. However, from the point in time that a child is no longer tracked (due to the termination of the study or to placement), she or he is considered "censored" and is automatically eliminated from computations. But up to that point in time, all information about censored children (and their families) is included in the data analysis and computation of the hazard rate. At the point of censoring, the child is classified as placed or missing (depending on the case outcome) and eliminated from computation. The EHA technique makes maximum use of the data and is analogous to aggregate logit analyses of success and failure for each day of a study (during which, of course, the sample size varies due to censoring). For more information on EHA, see Allison (1984) and Blossfeld et al. (1989).

Order of Entry. For the multivariate EHA analyses, the order of entry was structured. First, a large group of referral and intake characteristics plus mean goal achievement and service characteristics were allowed to enter equations using a $p \leq .05$ two-tailed criterion. All social and demographic variables that were found to be significantly related to the time-to-placement measure at the bivariate level were included in the pool of variables eligible for inclusion. Then, to explain additional variability in the hazard rate for placement, exit variables were allowed to enter. For all exit variables that entered the equations, the corresponding intake variable—if it was not already in the model—was forced into the equation. Only with such a control for intake characteristics was an exit variable allowed to remain in an equation. The order of entry was therefore designed to produce a list of intake and exit characteristics, including mean goal achievement, that might serve as predictors of time to placement.

Missing Information. The sample sizes vary across analyses because of missing information. No variable was used if information from more than 30% of the cases was missing. Across all major variables, less than 10% of the data by variable were missing. Means were substituted for missing values only when mean-substitution was found to be unbiased. By computing a dummy variable that was scored as 1 for all cases on a particular variable that had had the mean substituted for a missing value and by entering that dummy variable into the equation, it was possible to assess the influence of mean-substitution. When the coefficient for the dummy variable was found to be significant, mean-substitution was declared to be biased and the raw variable without the replacement of means for missing values was used. This reduced the sample size and, depending on the variables in equations, produced equations with slightly different sample sizes.

Sensitivity Analyses. To confirm the findings presented in this chapter, a second set of EHA analyses with data from the follow-up samples was undertaken. Use of the follow-up samples reduced sample sizes substantially, but it permitted the testing for censoring bias. Bias could be introduced because the first- and the second-year cohorts (of families) may have differed systematically. To test for this, analyses using only the first-year families (for whom complete follow-up information was available and therefore for whom in aggregate there was no censoring due to the termination of the study) were completed.

As there were fewer degrees of freedom, the sensitivity test models were somewhat smaller (i.e., they contained fewer explanatory variables) than the models based on the full sample of 581 children. But on balance, the sensitivity analyses corroborated the major findings based on the full data set. Therefore, the full models are presented in this chapter.

Limitations of the Study

Causal Attribution. The data are rich and descriptive, but the design does not permit causal attribution. In this kind of study, there are many possible confounds—regression to the mean, testing, maturation, etc. It is not clear that the bivariate and multivariate correlates of placement are causal in nature. Indeed, it is likely that some of the correlates mask causal relationships between placement and unmeasured variables. Similarly, some of the correlates may be spurious, due to associations with other variables that are correlated with both placement and other explanatory variables.

Reactivity and Limitations in Caretaker Recall. Although interviewers were carefully trained and confidentiality was guaranteed, it is possible that child caretakers and workers responded in socially desirable ways to sensitive questions regarding child placement. While worker and parent reports tended to corroborate each other, school authorities and other collateral persons were not interviewed to provide independent confirmation.

Conservative Measure of Treatment Success. Success was declared only when a child remained in her/his family or the family of a relative—an extended family member. Conversely, failure was declared when a child was placed or left home to live with a nonrelative for two weeks or longer. As discussed in Chapter 9, in comparison to previous studies this measure of success may have elevated failure or placement rates by the inclusion in the failure category of children who ran away from home and children who went to live with neighbors or friends. It is our sense, however, that family members and many practitioners consider these to be negative outcomes, and therefore placement was defined so as to include them.

In addition, although multiple-outcome measures were used to assess the effects of IFPS on family and child functioning, the dependent measure did not examine the stability of a child's living situation. Both the quality and stability of placement are important service outcomes, as discussed by Fanshel and others (Fanshel et al., 1989b). Readers are cautioned that the definition of placement and treatment success used by various research projects may make placement rates observed in different studies incommensurable.

Relatedly, the length of placement is not considered. Placements of two-weeks duration or more were counted as service failures. A few children returned to their families three to six weeks after removal. Thus, the placement outcomes reported here do not differentiate between short-term and long-term placements; and by including shorter term placements, placement rates are higher than may have been observed in earlier studies.

Finally, the social desirability of placements was not assessed. Consequently, it was not possible to distinguish between those placements that should have been prevented, and those that may have been in the best interest of the child and her/his family.

The Demographic Correlates of Placement

Overview

We conducted a variety of bivariate and multivariate analyses to identify the correlates of placement, or treatment success and failure. In this section, the bivariate relationship between child-family characteristics and treatment outcomes is described. Data for the total sample and for the two states are presented. We begin by examining the basic cross-tabular data for selected demographic categories by the dichotomous measure, placed versus not placed.

Are Ethnic Minority Children at Higher Risk of Placement?

Children of color are overrepresented in foster, group, and some other forms of out-of-home care. Recent data suggest that black children are three times more likely to be in foster care than white children (Children's Defense Fund, 1985, as cited in Morisey, 1990). Of the 122,315 children entering substitute care in 1985, 23% were black, 11% were Hispanic, 3% were Native American/Alaskan, and 1% were Asian/Pacific Islander (Maximus, 1985, p. II-13). In Washington State, minority children are also over represented in substitute care but exact figures are not available.

Child welfare advocates and researchers are justifiably concerned about the effectiveness of IFPS services for ethnic minority families given the higher risks that these families face in the United States, the large number of ethnic minority children entering substitute care, evidence of worker/agency racial bias, and lower rates of effectiveness of traditional child welfare services for minority families.[1]

As reported in Chapter 5, children from a variety of ethnic minority groups participated in the FIT project. They included:

- black 13 (2.2%)
- Filipino 5 (.9%)
- Hispanic origin 23 (4%)
- Native American 10 (1.7%)
- other ethnic minority 52 (9%)
- white, not Hispanic origin 476 (81.9%)
- missing data 2 (.3%)

The different ethnic groups were separated into the two categories ethnic minority and white, not Hispanic for this analysis because of the low cell sizes in the various subsamples. A number of cross-tabular comparisons were performed using both the family and target child (or potential removal—PR) data. In the *family* data, placement rates in Washington were lower for ethnic minority families than for white (and not Hispanic) families. The placement rate for ethnic minority families was 18.2% (10/55) versus 29.8% (75/252) for the white, non-Hispanic families (Yates corrected $\chi^2 = 2.473$, df = 1, $p < .12$; uncorrected Pearson $\chi^2 = 3.024$, df = 1, $p < .082$). In the Washington follow-up sample, ethnic minority families had a lower placement rate (29.0%; 9/31) than white, non-Hispanic families (37.0%; 57/154), but the difference was not statistically significant.

The ethnic minority families served by the Homebuilders program in Washington therefore experienced fewer home placements with the provision of IFPS, compared to white families. This pattern was found also when the child-based or PR placement data were examined. For the total sample of Washington children, a lower proportion of the ethnic minority children (14.1%; 11/78) as compared to white non-Hispanic children (24.6%; 81/329) experienced a placement (Yates corrected $\chi^2 = 3.408$, df = 1, $p < .07$; uncorrected Pearson $\chi^2 = 4.987$, df = 1, $p < .05$). When the 12-month, child-based, follow-up data for Washington were analyzed, a similar pattern was found, where the placement rate for children of color was 22.7% versus 31.7% for white, non-Hispanic children. The difference, however, was not significant.

In Utah, there were no significant differences in the total sample of 172 children at risk, but a *higher* proportion of ethnic minority children tended to experience placement (70.0%; 7/10), when compared to white, not Hispanic children (37.9%; 33/87), in the follow-up sample (Fisher exact p- value for a two-tailed test = .087). As with all of these cross-tabular analyses, caution must be exercised in interpreting the findings because the patterns are not consistent across all of the state subsamples, and the cell sizes are small. In addition, because of small sample sizes, the various ethnic minority groups were not analyzed separately in the bivariate and multivariate comparisons. However, in what must be considered exploratory analyses, we conducted a cross-tabular analysis for each of the separate minority groups in Washington, and we found that each group had a lower placement rate than the white, non-Hispanic group. Thus, the FIT data suggest that the Homebuilders model produced significantly better outcomes for all ethnic minorities. But the findings must be considered preliminary.

It is likely that IFPS may be more effective for some ethnic groups than others—depending upon the program model, staff training, therapist characteristics, community environment, and other factors. And it is also important to note that even within most ethnic minority groups, families may differ considerably in their level of acculturation and other characteristics. Making broad generalizations about treatment outcomes for ethnic minorities is difficult and ill-advised (Boyd-Franklin, 1989; Gibbs, Huang, & Associates, 1989).

Nevertheless, the Washington placement findings are curious. We hypothesize that the higher rates of placement prevention among minority families in the Washington programs is partially a result of the philosophy and structure of the service. The Homebuilders program provides a combination of concrete and clinical services in clients' homes. Moreover, services are intensive and brief. At least among black families, the Homebuilders approach may be more culturally acceptable than traditional child welfare and mental health services. In fact, Sue (1977) has shown that a greater proportion of ethnic minority clients receive unequal and poor mental health services compared to white, non-Hispanic clients. According to Solomon (1985) black families are more likely to seek help from someone else who has practical experience in problem-solving and can act as an advocate for them while empowering the family. In providing services to minority families, professional training and graduate degrees may not be as important as being a parent, having real experience in dealing with children, and being willing to give immediate practical assistance.

In fact, it may be that many ethnic minority families may need the concrete service assistance more than the clinical services, which may account for the differential success of home-based IFPS programs that deliver both types of service (V. Hodges, personal communication, March, 1990). The provision of concrete and clinical services within the context of a family's home is comparable to the type of help that is offered by friends and other sources of informal support. The intensity of Homebuilders, with roughly a one-month intervention and an average of 37 hours of face-to-face and telephone contact creates a context for interaction that is similar also to the help one might expect to receive from a friend.

The finding that ethnic minority families served by Homebuilders are as likely, or possibly more likely, to have a successful treatment outcome as white, non-Hispanic families is unusual in the field. While it warrants further exploration and study, it suggests that IFPS based on the Homebuilders model may be a potential solution to the problem of overrepresentation among minority children in foster care. With the exception of a few programs, insufficient effort has been made to develop and test FBS to prevent minority placements. The recent initiation of IFPS programs specializing in serving ethnic minority clients in California, Michigan, New York, Florida, Illinois, and elsewhere is encouraging, but few evaluation data are available from these relatively new programs.

Other program applications might be considered as well. For example, IFPS may be an effective approach to reuniting families after a minority child has been in placement and the goal has become reunification. Conversely, a recent pilot project using the Homebuilders model with special-needs adoptive children on the verge of dissolution indicates that IFPS can avoid these dissolutions in 86% of the cases, using a three-month follow-up period (Haapala et al., 1988b). Since many special-needs adoptions involve minority children, this service may be a useful strategy in providing ethnic minority children with permanent homes. It may be worth the investment of public child welfare agencies further to develop and test IFPS as strategies to reduce unnecessary minority placements and provide more permanent homes for minority children when placements do occur.

Are Older Children at Higher Risk of Placement?

With the exception of the recent influx of infants and children of cocaine-addicted mothers into foster care, the age of children in foster care has risen in the last ten years. The FIT data reflect this trend in that the average age of the children at risk was 11.4 in the PR sample, with 256 children (44.1%) aged 12 and under, compared to 325 (55.9%) aged 13 and older.

A variety of family-based and PR-based analyses were conducted to examine the relationship between child age and placement. The children were separated into two groups: children aged 12 and under versus children 13–17 years old. The placement rates for older children were higher than for younger children. For the total sample of 581 children, the placement rate for older children was 32.3% versus 16.4% for the younger children (Pearson $\chi^2 = 19.159$, df = 1, $p < .001$).

However, this pattern was driven by the Washington sites. The adolescents in the Washington subsample had higher placement rates (Pearson χ^2 = 15.642, df = 1, $p < .01$). The placement rate for children aged 13–17 was 31%, while for children less than 13, it was 14.6%. The findings in the combined data appear to be due to outcomes in Washington, for there were no significant age differences for the Utah subsample. The Utah therapists appear to have been as successful with older children as they were with younger children.

Are Boys or Girls at Higher Risk of Placement?

In failing to examine the influence of gender, researchers in the social sciences have been justifiably accused of exhibiting a form of methodological blindness. Gender blindness characterizes much of the research on casework processes and treatment effectiveness in terms of sample selection, data analysis, choice of measures, and scrutiny of the research findings (Gottlieb & Bombyk, 1987; Gottlieb, 1987).

While the FIT study did not examine directly the effect of gender on case decision-making, we were able to examine placement by gender. In the sample, 268 children (46.1%) were female, and the remaining 313 were male (53.9%). A gender by placement analysis was undertaken to explore the differential effect of treatment on girls and boys.

For the total sample, there were no significant differences in placement rates (27.2% for females, 23.6% for males). Individual state breakdowns yielded no significant differences as well. The difference in the placement rates for the children in the 12-month follow-up group was greater, but was not statistically significant (37.0% for females, 29.4% for males). Subsample analyses similarly yielded no significant findings. It appears that females and males fared about equally well in IFPS treatment, at least in terms of general placement outcomes.

Organizational Characteristics of Sites with High and Low Failure Rates

Using the worker survey data and other information, a number of site comparisons were made. Considering the number of IFPS sites ($N = 6$) and the number of statistical tests conducted, relatively few site differences were found. This indicates that the workers in the various program sites were similar in their ratings of services, use of clinical techniques, and other aspects of service. But the site differences found must be viewed with caution because, at some sites, they are based on low cell sizes ($N = 15$ therapists or less).

Therapist Education. The site in this study with the lowest failure rate had therapists who held, without exception, a masters degree in social work

(MSW), whereas the site with the highest failure rate had no MSW therapists. At this latter site, one therapist held a graduate degree in one of the
social sciences, and the remainder held only undergraduate degrees. These
data must be viewed with caution as the design of the study did not permit a
direct test of the causal relationship between therapist education and treatment outcome. However, these findings are curious in that they do not
replicate the data collected by Jones (1985) nor support the views of those
program administrators who argue that workers without masters-level training produce outcomes similar to those of advanced-degree-trained
therapists.

Concrete Services. The data also provide tentative support for the hypothesis that concrete services will be associated with treatment outcomes.
At the site with the highest proportion of failure cases, therapists rated
concrete services as significantly less important. In addition, workers from
the sites that had the highest proportion of treatment successes rated concrete services as significantly more important. Additional data supporting
the use of concrete services are presented later in this chapter and in Chapter 11.

Other Service Characteristics. The site in the study with the highest
failure rate had the lowest average number of total client contact hours,
lowest worker ratings of the importance of concrete services, the lowest
worker ratings of the importance of making services available 24 hours a day,
and the lowest worker morale (see Kohlert & Pecora, 1989, pp. 174–176).
These results are complicated by the fact that this same site was found to
have had families that, by all accounts, had more serious ratings of child and
family dysfunction. So this site may have had families with children who
were relatively more difficult to engage and more deeply involved in drugs
and delinquency.

Because of the design of the study, it is not possible to rule out the
explanation that the referral of more difficult cases may have caused a shift in
the service model used by therapists, or that therapists' attitudes at the start
of the program differed and this difference accounted for the varying rates of
success across the six sites. However, a second site with comparable clients
had the *highest* success rate of any site, so factors such as therapist education, agency and supervisor support of the IFPS model, and high program
morale may indeed be associated with treatment success.

Risk Factors for Placement: A Time-to-Placement Analysis

Using EHA, a number of child, parent, and home characteristics were
found to be associated with treatment outcomes. Based on EHA coefficients

(which express both the strength and direction of relationships between explanatory variables and the length of time to placement), the relative risk of service failure was computed for each factor. These risks and the bivariate coefficients from which they are derived are summarized in Tables 10.1 through 10.4.

Risk Factors at Referral

For the total or combined study sample of 581 children, a variety of demographic and referral characteristics was associated with placement. Referral characteristics are those family-related factors that were immediately known by intake workers or by IFPS therapists at their first meetings with families. They included the demographic characteristics of families, prior service histories, and the explicit reason(s) for referral to IFPS.

CPS Referral. As indicated in Table 10.1, PRs from families referred from CPS were found to be less likely to experience placement. Compared to children in families referred from other sources such as juvenile court, CPS children had a risk of service failure that was 32.5% lower. This implies that IFPS treatment may be more effective with CPS referrals, but there are many complicating factors. One must ask: What is it about CPS referrals that appears to make them more successful in treatment? In part, it may be easier to work with CPS referrals because of the "fit" between unique aspects of the IFPS treatment model and families' social and demographic characteristics. Referrals involving physical abuse, for example, may have had more successful outcomes because (1) in-home interventions allow therapists to capitalize on family crises as they arise (i.e., to make use of "teachable moments" that occur as a result of crisis); (2) the Homebuilders model emphasizes teaching parents new skills for child discipline, communication, and positive nurturing (elements of service known to be important for successful treatment of physical abuse); and (3) the in-home locus of service and ongoing coaching of parents facilitates both the generalization and maintenance of new parenting skills across time and settings. It is possible also that motivation from CPS clients is generally high because parents are afraid that their children may be taken from them. In contrast, the parents of older children (non-CPS) often appear to have requested placement at service intake, and they therefore may be less committed to keeping children at home.

The other type of CPS case commonly referred to the IFPS programs involves physical neglect. IFPS treatment appears to be well-suited to addressing the concrete service needs of neglect families. Treatment often includes focusing on acquiring housing, public assistance, and food stamps, as well as beginning to help parents understand their caretaking role and

Table 10.1. Risk Factors at Intake for Service Failure: Bivariate EHAs of the Demographic and Referral Characteristics of Children at Risk of Placement in Utah and Washington

	Coefficient[a]	Risk of service failure (%)
Utah and Washington combined (N = 581)		
Socioeconomic and demographic conditions		
CPS referral	−.393**	−32.5
Number of children in home	−.119*	−11.2
Aged 13–17	.780****	+118.2
Child is in home at referral	−.616****	−46.0
Child is at home at intake	−.607***	−45.6
Primary caretaker's age	.033***	+3.4
Male primary caretaker	.532**	+70.2
At least one family member is employed	.503***	+65.4
Child's service history		
Prior outpatient mental health services	.511***	+66.7
Prior inpatient mental health services	.427**	+53.3
Child characteristics		
Drug/alcohol involvement	.830****	+129.3
Truant from school 50% or more	.725****	+106.5
Utah only (N = 172)		
Socioeconomic and demographic conditions		
Low-income family (under $10,000 annually)	−.600*	−45.1
Male primary caretaker	.711**	+103.5
Child characteristics		
Drug/alcohol involvement	.613**	+84.6
Truant from school 50% or more	.856***	+135.5
Washington only (N = 409)		
Socioeconomic and demographic conditions		
Race/ethnicity (white, not Hispanic)	.622*	+86.3
CPS referral	−.775****	−43.9
Number of children in home	−.207**	−18.7
Aged 13–17	.816****	+126.2
Child is in home at referral	−.647***	−47.7
Child is at home at intake	−.768***	−53.6
Primary caretaker's age	.034**	+3.5
At least one family member is employed	.512**	+66.9
Child's service history		
At least one prior out-of-home placement	.473**	+60.5
Length of prior placement (months)	.041*	+4.2
Prior outpatient mental health services	.614**	+84.7
Child characteristics		
Drug/alcohol involvement	.861****	+136.6
Truant from school 50% or more	.605***	+83.1

[a] EHA coefficients are analogous to unstandardized coefficients in multiple regression.
*$p < .10$.   **$p < .05$.   ***$p < .01$.   ****$p < .001$.

fulfill it with greater competence. For many neglect families, IFPS may be but a major first step down a long road to improving family functioning.

Child Age.   As implied earlier in this chapter, children over the age of 12 were more than twice as likely to be placed during or after service. Reflecting the difficulty of working with adolescents and their families, the risk of service failure was 118.2% higher for children 13 years of age or more at referral. Child age may act as a proxy variable for problem behaviors—truancy, delinquency, and substance abuse—prevalent among older children. Like CPS referrals, one might ask: What is it about older children and their families that places them at greater risk of treatment failure? Because older children are likely to have more extensive service and problem histories, the effects of age may mask chronic problems that have not been treated successfully in the past. Consequently, age-related findings should be interpreted in the context of other risk factors.

Child Service History and Presenting Problems.   Children who were out of the home at referral or intake had approximately a 46% greater risk of service failure. This may be due to the weakening of parent-child attachment that occurs in many families once a child is placed. Parents may be less motivated to make efforts to keep their families together—to make behavioral changes—when the child has been removed from the home. Children who had mental health service histories had a risk of placement some 53% greater than children with no prior mental health service history. And suggesting that service failure rates may be higher for families with oppositional children, the risks of service failure were twofold higher for children who were truant (+106.5%) and who were suspected (or shown) to be involved with alcohol and drugs (+129.3%).

Caretaker Characteristics.   Curiously, families with male caretakers and families in which at least one caretaker was employed outside the home had a greater risk of placement. Children whose fathers were identified as the primary caregiver had a 70.2% greater risk of placement, but this finding must be viewed with caution because of the relatively small number of male primary caretakers (see the multivariate EHA section). Suggesting that work obligations complicate IFPS, children who came from homes where at least one parent was employed outside the home had a 65.4% greater risk of placement. These parents may simply be unable to monitor the activities of their children because work prevents close parent supervision. And the age of parents was positively correlated with the hazard rate. A one-year increase over the mean in the age of primary caretakers increased the risk of placement by 3.4%.

Comparison of Utah and Washington.   In the Utah subsample, poverty—defined as an annual family income of less than $10,000—was negatively associated with time to placement. This implies that poor families did some-what *better* in IFPS treatment. Their risk of service failure was approx-imately 45% lower than that of families with incomes greater than $10,000. In addition, families with a male primary caretaker were more than twice as likely (+103.5%) to experience service failure as families with females heads of household. As in the combined sample, children with drug/alcohol in-volvement (+84.6%) and poor school attendance (+135.5%) had a signifi-cantly higher risk of placement.

A wide variety of risk factors was identified for the Washington subsample, including child age over 12 years (+126.2%), primary caretaker's age (+3.5%), number of prior placements of children (+60.5%), and child loca-tion in the home at referral (−47.7%) or at intake (−53.6%). Placement rates were significantly greater for the family reconciliation cases compared to the cases referred by CPS. Drug and alcohol involvement (+136.6%) plus truan-cy (+83.1%) and prior mental health involvement (+84.7%) exerted a signif-icant influence on the risk of service failure. The data appear to suggest that noncompliant older children with substantial prior service involvement were more likely to experience placement.

Child, Parent, and Home Risk Factors at the
Start and Close of Treatment

As shown in Table 10.2, five characteristics of family members at intake were predictive of service outcomes, and 14 characteristics of families at termination were predictive of service outcomes. The findings suggest that parents who request out-of-home placement, who are openly hostile toward their children, and who have poor verbal discipline skills are more likely to fail in service. The findings suggest also that children who are truant and delinquent are more likely to be placed during or after IFPS.

By the close of service, this pattern is even more clear. If by the termina-tion of treatment, IFPS therapists rate parents' child management skills (including parental capacity to function, consistency of guidance, use of physical punishment, skill in verbal discipline, and parent-child attachment) as low, the risk of service failure is from two to four times higher. If parents failed to make gains in discipline skills during treatment, children were much more likely to be placed, reflecting a major program goal of ensuring child safety. If a parent continued to request out-of-home placement during service, the odds of placement and service failure were extraordinary, in-creasing the risk of placement by 739.1%.

By service termination, child-related factors also coalesce into a pattern. Truant, oppositional, and delinquent children, along with children who were mentally ill, appear to have had significantly higher risks of placement. Families that were disengaged and rigid had a slightly higher risk of service failure. This probably reflects a lack of effective parental monitoring and guidance.

Comparison of Utah and Washington.   These patterns are replicated in the analyses of the Utah and Washington subsamples. As shown in Tables 10.3 and 10.4, a few intake characteristics of parents and their children were associated with service outcomes, but many termination characteristics were predictive of outcomes. In Utah, four characteristics at intake were associated with placement, and nine characteristics at termination were associated with placement. In Washington, six intake and 14 exit correlates were identified.

While the findings across the two states were similar and corroborative, the Utah findings were-distinguished from the aggregate and Washington findings by an intriguing relationship between family/home characteristics and service outcomes. In Utah, children from families with inadequate residences (such that household functions like cooking and bathing are impaired) were more likely to be placed when corrective action had not been taken by IFPS termination. This raises an important question: What prevented IFPS therapists from taking corrective action? Perhaps the family situations were impossibly chaotic? Perhaps the home repair resources available to the therapists in Utah were inadequate? Or, as indicated in site comparisons, some Utah therapists may have placed less emphasis on concrete services. They may have failed to focus their efforts on critical household conditions and the absence of such a focus may have resulted in unacceptable physical risks to children. Whatever the reason, a similar finding did not emerge in Washington.

Service-Related Correlates of Time to Placement

In theory, the components of IFPS should be directly related to service outcomes. What therapists do should directly affect what children and parents do. We should observe this as a strong correlation between service activities and service outcomes. But as shown in Table 10.5 and as reported by Lewis (1990), few elements of service were directly and significantly related to time to placement. (A larger set of services, however, were associated with treatment goal achievement. See Chapter 11 of this book.)

Concrete Services.   The overall time spent providing concrete services that emphasize "doing" for clients significantly reduced the risk of failure in IFPS. Furthermore, greater amounts of all concrete service time were associated with the reduction of IFPS failure. Yet, in terms of specific types of concrete services, the greater use of only one of the 25 specific concrete-service activities, provide toys or recreation equipment, significantly reduced the chance of out-of-home placement. Three other activities approached a significant risk reduction ($p < .10$). The lack of individual concrete services emerging as specific correlates of placement prevention is likely due to the great diversity in their use, which resulted in small sample sizes in most service categories, but a large amount of concrete service time overall.

Table 10.2. Risk Factors at Intake and Termination for Service Failure: Bivariate EHAs of Child and Parent Characteristics in Utah and Washington (N = 581)

	At intake		At termination	
	Coefficient[a]	Risk of service failure (%)	Coefficient[a]	Risk of service failure (%)
Family/home characteristics				
Inadequate family residence; physical, structural, or sanitation problems pose threat to children; home is of questionable habitability	.176	+19.3	.520**	+68.2
Continuing financial problems	−.100	−9.5	−.327*	−27.9
Parent characteristics				
Parent's functioning impaired by mental illness; capacity to fulfill child caring role is limited	.229	+25.8	.662***	+93.9
Parent is inconsistent in or lacks child guidance and parenting skills; parent lacks capacity to control children	.260	+29.8	.867***	+137.9
Physical punishment is preferred; inappropriate or excessive use of punishment may have injured a child	−.051	−5.0	1.668****	+430.4
Verbal discipline of child is often negative, hostile, and unpredictable (i.e., one type of psychological maltreatment is present)	.584***	+79.3	.786****	+119.4
Parent is not motivated to solve problems; is indifferent, apathetic, or actually rejects parental role; may be hostile toward child care responsibilities	.105	+11.0	1.061****	+188.8

198

Parent prefers or requested out-of-home placement (but is willing to delay)	.987****	+168.3	2.127****	+739.1
Parent has fair to good understanding of child's physical needs but poor understanding in emotional, cognitive, and social areas	.146	+15.8	.465**	+59.2
Parent is not affectionate or approving; may openly reject child; child may demonstrate emotional trauma due, in part, to poor parent-child attachment	.751****	+112.0	.918****	+150.3
Child characteristics				
Moderate to serious mental disturbance or incapacitated due to mental illness	.208	+23.1	.629***	+87.5
Child attends school irregularly, performs poorly, and displays frequent oppositional behavior and misconduct	.499***	+64.7	.798****	+122.1
Delinquent behavior, including status offenses, truancy, property crime, and/or crimes against persons	.885****	+142.2	.927**	+145.3
Noncompliant behavior in the home; may include behavior that is dangerous to self and others	.664	+94.3	1.191****	+228.9
Child minimally involved or rejects any involvement with agency	.143	+15.4	.648***	+91.2
Family adaptability and cohesion				
Low cohesion; family is disengaged	.388*	+47.3	.198	+21.9
Family is rigid	−.503**	−39.5	.152	+16.4

[a] EHA coefficients are analogous to unstandardized coefficients in multiple regression.
$*p < .10.$ $**p < .05.$ $***p < .01.$ $****p < .001.$

Table 10.3. Risk Factors at Intake and Termination for Service Failure: Bivariate EHAs of Child and Parent Characteristics in Utah Only (N = 172)

	At intake		At termination	
	Coefficient[a]	Risk of service failure (%)	Coefficient[a]	Risk of service failure (%)
Family/home characteristics				
Family residence was inadequate for the performance of household functions (e.g., preparing meals, bathing)	.484	+62.3	.973***	+164.6
Parent characteristics				
Parents are isolated; no close friends or relatives can be counted on for help	.619**	+85.7	−.532	−41.3
Parent is inconsistent in or lacks child guidance and parenting skills; parent lacks capacity to control children	−.103	−9.8	.764***	+114.8
Parent is not motivated to solve problems; is indifferent, apathetic, or actually rejects parental role; may be hostile toward child care responsibilities	−.252	−22.3	1.012***	+175.0
Parent prefers or requested out-of-home placement (but is willing to delay)	.602**	+82.7	1.081****	+194.7
Parent is neither fully nor actively involved in case planning, services, and/or treatment	.168	+18.3	.609**	+83.8

Child characteristics			
Child demonstrates symptoms (nightmares, loss of appetite, difficulty concentrating) of stress; may evidence more serious mental health symptoms (e.g., avoidance, excessive aggression, refusal to attend school, mood swings, and talk of suicide)	.113	+11.9	.748**	+111.3
Child attends school irregularly, performs poorly, displays frequent oppositional behavior and serious misconduct	.654*	+92.3	1.152****	+216.6
Parent is not affectionate or approving; may openly reject child; child may demonstrate emotional trauma due, in part, to poor parent-child attachment	.530*	+70.0	.872***	+139.2
Delinquent behavior, including truancy, status offenses, property crimes, and/or crimes against persons	1.064**	+189.8	1.308*****	+270.0
Child does not cooperate with agency	.431	+53.9	.580*	+78.5
Family cohesion and adaptability			
Secondary caretakers are disengaged	.574 (n = 81)	+77.6	.797* (n = 56)	−55.0
Families are rigid	−.698	−50.3	.701*	+101.7
Secondary caretakers have extreme adaptability: chaotic or rigid	−.938** (n = 81)	−60.8	−.672 (n = 56)	−48.9

a EHA coefficients are analogous to unstandardized coefficients in multiple regression.
*p < .10.   **p < .05.   ***p < .01.   ****p < .001.

201

Table 10.4. Risk Factors at Intake and Termination for Service Failure: Bivariate EHAs of Child and Parent Characteristics in Washington Only ($N = 409$)

	At intake		At termination	
	Coefficient[a]	Risk of service failure (%)	Coefficient[a]	Risk of service failure (%)
Family/home characteristics				
Continuing financial problems	-.148	-13.7	-.390*	-32.3
Parent characteristics				
Parent's functioning impaired by mental illness; capacity to fulfill child-caring role is limited	.462*	+58.7	.678**	+96.9
Physical health problems (one or more physical diseases or disabilities)	-.448*	-36.1	-.414*	-33.9
Parent is inconsistent in or lacks child guidance and direction skills; parent lacks capacity to control children	.130	+13.9	.828***	+118.8
Physical punishment is preferred; inappropriate or excessive use of physical punishment may have injured a child	-.407*	-33.4	-.524**	+40.8
Verbal discipline of child is often negative, hostile, unpredictable (i.e., one type of psychological maltreatment is present)	.721**	+105.7	.997****	+171.1
Parent is not motivated to solve problems; is indifferent, apathetic, or actually rejects parental role;	.188	+120.7	1.121****	+206.7

202

may be hostile toward child care responsibilities				
Parent prefers or requested out-of-home placement (but is willing to delay)	1.020****	+177.4	2.657****	+1325.1
Parent has fair to good understanding of child's physical needs, but poor understanding of child's emotional, cognitive, and social needs	.127	+13.5	.439*	+55.2
Parent is not affectionate or approving; may openly reject child; child may demonstrate emotional trauma due, in part, to poor parent-child attachment	.815****	+125.9	.913***	+49.2
Child characteristics				
Child demonstrates moderate to serious symptoms of mental illness (e.g., avoidance, excessive aggression, refusal to attend school, mood swings, and talk of suicide)	.234	+26.4	.589**	+80.2
Unmet physical needs; clothing, nutrition, and hygiene may be marginal	−.469*	−37.4	−.640**	−47.2
Child attends school irregularly, performs poorly, and displays frequent oppositional behavior and serious misconduct	.300 (n = 279)	+35.0	.519** (n = 285)	+68.1
Delinquent behavior, including truancy, status offenses, crimes	.786****	+119.4	.670****	+95.4

(continued)

Table 10.4. (Continued)

	At intake		At termination	
	Coefficient[a]	Risk of service failure (%)	Coefficient[a]	Risk of service failure (%)
against property, and/or crimes against persons				
Noncompliant behavior in the home; may include behavior dangerous to self and others	.592	+80.7	.893****	+144.3
Child rejects any involvement with agency	−.122 (n = 295)	−11.4	1.230*** (n = 308)	+242.2
Current or recent sexual abuse or exploitation	−.891** (n = 312)	−59.0	−.336 (n = 334)	−28.4
Family cohesion and adaptability Family is disengaged	.134	+14.3	.698***	+101.1
Social support Extended family/nonkin coaching relation; about twice a week or more	.490** (n = 406)	+63.3	.135 (n = 371)	+14.5

[a] EHA coefficients are analogous to standardized coefficients in multiple regression.

*p < .10.   **p < .05.   ***p < .01.   ****p < .001.

In the other direction, increased time spent in the concrete service activity, "help obtain legal aid," was significantly associated with increased risk of placement. Clearly, the provision of legal aid in and of itself is not a cause of placement. Rather it probably suggests that divorce, financial difficulties, delinquency, and other problems that require legal help increase the risk of service failure.

Clinical Services. Only one aggregate clinical measure and four of the 75 specific clinical service interventions were predictive of service success. The aggregate measure was time/money management. Specific clinical activities were listening to client, encouraging, providing literature, and money management. Seven clinical variables, including the summated measure, solve problems/reduce conflict, and the two-variable index, crisis intervention, were associated with increases in the risk of service failure. The use of these interventions appears to signal the presence of family crises or external stressors conducive to service failure.

Of all measures of service time, only hours in telephone contact with IFPS families in the second week of service was associated with placement. It increased the risk of placement by 17.3%. Greater use of telephone contacts early in treatment appears to suggest that cases with a lack of ongoing engagement or with early deterioration are at a slightly greater risk of failure.

Goal Achievement. Other than aggregate concrete service measures, among all the types of service-related variables in the study, service goal attainment ratings were most consistently associated with time to placement. Ten of the 16 IFPS goals were significantly related to reducing the chance of service failure. Attainment of the goals, decrease depression, increase social support, increase use of community resources, decrease running away, increase parenting skills, and decrease depression significantly predicted service success. Goal achievement for establish trust, increase communication, improve parenting skills, increase school performance, and increase compliance with house rules also was significantly associated with decreased risk of placement. The composite measure, mean goal achievement, was significantly predictive of service success. Thus, while some isolated elements of service were predictive of outcomes, goal achievement appears to be broadly and highly correlated with service success.

Comparison of Utah and Washington. The Utah and Washington subsamples differed little. One aggregate concrete service measure approached significance for each state. Time/money management remained a predictor of success for both subsamples. When the states were examined individually, length of service became significant for both groups, suggesting the importance of providing the full term of service, however defined.

Table 10.5. Characteristics and Elements of Service Related to Time to Placement

	Cases	Coefficient[a]	Risk of failure (%)
Combined Utah and Washington			
Concrete services			
Provide food	579	-.312*	-26.8
Help get food	581	-.253*	-22.4
Provide child care	581	-.098*	-9.4
Help obtain legal aid	580	.224***	25.1
Do housework with client	581	-.118*	-10.5
Provide toys or recreation equipment	579	-1.133***	-67.8
All "doing" services[b]	581	-.050***	-4.9
All concrete services[b]	581	-.018***	-1.2
Clinical services			
Use of reinforcement	581	-.181*	-16.5
Anger management	581	.262***	29.9
Handle frustration	581	.176*	19.2
Impulse management	581	.185*	20.3
Use of crisis card	581	.191*	21.0
Give and accept feedback	581	.221**	24.8
Accepting no	581	.174*	19.0
Improve compliance	581	.172*	18.8
Listening to client	581	-.458****	-26.7
Encouraging	581	-.234**	-20.9
Family council	581	.238***	26.8
Defusing crises	581	.333****	39.5
De-escalating	581	.272***	31.2
Clarify family rules	581	.197*	21.8
Provide literature	581	-.332***	-28.3
Multiple-impact therapy	581	.457*	57.9

206

Meet with other providers	581	.177*	19.4
Attend/testify at court	581	.354***	42.4
Money management	581	-.812****	-56.6
Solve problems/reduce conflict[b]	581	.023**	2.4
Time/money management[b]	581	-.390****	-32.3
Crisis intervention[b]	581	.180****	19.8
Time and service response			
Hours face-to-face contact in first two weeks of service	568	-.025*	-2.3
Hours telephone contact in first two weeks of service	569	.076*	7.9
Hours face-to-face contact in second week of service	565	-.030*	-3.0
Hours telephone contact in second week of service	564	.160**	17.3
Goal attainment			
Establish trust	260	-.295**	-25.5
Increase communication	304	-.436****	-35.3
Increase parenting skills	461	-.428****	-35.9
Increase anger management	337	-.352****	-29.7
Increase school performance	188	-.205**	-18.5
Decrease depression	106	-.738****	-52.2
Increase compliance with house rules	289	-.237**	-21.1
Decrease running away	60	-.601****	-45.1
Increase social support	74	-.659****	-48.3
Increase use of community resources	98	-.610***	-45.7
Mean goal achievement[b]	575	-.550****	-42.3
Utah only			
Concrete services			
Provide transportation	172	-.119*	-11.2
Provide toys or recreation equipment	172	-2.040****	-87.0
Arrange recreation activities	172	-.884*	-58.7
All concrete services[b]	172	-.031*	-4.1

(continued)

Table 10.5. (Continued)

	Cases	Coefficient[a]	Risk of failure (%)
Clinical services			
Use of reinforcement	172	-.627**	-46.6
Natural/logical consequences	172	-.562*	-43.0
Anxiety management	172	-.975*	-62.3
Build self-esteem	172	-1.241***	-71.1
Rational-emotive therapy techniques	172	-.691*	-49.9
Listening to client	172	-.944****	-61.1
Build structure/routine	172	-.717*	-51.2
Provide literature	172	-1.402**	-75.4
Refer to social service	172	-1.078***	-66.0
Consultation with other services	172	-.734***	-52.0
Teach use of leisure	172	-1.138***	-68.0
Time/money management[b]	172	-.394**	-32.6
Time and service response			
Days from receipt of case to termination	165	-.047****	-5.6
Goal attainment			
Establish trust	66	-.261*	-23.0
Increase communication	60	-.739***	-52.2
Increase parenting skills	114	-.468****	-37.4
Increase anger management	88	-.466**	-37.3
Increase school performance	64	-.440***	-35.6
Decrease depression	17	-1.613**	-80.1
Decrease running away	19	-.654***	-48.0
Decrease delinquent behavior	19	-1.256***	-71.5
Mean goal achievement[b]	167	-.405***	-33.3

Washington only

Concrete services

Provide food	407	−.796*	−54.9
Help obtain legal aid	409	.249****	28.3
Help obtain utility benefits	409	−.777*	−54.0
Provide a job	409	.353**	42.4
Provide toys or recreation equipment	407	−.763*	−53.4
Arrange life skill classes	407	.212*	23.6
All "doing" services[b]	407	−.053*	−5.2

Clinical services

Time out	409	−.573*	−43.6
Active listening skills	409	−.730***	−51.2
No-lose problem-solving	409	.434*	54.4
Anger management	409	.404*	49.7
Handle frustration	409	.557**	74.6
Give and accept feedback	409	.549*	73.0
Appropriate sexual behavior	409	.947***	157.8
Improve compliance	409	.530***	69.8
De-escalating	409	.568***	76.4
Clarify family rules	409	.413*	51.1
Behavioral rehearsal/role play	409	−.842***	−56.9
Attend/testify at court	409	1.073****	192.3
Teach use of leisure	409	.788***	119.9
Solve problems/reduce conflict[b]	409	.040***	4.0
Manage depression/stress[b]	409	.046***	4.8
Time/money management[b]	409	−.472*	−37.7
Crisis intervention[b]	409	.186***	20.4
Alleviate sexual abuse/dysfunction[b]	409	.239*	27.0

(continued)

209

Table 10.5. (Continued)

	Cases	Coefficient[a]	Risk of failure (%)
Time and service response			
Hours telephone contact in first two weeks of service	408	.152**	16.4
Hours telephone contact in second week of service	408	.299****	34.8
Days from receipt of case to termination	408	−.058****	−5.7
Average hours direct service per quarter in last three quarters	408	.067**	6.9
Goal attainment			
Establish trust	194	−.272*	−23.8
Increase communication	244	−.430***	−35.0
Increase parenting skills	347	−.375****	−31.3
Increase anger management	249	−.304**	−26.2
Decrease depression	89	−.601**	−45.2
Increase compliance with house rules	229	−.252*	−22.3
Decrease running away	41	−.560*****	−42.9
Increase social support	62	−.731***	−51.8
Increase use of community resources	90	−.582****	−44.1
Mean goal achievement[b]	408	−.659*****	−48.3

[a] EHA coefficients are analogous to unstandardized coefficients in multiple regression.
[b] Summated scale or index.
*p < .10.   **p < .05.   ***p < .01.   ****p < .001.

Goal attainment variables remained the measures most highly predictive of success. Mean goal achievement was significantly correlated with outcomes in both states. For Utah, seven specific goals were related to reduction of placement risk. For Washington sites, service success was predicted by eight of the goals.

Multivariate Risk Factors: Models of Time to Placement

Now we take a slightly different approach to describing factors associated with treatment failure. This section will build on the bivariate findings from Tables 10.1–10.5 to develop models or lists of variables that contribute uniquely to the hazard rate for placement. Many of the variables discussed in the previous sections are correlated with one another. And although clear patterns emerged, the aggregate bivariate findings are useful but not sufficient for developing a parsimonious list of relatively independent risk factors. To create such a list, we used an EHA procedure that allowed us to identify a set of variables or a model that summarizes the bivariate findings.

Multivariate models are dependent on the strength of bivariate correlations and the degree to which a variable that is already in a model is correlated with a variable that is eligible for inclusion in a model. On balance, variables with high relative risks that are independent of other variables are first to enter models. For example, while the risks are high for children who are truant from school, delinquent in the community, and noncompliant in the home, all three of these risk factors probably measure a similar underlying construct, oppositional behavior. Although not always true, it is likely that a child who is truant from school is oppositional in the home and noncompliant in the community. Because they are correlated, it would take an unusually strong relationship with placement for, say, delinquency (child's behavior in the community) to enter a model if truancy were already included in the model. Given similar variables, one usually will enter a model and the others will not. In creating multivariate models, parsimony is gained but richness is lost. Thus while multivariate models can be thought of as extremely economic ways of expressing many, many individual findings, readers should also refer to the bivariate analyses.

Combined Utah and Washington Multivariate Model

A large number of alternative multivariate models were generated to (1) identify a set of variables that economically reflected the bivariate demographic, service, and family functioning correlates of outcome, (2) control for intake characteristics for those exit measures related to outcome, and (3) minimize the number of missing cases. Models were selected on the basis of goodness of fit (chi-square), the sample sizes (as large as possible), and construct validity (applicability to treatment and public policy).

The eight factors shown in Table 10.6 were significantly correlated with the risk of placement across the combined Utah and Washington samples (N = 551). Controlling for other variables in the model—holding other variables constant—modest mean goal achievement during treatment was highly correlated with service success/failure. Children from families where goal achievement of at least 25% was reported had a risk of placement almost 64% lower than children from families where little or no progress was made.[2] This is fresh support for the argument that the clinical nature of the IFPS service model—as well, perhaps, as its unique service characteristics such as 24-hour-a-day availability—is responsible for behavioral changes that in turn reduce the risk of placement.

With goal achievement held constant, a number of child-related factors appear to have contributed to treatment success/failure. Children who were in their homes, as opposed to in a placement, at the time of referral were less (−40.4%) likely to be placed during and subsequent to family treatment. Children in homes where the parents had requested placement had a risk of service failure that was 71.6% higher than children from homes where parents were more committed to family preservation. Holding other factors such as living situation at IFPS referral constant, the risk of treatment failure appears to be higher for children who had been placed out of the home at least once (+48.9%). And suggesting that delinquent and noncompliant children may constitute a higher risk group within the population of children referred to IFPS, the risk of service failure was 78.3% higher for children who at intake were suspected or known to have drug and alcohol involvement.

IFPS appear to be more complicated to deliver when at least one parent is employed outside the home. There is recent evidence that this problem may not be unique to IFPS. In fact, scheduling problems appear to complicate the provision of many human services, especially office-based services that operate on an 8:00-to-5:00 schedule (see, e.g., Lazar, Sagi, & Fraser, 1991). In addition to scheduling, other complications due to parental employment—such as work-related stress and the lack of time to supervise and discipline children consistently—may affect treatment outcomes. In spite of the apparently flexible schedule and pragmatic orientation of family preservation services, the risk of service failure was significantly higher (+62.9%) for children whose parent(s) reported outside work obligations. Frankly, we are puzzled by the strength of this finding because of the benefits usually associated with increased family income through parent employment. Readers should view this finding with caution until additional confirmatory research is conducted.

Table 10.6. Risk Factors at Intake and Termination for Service Failure: Multivariate EHAs of Demographic, Child, Parent, and Service Characteristics

	Coefficient[a]	Risk of failure (%)
Combined Utah and Washington (N = 551)[b]		
Mean service goal achievement (25% or more)	−1.015****	−63.8
Child was in home at referral	−.518**	−40.4
Child has at least one prior placement	.398**	+48.9
Caretaker (at least one) is employed outside of home	.488**	+62.9
Enabling concrete services (teaching, going with, modeling, etc.) were provided to help the family procure a resource on its own	−.398**	−32.8
Child was drug or alcohol involved at referral	.578****	+78.3
Parent preferred out-of-home placement; may have requested immediate placement, but was willing to delay at intake	.540***	+71.6
Physical, structural, or sanitation problems existed in the home and affected its habitability at exit	1.122***	−207.1
Utah only (N = 160)[c]		
Mean service goal achievement	−.476***	−37.8
Family residence was inadequate for the performance of household functions (e.g., preparing meals, bathing) at intake	.703**	+101.9
Primary caretaker was male	.745**	+110.5
Parent preferred out-of-home placement; may have requested immediate placement, but was willing to delay at intake	.597*	+81.6
Child was truant from school 50% or more at intake	.776***	+117.3
Enabling concrete services (teaching, going with, modeling, etc.) were provided to help the family procure a resource on its own	−.569*	−43.4
Washington only (N = 380)[d]		
Mean service goal achievement (25% or more)	−1.574****	−79.3
Child is between 13 and 17 years of age	.571**	+77.0
Ethnic minority	−.787**	−54.5
Child was in the home at intake	−.769**	−53.6
Child has at least one prior placement	.514**	+67.2
Parent preferred out-of-home placement; may have requested immediate placement; but was willing to delay at intake	1.091****	+197.7
Parent's functioning impaired by mental illness; capacity to fulfill child-caring role is limited	.704**	+102.2

(continued)

Table 10.6.   (Continued)

	Coefficient[a]	Risk of failure (%)
Child's physical needs were marginally or inadequately met by parent(s)	−737**	−52.2
Child is drug or alcohol involved at referral	.491**	+63.4

[a] EHA coefficients are analogous to unstandardized coefficients in multiple regression.
[b] This model contained a control for home habitability at intake. All variables met the assumption of proportionality. The model has the following statistical characteristics: log likelihood = −804.4465, global χ^2 = 77.91, df = 9, p < .000. A second model using goal achievement as an interval scale—that is, in its raw form—was estimated and, although proportionality was violated for goal achievement, the resulting model was similar to but slightly larger than the model above. This second model had 552 valid cases and included mean goal achievement (−.472****), child was in the home at referral (−.496, −39.1%), child is between 13 and 17 years of age (.481**, +61.7%), child has at least one prior placement (.455**, +57.7%), caretaker is employed outside home (.470**, +60.0%), parental lack of affection for and rejection of the child (.531***, +70.0), provision of enabling concrete services (−.365**, −30.6%), child's home-related behavior was noncompliant and disobedient at exit (.644***, +90.5%), and home habitability at exit (.848**, +133.6%). Controls for child's home-related behavior at intake and home habitability at intake were forced into the model. This model had the following statistical characteristics: log likelihood = −801.6737, global χ^2 = 103.78, df = 11, p < .001).
[c] All variables in this model and the one presented below satisfied proportionality. Mean goal achievement was used as an interval-level variable and satisfied proportionality. This model contained a control for child behavior in the community (unconventional and unacceptable, including truancy or delinquency). Due to missing values, 12 cases were deleted. The model has the following statistical characteristics: log likelihood = −222.6475; global χ^2 = 36.99, df = 7, p < .001. A more parsimonious model without a control also had 12 missing cases. It had three significant and three trend-level explanatory variables (coefficient, risk): mean service goal achievement (−.533***, −41.3%), truancy at intake (.863***, +137.1%), parent preferred placement at intake (.639**, +89.5%), home suitability (residence inadequate) at intake (.690*, +99.5%), male primary caretaker (.687*, +98.7%), and enabling concrete services were provided (−.577*, −43.8%). This second model had the following statistical characteristics: log likelihood = −223.5816, global χ^2 = 35.64, df = 6, p < .001.
[d] All variables in this model met proportionality. The model has the following statistical characteristics: log likelihood = −441.5472, global χ^2 = 91.54, df = 10, p < .000. "Enabling" concrete services was entered in this model, but it failed to reach significance (t = −1.388). A second model using goal achievement as an interval variable was estimated. While the goal achievement variable failed a test of proportionality, the model was remarkably similar to the one reported above. This model had 390 valid cases and included mean goal achievement (−.685****), child age (.546*, +72.6%), ethnic minority (−.654**, −48.0%), child is home at intake (−.877**, −58.4%), prior placement (.498**, +64.5%), parent preference for out-of-home placement (1.060****, +188.7%), parental mental illness (.530*, +69.9%), and enabling concrete service (−.476*, −37.9%). This model had the following statistical characteristics: log likelihood = −464.9345, global χ^2 = 78.23, df = 8, p < .001.
*p < .10.   **p < .05.   ***p < .01.   ****p < .001.

Service success also was correlated significantly with the use of concrete services. Controlling for the behavior of children and their parents plus goal achievement, families that received an enabling concrete service had a 32.8% lower risk of placement. Concrete services appear to be a critical ingredient in providing effective treatment. The model summarized in Table 10.6 suggests that the delivery of treatment by therapists who attend to the social, psychological, *and* environmental needs of families is more likely to succeed. More successful therapists appear to have trained family members to seek and obtain tangible help from community agencies. They provided enabling concrete services.

Holding the service, demographic, and social characteristics of service participants constant, one service exit factor emerged as a predictor of placement. If a child's home at termination had serious structural problems that affected its habitability, the risk of placement trebled (+207.1%). Thus even if families had relatively high goal achievement and a low risk profile otherwise, poor home environmental conditions at service exit were highly correlated with service outcomes. Home habitability may be a risk factor that therapists can use as an indicator that, as IFPS draw to a close, referral for on-going services are necessary to ensure the well-being of children and their families.

As indicated in note b in Table 10.6, a second model was estimated using goal achievement in its raw form, i.e., as an interval variable with a range from 1.0 to 5.0. This second model is not being emphasized because, according to a statistical test that has been recently criticized as misspecified, proportionality was not met for mean goal achievement in raw form. We present the findings because it is not clear, at this time, whether the test is valid. Moreover, the log-log plots of the survival estimates by levels of goal achievement did not look widely disproportional (for more information, see Fraser et al., 1992). If the test is not valid, then the findings may be substantively interesting to readers and valid from a statistical point view.

The second model contained nine variables. Of the nine findings, mean goal achievement, child location at referral, prior placement, caretaker employment, concrete services, and home habitability replicated the first model. Controlling for these factors, three new variables entered the model. Teenagers appear to have had a risk of service failure some 61.7% higher than younger children. Parental lack of affection for and emotional bonding to their children also appeared significantly to increase the risk of placement (+70.0%). Lastly, children who by the close of services were noncompliant and disobedient in the home, controlling for their behavior at intake, were nearly twice (+90.5) as likely to be placed. Like home habitability at exit, the home-related behavior of children at exit may serve as an indicator to practitioners of the need for referral at the close of IFPS for ongoing services.

Utah-Only Multivariate Model

Because the sample sizes are smaller, the subsample analyses produced smaller models. Four variables were significantly correlated with treatment outcome and two variables were correlated with outcome at the trend level ($.05 < p < .10$). In Utah, mean service goal achievement was significantly related to treatment outcomes. Holding other measures constant, home conditions (e.g., inadequate furniture, appliances, plumbing) that were judged by therapists as rendering difficult the performance of essential daily living tasks increased the risk of service failure by 101.9% Interpreted as an odds, families where home conditions interfered with the cooking of meals, with bathing, or with safe food storage were about twice as likely to fail in treatment.

Compared to female caretakers, male primary caretakers were more than twice as likely ($+110.5\%$) to have children placed subsequent to the start of treatment. Further analysis showed that the simple failure rate for the 21 male primary caretakers in Utah was 52.4% (11/21), while for the 151 female caretakers, it was 29.1% (44/151). Although significant ($\chi^2 = 4.578$, df = 1, $p < .05$), caution is warranted in interpreting this finding, for the sample size of male caretakers was quite small. It is possible that the failure rate for fathers was influenced by a small number of idiosyncratic home situations.

Holding these factors constant, truancy increased the risk of service failure more than twofold ($+117.3\%$). Consistent with the bivariate findings, this suggests that the risk of service failure was higher overall for oppositional children. Because the Utah program served families that tended to have older, more noncompliant children, one might be tempted to generalize to the broader population of IFPS programs that work with truant and drug-involved children. However, as discussed in Chapter 5, the sample in Utah contained a small group of extremely oppositional, court-referred children who may not be representative of children referred to other IFPS programs.

Finally, two trends emerged. There was a tendency for enabling concrete services to decrease the risk (-43.4%) of service failure and for positive parental attitudes toward placement to increase the risk ($+81.6\%$) of service failure. As in the combined model, the provision of concrete services appears to be an integral component of IFPS and their success. Concrete services appear to contribute to treatment outcomes even when household characteristics such as habitability are controlled. This suggests that the function of concrete services may be broader than environmental improvement. They may exert an independent effect on the rapport that develops between family members and the therapist during the treatment process. If so, concrete services indirectly promote a more positive therapeutic relationship and, in a stage-setting sense, create a home climate oriented toward more effective problem-solving and learning.

Separate from concrete services and the social characteristics of children and their parents, the attitudes that caretakers assumed toward placement were correlated with treatment outcomes. As discussed earlier, this is an intriguing finding, for it appears to reflect the degree to which parents approached the learning opportunities presented by IFPS therapists. Discouraged and hopeless parents who viewed placement as their family's best alternative appear to have been less likely to participate fully in the treatment process and, consequently, to benefit from treatment.

In interpreting the findings, each variable in the multivariate models may be thought of as exerting a relatively independent but multiplicative effect on the hazard rate. The total effect can be estimated by exponentiating EHA coefficients and multiplying values of relevant variables (see Blossfeld et al., 1989, pp. 151–152). And so one might say, for example, that a Utah child who was truant [exp.(776) = 2.17], who had a male primary caretaker [exp.(745) = 2.11], and who lived in an inadequate residence [exp.(703) = 2.02] was approximately 9 times (2.10 × 2.17 × 2.02 = 9.21) more likely to be placed than a child who was attending school, had a female primary caretaker, and lived in an adequate residence. Given such knowledge, one might legitimately ask, If some families are at higher risk of placement, what can we do to improve services to them? After we review the Washington-only findings in the next section, we will examine the elements of service that are correlated with goal achievement in Chapter 11. Because goal achievement appears to be a stable predictor of treatment outcomes, services that promote achievement are likely to reduce the risk of placement and may constitute a frame of reference for making these improvements.

Washington-Only Multivariate Model

In Washington, nine variables were associated with service outcomes. Modest mean goal achievement and parental attitudes toward placement were highly correlated with placement. As in earlier analyses, mean goal achievement appears to have acted as a buffer against other risk factors. It reduced the risk of placement by 79.3%. In contrast, parental attitudes favorable toward placement trebled (+197.7%) the risk of service failure. Teens were more likely to be placed (+77.0%) as were children who had at least one prior placement (+67.2%). Children who were suspected or known to have drug and alcohol involvement at intake were some 63.4% more likely to be placed. And children from homes where a parent's caretaking capacity was impaired by mental illness were at greater risk (+102.2%).

Controlling for other factors, ethnic minority children who received Homebuilders services had a significantly lower risk (−54.5%) of service failure when compared to white, non-Hispanic children. Two other child characteristics were associated with a reduced risk of service failure. Children who were in their homes at intake were less likely (−53.6%) to be placed and, curiously, children whose needs were marginally or inadequately meet by parents were less likely (−52.2%) to be placed. That is, children with *less* adequate physical resources at intake were somewhat *less* likely to be placed when compared to children whose needs were adequately met. This finding probably represents the broader pattern that less positive outcomes were observed for cases where physical needs were met, but emotional maltreatment, severe corporal punishment, and parent-child conflict were the source of referral.

But it may also be related to findings regarding concrete services. In this model, the physical needs variable appears to have replaced the enabling concrete services variable (see Table 10.6, footnote d). The provision of concrete services to families that lack resources to meet the physical needs of their children is an age-old treatment strategy (see, e.g., Kadushin, 1974). Thus, what appears at first to be an odd finding may represent the importance of concrete services for referrals involving neglect. The negative direction of the "needs" coefficient also suggests that services to meet physical needs fulfill a supplementary, rather than primary, function in IFPS. Modest physical needs—such as worn and patched clothing, poor preventive health care habits, and physical illness (that is likely to heal on its own)—may not be a sufficient reason for provision of ongoing service or referral at the close of service.

In a second model using goal achievement as an interval variable (see Table 10.6, footnote d), eight variables—two just barely above the $p < .05$ level of statistical significance ($p < .053$) and at a trend level—were correlated with outcome. In addition to *goal achievement, enabling concrete services* were correlated with outcomes. Provision of enabling concrete services reduced the risk of placement by 37.9%. As suggested above, the child physical needs variable did not enter in the presence of concrete services. Controlling for the demographic and social characteristics of families, goal achievement and concrete services appear to have promoted placement prevention.

In contrast, a number of factors increased the risk of placement. Older children were more likely (+72.6%) to be placed. Children with at least one prior out-of-home placement were more likely (+64.5%) to be placed. Children in the home at intake were less likely (−58.4%) to be placed, and conversely, children out of the home who were being reunified with their parents were more likely to be placed. Consistent with other findings, parent characteristics such as mental illness (+69.9%) and positive attitudes toward placement (+188.7%) exerted strong effects on the outcome of treatment. Finally, as in the model with a dichotomized goal achievement variable, ethnic minority children were markedly less likely to experience placement.

Study Hypotheses

A number of hypotheses developed by the project and discussed in Chapter 3 were tested in these analyses. The findings related to each hypothesis are summarized below.

1. Prior placement in foster, group, or institutional care will be positively associated with treatment failure. This hypothesis was supported by a number of findings. Prior placement was a risk factor identified in the bivariate and multivariate EHA analyses; prior inpatient mental health services was predictive of placement at intake in the aggregate sample; and for the Washington subsample, prior out-of-home placement was associated with placement (see Table 10.1). In the aggregate and Washington samples, placement out of the home at referral and intake was also associated with treatment failure. The location of children at the start of services was both a bivariate (see Table 10.1) and a multivariate correlate (see Table 10.6) of outcome.

2. Greater attainment of specific treatment goals during IFPS will be positively associated with treatment success. Treatment goal attainment was strongly related to a reduction of placement risk in bivariate and multivariate analyses (see Tables 10.5 and 10.6).

3. Greater provision of concrete services will be associated with treatment success. This hypothesis was supported. A small number of concrete services was associated directly with a reduction in placement risk (see Table 10.5) for the aggregate sample and both states individually. Two summated measures composed of all "doing" concrete services as well as all enabling concrete services were associated with a reduction in the risk of placement for the aggregate sample in the bivariate analysis (see Table 10.5). Enabling concrete services were associated with a reduction in the risk of placement in the aggregate, and individual state multivariate EHA analyses (see Table 10.6).

4. Lack of social support will be positively associated with treatment failure. On balance, this hypothesis was not supported. However, in the Utah subsample, parents who were socially isolated at the beginning of IFPS treatment had a higher risk of failure (see Table 10.3). Curiously, this same relationship was not found at service termination, possibly indicating that the actions of IFPS therapists offset social isolation.

5. The amount of time elapsing between referral and IFPS therapist response will be positively correlated with treatment failure. This hypothesis was not supported, but the lack of support may be due to a methodological limitation. The small amount of variation across service response times reduced the possibility of detecting significant differences. Even when a cross-tabular analysis of the cases with unusually slow by fast response times was conducted, no differences emerged.

Discussion

Many parent, child, and treatment characteristics were associated with service outcomes but one of the more intriguing correlates of placement was mean goal achievement. It was consistently predictive of treatment success and failure. Children in families that were modestly to fully successful in completing treatment goals were significantly more likely to remain at home with their parents. They had a risk of treatment failure some 63.8% lower than families that failed to achieve treatment goals.

The findings imply also that IFPS are less effective with families where children are drug involved and have extensive service histories. The aggregated risk of placement for a child with at least one prior placement and drug involvement was +165.4% ([exp(.398) × exp(.578) −1] × 100). In addition to child-related factors, however, parent-related factors were predictive of outcomes. Parents who had requested out-of-home placement and whose homes had physical problems that rendered them of marginal habitability were far more likely to be unresponsive to treatment. These factors alone increased the risk of placement fivefold [exp(.540) × exp(1.122)]. The data also suggest that employment outside the home has an impact on the ability of parents to benefit from IFPS. While one could hardly advocate parent unemployment, when the effect of employment is factored into the other parent-related risks, the risk of placement jumps to 758.5% ([exp(.540) × exp(1.122) × exp(.488) − 1] × 100). Families with a high risk profile on all child- and parent-related variables were some 22.8 times more likely to fail in treatment. Expressed as a percentage, their risk was 2178.3% higher than families that had a low risk profile.[3]

The Effect of Goal Achievement on Risk Factors

Some factors—goal achievement and enabling concrete services—reduced the risk of placement, and in so doing, they weakened the effect of the risk factors. Assuming only modest goal achievement, goal attainment and concrete services reduced the risk of treatment failure by 75.7% ([exp(−1.015) × exp(−.398) − 1] × 100). But in combination with other factors, their impact is multiplicative. Assuming, for example, that an adolescent with one prior placement was in the home at referral, that her/his parents had the highest possible risk profile, that the child was drug involved at intake, *and* further that the family completed only about half of its treatment goals while receiving enabling concrete services, the risk of service failure would decline from 2178.3 to only 230.4%.[4] Thus, in the presence of extraordinary and unlikely risk, the two service-related negative coefficients function as important "risk reduction" factors that can substantially affect treatment outcomes for the highest risk families. The findings demonstrate the relative importance of working intensively with family members to meet treatment goals, while providing concrete services.

State by state, service differences may have accounted for the different EHA models. Therapists in both states received satisfactory or better ratings on virtually all aspects of service delivery. But compared to Washington, the Utah IFPS therapists were rated by Utah primary caretakers as significantly less available, less helpful in providing explanations of the treatment process, and less able to be relied on when the client had a problem (we will discuss this more in Chapter 12). That Utah children with male primary caretakers were about twice as likely to be placed may be related to the relatively less flexible and responsive service that was delivered in one or both of the Utah sites. And this may be due, in part, to the higher caseloads in that state. The relatively more flexible and responsive service that was delivered in Washington may have promoted success among fathers who were primary caretakers.

Program differences, too, may have played a role in explaining the startling finding that, compared to non-Hispanic white children, ethnic minority children had significantly lower service failure rates in Washington. A minority child with the highest risk profile in Washington and modest goal achievement had a risk of service failure of 1225.0%, in contrast to a comparable white, non-Hispanic child, who had an aggregate risk of 2810.8%.[5] In Utah a high-risk child was 16.8 times (+1,579.4%) more likely to go into placement than a low-risk child.

The effect of goal achievement on these risks is large. In Washington, a high-risk minority child whose family had made modest goal attainment would have a 174.6% risk of placement. A white, non-Hispanic child whose family made at least modest progress in treatment—as measured by goal achievement—would have a 503.2% risk of placement. And in Utah, a similar child with the highest possible risk profile but with average goal attainment would have a 302.7% risk. In sum, goal achievement appears to exert a remarkable buffering effect on the risk factors; and across the highest risk profiles, ethnic minority children in Washington were the least likely to be placed.

Need for Additional Research

To confirm these findings, the field needs both rigorous follow-up studies and, to address questions of comparative effectiveness, experimental studies across all the competing models of family-based child welfare services. These models include the Homebuilders IFPS model, which is (as far as we know) the shortest and most intensive intervention. It is contrasted by a variety of longer-term, multiple-worker, office- and home-based service models. The critical elements of the Homebuilders IFPS model—relationship building; an ecological focus on child, family, and community environment; explicit in-home training in child management; offering concrete services; treating clients as colleagues; and brief, intensive service—are not used in the same combinations in most other FBS models. Research studies using comparable clients, control conditions, success criteria, and follow-up periods are necessary both (1) to corroborate the correlates of success/failure found here, and (2) to determine if the IFPS models based on the Homebuilders model are any more or less effective than other family-based therapies.

One finding in particular bears careful examination and replication. As we have noted, ethnic minority children in Washington had higher success rates compared to white, non-Hispanic children. The simple failure rate, the bivariate hazard rate, and the multivariate hazard rate with controls for child and parent characteristics were lower for ethnic minorities. Suggesting that this finding is not a statistical artifact, additional analyses indicated that the proportionality assumption fundamental to the proportional hazards model was met for the ethnic minority variable (see Allison, 1984; Fraser et al., 1992). While we must consider the finding preliminary, it is provocative and as such warrants cautious interpretation. Perhaps the home focus and brevity of service help to make Homebuilders a more culturally sensitive service model. It may be that therapists who have received extensive training in in-home intervention and who view themselves as colleagues of clients are able to develop a stronger rapport with ethnic minority clients. Perhaps they are more culturally competent. Or perhaps the 24-hour availability, provision of concrete services, and training orientation of service are particularly effective with ethnic minorities. Conversely, the finding may be due to a one-time-only sampling bias and will not be replicable. Whatever the reason, it is clear that something rather unusual occurred and replication studies are merited.

Of What Use Are These Findings?

As mentioned in Chapter 9, from the perspective of staff members, better screening at intake is often identified as requisite to reduce failure rates, and the findings might be used to create intake or screening guidelines. However, at this point, we believe activity along these lines to be premature. It is too early to utilize findings from this and other studies to eliminate higher risk client populations from eligibility for IFPS. Many children of families with high-risk profiles were treated successfully, and risk factors appear to be largely negated by returning a child to her/his home (if s/he were out of the home prior to the start of service), by delivering enabling concrete services, and by achieving modest success in meeting treatment goals. Using these data as a point of departure, a clearer understanding of the critical elements of this program model is necessary, for programs may be modified to serve different or difficult clientele.

In this respect, a strong relationship between service participation and family preservation emerged in the data. Goal attainment across the 16 treatment goals appears to mediate distal service outcomes. In the context of mean goal achievement, the Washington Homebuilders model produced better outcomes in ethnic minority families and families with younger children who at referral were not known (or suspected) of drug involvement and whose parents were not impaired by mental illness. In Utah, truant children were at greater risk, suggesting that younger children also may have fared somewhat better in treatment. Across both states, parents who were relatively more willing to delay a placement decision in order to participate in IFPS had significantly better outcomes. As shown in Chapter 8, both the Utah and Washington families made significant gains during participation in IFPS; and as shown in Chapter 9, IFPS participants had significantly higher placement prevention rates when contrasted with a matched case overflow comparison group. In this chapter, families that were more responsive to treatment (in terms of goal achievement) were found to be less likely to experience placement. Even modest goal achievement appears to affect service outcomes. Among high-risk families then, the challenge may be to promote goal achievement, for goal achievement seems to buffer child- and parent-related risk factors for placement. To describe more fully the elements of service that produced goal achievement, we might now ask, What are the correlates of goal achievement?

Notes

1. For more information about the challenges and problems in serving ethnic minority families in child welfare, see Billingsley and Giovannoni (1972), Boyd-Franklin (1989), Chestang (1978), Gibbs et al., (1989), Green (1982), Morisey (1990), Solomon (1985), and Sue (1977).

2. Goal achievement was measured on a scale with five levels, but for these analyses it was dichotomized in order to satisfy the assumption of proportionality. Log-log plots of various levels of mean goal achievement by time and placement indicated that a 1.00–1.99 versus 2.00–5.00 dichotomy produced proportionality while other combinations did not. The risk of failure for a level change is given by

$$[\exp(\text{coeff})]^x - 1) \times 100$$

where exp indicates that the coefficient is being exponentiated, and x is the number of level changes.

3. A high risk profile was defined as a positive score on each of the child- and parent-related risk factors. Thus:

[exp(.398) × exp(.488) × exp(.578) × exp(.540) × exp(1.122) − 1] × 100 = 2178.3%

4. Estimated by

[exp(−1.015) × exp(−.518) × exp(.398) × exp(.488) × exp(−.398) × exp(.578) × exp(.540 × exp(1.122) − 1] × 100 = 230.4%

The risk for an equivalent child who was out of the home at referral would be estimated as

[exp(−1.015) × exp(.398) × exp(.488) × exp(−.398) × exp(.578) × exp(.540) × exp(1.122) − 1] × 100 = 454.6%

5. White, non-Hispanic child out of home at intake and with highest risk profile in Washington:

[exp(.571) × exp(.514) × exp(1.091) × exp(.704) × exp(.491) − 1] × 100 = 2810.8%

Minority child out of home at intake and with highest risk profile in Washington:

[exp(.571) × exp(−.787) × exp(.514) × exp(1.091) × exp(.704) × exp(.491) − 1] × 100 = 1225.0%

White, non-Hispanic child out of home at intake with modest goal achievement in Washington:

[exp(−1.574) × exp(.571) × exp(.514) × exp(1.091) × exp(.704) × exp(.491) − 1] × 100 = 503.2%

Minority child out of home at intake with modest goal achievement in Washington:

[exp(−1.574) × exp(.571) × exp(−.787) × exp(.514) × exp (1.091) × exp(.704) × exp(.491) − 1] × 100 = 174.6%

Chapter 11

What Elements of Service Relate to Treatment Goal Achievement?

ROBERT E. LEWIS

In the few studies of FBS and IFPS literature that have focused on correlates of treatment success, service goal achievement has surfaced as one of the more important predictors of success. Attainment of service goals was found to predict service success among FBS programs surveyed by Nelson et al. (1988). Willems and DeRubeis (1981) found that treatment group cases had higher child and parent goal achievement scores than control group families. The Hennepin County Community Services study (AuClaire & Schwartz, 1986) also provided some support for this conclusion in that successful families from the treatment group had higher goal attainment ratings at six months when compared to other groups.

As reported in Chapter 10, *mean goal achievement*—the average attainment score across all service goals—was a significant factor in the multivariate EHA models predicting reduction in the risk of out-of-home episodes for target children. *Mean goal achievement* was significantly correlated with success in the model for the entire sample of children-at-risk, as well as for the models for the Washington and Utah state subgroups, and it had a large moderating effect on other risk factors (see Chapter 10). When considered individually, goal attainment for 10 of the 16 IFPS goals significantly reduced the chance of service failure (see Chapter 10; and Lewis, 1990). In contrast, very few specific clinical or concrete services, including measures of time and case response, were directly associated with significant reductions in the risk of placement. As will be shown in this chapter, however, a wide range of these services were strongly associated with goal achievement itself. Thus, goal achievement appears to have played an important and discriminative role in mediating various IFPS components and the overall success or failure of treatment. Therefore, understanding which elements of service are associated with which specific kinds of goal achievement has a great deal of significance for understanding the efficacy of IFPS. Paraphrasing Videka-Sherman (1985), information is needed to answer the question of *which* interventions achieve *which* goals for *which* types of clients in *which* situations to produce *which* ultimate outcomes. This chapter addresses a portion of this need by estimating the correlation between particular interventions and the achievement of specific IFPS goals.

Method and Limitations

Subjects of this analysis were the 581 children identified at the time of referral of their families for IFPS as being in danger of imminent removal from home. Four instruments completed by the IFPS therapists at service completion served as the sources of data for this analysis. As discussed in Chapter 4, the instruments were the Goal Checklist, the Concrete Services Checklist, the Clinical Services Checklist, and the Case Termination Survey. Summated clinical scales described in Chapter 6 were given emphasis in the analysis.

The use of individual children at risk of placement as the unit of analysis for this chapter provides consistency with most of the rest of the analyses in this book. Since goals set and service provided were only identified in relation to entire families, some imprecision may result from this choice. Specific goals and services were linked to families and not to specific children. Families with multiple children constituted less than one-fourth of the total (101/453), suggesting at most a minor distortion from the child-based analysis. Multiple goals and services were also the norm (see Chapter 6). Because of the way in which the data were collected, it was not possible, in each case, to specify which service activities were specifically directed to which goals. Finally, although IFPS therapists worked with 16 goals, this analysis was limited to nine goals because of subsample size limitations. Analyses were performed where there were at least 100 cases.

Multiple approaches were used to estimate the relationship between specific interventions and achievement of the nine treatment goals. These approaches include the following:

1. Significant correlations with goal achievement. The interventive strategies that correlated significantly with the nine high usage goals were identified.

2. Services used most often (in over 50% of cases) where goal achievement = 3 or more. On the five-point scale of goal achievement a rating of 3 represented the first anchored point expressing predominant attainment. Within this goal achievement subsample, a core or cross-cutting set of services was defined. These core services were excluded from analysis for individual goals unless 5% or more above the mean percent usage. Core services were defined as those used in more than 50% of cases for at least seven of the nine high usage goals.

3. *Regression models.* Service-related regression equations were developed for each of the nine high use IFPS goals.

Results are shown for the total sample and for the Washington Homebuilders subset of children.[1]

Core Services Related to Goal Achievement

Usage of specific concrete and clinical interventions was examined for goals, that met two criteria: (1) average goal achievement must have been 3 or more (where 3 is 'half achieved' on the five point scale of goal achievement); (2) the activity must have been used in at least 50% of cases across at least seven of the nine goals. Shown in Table 11.1, among the specific interventions one concrete service, *provide transportation,* and 31 clinical services met both criteria. This set of services appears to represent an IFPS core of services used successfully by therapists no matter which goals had been established.

Within this core of interventions, mean usage of individual services ranged from 55 up to a high of 98%. The five service activities with the highest mean usage were associated with the summated scale *develop treatment relationship.* Eleven of the 31 core services were related to this dimension. This cluster of services included relationship building activities, problem clarification and treatment plan development, and crisis defusing. This suggests that "soft" clinical skills-the ability to form working bonds of attachment and problem focus-are central to the Homebuilders intervention strategy.

Seven core interventions were from the *improve parent effectiveness* dimension. Behavioral in orientation, these activities are largely concerned with family communication and parent skill training.

Six service activities from the dimension *modify problem behaviors* were also in the core set. These services involved the establishment of behavior-monitoring devices and structure in client families, and a teaching component to help parents learn how to choose and administer behavior management approaches in their home.

Other important specific interventions that were used for a major proportion of clients included *child development* (teaching age-appropriate behaviors), *build self-esteem,* and *consultation with other services.*

The greatest number of the core services were of the applied therapeutic variety, with roots in Rogerian theory. However, 13 (42%) of the core services had a skills-training or educational component. In conjunction with an emphasis on relationship building, the use of skill building approaches was central to goal achievement.

In spite of the general applicability of the core services across the majority of cases, workers used them with some selectivity, as shown by variation in

Table 11.1. Usage (%) of Core IFPS by Goal

			Service goal[b]									Mean
Service[a]	Scale[c]	Focus[d]	1 %	2 %	3 %	4 %	5 %	6 %	7 %	8 %	9 %	usage (%)
Concrete services												
Provide transportation			65	54	62	61	56	73	58	62	60	61
Clinical services												
Listening to client	TXREL	A	97	98	97	99	98	97	100	97	97	98
Encouraging	TXREL	A	93	96	93	85	94	94	99	93	91	93
Offer support/understanding	TXREL	A	88	91	86	90	92	91	94	93	86	90
Relationship building	TXREL	A	91	87	86	87	90	88	91	82	84	87
Setting treatment goals	TXREL	S	85	87	82	86	83	82	84	86	81	84
Use of reinforcement	COMMUN	S	87	82	90	84	85	76	81	70	88	83
Reframing	TXREL	A	75	84	74	84	76	83	89	85	77	81
Provide literature	COMMUN	A	74	80	75	80	77	84	79	80	74	78
Clarify problem behaviors	TXREL	A	69	80	73	82	80	75	81	86	76	78
Natural/logical consequences	COMMUN	S	71	80	80	83	80	65	74	70	82	76
Child development		S	68	73	74	73	74	74	66	72	71	72
RET concepts	COMMUN	S	61	84	67	82	65	71	79	70	72	72
Building hope	TXREL	A	74	68	69	72	74	69	72	55	71	69
Monitoring clients	BEMOD	A	74	62	68	67	73	70	62	61	73	68
"T" statements	COMMUN	S	63	84	66	78	67	60	67	65	65	68
Providing reinforcers	BEMOD	A	66	60	65	64	67	66	69	68	67	66
Build self-esteem	DEPMGT	AS	54	57	57	63	64	89	62	79	55	64
Anger management	PRBSLV	S	55	73	65	86	64	54	58	51	67	64
Clarify family rules	TXREL	A	61	70	61	69	64	60	52		72	64
Improve compliance	BEMOD	AS	56	61	63	71	67	52	61	52	76	62

Service[c]	[d]	1	2	3	4	5	6	7	8	9
RET techniques	COMMUN	AS		74	68	53	55	65	63	60	62
Consultation with other services	REFER	A	61	53	59	63	62	57	80	56	61
Active listening skill	COMMUN	S	54	76	70	59	53	52		58	60
Build structure/routine	BEMOD	A	57	60	55	70	61	54	59	58	59
Defusing crises	TXREL	A	56	62	63	64	57	60	58	58	59
Make treatment plans	TXREL	A	66	54	61	60	56	56	51	60	59
Tracking behaviors	BEMOD	S		53	57	65	57	56	56	61	58
Track/chart behaviors	BEMOD	A		57	58	63	57	54	55	61	57
Handle frustration	PRBSLV	S	51	57	64	59	53	57		53	56
Clarify family roles	PRBSLV	AA	51	51	58	61	53		55	53	56
Process of change	PRBSLV	S	55		58	59	52	59		53	55

[a] For children in cases with specific goal achievement levels of 3 or above, with usage 50% or above. Core services are those with usage at 50% or above for at least seven of the nine predominant goals.

[b] Goals included where number of subjects is greater than 100. Goal definitions are
1 establish trust and functional working relationships with client
2 increase communication skills
3 increase parenting skills
4 increase anger management/conflict resolution skills
5 improve school performance and/or attendance
6 increase self-esteem
7 decrease anxiety, worry, or fear
8 decrease depression and/or suicide thoughts or behaviors
9 increase compliance with house rules

[c] Summate scale (see Chapter 6)
TXREL: develop treatment relationship
COMMUN: improve parent effectiveness
BEMOD: modify problem behaviors
PRBSLV: solve problems/reduce conflict
DEPMGT: manage depression/stress
REFER: make referrals/advocacy

[d] Clinical service intervention focus (see Chapter 6) A, applied therapeutic; S, skill training; AS, applied therapeutic and skill training.

the percentage utilization across the presence of various goals. For example, for the service *build self-esteem*, an activity that includes teaching clients to use positive self-talk, the reinforcement of client strengths, and involving persons in esteem-building activities, a fairly wide range of service utilization was found. Where the goals *improve self-esteem* and *decrease depression* were established, utilization was 89 and 79% respectively. On the other hand, utilization was less than 60% for the five other goals. Therefore, even for services with high rates of usage across cases, some variation according to treatment direction was observed.

Specific Services Associated with Specific Goal Achievement

In the following section, service measures are identified by their association with the achievement of specific treatment goals. Both specific interventions and summated service scales are considered. Services significantly correlated with specific goal achievement are shown. Also included in the analysis are interventions used over 50% of the time, when goals were reported as being at least "half achieved." The core set of individual services was removed from consideration unless the rate of usage was at least 5% above the mean usage for the specific service. Finally, service-related regression models for each goal are noted. Like the EHA models, these regression models are parsimonious, but less rich and descriptive, ways to summarize the predictors of goal success.

Goal 1: Establish trust and functional working relationships with clients (e.g., family members see the value of working with the therapist; client hostility toward counseling is reduced; clients agree to try to do something)

The aggregate concrete service measures were present for a substantial percentage of children (and their families) with the goal *establish trust* (see Table 11.2). Also, one specific concrete service, *give financial assistance*, was significantly correlated with achievement of this goal.

The majority of the summated clinical treatment scales and indices (8 of 11) were significantly correlated with establishing trust. The highest correlation ($r = .404$) was with the scale *improve parent effectiveness*. This cluster of clinical activities emphasizes improving family communication, responsibility, and functioning by teaching parents (and possibly other family members) active listening skills, the use of "I" statements, assertiveness, and territoriality concepts. The scale *develop treatment relationship* reached the significance level along with other scales involved with the application of techniques to specific problems, e.g., modifying problem behaviors, solving problems, and managing depression or stress. Specific indices applying rational-emotive therapy techniques and teaching assertiveness and time/money management also had correlations with the goal that proved statistically significant.

Among the individual clinical activities, a relatively even balance appeared between applied therapeutic techniques-largely directed toward support of clients and relationship building-and teaching parent skills and self-management to family members. High-use core services included were *monitoring clients, building hope, make treatment plans,* and teaching the *use of reinforcement.*

The overall regression equation for establishing trust in the IFPS therapist-client relationship consisted of five measures. As noted in Table 11.2, these items included two summated scales, two specific clinical variables, and one measure of service time. The equation accounted for about 40% of the variance in the attainment of the establishing trust and working relationship goal.

The most dominant positive correlate of establishing a trusting working relationship was the summated scale *improve parent effectiveness.* The other positive correlate of establishing trust was a composite measure, *give financial services,* which underscored the importance of tangible help, including monetary concerns, in achieving a trusting, working relationship. This variable included the education-oriented intervention *teach money management,* and two concrete service activities: *give financial assistance,* and *help client get a job.* The inclusion in the equation of a set of variables relating in various ways to improving family finances suggests that help that resulted in a better financial base for the family served as a powerful reinforcer of the image of therapists as concerned and competent helpers who could be entrusted to assist family members with their problems. It is also possible that financial difficulties may be at the base of much of the other problems being experienced by families, and the easing of families' financial concerns freed them from those burdens sufficiently to allow the formation of trustful relationships with the IFPS therapists or for added parental focus on resolving other difficulties.

In summary, these findings seem to indicate that a wide variety of Rogerian, behavioral, and concrete interventions are used to develop client trust and a good working treatment relationship. Techniques usually employed to develop therapeutic relationships, such as empathetic listening and supportive responses, were ubiquitous and their greater use was associated with goal achievement. However, the relative significance for establishing trust by teaching specific communication and interpersonal skills and intervening to help improve a client's financial situation seems to have added implications. These trust-building activities focus on improving client situations and capabilities as opposed to being aimed at building relationships per se. Therefore, relationship enhancement appears to be at least as much a function of applying various helping strategies as of the use of affect-oriented

Table 11.2. Service Relationships with Goal: Establish Trust[a]

	Total sample			Homebuilders Washington only		
	Service used for goal achievement of 3 or more (N = 183)		Significant correlation with goal achievement (N = 260)	Service used for goal achievement of 3 or more (N = 136)		Significant correlation with goal achievement (N = 194)
Service measures[b]	No.	(%)		No.	(%)	
Concrete services						
All doing services	101	55.2		70	51.5	
All enabling services	95	51.9		69	50.7	
All concrete services	146	79.8		107	78.7	
Give financial assistance	30	16.4	.135*			
Help secure child care	20	10.9				.216**
Clinical services—Summated scales/indices						
Solve problems/reduce conflict	182	99.5	.247**	135	99.3	.216**
Develop treatment relationship	182	99.5	.283***	135	99.3	.220**
Modify problem behaviors	179	97.8	.266***	132	97.1	.296***
Improve parent effectiveness	178	97.3	.404***	134	98.5	.400**
Manage depression/stress	160	87.4	.125*	119	87.5	
Make referrals/advocacy	146	79.8		105	77.2	.274**
Rational-emotive therapy	113	61.7	.280**	86	63.2	
Crisis intervention	107	58.5		80	58.8	0.205**
Teach assertiveness	57	31.1	.223**	36	26.5	0.268**
Time/money management	53	29.0	.227**	38	27.9	
Clinical services—Applied therapeutic						
Listening to client	178	97.3	.161**	133	97.8	.163*
Encouraging	171	93.4	.244***	132	97.1	.195**
Relationship building	166	90.7	.184***	131	96.3	
Offer support/understanding	161	88.0	.138*	127	93.4	

232

Monitoring clients[c]	136	74.3	.142*	103	75.7	.154*
Building hope[c]	135	73.8	.171**	106	77.9	.147*
Make treatment plans[c]	121	66.1		92	67.6	
Build structure/routine	105	57.4		88	64.7	.179*
Track/chart behaviors	93	50.8		73	53.7	.205**
Behavior rehearsal/role play	69	37.7		52	38.2	.206**
Advocacy with utilities	18	9.8		10	7.4	.142*
Clinical services—Skill training						
Use of reinforcement[c]	159	86.9	.210**	120	88.2	.277**
"I" statements	115	62.8	.336***	86	63.2	.373***
RET concepts	112	61.2	.292**	86	63.2	.317***
Anger management	101	55.2	.148*	67	49.3	
Active listening skill	99	54.1	.217**	69	50.7	.167*
Time out	94	51.4		69	50.7	.143*
Tracking behaviors	91	49.7		63	46.3	.158*
Negotiation skills	87	47.5	.157*	53	39.0	
No-lose problem-solving	66	36.1	.238***	41	30.1	.181*
Give and accept feedback	60	32.8	.162**	34	25.0	
Territoriality concepts	20	10.9	.128*	15	11.0	.165*
Clinical services—Applied therapeutic and skill training						
RET techniques	87	47.5	.274**	69	50.7	.318**
Money management	34	18.6	.177**	26	19.1	.209**

[a] Total sample multiple-regression analysis for the goal *establish trust* included the variables *give financial services, improve parent effectiveness, referral to social service* (negative loading), *recognize suicide potential* (negative loading), and *percent direct hours first quarter* (negative loading); multiple $R = .638$, adjusted $R^2 = .395$. Washington subgroup only, multiple-regression analysis for the goal *establish trust* included the variables *give financial sevices, improve parent effectiveness, referral to social service* (negative loading), *recognize suicide potential* (negative loading), *percent direct hours first quarter* (negative loading), *encouraging, behavior rehearsal/role play, behavior modification, help secure child care,* and *days in service*; multiple $R = .640$, adjusted $R^2 = .381$.

[b] Services shown are those used in 50% or more of the cases where goal achievement equaled 3 or above, or that correlated significantly with the goal.

[c] Core service with utilization 5% or more above overall mean usage for that service (for total sample).

* $p < .05$. ** $p < .01$.

233

relationship-building procedures. Particularly noteworthy for trust-building is the importance of helping clients meet basic physical or financial needs.

Washington Only. The profile of services associated with *establish trust* goal achievement from the Homebuilders Washington programs was similar to the overall sample. However, the regression model for Washington children contained more variables than for the overall sample. It included the five variables present in the total sample model plus five additional measures. Three clinical measures added to the model were the summated clinical scale *modify problem behaviors,* and specific variables *encouraging* and *behavior rehearsal/role play* (trend only). Also added were the concrete services variable *help secure child care* and *number of days in service.* The Washington model accounted for approximately the same proportion of variance as the total sample model.

The addition of the measure *modify problem behaviors* appears to strengthen the emphasis observed above that direct intervention into family problems was a source of improved working relationships. Likewise, the presence of another concrete services variable in the equation provides more support for the importance of tangible assistance in IFPS intervention. The inclusion of number of days in service suggests that better working relationships are achieved when the full course of treatment is able to be provided.

Goal 2: Increase communication skills (e.g., "I" messages, active listening, problem solving, family council, describing behavior, avoiding labels and blaming)

As shown in Table 11.3, aggregate concrete service measures were less evident as important correlates of the goal *increase communication* as compared to *establish trust.* Three specific concrete variables were significantly correlated with achievement of the communication goal but the very small number of cases were suggestive of chance relationships.

The highest significant correlations with summated clinical scales were with *improve parent effectiveness* (r .312) and *solve problems/reduce conflict* ($r = .275$). Activities encompassed within the former approach include the teaching of communication and child management skills; the latter activities would appear to attempt to reduce extrafamilial stress and interpersonal conflict within the family and so indirectly improve the communication climate, but also include training in personal and familial problem-solving techniques. Twenty specific clinical interventions correlated significantly with the goal. As above, these services particularly reflect the importance of skills-training for communication and problem-solving. Highest correlations were with the teaching of *no-lose problem solving* and *active listening skills,* of the use of *behavior rehearsal/role play,* and of *problem-solving* with family members.

Core clinical variables that were used disproportionately were *clarify family rules*, the teaching of the use of *"I" statements* and *active listening skill*, and *anger management*. Several noncore services were used in over half of these cases, notably *negotiation skills* (at 60%), which involves teaching family members techniques to avoid conflict and powerstruggles. Other noncore service activities in this group were *problem ownership, problem solving, behavior rehearsal/role play*, and *no-lose problem-solving*. These interventions re-emphasize the importance of the teaching of better communication and problem-solving skills in the Homebuilders model. In addition, they point to the importance of working with families to reduce conflict, by increasing internal controls of each family member and improving structure in the family.

The overall regression equation for predicting achievement of the goal had five significant variables, all clinically related. The equation accounted for 21% of the variability associated with the goal.[2] Two summated scales, *solve problems/reduce conflict* and *improve parent effectiveness*, were significant positive correlates in the equation. One clinical activity not included in the above scales, *behavior rehearsal/role play*, was added to the equation. This intervention would appear to add to the emphasis on teaching skills to parents, while the addition of another service technique, *money management*, addressed another type of family problem. Finally, the summated scale *make referrals/advocacy* was a strong *negative* correlate of goal attainment for communication skills. This scale includes variables involved with making referrals, consulting, and advocacy with schools and community service providers. Apparently, situations where extensive outside agency involvement is required were less susceptible to change in the area of family communication skill.

In summary, skills-training approaches appeared to be central for achieving the goal *increase communication skills*. The content of such training included a focus on listening skills, the use of "I" messages, anger management, and family problem-solving techniques. Direct intervention with problems of the family also supported this goal achievement, perhaps by controlling conflict between family members or reducing outside pressures. Concrete services appeared not to have a strong impact regarding this goal.

Washington Only. The profile of services associated with achievement of the goal increase communication for the Washington subsample was nearly identical with the overall sample. The regression model for the Homebuilders Washington subset included four of the variables present in the total sample model. In addition, two more measures were identified, the concrete variable *arrange life skill classes* and the clinical intervention *anxiety management*. The dominant measure in the equation was *improve parent effectiveness*. The equation accounted for a very slight increase in variance as compared to the total sample model.

Table 11.3. Service Usage and Correlation with Goals: Increase Communication[a]

	Total sample			Homebuilders Washington only		
	Service used for goal achievement of 3 or more (N = 230)		Significant correlation with goal achievement (N = 347)	Service used for goal achievement of 3 or more (N = 183)		Significant correlation with goal achievement (N = 304)
Service measures[b]	No.	(%)		No.	(%)	
Concrete services						
All concrete services	168	73.0		131	71.6	.132*
Arrange life skill classes	15	6.5	.116*	17	9.3	.152*
Help obtain utility benefits	7	3.0	.115*	13	7.1	.147*
Help secure child care	6	2.6	.162**	15	8.2	
Help obtain legal aid						
Provide clothing						
Clinical services—summated scales/indices						
Solve problems/reduce conflict	224	97.4	.275**	177	96.7	.304**
Develop treatment relationship	228	99.1	.142*	181	98.9	.179**
Manage depression/stress	222	96.5		176	96.2	
Modify problem behaviors	223	97.0		176	96.2	
Improve parent effectiveness	227	98.7	.312**	181	98.9	.364**
Make referrals/advocacy	181	78.7	.203**	137	74.9	.287**
Rational-emotive therapy	197	85.7	.220**	160	87.4	.245**
Teach assertiveness	74	32.2		55	30.1	
Crisis intervention	149	64.8		117	63.9	
Clinical services—Applied therapeutic						
Relationship building	199	86.5	.137*	156	85.2	
Provide literature	183	79.6	.187**	154	84.2	.170**
Clarify family rules[c]	160	69.6		116	63.4	

236

Service	N	%	r	N	%	r
Building hope	157	68.3		126	68.9	.147*
Make treatment plans	142	61.7	.151**	107	58.5	.142*
Behavior rehearsal/role play	119	51.7	.238**	99	54.1	.265**
Provide paper/pencil tests	59	25.7	.142*	41	22.4	.144*
Anxiety management	58	25.2	.118*	39	21.3	.153*
Advocacy with utilities	13	5.7	.136*			
Clinical services—Skill training						
"T" statements[c]	192	83.5	.196**	153	83.6	.216**
RET concepts	192	83.5	.193**	156	85.2	.259**
Active listening skill[c]	175	76.1	.221**	134	73.2	.226**
Anger management[c]	168	73.0	.193**	126	68.9	
Negotiation skills	139	60.4	.130*	97	53.0	.167**
Handle frustration	130	56.5	.245**	97	53.0	.144*
No-lose problem-solving	117	50.9	.195**	85	46.4	.292**
Give and accept feedback	88	38.3	.123*	55	30.1	.175**
Assertiveness	71	30.9		53	29.0	.134*
Clinical services—Applied therapeutic and skill training						
RET techniques[c]	170	73.9	.168**	138	75.4	.245**
Problem-solving	123	53.5	.228**	83	45.4	.229**
Impulse management	84	36.5	.145*			
Develop informal supports	35	15.2	.114*			
Money management	33	14.3	.117*	25	13.7	.136*

[a] Total sample multiple-regression analysis for the goal *increase communication* included the variables *solve problems/reduce conflict, improve parent effectiveness, make referrals/advocacy* (negative loading), *Behavior rehearsal/role play,* and *money management;* multiple R = .453, adjusted R^2 = .205. Washington subgroup only, multiple-regression analysis for the goal *management;* multiple R = .205. *improve parent effectiveness* included the variables *improve parent effectiveness, make referrals/advocacy* (negative loading), *increase communication* included the variables *behavior rehearsal/role play, money management, anxiety management,* and *arrange life skill classes;* multiple R = .499, adjusted R^2 = .230.

[b] Services shown are those used in 50% or more of the cases where goal achievement equaled 3 or above, or that correlated significantly with the goal.

[c] Core service with utilization 5% or more above overall mean usage for that service (for total sample).

* $p < .05$.   ** $p < .01$.

Goal 3: Increase parenting skills (e.g., use of positive consequences, consistency in discipline, charting and contracting, setting limits, giving clear expectations, reducing physical punishment, bargaining, knowledge of child-adolescent development)

As compared to *increase communication*, concrete services were used somewhat more extensively for the children at risk in families with whom the goal *increase parenting skills* had been established. Also, two specific concrete services associated with the acquisition of family resources, e.g., child care and clothing, were significantly correlated with this goal (see Table 11.4).

The summated clinical scale correlated most strongly with the goal *increase parenting skills* was *modify problem behaviors* ($r = .266$), which includes therapist activities of both teaching skills in child management and discipline as well as directly applying such procedures in child or family counseling contacts. Specific service activities in this scale include teaching parents how to use reinforcement and environmental controls such as the use of natural and logical consequences, strengthening parent efforts to improve child compliance, therapist provision of reinforcers, helping the family build structure and daily routine, and tracking or charting of behaviors. Also correlated were the scales *improve parent effectiveness, solve problems/reduce conflict,* and *develop treatment relationship.*

Seventeen clinical interventions correlated significantly with *increase parenting skills,* showing a mix of applied therapeutic and skill-training approaches. The strongest correlations were for *use of reinforcement* ($r = .271$), which focused upon teaching parents how to implement reinforcement schedules and follow through in the disciplining and management of their children, and *track/chart behaviors* ($r = .243$), in which therapists create behavioral charts and follow behavioral contracts with clients. Content of the remainder of these services included several activities involved with the teaching of behavioral management approaches, the direct establishment of structure, and supportive, relationship-building activities.

Only one core service was used in excess of 5% above mean usage for that service, *use of reinforcement.* The one noncore service used above the 50% level for this goal was *time out,* the teaching of these techniques for parents to use as a behavioral consequence and also as a personal coping skill.

The overall regression model for the goal *increase parenting skills* was comprised of five measures, including two summated clinical scales, one specific clinical activity, one concrete service variable, and one measure of service time. The overall equation, while statistically significant, accounted for only about 12% of the variance associated with achievement of this goal. This suggests that other factors, in addition to the variables entering into the equation, affect parenting skills.

The dominant correlate of increasing parental skills was the summated scale *modify problem behaviors*. A second aggregate measure was also significant, *increase parent effectiveness*. As discussed earlier, this measure places emphasis on the teaching of communication skills in families. This variable was also a significant correlate for the somewhat related goal, *increase communication skills*. A major difference in the models for the two goals was the added presence of behavior modification interventions for the parenting skills goal.

Another clinical scale that entered in the equation, *anxiety management*, suggests that efforts to reduce anxieties were helpful in facilitating the parent's learning process. The inclusion of the concrete service activity *help secure child care* may imply that helping mothers have more time away from child care pressures allowed them to be more relaxed with children, likely increasing the successful use of the new parenting techniques.

Finally, one time measure, *average direct service hours per quarter for the last three quarters*, was negatively associated with goal achievement. This suggests that when the need exists to maintain a high level of involvement with a family over the entire course of IFPS treatment, the goal relating to achieving greater parenting skill is less successful (i.e. more difficult to achieve).

In summary, interventions associated with the goal *increase parenting skills* were behaviorally oriented. There was strong emphasis upon training parents in behavior management skills, and to a lesser degree teaching communication skills. Some strategies associated with the direct application of behavior management techniques were also correlated with this goal, as were several supportive and anxiety reducing service activities.

Washington Only. Correlates of *increase parenting skills* for the Washington subsample were similar to the overall profile, and in the cases of the scale *modify problem behaviors* and the specific intervention *use of reinforcement*, higher correlations were evidenced. One more variable, *time out*, was included at a trend level, providing further evidence that learning theory approaches to child management can be delivered in IFPS.

Goal 4: Increase anger management/conflict resolution skills (e.g., negotiating areas of conflict, problem-solving, assertiveness, taking no for an answer; reducing "back-talk," hitting, yelling, swearing, and property damage)

Most of the summated clinical scales were significantly correlated with the *increase anger management/conflict resolution skills* goal, the strongest of which were *improve parent effectiveness* ($r = .314$) and *solve problems/reduce conflict* ($r = .313$), as shown in Table 11.5. The former, as discussed above, largely involves teaching of communication and child management skills to parents. The latter aggregates a number of clinical service

Table 11.4. Service Relationships with Goal: Increase Parenting Skills[a]

	Total sample			Homebuilders Washington only		
	Service used for goal achievement of 3 or more (N = 358)		Significant correlation with goal achievement (N = 461)	Service used for goal achievement of 3 or more (N = 230)		Significant correlation with goal achievement (N = 347)
Service measures[b]	No.	(%)		No.	(%)	
Concrete services						
All doing services	181	50.6		130	49.1	.147**
All enabling services	186	52.0		130	49.1	
All concrete services	288	80.4		209	78.9	
Help secure child care	56	15.6	.122**	47	17.7	
Provide clothing	18	5.0	.106**	5	1.9	
Clinical services—Summated scale/index						
Solve problems/reduce conflict	353	98.6	.107*	260	98.1	.112*
Develop treatment relationship	354	98.9	.096*	261	98.5	
Manage depression/stress	329	91.9		242	91.3	
Modify problem behaviors	351	98.0	.266**	259	97.7	.310**
Improve parent effectiveness	354	98.9	.192**	261	98.5	.190**
Make referrals/advocacy	284	79.3		200	75.5	
Rational-emotive therapy	245	68.4		182	68.7	
Crisis intervention	226	63.1		162	61.1	
Clinical services—Applied therapeutic						
Listening to client	348	97.2		258	97.4	.110*
Encouraging	332	92.7		251	94.7	.106*

240

	N	%		N	%	
Offer support/understanding	309	86.3	.111*	238	89.8	
Relationship building	306	85.5	.097*	231	87.2	
Provide literature	270	75.4	.098*	212	80.0	
Building hope	248	69.3	.125**	188	70.9	
Monitoring clients	243	67.9	.116*	179	67.5	
Track/chart behaviors	208	58.1	.243**	154	58.1	.235**
Behavior rehearsal/role play	165	46.1	.160*	124	46.8	.163*
Anxiety management	92	25.7	.116*	58	21.9	.123*
Clinical services—Skill training						
Use of reinforcement[c]	322	89.9	.271**	239	90.2	.335**
Natural/logical consequences	285	79.6	.162**	209	78.9	.169**
RET concepts	238	66.5	.141**	176	66.4	.168**
Tracking behaviors	206	57.5	.161**	139	52.5	.172**
Handle frustration	190	53.1	.110*	125	47.2	.157**
Time out	189	52.8		140	52.8	.136*
No-lose problem-solving	141	39.4	.102*	81	30.6	
Clinical services—Applied therapeutic and skill training						
Improve compliance	224	62.6	.118*	156	58.9	
RET techniques	197	55.0	.117*	157	59.2	
Problem-solving	169	47.2	.093*	100	37.7	.186**

[a] Total sample multiple-regression analysis for the goal *increase parenting skills* included the variables *behavior modification, improve parent effectiveness, help secure child care, anxiety management, average direct hours per quarter in last three quarters* (negative loading); multiple $R = .367$, adjusted $R^2 = .125$. Washington subgroup only, multiple-regression analysis for the goal *increase parenting skills* included the variables *behavior modification, improve parent effectiveness, help secure child care, anxiety management, average direct hours per quarter in last three quarters* (negative loading), and *time out*; multiple $R = .417$, adjusted $R^2 = .159$.

[b] Services shown are those used in 50% or more of the cases where goal achievement equaled 3 or above, or that correlated significantly with the goal.

[c] Core service with utilization 5% or more above overall mean usage for that service (for total sample).

*$p < .05$. **$p < .01$.

Table 11.5. Service Relationships with Goal: Increase Anger Management/Conflict Resolution Skills[a]

Service measures[b]	Total sample			Homebuilders Washington only		
	Service used for goal achievement of 3 or more (N = 260)		Significant correlation with goal achievement (N = 337)	Service used for goal achievement of 3 or more (N = 190)		Significant correlation with goal achievement (N = 249)
	No.	(%)		No.	(%)	
Concrete services						
All concrete services	201	77.3		143	76.1	
Provide recreation activities	57	21.9	.131*	37	19.7	
Arrange life skill classes	22	8.5	.113*	15	8.0	
Clinical services—Summated scale/index						
Solve problems/reduce conflict	257	98.8	.313**	185	98.4	.342**
Develop treatment relationship	258	99.2	.239***	186	98.9	.219***
Manage depression/stress	250	96.2	.163***	184	97.9	
Modify problem behaviors	253	97.3	.200**	182	96.8	.200**
Improve parent effectiveness	257	98.8	.314***	186	98.9	.294**
Make referrals/advocacy	207	79.6		141	75.0	
Rational-emotive therapy	243	93.5	.212***	164	87.2	.210**
Teach assertiveness	81	31.2	.160**	54	28.7	.156*
Crisis intervention	179	68.8		124	66.0	
Clinical services—Applied therapeutic						
Listening to client	257	98.8	.123*	185	98.4	
Encouraging	247	95.0	.139*	180	95.7	.169**
Offer support/understanding	235	90.4	.144**	173	92.0	
Setting treatment goals	223	85.8	.152**	159	84.6	.137*

Reframing	219	84.2	.114*	157	83.5	.165**
Clarify problem behaviors^c	212	81.5	.118*	156	83.0	.158*
Provide literature	209	80.4	.228***	159	84.6	.184***
Building hope	186	71.5		137	72.9	.127*
Clarify family rules^c	180	69.2		125	66.5	
Make treatment plans	158	60.8	.165***	115	61.2	.137*
Track/chart behaviors	151	58.1	.189***	108	57.4	.190**
Refer to other counseling	146	56.2		105	55.9	
Behavior rehearsal/role play	137	52.7	.129*	104	55.3	.134*
De-escalating	135	51.9		95	50.5	
Use of crisis card	134	51.5		97	51.6	
Anxiety management	66	25.4		39	20.7	
Provide paper/pencil tests	65	25.0	.109*	49	26.1	.136*
Advocacy with utilities	10	3.8	.157**	6	3.2	
Clinical services—Skill training						
Anger management	223	85.8	.173**	155	82.4	.160*
Use of reinforcement	219	84.2	.202***	158	84.0	.197**
Natural/logical consequences^c	215	82.7	.163***	149	79.3	.130*
RET concepts^c	212	81.5	.185***	160	85.1	.191**
"I" statements^c	202	77.7	.118*	144	76.6	
Active listening skill^c	182	70.0		125	66.5	
Handle frustration^c	165	63.5	.173***	110	58.5	.176**
Negotiation skills	154	59.2	.214***	91	48.4	.185**
Process of change	150	57.7	.135*	100	53.2	.163*
Problem ownership	148	56.9		91	48.4	
No-lose problem-solving	129	49.6	.185***	77	41.0	.159*
Clinical services—Applied therapeutic and skill training						
Improve compliance^c	185	71.2	.114*	127	67.6	.219**

(continued)

243

Table 11.5. *(Continued)*

Service measures[b]	Total sample				Homebuilders Washington only			
	Service used for goal achievement of 3 or more (N = 260)		Significant correlation with goal achievement (N = 337)		Service used for goal achievement of 3 or more (N = 190)		Significant correlation with goal achievement (N = 249)
	No.	(%)			No.	(%)	
RET techniques[c]	176	67.7	.163**		139	73.9	.219**
Build self-esteem	164	63.1	.177**		114	60.6	.129*
Problem-solving	141	54.2	.201**		81	43.1	.165**
Impulse management	115	44.2	.164**		66	35.1	

[a] Total sample multiple-regression analysis for the goal *increase anger management* included the variables *solve problems/reduce conflict, improve parent effectiveness, build self-esteem, track/chart behaviors, percent direct hours first quarter* (negative loading); multiple $R = .405$, adjusted $R^2 = .151$. Washington subgroup only; multiple-regression analysis for the goal *increase anger management* included the variables *solve problems/reduce conflict, build self-esteem, use of reinforcement, RET techniques*; multiple $R = .404$, adjusted $R^2 = .149$.

[b] Services shown are those used in 50% or more of the cases where goal achievement equaled 3 or above, or that correlated significantly with the goal.

[c] Core service with utilization 5% or more above overall mean usage for that service (for total sample).

*p < .05.   **p < .01.

activities including teaching clients such skills as problem solving, problem ownership, negotiation skills, how to give and accept feedback, how to accept no from others, "fair-fighting" rules, helping clients to manage frustration and impulsivity, establishing family councils for decision-making, helping clarify family roles and rules, and intervening directly to resolve family difficulties. Other correlates in this group were *develop treatment relationship, modify problem behaviors, manage depression/stress, rational-emotive therapy,* and *teach assertiveness.*

Two of the specific concrete variables, *provide recreation activities* and *arrange life skill classes,* were correlates of *increase anger management/conflict resolution skills* goal achievement. A large number (26) of specific clinical interventions were correlated with the goal. Highest coefficients were for *negotiation skills, use of reinforcement, problem-solving,* and *provide literature.* Similar to the two previous goals, a balance was demonstrated between applied therapeutic and skills-training approaches.

A considerable number (10) of the core clinical interventions were selectively high in terms of percentage of usage. Activities defined as *anger management,* i.e., teaching parents (and older children) how to identify anger at earlier stages, interrupt anger chains, and de-escalation techniques, were used for 86% of children in families with an anger management goal as compared to a mean usage of 64%. Other services in this higher use group were *"I" statements, improve compliance, active listening skill, handle frustration, natural/logical consequences, RET concepts, RET techniques, clarify problem behaviors,* and *clarify family rules.* Seven noncore services were also above the 50% level in usage: *negotiation skills, problem ownership, refer to other counseling, problem-solving, behavior rehearsal/role play, use of crisis card,* and *de-escalating.*

Five variables were included in the regression equation for the goal: two clinical scales, two additional specific clinical activities, and one time-related variable. The overall equation accounted for approximately 15% of the total variability in the goal.

Solve problems/reduce conflict was the most dominant correlate of successfully training clients to manage anger. The presence of this measure suggests the utility of dealing with anger difficulties through teaching skills to handle conflict and negative feelings, and by direct intervention into problem situations.

Inclusion of the summated measure *improve parent effectiveness* implies that teaching parents better communication and child management skills may have derivative effects such as reducing episodes of anger or conflict. Additionally, supporting parents is important, accounting perhaps for the significance of the clinical activity *build self-esteem* in this model.

One measure of service time, *percentage of direct client contact hours in the first quarter,* entered into the equation negatively. It would appear that interventions to improve anger management may be less effective in a type of crisis situation that requires an extraordinary amount of initial client contact.

In summary, many specific strategies were associated with the attainment of improved anger management and conflict resolution. This shows, perhaps, the complexity of intervening when anger and overt conflict exist in families. A mix of skills-training and applied therapeutic interventions are involved in goal achievement. Training approaches include building a wide range of skills: problem-solving, reduction of frustration and fighting, communication, and child management. Applied therapeutic interventions focus on establishing treatment directions, building relationships, helping families establish rules and structure, and supplying a supportive base for learning and change to occur.

Washington Only. Services associated with achievement of the *anger management* goal for Homebuilders Washington clients followed the pattern observed in the overall sample. The regression model contained some of the same elements as the full sample equation and accounted for a very modest proportion of variance. As with the total sample, *solve problems/reduce conflict* was the dominant correlate of goal achievement. The use of *RET techniques* was significant in the equation, and *build self-esteem* and *use of reinforcement* entered the equation at a trend level.

Goal 5: Improve school performance and/or attendance (e.g., school allows child to return, child attends regularly, child on-time to school, homework is completed, child gets along with schoolmates and teachers)

The services predictive of achievement for the goal *improve school performance* were more limited than for some other goals. The strongest correlate ($r = .283$) was *time/money management*, a two-variable index involving a skill building approach to help a family organize and manage their time, particularly as a way of improving bedtime and wake-up routines to increase child punctuality and school attendance. Modest correlations were also identified with the scales *manage depression/stress, make referrals/advocacy,* and *modify problems behaviors* (see Table 11.6).

For the total sample, two specific concrete services were correlated with goal achievement for *improve school performance: help obtain medical/dental services* and *provide toys or recreation equipment*. Nine specific clinical services had significant correlations. The largest coefficients were for *protect from sexual abuse, build self-esteem, consultation with other services,* and *refer to other counseling*. Skill-training approaches appeared less important than direct intervention.

Core clinical services with disproportionately high usage readings for this goal were largely connected with behavioral structuring and monitoring

(*monitoring clients, build structure/routine*, [teach parents] *tracking behaviors, clarify family roles*). *Building hope* added an emotional support element.

Nine noncore services rose to usage for more than half of *improve school performance* clients. Several of these involved advocacy (*advocacy with schools, refer to other counseling, meet with other providers*). Others concerned problem-solving or problem management (*negotiation skills, problem ownership, problem-solving, de-escalating, environmental controls*).

The regression equation for predicting achievement of the goal *improve school performance* had six significant measures. Five of these measures were clinically related and the other was a concrete service activity. The equation accounted for a relatively small proportion (about 16%) of the variability associated with the goal.

The clinical index *time/money management* was the most significant correlate in this equation. Closely related to this was the clinical variable *track/chart behaviors*, perhaps indicating value in the use of very specific techniques for monitoring child behavior with respect to school attendance and academic performance.

Protect children from sexual abuse also had a significant effect in relation to performance in school. Perhaps attempts to ameliorate the threat of such abuse (or reabuse) within families served to free children to function normatively in a school setting. Implementing the concrete service *help obtain medical/dental services* may have had a similar effect. Therapist efforts to help families acquire medical treatment (including eye exams and glasses) were correlates of better school performance. Finally, two clinical interventions aimed at affective change were included in the model, *build self-esteem* and *anxiety management*. This finding suggests that child self-esteem difficulties related to school performance contributed to truancy and other school-related problems.

In summary, the elements that appear to be important in IFPS for strengthening school performance goal achievement include the development of structure and routine in the home, particularly the management of routines and time, i.e., getting up and to school, keeping a schedule for homework; working with parents to establish reinforcers for school attendance and performance; taking steps to protect a child from sex abuse; helping the family (or child) build hope, deal with depression, improve self-esteem; acquire needed medical or dental treatment for the child; use collaborative efforts or advocacy with other resources, perhaps with school counselors, medical providers, child abuse workers, or community mental health resources.

Washington Only. Findings from the Washington subsample included some added elements, and appeared to have a slightly sharper focus than for

Table 11.6. Service Relationships with Goal: Improve School Performance[a]

Service measures[b]	Total sample			Homebuilders Washington only		
	Service used for goal achievement of 3 or more (N = 135) No.	(%)	Significant correlation with goal achievement (N = 188)	Service used for goal achievement of 3 or more (N = 85) No.	(%)	Significant correlation with goal achievement (N = 124)
Concrete services						
All doing services	70	51.9		43	50.6	.199*
All concrete services	102	75.6		67	78.8	.194*
Provide child care	17	12.6		13	15.3	.178*
Help secure child care	16	11.9		10	11.8	.185*
Help secure clothing	11	8.1		7	8.2	
Help obtain medical/dental services	20	14.8	.1826*	13	15.3	.223*
Provide toys or recreation equipment	20	14.8	.1538*	11	12.9	.218*
Clinical services—Summated scale/index						
Solve problems/reduce conflict	134	99.3		84	98.8	
Develop treatment relationship	133	98.5		85	100.0	
Manage depression/stress	126	93.3	.198**	79	92.9	
Modify problem behaviors	134	99.3	.147*	84	98.8	
Improve parent effectiveness	131	97.0		81	95.3	.287**
Make referrals/advocacy	119	88.1	.166*	73	85.9	
Rational-emotive therapy	88	65.2		54	63.5	.260**
Time/money management	49	36.3	.283**	24	28.2	.283**
Crisis intervention	93	68.9		57	67.1	
Sexual behavior/abuse	39	28.9	.193**	21	24.7	.185*
Clinical services—Applied therapeutic						
Building hope[c]	100	74.1		65	76.5	
Monitoring clients[c]	98	72.6		61	71.8	

248

Service						
Build structure/routine[c]	94	69.6	.160*	65	76.5	.184*
Providing reinforcers	91	67.4	.145*	60	70.6	.294**
Track/chart behaviors[c]	85	63.0	.184*	54	63.5	.235**
Consultation with other services	85	63.0	.207**	47	55.3	
Clarify family roles[c]	83	61.5		44	51.8	
Refer to other counseling	79	58.5		43	50.6	.194*
Advocacy with schools	79	58.5		43	50.6	
Meet with other providers	75	55.6		39	45.9	
Use of crisis card	68	50.4		37	43.5	
De-escalating	68	50.4		42	49.4	.205*
Environmental controls	68	50.4		39	45.9	.375**
Refer to other counseling	67	49.6	.201**	42	49.4	
Anxiety management	45	33.3	.151*	19	22.4	
Clinical services—Skill training						
Use of reinforcement	115	85.2		73	85.9	.280**
Tracking behaviors[c]	88	65.2		48	56.5	.252**
Process of change	80	59.3	.149*	45	52.9	
Handle frustration	79	58.5		43	50.6	.180*
Problem ownership	78	57.8		36	42.4	
Negotiation skills	76	56.3		34	40.0	
Protect from sexual abuse	14	10.4	.228**	11	12.9	.256**
Clinical services—Applied therapeutic and skill training						
Build self-esteem	86	63.7	.201**	51	60.0	.190*
Problem-solving	71	52.6		31	36.5	

[a] Total sample multiple-regression analysis for the goal *improve school performance* included the variables *time/money management, help obtain medical/dental services, anxiety management, build self-esteem, track/chart behaviors, protect from sexual abuse*; multiple R = .436, adjusted R^2 = .163. Washington subgroup only; multiple-regression analysis for the goal *improve school performance* included the variables *time/money management, build self-esteem, track/chart behaviors, protect from sexual abuse, use of reinforcement*; multiple R = .521, adjusted R^2 = .241.

[b] Services shown are those used in 50% or more of the cases where goal achievement equaled 3 or above, or that correlated significantly with the goal.

[c] Core service with utilization 5% or more above overall mean usage for that service (for total sample).

*$p < .05$. **$p < .01$.

the overall sample. For one thing, the total hours of concrete service delivery were correlated with *improve school performance*, and three more specific concrete interventions involving the provision or securing of child care and clothing were correlated with goal achievement. Higher correlations were also noted for *modify problem behaviors* and *make referrals/advocacy*.

The regression equation for the Washington Homebuilders program contained four of the same variables as the model for the total sample, including the index *time/money management*, and the specific clinical variables *protect from sexual abuse, build self-esteem,* and *track/chart behaviors*. An added clinical variable in the Washington model was *use of reinforcement*, providing additional support for the need for home-based contingencies for school behavior. The proportion of variance accounted for was also slightly greater than for the total sample equation.

Goal 6: Increase self-esteem (e.g., client sees positives about self, client uses affirmations)

Concrete services were somewhat more in evidence where the goal *increase self-esteem* had been identified as a treatment objective. Aggregate measures displayed high rates of usage (shown in Table 11.7). Three specific concrete services were correlated significantly with the goal, although the number of subjects where these services were used was not large. The overall positive association of concrete services with this goal suggests that the provision of tangible resources helps parents feel better about themselves. Specific concrete correlates of the goal seem to emphasize the importance of new outlets for recreation and learning.

In the overall sample, only three summated clinical scales and seven specific clinical interventions were correlates of *increase self-esteem*. Summated measures were *solve problems/reduce conflict, improve parent effectiveness*, and *teach assertiveness*. Highest correlates among the specific interventions were with *make treatment plans, anxiety management*, and *RET concepts*.

Of the core clinical variables, only one fit the criteria for selectively high usage, *build self-esteem*. As noted earlier, this intervention included teaching clients to use positive self-talk, reinforcing client strengths, and involving clients in esteem-building activities. *Build self-esteem* was identified as being used with 88.89% of the subjects in families with the *increase self-esteem* goal, a full 25 percentage points above the mean percent usage for this intervention across all goals.

One noncore service, *refer to other counseling*, was used in more than 50% of cases. Apparently, therapists chose to make referrals to outside counseling resources at a relatively high rate for persons identified with self-esteem difficulties.

The regression model for the goal *increase self-esteem* included one two-variable clinical index, three additional specific clinical activity variables, and two concrete service measures. The overall equation accounted for one-fourth of the variance associated with achievement of this goal.

The strongest correlate of increasing client self-esteem was the therapist activity *make treatment plans*, suggesting the importance of careful assessment and planning in dealing with self-esteem difficulties. Specific treatment approaches to teach *assertiveness, anxiety management,* and *anger management* to clients were also significant in this equation. These clinical approaches all focus on helping a person exercise more conscious control over feelings and behaviors. Also included was the concrete variable *arrange life skill classes*, which might suggest the value to a client's self-esteem of using community-based educational approaches. Alternatively, just leaving the home for an evening class and meeting other adults may have a positive effect on self-esteem. A final variable included in the model was the concrete service *provide toys or recreation equipment.* The inclusion of this measure might imply some effect from the parents receiving additional resources to engage in more recreational activities with their children. It is more likely, however, that the inclusion of this service reflects those cases where the goal was set for *children.* Thus, the receipt of such gifts may have had a positive effect on the self-esteem of some of the children.

In summary, careful assessment and planning, developing good therapist-client relationships, and providing structure in treatment appear to promote self-esteem. Therapists tended to refer to outside counseling resources at a higher rate than for most other goals. Specific treatment approaches to teach assertiveness and anxiety and anger management were also related to successful esteem-building. This suggests that helping a person exercise more conscious control over feelings and behaviors may strengthen feelings of self-worth. The overall provision of concrete services was also important. Therapists were successful in building self-esteem of clients (parents and children) when they provided physical resources and new outlets for recreation and learning.

Washington Only. The findings for Homebuilders Washington cases provided a somewhat more focused depiction of services associated with reports of increased self-esteem in IFPS subjects. For several clinical measures, considerably higher correlations were noted and more correlates of the goal were identified. In the regression model, four of the six variables in the total sample model were retained and three other variables were added, resulting in a relatively higher adjusted R^2 as compared to the total sample figure (.375 as opposed to .253). Most dominant of the new variables was the aggregate measure *solve problems/reduce conflict.* Also added were the clinical variable *monitoring clients* and a further concrete service *provide recreation activities.*

Table 11.7. Service Relationships with Goal: Increase Self-Esteem[a]

| Service measures[b] | Total sample | | Homebuilders Washington only | |
	Service used for goal achievement of 3 or more (N = 89) No. (%)	Significant correlation with goal achievement (N = 115)	Service used for goal achievement of 3 or more (N = 80) No. (%)	Significant correlation with goal achievement (N = 103)
Concrete services				
All doing services	53 59.6		47 58.8	
All enabling services	50 56.2		45 56.3	
All concrete services	78 87.6		71 88.8	
Provide transportation	65 73.0		80 100.0	
Provide toys or recreation equipment	14 15.7	.216*	13 16.3	.219*
Provide recreation activities	16 18.0	.199*	15 18.8	.225*
Arrange life skill classes	12 13.5	.240*	11 13.8	.276**
Clinical services—Summated scale/index				
Solve problems/reduce conflict	82 92.1	.299**	73 91.3	.433**
Develop treatment relationship	86 96.6		77 96.3	.211*
Manage depression/stress	84 94.4		77 96.3	
Modify problem behaviors	86 96.6		77 96.3	.219*
Improve parent effectiveness	84 94.4	.266**	77 96.3	.377**
Make referrals/advocacy	71 79.8		62 77.5	
Rational-emotive therapy	63 70.8		59 73.8	.238*

Teach assertiveness	58	65.2	.294**	25	31.3	.312**
Crisis intervention	53	59.6		48	60.0	
Clinical services—Applied therapeutic						
Clarify problem behaviors	67	75.3		58	72.5	.235*
Monitoring clients	62	69.7	.220*	57	71.3	.252*
Make treatment plans	50	56.2	.269**	44	55.0	.296**
Refer to other counseling	48	53.9		41	51.3	
Pleasant events	44	49.4		42	52.5	
Anxiety management	25	28.1	.244**	21	26.3	.264**
Clinical services—Skill training						
Child development	66	74.2		60	75.0	.234*
RET concepts	63	70.8	.239**	59	73.8	.313**
Anger management	48	53.9		43	53.8	.237*
Handle frustration	47	52.8	.185*	43	53.8	.252*
Assertiveness	28	31.5	.225*	25	31.3	.225*
Clinical services—Applied therapeutic and skill training						
Build self-esteem[c]	79	88.8		72	90.0	
RET technique	49	55.1		45	56.3	.213*
Teach job hunting	14	15.7	.200*	13	16.3	

[a] Total sample multiple-regression analysis for the goal *increase self-esteem* included the variables *teach assertiveness, provide toys or recreation equipment, arrange life skill classes, anger management, anxiety management, make treatment plans*; multiple R = .542, adjusted R^2 = .253. Washington subgroup only; multiple-regression analysis for the goal *increase self-esteem* included the variables *teach assertiveness, provide toys or recreation equipment, arrange life skill classes, anxiety management, monitoring clients, solve problems/reduce conflict, provide recreational activities*; multiple R = .647, adjusted R^2 = .375.

[b] Services shown are those used in 50 percent or more of the cases where goal achievement equaled 3 or above, or that correlated significantly with the goal.

[c] Core service with utilization 5 percent or more above overall mean usage for that service (for total sample).

*p < .05. **p < .01.

253

Three of the variables were concrete in nature, with an emphasis on recreation. Inclusion of the summated scale *solve problems/reduce conflict* suggests that self-esteem should be viewed as a function of environmental and family conditions. Self-esteem may be, in part, a function of systemic problems in the home. From a systems perspective, resolving family conflict probably has significant effects on parents' and childrens' self-esteem.

Goal 7: Decrease anxiety, worry, or fear (decrease feelings of fear, worry, and panic; ruminate less, feel more relaxed)

Shown in Table 11.8, no specific concrete service correlates of the goal *decrease anxiety, worry, or fear* were identified. Clinical correlates of this goal were also limited. Two summated clinical measures were significantly correlated with the goal, *develop treatment relationship* and *rational-emotive therapy* (a two-variable index), and seven specific clinical interventions. Of the latter, *offer support/understanding* had the largest coefficient, followed by *child development, handle frustration,* and *anxiety management.*

Core clinical services used at selectively higher rates than average were *encouraging, offer support/understanding, reframing,* and *RET concepts.* Noncore services used in more than half of these cases were *refer to other counseling, anxiety management, time out,* and *behavior rehearsal/role play.*

Among the themes suggested by the significant clinical interventions is the importance of a supportive treatment relationship. Apparently, anxious or fearful clients respond positively to therapists who provide understanding and encouragement, and actively attempt to foster hope. A second theme is the direct confrontation of the problems thought to produce anxiety and frustration through teaching self-management techniques such as positive self-talk and relaxation. Third, providing added knowledge of normal child development appears to be important for this goal. This suggests that many of the parents had concerns and/or misconceptions about child development (e.g., toilet training, bed-wetting, tantrum behaviors, age-typical difficulties of adolescents), and an educational approach may have salience.

Five variables comprised the regression model for the goal *decrease anxiety, worry, or fear:* four specific clinical activities and one time dimension. The overall equation accounted for approximately 29% of the total variability in the achievement of the goal.

The intervention with the highest weighting in the equation was *offer support and understanding.* As stated above, this finding appears to confirm the usefulness of Rogerian supportive and relation-building techniques with anxious clients. The next strongest correlate was improving understanding about child development issues. Knowledge that bothersome behaviors may be maturationally based and likely to be outgrown may reduce fears on the part of parents. Other correlates of successful anxiety reduction were two clinical interventions that attempt to address the problem directly. One was to teach the client anxiety management skills; the other was the use of rational-emotive therapy techniques, which typically aim at increasing clients' cognitive control of their emotional states. A time dimension, *average direct service hours per quarter for the last three quarters*, was also highly significant in the equation, but in a negative direction. This suggests that family preservation services are more effective in dealing with problems of anxiety, worry, or fear through a brief period of intensity or crisis intervention, rather than with a high level of service lasting the entire treatment period. After the first or second week, service efficiency appears to decline. If a need existed to maintain a high level of involvement with the client over the entire course of IFPS treatment (that is, the problems may be more chronic or deep-seated), there is less chance to positively impact client levels of anxiety, worry, or fear.

In summary, the strongest correlates with the goal *decrease anxiety, worry, or fear* were with Rogerian supportive and relationship-building techniques. Other important interventions involved providing knowledge of child development matters, and helping clients with emotional self-management through rational-emotive therapy approaches and through teaching the use of such techniques as positive self-talk and relaxation.

Washington Only. The service correlates of achievement for the goal *decrease anxiety, worry, or fear* for Homebuilders Washington clients were nearly identical with the total sample.

Goal 8: Decrease depression and/or suicidal thoughts or behaviors (client feels less hopeless or helpless, and more in control of her/his life; engages in pleasant events; reduces talk about depression or self-destruction)

A higher level of concrete services was used for subjects with the goal *decrease depression* (see Table 11.9) as compared to most other goals. Aggregate measures displayed very high rates of usage and five specific concrete services were correlated significantly with the goal, although utilized with relatively small numbers of subjects. Specific focus of these specific concrete services was around the provision or acquisition of tangible resources, including food, clothing, utilities, and child care. The heavy involvement of concrete services in achieving the *decrease depression* goal suggests that at least a portion of what therapists were defining as depression may have been situational and related to the lack of basic necessities.

Only one clinical summated measure was correlated with *decrease depression: solve problems/reduce conflict.* Seven specific clinical variables were significant, the strongest correlations being with *relationship building* and *provide literature.* IFPS therapists defined the former as involving active listening and demonstrations of concern and understanding, helpfulness including the provision of concrete services, and general accessibility and

Table 11.8. Service Relationships with Goal: Decrease Anxiety/Worry/Fear[a]

	Total sample		Homebuilders Washington only	
	Service used for goal achievement of 3 or more (N = 95)	Significant correlation with goal achievement (N = 123)	Service used for goal achievement of 3 or more (N = 85)	Significant correlation with goal achievement (N = 113)
Service measures[b]	No. (%)		No. (%)	
Concrete services				
All enabling services	56 58.9		48 56.5	
All concrete services	72 75.8		63 74.1	
Clinical services—Summated scale/index				
Solve problems/reduce conflict	92 96.8		82 96.5	
Develop treatment relationship	95 100.0	.180*	85 100.0	
Manage depression/stress	94 98.9		84 98.8	
Modify problem behaviors	93 97.9		83 97.6	
Improve parent effectiveness	95 100.0		85 100.0	
Make referrals/advocacy	77 81.1		67 78.8	
Rational-emotive therapy	78 82.1	.203*	71 83.5	.196*
Crisis intervention	58 61.1		53 62.4	
Clinical services—Applied therapeutic				
Encouraging[c]	94 98.9		84 98.8	

256

Offer support/understanding[c]	89	93.7	.364**	79	92.9	.378**
Building hope	68	71.6	.183*	59	69.4	
Reframing[c]	85	89.5		75	88.2	
Refer to other counseling	62	65.3		53	62.4	
Anxiety management	56	58.9	.251**	46	54.1	.213*
Behavior rehearsal/role play	48	50.5		43	50.6	
Clinical services—Skill training						
RET concepts[c]	75	78.9	.207*	68	80.0	.193*
Child development	63	66.3	.290**	66	77.6	.306**
Handle frustration	54	56.8	.255**	50	58.8	.269**
Time out	50	52.6		41	48.2	
Clinical services—Applied therapeutic and skill training						
RET techniques	62	65.3	.253**	58	68.2	.242**

[a] Total sample multiple-regression analysis for the goal *decrease anxiety/worry/fear* included the variables *anxiety management*, *RET techniques*, *child development*, *offer support/understanding*, *average direct hours per quarter last three quarters* (negative loading); multiple $R = .569$, adjusted $R^2 = .294$. Washington subgroup only, multiple-regression analysis for the goal *decrease anxiety/worry/fear* included the variables *anxiety management*, *RET techniques*, *child development*, *offer support/understanding*, *average direct hours per quarter last three quarters* (negative loading); multiple $R = .560$, adjusted $R^2 = .281$.

[b] Services shown are those used in 50 percent or more of the cases where goal achievement equaled 3 or above, or that correlated significantly with the goal.

[c] Core service with utilization 5 percent or more above overall mean usage for that service (for total sample).

* $p < .05$.   ** $p < .01$.

Table 11.9. Service Relationships with Goal: Decrease Depression[a]

Service measures[b]	Total sample		Homebuilders Washington only	
	Service used for goal achievement of 3 or more (N = 71) No. (%)	Significant correlation with goal achievement (N = 106)	Service used for goal achievement of 3 or more (N = 59) No. (%)	Significant correlation with goal achievement (N = 89)
Concrete services				
All doing services	45 63.4		37 64.9	
All enabling services	48 67.6		39 68.4	
All concrete services	64 90.1		53 93.0	
Help get food	17 23.9	.323**	14 24.6	.396**
Provide food	16 22.5	.284**	13 22.8	.350**
Help obtain utility benefits	16 22.5	.207*	10 17.5	
Provide child care	14 19.7	.197*	11 19.3	
Help secure child care	11 15.5		8 14.0	.234**
Provide clothing	3 4.2	.212*	2 3.5	.291**
Clinical services—Summated scales/indices				
Develop treatment relationship	69 97.2		55 96.5	
Modify problem behaviors	68 95.8		54 94.7	
Manage depression/stress	67 94.4		55 96.5	
Improve parent effectiveness	67 94.4		55 96.5	
Solve problems/reduce conflict	66 93.0	.203*	52 91.2	
Make referrals/advocacy	64 90.1		50 87.7	
Rational-emotive therapy	51 71.8		42 73.7	

Clinical services—Applied therapeutic						
Clarify problem behaviors[c]	61	85.9		47	82.5	.285**
Relationship building	58	81.7	.293**	46	80.7	.263**
Provide literature	57	80.3	.249**	47	82.5	
Consultation with other service[c]	57	80.3		43	75.4	
Depression management	54	76.1		43	75.4	
Pleasant events	45	63.4		38	66.7	
Building hope	39	54.9	.233*	29	50.9	
Use of crisis card	39	54.9		30	52.6	
Refer to social service	39	54.9		31	54.4	
Refer to other counseling	39	54.9		30	52.6	
Behavior rehearsal/role play	34	47.9	.206*	26	45.6	
Provide paper/pencil tests	24	33.8	.223*	15	26.3	
Clinical services—Skill training						
Self-criticism reduction	41	57.7		29	50.9	
Negotiation skills	36	50.7	.204*	24	42.1	
Accepting no	26	36.6		19	33.3	
Clinical services—Applied therapeutic and skill training						
Build self-esteem[c]	56	78.9		45	78.9	
Problem-solving	36	50.7	.209*	25	43.9	
Teach use of leisure	35	49.3		30	52.6	

[a] Total sample multiple-regression analysis for the goal *decrease depression* included the variables *solve problems/reduce conflict, total concrete services, average direct services hours per quarter last three quarters* (negative loading); multiple R = .554, adjusted R² = .285. Washington subgroup only; multiple-regression analysis for the goal *decrease depression* included the variables *solve problems/reduce conflict, total concrete services, average direct services hours per quarter last three quarters* (negative loading), *develop treatment relationship*; multiple R = .607, adjusted R² = .339.

[b] Services shown are those used in 50% or more of the cases where goal achievement equaled 3 or above, or that correlated significantly with the goal.

[c] Core service with utilization 5% or more above overall mean usage for that service (for total sample).

* p < .05. ** p < .01.

availability, while the latter typically involved providing topical problem-focused handouts for home study.

Core services used at a selectively higher rate were *clarify problem behaviors, build self-esteem,* and *consultation with other service.* Noncore services used for more than half of decrease depression subjects with high goal attainment ratings were depression management, pleasant events, self-criticism reduction, use of crisis card, refer to other counseling, refer to social service, problem solving, and negotiation skills. These services show therapist emphasis on helping clients learn specific techniques for altering moods, attention to self-esteem building, the involving of other agencies and experts in planning or treatment, and direct involvement in helping families solve problems.

The overall regression equation for predicting decreased depression had only three significant variables: the aggregate clinical scale *solve problems/reduce conflict,* the total time spent in providing concrete services, and *average direct client contact hours per quarter for the last three quarters.* The equation accounted for a moderate proportion (about 30%) of the variability associated with the goal.

Approaches that resolve current concerns, reduce stress, or provide needed resources were underscored by the regression analysis as useful interventions when depression was identified as a target for treatment. As in the case of reducing anxiety/worry/fear, the time dimension *average direct client contact hours per quarter for the last three quarters* was a strong negative correlate for successfully dealing with depression. Apparently depression, as identified by the IFPS therapists, was best handled when an unusually high level of continuing client involvement was not required. This finding also suggests that the source of depression (or mood difficulty) for these families may have been exogenous in that it could be addressed through brief problem-solving and concrete service interventions, with about 4–6 hours of client contact in the latter weeks of the treatment.

Summarizing the findings, use of techniques for depression management, building self-esteem, self-criticism reduction, plus attention to relationship building and careful problem diagnosis by IFPS therapists were associated with reported success in decreasing depression. Problem-solving and concrete services were also important correlates of the goal. Finally, workers made use of outside clinical resources, either for consultation or referral.

Washington Only. Findings for the Homebuilders Washington subsample were less definitive than the overall sample, in that fewer services were correlated significantly with goal achievement. The regression model for Washington was similar to the total sample equation, with addition of the summated clinical variable *develop treatment relationship.* The Washington model also had a slightly higher adjusted R^2.

Goal 9: Increase compliance with house rules (e.g., chores, smoking, bedtime, curfew, dating)

Shown in Table 11.10, concrete service measures were not important correlates of achieving the *increase compliance with house rules* goal. Two summated clinical measures, *modify problem behaviors* and *solve problems/reduce conflict*, were important. *Modify problem behaviors* is a summation of eight clinical variables emphasizing the teaching and implementing of behavior tracking and reinforcement, environmental controls, natural and logical consequences, and building structure. *Solve problems/reduce conflict* is comprised of 13 variables, which attempt to reduce extrafamilial stress and interpersonal conflict within the family through teaching specific techniques to family members and by direct counseling and intervention around family problems.

Nine specific interventions were also correlated with the goal. Specific interventions most strongly associated with goal achievement were *use of reinforcement* (teaching parents the techniques), *handle frustration*, and *anxiety management*. Other significant correlates also were largely concerned with helping parents with child management and providing more structure in their homes.

Core services used at a higher than average rate were *monitoring clients, clarify family rules, use of reinforcement, natural/logical consequences*, and *improve compliance*. The only noncore services used at 50% or greater rate were *problem ownership* and *refer to other counseling*. These services point to the importance of helping families improve the structure in their home through the definition of rules and effective use of behavioral reinforcers. Also of value is helping individuals to take more responsibility for self-management. For the specific services above, those that involve the direct application of clinical techniques and those that promote increased skills on the part of subjects were about equally represented.

The overall regression model for the goal *increase compliance with house rules* contained five measures, including two summated clinical scales, two additional specific clinical activity variables, and one measure of service time. The equation accounted for only about one-seventh of the variance associated with achievement of this goal. The strongest positive correlate in this equation was the measure *modify problem behaviors*. Two other clinical variables, *anxiety and confusion management* and *handling frustration*, also were important, suggesting that therapist concern for client feelings was needed to motivate or assist clients to implement these child management procedures.

A second summated clinical measure, *make referrals/advocacy*, influenced the goal of household rule compliance negatively. This finding may suggest that in certain cases, the problem situation may have been

Table 11.10. Service Relationships with Goal: Increase Compliance with House Rules[a]

Service measures[b]	Total sample		Homebuilders Washington only	
	Service used for goal achievement of 3 or more (N = 218) No. (%)	Significant correlation with goal achievement (N = 289)	Service used for goal achievement of 3 or more (N = 172) No. (%)	Significant correlation with goal achievement (N = 229)
Concrete services				
All concrete services	169 77.5		135 78.5	
Clinical services—Summated scale/index				
Solve problems/reduce conflict	215 98.6	.127*	169 98.3	.212**
Develop treatment relationship	216 99.1		170 98.8	
Manage depression/stress	201 92.2		160 93.0	
Modify problem behaviors	216 99.1	.194*	170 98.8	.235**
Improve parent effectiveness	212 97.2		169 98.3	
Make referrals/advocacy	164 75.2		126 73.3	
Rational-emotive therapy	163 74.8		136 79.1	
Crisis intervention	140 64.2		112 65.1	

Clinical services—Applied therapeutic					
Monitoring clients[c]	160	73.4	.136*	124	72.1	
Clarify family rules[c]	156	71.6	.137*	121	70.3	.130*
Track/chart behaviors	134	61.5	.157*	113	65.7	.181**
Refer to other counseling	112	51.4		92	53.5	
Anxiety management	47	21.6	.176**	36	20.9	.192*
Clinical services—Skill training						
Use of reinforcement[c]	192	88.1	.230**	155	90.1	.248**
Natural/logical consequences[c]	178	81.7	.166*	141	82.0	.172*
Handle frustration	116	53.2	.199**	87	50.6	.254**
Problem ownership	111	50.9		79	45.9	
Clinical services—Applied therapeutic and skill training						
Improve compliance[c]	165	75.7	.144*	131	76.2	
Problem-solving	104	47.7	.120*	77	44.8	

[a] Total sample multiple-regression analysis for the goal *increase compliance with house rules* included the variables *anxiety management, handle frustration, behavior modification, make referrals/advocacy* (negative loading), *percent direct service hours first quarter* (negative loading); multiple $R = .402$, adjusted $R^2 = .146$. Washington subgroup only, multiple-regression analysis for the goal *increase compliance with house rules* included the variables *anxiety management, handle frustration, behavior modification, make referrals/advocacy* (negative loading), multiple $R = .370$, adjusted $R^2 = .122$.

[b] Services shown are those used in 50% or more of the cases where goal achievement equaled 3 or above, or that correlated significantly with the goal.

[c] Core service with utilization 5% or more above overall mean usage for that service (for total sample).

263

beyond the therapist's skill level or personal resources, as evidenced by referrals to other treatment providers. Or it may be that certain situations warranting outside referral involved greater problem severity and were less amenable to IFPS treatment.

One measure of service time, *percentage of direct client contact hours in the first quarter*, was also a negative correlate of increased rule compliance. Thus, it would appear that services to influence compliance with house rules are less effective when delivered in a crisis mode or not continued at a high level over the entire course of treatment.

In summary, the most common interventions associated with success for the goal *increase compliance with house rules* dealt directly with the management of problem behaviors. These activities included behavior tracking, improving environmental controls and structure in the home, implementing reinforcement techniques, and the use of natural and logical consequences for behavior difficulties. Therapists used both direct therapeutic and skills-training approaches to deal with problem behaviors. In addition to behavior management strategies, direct problem-solving was useful. Finally, attention to client anxiety and frustrations appeared to strengthen the achievement of increased rule compliance.

Washington Only. Service correlates of *increase compliance with house rules* for Washington corresponded closely to those for the overall sample, but were slightly fewer in number. The regression model for the Washington Homebuilders subset lost one variable from the total sample model and accounted for slightly less variance.

Discussion

Service Predictors of Goal Achievement

A large variety of clinical and concrete service techniques were associated with or contributed significantly to the achievement of IFPS treatment goals. These associated measures were identified in several ways: (1) correlation of services with achievement of the various goals; (2) usage of services in the case of subjects where achievement of specific goals was rated at least partly attained, identifying for each goal the core services used at higher than typical rates and the noncore services used for a majority of subjects; and (3) service-related regression models for each goal.

A set of core IFPS was identified. Services were categorized as core techniques when they were used extensively across the full range of treatment goals. The most common services in this grouping were relationship building and supportive activities consistent with Rogerian theory. The next most common set of interventions included among the "core" services were behaviorally oriented, concerned with family communication, parent skill training, and the establishment of behavior monitoring and structure in client families. Other important specific interventions that were used for a major proportion of clients included teaching age-appropriate behaviors and helping build client self-esteem. One concrete service, providing transportation, was used the majority of time in connection with all major goals, with additional types of concrete interventions present in the majority of cases.

Major service clusters for each of the treatment goals are summarized below:

Building Client-Therapist Relationships. For the goal *establish trust and functional working relationships,* a wide variety of Rogerian, behavioral, and concrete interventions support the development. Techniques that might logically be employed to develop therapeutic relationships, such as empathetic listening and supportive responses, were, in fact, associated with goal achievement. However, many of the trust-building activities focused on improving household conditions and client capabilities, as opposed to being aimed at building relationships. Of note is the importance for trust-building of helping clients meet basic financial needs.

Training in Communications. Skills-training approaches appeared to be central for achieving the goal *increase communication skills.* The content of such training included a focus on listening skills, the use of "I" statements, anger management, and family problem-solving techniques. Direct problem-solving with the family also supported this goal achievement.

Training in Parenting and Child Management. Interventions associated with the goal *increase parenting skills* were largely behaviorally oriented, with emphasis upon training parents in behavior management skills, and to a lesser degree teaching communication skills. Some direct applications of behavior management techniques were also correlated with this goal, as were supportive and anxiety reducing activities.

Training in Anger Management and Conflict Resolution. A number of strategies were associated with the attainment of the goal *improve anger management and conflict resolution skills.* Skills-training approaches include problem-solving, reduction of frustration and fighting, communication, and child management. Applied therapeutic interventions focus on establishing treatment directions, building relationships, helping families establish rules and structure, and establishing a supportive base for learning and change to occur.

Strategies Related to Truancy and School Performance. IFPS interventions important for *improve school performance* goal achievement included the development of structure and routine in the home, particularly the management of time; working with parents to establish reinforcers for school attendance and performance; taking steps to protect a child from sexual abuse; helping the family (or child) build hope, deal with depression, and improve self-esteem; acquire needed medical or dental treatment for the child; and use of collaborative efforts or advocacy with other resources.

Esteem-Building. Achieving the goal *increase self-esteem* was most highly correlated with problem-solving activities. Interventions specifically designed to increase self-esteem were important. Careful assessment and planning, and developing a good therapist-client relationships also were associated with goal success. Therapists tended to refer to outside counseling resources at a higher rate to achieve this goal than for most other goals. Specific treatment approaches to teach assertiveness and anxiety or anger management were also related to successful esteem-building. The overall provision of concrete services was important and therapists were more successful in building self-esteem of clients (parents and children) when they provided physical resources and new outlets for recreation and learning.

Strategies to Reduce Anxiety, Worry, and Fear. The strongest correlates with the goal *decrease anxiety, worry, or fear* were supportive and relationship-building techniques. Other important interventions involved providing knowledge of child development, helping clients with self-management through rational-emotive therapy and through teaching the use of such techniques as positive self-talk and relaxation.

Strategies Related to Depression. Depression management, self-esteem building, self-criticism reduction, relationship building, and careful problem assessment by IFPS therapists were associated with reported success for cases with the goal *decrease depression*. Problem-solving activities and concrete services were also important correlates of the goal. Finally, therapists reported extensive contact with outside clinical resources for consultation and referral.

Strategies Related to Oppositional Behavior in the Home. The most common interventions associated with success for the goal *increase compliance with house rules* dealt directly with the management of problem behaviors. These activities included tracking behaviors, improving environmental controls and structure in the home, implementing reinforcement techniques, and teaching parents the use of natural and logical consequences for behavior difficulties. Therapists used both direct therapeutic and skills-training approaches to deal with problem behaviors. In addition to behavior management strategies, direct problem-solving was useful. Finally, attention to client anxiety and frustrations appeared to strengthen the achievement of increased rule compliance.

The Central Elements of Treatment: Behavioral Strategies
in the Context of Concrete and Clinical Services

These findings provide clues to the elements of success in the Home-builders IFPS model. From the perspective of services that are salient in producing goal achievement, the Homebuilders model appears to be a synthesis of three major treatment or practice approaches. First, the model is grounded in Rogerian theory and practice (Pray, 1991; Rogers, 1961). The use of "soft" clinical skills, aimed at forming working attachments with clients and setting treatment expectations, is a constant thread running through every therapist's endeavors. These activities have a primary intent to establish treatment relationships, but they also function as supports to promote client cooperation and utilization of specific treatment regimes. Reciprocal connections were also found between relationship development and the use of behaviorally oriented skill-building and concrete services. Concrete services, particularly, appear to be used to enhance trust and solidify working relationships with clients.

Behavioral interventions constitute a second theoretical base for IFPS success. Diverse approaches successfully incorporated into IFPS include training clients in mood and self-management skills to relieve anxiety, control anger, improve self-esteem, and lessen depression. Also, parenting training approaches are used to improve communication and child management skills. In addition, some activities appear to emphasize the didactic presentation of information to improve client understanding and performance. These include teaching stages of child development and providing literature to increase family capabilities. As a part of their treatment role, therapists also give assistance to parents to establish structure and reinforcers, or they may set up behavior-monitoring mechanisms directly.

As suggested above, a third critical component of the model is the use of concrete services. Transporting clients was ubiquitous across all goals, and other specific concrete services were associated with goal achievement in specific areas. Giving financial assistance was correlated with establishing trust, helping secure child care with increasing communication and parenting skills, providing recreational activities and arranging life skill classes with increasing anger management, obtaining medical services and toys or recreation equipment with improving school performance, providing recreational resources and arranging life skill classes with increasing self-esteem, and helping families get food, clothing, child care, and utility benefits with decreasing depression. These findings appear to confirm the extensive use and central role of concrete services in Homebuilders IFPS model success. Concrete services are used strategically both to stabilize families and to build treatment relationships.

The diverse combination of services encompassed within the Home-builders IFPS 'model is unusual, but has its parallels in developments in other or broader fields of practice. One such affinity is with the ecological systems model (Germain, 1977, 1979, 1981). This model views cases from the perspective of the systems involved in the interaction of people with their environments. These systems may include intrapersonal, family, social, cultural, organizational/community, and physical-environmental. Connections may also be drawn between the Homebuilders model and task-centered treatment (Fortune, 1985; Reid, 1985; Reid & Epstein, 1977; Tolson & Reid, 1981). Task-centered treatment is usually described as an eclectic model of practices which emphasizes short-term, structured, problem-solving approaches. Tolson's discussion of the need for a practice metamodel is also instructive (1988). A metamodel attempts to provide a structure to allow practitioners to have knowledge about a range of treatment models and to draw from them flexibility according to need. Similarly, Fischer (1978) has argued for a multi-method or eclectic model, where practitioners may draw from many sources to find techniques that are useful and of proven effectiveness. All of these developments have congruence with the Homebuilders IFPS model and provide a measure of theoretical support for such a broad and intensive approach to family problem-solving.

Summary of Homebuilders Washington Subsample Analyses

The Homebuilders program originated in Washington state and was a major source for training and technical assistance in the development of the Utah Family Preservation programs. Some reasons exist to suggest that some of the Washington programs may have delivered a more finely honed treatment, such as lower rates of staff turnover, more experienced supervision, and higher placement prevention rates. To view separately the Washington Homebuilders program, analyses were conducted on Washington cases alone.

For the Washington subsample, several regression models tended to have slightly higher R^2s and to include more variables. This implies that the Washington sites may have provided a slightly more internally coherent service. These findings are suggestive of the possible influence of a more stable (in terms of turnover) and experienced workforce in the Washington program. Caution must be exercised about this interpretation, however. Washington therapists were dealing with a slightly younger population of children at risk of placement compared to the Utah caseload and, in a separate analysis, the younger age-group provided equations that were better configured than models for adolescents (Lewis, 1990). Additionally, use of a smaller number of subjects tends to inflate R^2s.

What are the Implications for IFPS Therapists?

In this and earlier chapters we have presented a large amount of descriptive and correlational data about how services under the Homebuilders IFPS model relate in a variety of ways to successful goal achievement. Taken as a whole, this mass of data appears to demonstrate the richness, complexity, and intensity of the IFPS service approach.

So what practical conclusions can be drawn to benefit the work of IFPS therapists? As we have noted above, this model is an unusual interweave of services, including Rogerian approaches to building trust, use of learning theory and skill building, and concrete services. All major aspects of the model appear correlated with goal achievement. There was no suggestion in the findings that specific aspects of the model were insignificant or inconsequential. Thus, it would appear that an IFPS therapist may not dismiss or neglect any aspect of this model without risking the possibility of degrading service effectiveness.

In any treatment model, there is a tendency for therapists to develop personal preferences regarding the use of various techniques and strategies. The diversity of tools and interventions present in the Homebuilders approach may make it especially prone to "model drift." Yet, evidence compiled in this study suggests caution in dismissing any aspects of the model. Maintaining a high level of intensity in IFPS through very small caseloads is particularly important.

These findings strongly support the centrality of concrete services within the treatment model. While high professional status has not been traditionally accorded to persons who deliver concrete services, IFPS therapists should not underestimate the importance of including such approaches in their practice. Concrete services, combined with psychological interventions, should be utilized in treating the majority of families, as opposed to just being the treatment of choice for less severely disturbed families, or used as secondary services, or a set of interventions of last resort.

Likewise, skill building interventions were demonstrated to be an essential part of the IFPS therapist's treatment armamentarium and should be given equal credence with Rogerian techniques. As noted above, any attempts to delineate such services as less "professional" should be avoided. Alternatively, therapists would seem well-advised to undertake the effort to gain mastery in the use of a range of specific skill-building tools including those which assist individuals to achieve greater emotional and behavioral self-management, to improve social skills, to attain better understandings of child development needs, and to improve skills in communication, problem-solving, and child management.

In many cases, practitioners may need to look beyond the boundaries of intervention theories presented in their professional education to grasp the scope of IFPS, although as we have noted above, there are some developing practice models with which the Homebuilders approach has affinity. IFPS therapists need to be willing to incorporate a broad range of techniques drawn from a variety of sources into their system of practice. IFPS staff must be flexible and open to continuing education.

What Are the Implications for IFPS Supervisors and Trainers?

These findings suggest certain areas of emphasis on the part of persons in direct support of IFPS, particularly IFPS supervisors and trainers. First, the range of interventions in the Homebuilders model suggests that a supervisor must have a broad understanding of techniques within the model, but more than that, he or she should encourage broad usage of these interventions by therapists. Overall understanding of the treatment model and its techniques on the part of supervisors is important in avoiding unplanned, unintended changes in the nature of services.

Second, because workers must attain mastery of the use of a variety of skill building and instructional techniques, worker training and skill-building is important. Since the IFPS therapists do not typically work standard five-days-a-week daytime shifts, and since almost all the work is performed away from the office, conventional methods of training and supervision must be reconsidered. Supervisors must plan to be in the field at least a portion of the time. Much of the training opportunity is best obtained by joining therapists in their in-home contacts with families. In addition, because of the level of stress on therapists brought about by the demands of the work schedule, plus type of clientele and service delivery model, a culture of positive peer support must be developed. Supervisors can encourage the development of positive support by co-workers through such things as weekly case staffing by peers and regular group discussion of stressors experienced in the work.

Additionally, as identified in Chapter 10, cultural competence may be an important issue for supervisors. Supervisors must assist workers to see their practice in the context of the cultures of the families they serve. Both problems and problem amelioration are strongly influenced by ethnicity and poverty, and workers must be skillful in engaging families from a variety of backgrounds.

One important implication of these findings for persons in IFPS staff training roles is the need to develop libraries of skill training tools (videos, audio tapes, written materials, approaches, techniques, lesson plans, etc.) and to make sure workers are comfortable with their use. This latter issue implies that trainers go beyond an informational approach in presenting such tools. Rather, a mastery approach seems advisable, in which the use of resource materials becomes "second-nature" to practitioners.

Finally, this chapter might be used as a conceptual tool for training, to communicate the scope of the delivery model. At first, many workers tend to underestimate the complexity of the IFPS treatment model. The findings provide important clues on how to conceptualize the Homebuilders approach.

Conclusion

In this chapter, we examined the relationship between the provision of specific services and treatment goal achievement. Models were developed encompassing service variables predictive of goal attainment for the entire sample of children and for Homebuilder's cases in Washington state. Core or cross-cutting services that appear to be fundamental to IFPS practice were identified. Then across nine treatment goals, services predictive of specific outcomes were identified. Concrete services played an important role in IFPS goal attainment, including establishing trust, increasing communication and parenting skills, anger management, improving school performance, increasing self-esteem, and decreasing depression. An even larger group of clinical techniques, including both direct clinical interventions and behaviorally focused educational approaches, was instrumental in achieving service goals.

Notes

1. See Lewis (1990) for further subsample regression analyses (age, gender, referral source).
2. The proportion of variance accounted for by the regression models for the several goals was modest at best. Methodological reasons may exist for the moderate R^2s. First, EHA results, reported in Chapter 10, clearly demonstrate that client characteristics and situations are important predictors of IFPS success. In this chapter, we only focused upon service-related correlates of achievement of specific treatment goals. By restricting the type of variables eligible for inclusion in the regression models, the proportion of variance may have been constrained. Models with social and demographic variables could have been developed, but our interest here was primarily in the kind of services that were predictive of goal attainment. Second, methodological limitations may have tended to confound distinctions and to result in reduced explanatory power in the data. Services and goals were tied to families rather than children (the unit of analysis for this chapter) and this may have introduced measurement error that depressed the R^2s.

Chapter 12

How Consumers View Intensive Family Preservation Services

PETER J. PECORA, JEFFREY A. BARTLOME, VICKY L. MAGANA,
and CONNIE K. SPERRY

Previous chapters have presented findings related to a variety of client
outcomes and levels of functioning. These findings were obtained largely
through therapists' paper-and-pencil ratings of parent, child, and family
functioning, as well as through caretakers' ratings of family problems, conditions, and social support. Building on data collected directly from parents,
this chapter will focus on the results of interviews with primary caretakers
who were asked to evaluate IFPS. These data will be presented following a
brief review of consumer satisfaction research and a summary of the interview procedures.

Involving Consumers in Evaluation Studies of Social Services: A Brief Review

Rapp and Poertner (1987) recently argued that the central challenge facing
human service managers today is "moving clients to center stage." This
involves adopting a client-centered philosophy and renewed attention to two
aspects of service delivery—process and outcome:

> There are two major elements in what we are referring to as client centered-
> ness. The first focuses attention on the "process" of service provision—the
> degree to which the practice and the behavior of personnel, and the organiza-
> tional structures and operating processes reflect a preoccupation with clients
> and their well being. It includes having the client treated with the highest
> degree of dignity, respect, and individuality. It involves the design and imple-
> mentation of intake procedures, service accessibility, courtesy of receptionists,
> provisions for client input into individual case and programmatic decisions,
> flexibility to tailor services to individual client needs and desires, etc. The list
> can be extended tenfold.
> The second element of client centeredness is the organizational focus on

service effectiveness, client outcomes, [and] results. While the terms vary by author, the central notion is that the centerpiece of agency performance is the benefits accrued by clients as a result of our efforts. (Rapp & Poertner, 1987, p. 23)

Obtaining the client's perspective in assessing service effectiveness has been emphasized by a number of program evaluation experts in child welfare and other fields (see for example, Ellsworth, 1975; Hargreaves & Attkisson, 1978; Magura & Moses, 1984; Maluccio, 1979a,b; Millar & Millar, 1981). These and other researchers have highlighted a number of benefits associated with consumer evaluation data: (1) client empowerment is modeled; (2) attainment of organizational goals is increased through improved organization-client relations; (3) client observations and recommendations may identify areas for improvement and solutions that other evaluation methods did not discover, in effect broadening the range of measures that are used to quantify "agency effectiveness;" and (4) clients bring an outside perspective to the evaluation process compared to using only worker-generated data (Giordano, 1977, pp. 34–35).

There are a variety of ways to include consumers in program evaluation, including assessing their satisfaction with services, as well as obtaining client self-reports of change as a result of services. Previous studies of client or consumer satisfaction have concentrated on assessing general levels of satisfaction and overall quality of life. Recently, social scientists have highlighted client satisfaction as an additional method of determining agency effectiveness (Gutek, 1978). For example, a major focus of Katz, Gutek, Kahn, and Barton's (1975) survey of 1431 Americans was their satisfaction with seven different helping agencies. They found that accessibility of services was strongly related to citizens' satisfaction with the outcome of services.

Moch (1975, as cited in Gutek, 1978) studied several social security offices and found high consumer satisfaction with the services of these offices. Seventy-two percent of respondents reported satisfaction with the outcome of their last visit to the office. Ninety-three percent said they were satisfied with how they were treated during their last visit. Gerber, Brenner, and Litwin (1986) found that of a sample size of 96, 80% of social service clients and their families rated staff positively in helpfulness, and more than 75% noted improvement in 13 identified problem resolution areas. Services effectiveness was particularly apparent in illness counseling, in a range of concrete services, and in the provision of follow-up care.

Using a social problem classification system for social health care evaluation that had been developed and validated previously (Berkman, 1980; Rehr, 1989), the Mount Sinai Hospital Social Work Department evaluated its services. In making the evaluation, researchers considered both social worker and client perceptions of the social problems dealt with and the assessments of outcomes of intervention. Using the social problem contracts as the method of judging service outcome, the departmental study results indicated "substantial agreement between clients and social workers on the problems (N = 112) dealt with and the outcomes of intervention (91% [N = 102] and 86% [N = 96] agreement, respectively)" (Rehr & Berkman, 1979, p. 105). Positive outcomes—either resolved or improved as perceived by both client and therapist—were found in almost 80% (N = 90) of those problems contracted for by both parties (Rehr & Berkman, 1979).[1]

Traditionally, program evaluation studies in child welfare have not focused on client satisfaction or client reports of improvement. Part of the reason for this may be the problems associated with consumer recall and various types of response bias (Austin et al., 1982; Sudman & Bradburn, 1974). In fact, most program evaluators advise that consumer surveys be used primarily as sources of information for overall client satisfaction and program improvement. One example of this approach was an evaluation by the Child Welfare League of America of the Family Reception Center, a multiservice program designed to divert youth from the juvenile justice system and to avert out-of-home placement. Information from staff, clients, and the community suggested a high degree of satisfaction with the program and identified major service components that consumers felt made the program effective (Shyne, 1976).

Furthermore, with few exceptions, the viewpoints of children as consumers are rarely gathered. Yet some research studies in foster care have demonstrated how information gathered from children is essential for program planning. Barth and Berry reviewed a number of recent research studies regarding preferred permanency planning outcomes (reunification, adoption, guardianship, and long-term foster care). Studies of child satisfaction were included as part of their review, which concluded:

1. All but one of the children who returned home preferred their present home to their foster home.

2. Most children preferred their current setting compared to their previous setting, with satisfaction highly associated with the child's sense of permanence.

3. Children who had multiple placements and who sought a sense of belonging, preferred adoption.

4. Children living in institutions felt less comfortable, not as happy, less loved, less looked after, less trusted, and less cared about than did children in other forms of surrogate care or children reunified with their families.

5. Children who had some choice in their foster care placement were significantly more satisfied in their placements than were children with no choice (Barth & Berry, 1987).

Consumer-Focused Research in Family-Based Services

Recently, a few studies have attempted to address client satisfaction or views of service with FBS treatment. Hayes and Joseph (1985) attempted to determine client satisfaction through mail and telephone surveys. They found the majority of clients were positive about the service. Willems and DeRubeis (1981) studied clients' degree of understanding and therapist-client consistency regarding family problems, service plans, work roles, and case satisfaction. In-person interviews at case closure indicated that the experimental group had substantially more understanding and agreement in many areas compared to the control group (which had received more traditional types of child welfare services).

In a study by Haapala (1983), critical incidents were collected from 41 children, each child's mother, as well as the therapists working with these families during Homebuilders treatment (see also, Fraser & Haapala, 1988). Once a week each research participant was asked to identify especially helpful events that occurred during targeted sessions involving the therapist and one or more family member. As discussed in Chapter 3, the more time mothers reported incidents that were classified as "concrete services" or "interruptions and disruptions of the counseling session" the greater was the chance that the child targeted for placement remained at home. A similar procedure used for collecting data from the *child* in danger of placement for this same study revealed that higher frequency of child reports of "concrete services" offered or provided by the Homebuilders was significantly correlated with better service outcomes.

In another study, Kinney and Haapala (1984) requested that parents and therapists rate 34 problem areas at the end of IFPS. A high proportion (81.5%) of the problem areas were rated by the consumers and therapists as having improved. Another study conducted by the Child Welfare League of America focused on 11 different problem areas, and parents were asked to report the degree of change between the start and completion of HBS. A five-point scale was used with two scale anchors: 1, a lot better; and 5, a lot worse. The percentage of clients rating various problem areas as "a lot better" ranged from a low of 15% for children's symptomatic behavior to 36% for school adjustment and 60% for sexual abuse (Magura & Moses, 1984, p. 103).

The reason why data related to client satisfaction or self-reports of improvement have not been included in more evaluations of FBS is, in part, explained by the fact that the field is so young. Many FBS administrators have focused all their energies on implementing and maintaining their programs. Thus the few FBS agencies that are gathering client satisfaction data generally use it only to gauge consumer satisfaction rather than as a formal means of program evaluation.

In addition, there are a variety of difficulties associated with assessing consumer viewpoints of services received. In contrast to the above studies, most consumer outcome research has used global measures of client satisfaction instead of problem-specific questions or behaviorally anchored scales. Interpreting satisfaction scores is also difficult because of an absence of normative data (Hargreaves & Attkisson, 1978) and a general distrust of satisfaction measures (Miller & Pruger, 1978). More specifically, there are a variety of methodological limitations associated with consumer satisfaction and outcome research, including:

1. People seem satisfied with everything they are asked about.
2. Clients do not show high levels of dissatisfaction in areas where it is "common knowledge" that people are dissatisfied (e.g., 61% of respondents reported satisfaction with public assistance offices). Thus in some service arenas, some clients may not respond honestly for fear that future services may be withheld or sanctions of some kind (e.g., child placement, restricted child visitation) may be imposed.
3. There exists a discrepancy between the evaluation of one's own experience and the evaluation of a program in general (Gutek, 1978).
4. The pre-existing negative attitudes that people hold about an organization or program may contrast greatly with the actual results of service, resulting in inflated satisfaction ratings—a "contrast effect" (Katz et al., 1975, as cited in Gutek, 1978).
5. Distinctions are rarely drawn between whether clients like, relate to, or trust certain groups of professionals, and whether those professionals are effective in treating or helping their clients (Giordano, 1977, p. 36).
6. Evaluation studies rarely take into account the influence of the organization (e.g., coercive power), client backgrounds, and other "intervening variables" upon client responses (Giordano, 1977).

One recommendation for improving satisfaction studies involves using a combination of more specific satisfaction measures instead of one subjective or global question. However, studies of job satisfaction using this approach have found that specifying various facets of satisfaction account for only about 50% of the variance in global satisfaction (Gutek, 1978). Yet the use of more specific measures may provide more information about determinants of consumer satisfaction.

Developing more objective outcome measures that focus on specific areas of child, parent, or family functioning may also improve satisfaction outcome studies. In addition, approaches that attempt to incorporate the client's opinion about quality of service or their "cognitive meaning" of satisfaction appear worthwhile. These approaches take into account how consumers conceptualize satisfaction, and use a variety of questions to take into account the dynamics involved in interviewing consumers (e.g., clients may or may not identify suggestions for improvement, people rate satisfaction in comparison to what they or others they know have experienced, "happiness" or "contentment" with a service is viewed as being different than "satisfaction") (Gutek, 1978).

We attempted to address some of the methodological limitations associated with client satisfaction research by interviewing primary caretakers about a range of specific aspects of the services that they had received. In assessing client self-reports of change, both global and specific problem inventories were used (these data were reported in Chapter 8). The next sections of this chapter will summarize the data-gathering procedures and findings of the consumer satisfaction interviews.

Method

Subjects and Data Collection Procedures

Primary caretakers for each of the families that participated in the study were interviewed by telephone or in person by a research assistant or site coordinator within two weeks after IFPS were completed. The primary caretaker for each family received a letter explaining the purpose of the "consumer outcome" interview and a checklist of problem areas (two pages of the interview schedule that contained the problem checklist were copied and sent to each person) to assist them in responding to the interview. Interviews required 30–45 minutes to complete.

Primary caretakers of 290 families in Washington and 106 families in Utah were interviewed (total sample, 396). Thus consumer outcome and satisfaction data were collected for 87% (396/453) of the families who participated in the FIT study.

Instrument

The Consumer Satisfaction Survey focused on the type of services received and the client's perception of the relative value of different elements of HBS. The instrument was based upon a form that BSI's Homebuilders program has been using since about 1977 (see Chapter 4). More specifically, the interviews focused on what clients thought were the most important treatment goals, what was most helpful about the service, comparisons of family functioning between now and before services were provided, as well as satisfaction with specific aspects of the therapist's behavior and the service itself.[2] A mix of close- and open-ended questions were incorporated into the instruments. A multistage content analysis involving two groups of project staff was used to identify common response categories for each of the open-ended questions.

Study Limitations

One of the limitations of this aspect of the study is that children and secondary caretakers were not interviewed regarding consumer satisfaction. Secondary caretakers, however, were interviewed if the child was placed, and these data are reported in the placement outcomes chapter (Chapter 9). The response biases of social desirability and partial recall should not be underestimated when examining these types of data. As suggested in the literature review section of this chapter, there is a tendency for clients in many treatment settings to increase their ratings of satisfaction because of social desirability. In addition, because of their gratitude to the therapist, parents may report greater amounts of improvement compared to what actually has occurred. Assessing the extent to which the social desirability bias affected the accuracy of the client ratings of change is difficult. But as mentioned by Magura and Moses (1986, p. 240), "one indication of the clients' general truthfulness is simply their observed willingness to admit to problems." As was discussed in Chapter 8, caretakers did state that some problem areas were still present; and some problem areas were rated as serious, despite the provision of IFPS.

Regarding partial recall, clients may have difficulty in stating specifically what goals were set and what aspects of service or therapist behaviors were most helpful. Separating memory limitations from poorly articulated case goals and methods is a challenge in general, but it should (in theory) be reduced in FIT because of the use of a collaborative goal-setting procedure in which clients and therapists used the Goal Checklist to designate service objectives.

Findings

Primary Caretaker Reports of Treatment Goals and Degree of Attainment

Primary caretakers in each family were asked to identify the treatment goals they were working on with the IFPS therapist. Unexpectedly, less than 62% of the respondents from both states were able to identify a treatment goal in response to this open-ended question. This may be due to problems in the interview schedule or to the lack of "probe" or follow-up questions. More respondents would have likely identified at least one goal if a sample list of goals were available to them. So these findings must be viewed with caution. Of interest is the variety of treatment goals identified by primary caretakers; for the total sample, only one goal was reported by over 10% of the respondents.

The goals related to *increasing communication skills, improving the child's behavior,* and *increasing compliance with house rules* were identified by the highest proportion of respondents. These treatment goals were also reported by a high proportion of respondents when the data were analyzed by state, with the exception of Washington, where *increasing anger management and conflict resolution skills* was ranked second (see Table 12.1).

While the treatment goal of anger management/conflict resolution skills was rated second among Washington respondents, both *improving child's behavior* and *increasing compliance with house rules* were rated second among Utah respondents. Project participants in both states seemed to identify goals that centered on helping parents improve their communication skills and parenting of their children. Communication skills included such things as reflective and active listening, use of "I" statements, learning to express feelings, developing competency in stating one's own needs/wants to other family members, talking to one another more openly, and clarifying messages.

Primary caretakers generally perceived the degree of goal achievement as positive. The goals were rated according to degree of accomplishment using a 5-point scale with two scale anchors: 1 not at all; 5, greatly. Improving family relationships (3.9), improving the child's behavior (3.6), and increasing anger management skills (3.5) were all rated high in goal accomplishment. Utah and Washington goal achievement ratings varied, but the number of cases in each state was generally small (see Table 12.1).

Parent Satisfaction with the Location of Target Children at Case Termination

One of the most important treatment goals of IFPS is to prevent unnecessary out-of-home placements or runaway behavior. Therefore, as part of the client satisfaction interviews, data were obtained regarding the desirability of the child's current location from the primary caretaker's perspective.

The interviewers asked primary caretakers if they thought that having the target child(ren) living at home at case termination was best for the family. A higher percentage of respondents (89.1%) were satisfied with target child(ren) living at home although there were differences between the Washington and Utah sites. Approximately 10% more primary caretakers in Washington (91.8%) were satisfied with target child(ren) living at home than primary caretakers living in Utah (81.7%).

While a high proportion of primary caretakers felt their family was better served with the child in the home, how did primary caretakers perceive the case situation if their child was *not* living at home? Among the small number ($N = 39$) of families who had target children living outside the home at the time of case termination and who were interviewed, 29 (74.4%) felt that having the child *not* living at home was best for their families. Given placement then, the majority of primary caretakers were satisfied with case outcomes.

Table 12.1. Most Frequently Reported Treatment Goals and Degree of Accomplishment Reported by Primary Caretaker[a]

Treatment goal	Utah			Washington			Total sample		
	N	Respondents reporting goal (%) (N = 102)	Degree of accomplishment M (SD)	N	Respondents reporting goal (%) (N = 230)	Degree of accomplishment M (SD)	N	Respondents reporting goal (%) (N = 332)	Degree of accomplishment M (SD)
A. Increase communication skills	15	14.7	2.87 (1.51)	35	15.2	3.67 (1.09)	50	14.8	3.46 (1.14)
B. Improve child's behavior	12	11.8	3.75 (1.22)	21	9.1	3.46 (1.14)	33	9.9	3.56 (1.16)
C. Increase compliance with house rules	12	11.8	2.58 (1.24)	19	8.3	3.40 (1.16)	31	9.3	3.10 (1.23)
D. Increase anger management/ conflict resolution skills	7	6.9	2.71 (1.38)	23	10.0	3.67 (1.16)	30	9.0	3.50 (1.24)
E. Improve school performance and/or attendance	7	6.9	2.25 (1.75)	20	8.7	3.50 (1.34)	27	8.1	3.12 (1.56)
F. Improve family relationships (help family get along better)	10	9.8	3.80 (.80)	14	6.1	4.00 (1.35)	24	7.2	3.91 (1.12)

[a] Degree of accomplishment was measured on a five-point scale with the following scale anchors: 1, not at all; 5, greatly.

Consumers who reported one or more target children *not* living at home when termination occurred were also asked where they would prefer to see their child living. Utah respondents ranked "residential treatment" and "other" as the two most preferred locations for their children. Washington respondents ranked "relatives" as their top choice with both "in-home" and "foster care" ranked second. Reasons for differences between the two sites in regards to placement preference may be indicative of differences in problem severity, treatment outcome, and resource availability (e.g., a number of additional private inpatient hospital programs for adolescents were started towards the end of the FIT project in Utah, with a significant increase in the number of advertisements promoting inpatient hospitalization as a treatment method). Consumer awareness of community resources may also be a factor in explaining the variance in preferred placements.

In summary, the primary caretakers reported generally high rates of goal achievement and satisfaction with the location of their child at case termination, even if the child was not living at home. The next sections will present the perceptions of primary caretakers regarding satisfaction with various aspects of the IFPS therapist and services. These findings may help to explain the mix of generally positive findings noted above.

General and Specific Satisfaction with IFPS Therapists

When asked about how they and their therapist "got along," respondents indicated high satisfaction with IFPS therapists in both Utah ($M = 1.5$, SD $= 1.3$) and Washington ($M = 1.2$, SD $= 0.6$), when satisfaction was rated on a five-point scale with 1 as "very satisfied" and 5 as "very dissatisfied." The consumer satisfaction rating for the total sample was 1.3 (SD $= 0.8$). Differences between the two states were not significant, but there was much greater variation among the respondents in Utah.

Therapist performance in various areas was also rated by the primary caretaker according to how often certain descriptive statements applied to their therapist. Specific aspects rated were:

• Therapist scheduled appointments for times that were convenient.
• Therapist explained what he/she was doing and why.
• Therapist listened and understood the client's situation.
• Therapist was available when needed.
• Client felt the therapist cared about her/him as a person.
• Client felt the therapist cared about the family.
• Client felt that the therapist could be relied upon when the client had a problem.
• The client felt that the therapist was organized and knew what she/he was doing.

The IFPS therapists in both states received high ratings, indicating that primary caretakers perceived their workers as frequently fitting the characteristics outlined above. When *t*-tests were conducted, levels of satisfaction for the Washington sites were significantly higher in all but one area, scheduling appointments at times convenient for the clients (see Table 12.2). But worker ratings for each state were 4.3 or higher when measured on a five-point scale, indicating a high degree of satisfaction.

General and Specific Satisfaction with IFPS

Primary caretakers also rated the degree of helpfulness of the counseling and other services that they received on a five-point scale with the following scale anchors: 1, least helpful; 5, extremely helpful. The services provided by the Utah therapists (M = 3.9, SD = 1.3) and the Washington therapists (M = 4.6, SD = 0.8) were rated as very helpful; with Washington services being rated as significantly more helpful ($p < .001$). The average rating of helpfulness for the total sample rating was 4.4 (SD = 1.0).

Two major program components of the service were also rated positively: clients felt that it was important that the therapist went to their house for appointments; and clients valued the new skills and ways of doing things which they were taught (see Table 12.3). The responses to the first question provide evidence that when *consumers* are asked about services, they prefer the delivery of services in the home. With the Homebuilders model, both clients and therapists believe in the efficacy of in-home interventions, in contrast to some of the worker attitudes and program philosophies reported in other evaluation studies (e.g., Nelson et al., 1988).

While Washington participants indicated a higher level of satisfaction with the services than did the Utah participants on both general and specific aspects of services offered, a high percentage of respondents in both states "would recommend home-based service to a family in a similar situation":

- Utah: 93 or 93.9% of respondents
- Washington: 271 or 98.2% of respondents

Aspects of Service Reported as Most Helpful

Using an open-ended question format, primary caretakers were asked to identify what was "most helpful in your counseling with the therapist?" The answers to these questions were subjected to a content analysis by two project staff. The classifications were then reviewed by two of the principal investigators.

Table 12.2.   Primary Caretaker Ratings of IFPS Therapist Performance

Therapist performance areas[b]	Utah (N = 101) M (SD)	Washington (N = 285) M (SD)	Total sample[a] (N = 386) M (SD)
1. Did (therapist) schedule appointments for times that were convenient for you?	4.8 (0.6)	4.9 (0.5)	4.9 (0.5)
2. Did (therapist) explain to you what she/he was doing and why?	4.5 (1.0)	4.9 (0.5)	4.8 (0.7)***[c]
3. Do you think (therapist) listened to you and understood your situation?	4.4 (1.0)	4.8 (0.6)	4.7 (0.8)***
4. Do you feel that (therapist) cared about you as a person?	4.7 (0.7)	4.9 (0.5)	4.8 (0.5)*
5. Do you feel that (therapist) cared about your family?	4.7 (0.7)	4.9 (0.4)	4.8 (0.5)*
6. Was (therapist) available to you when you needed her/him?	4.4 (0.9)	4.9 (0.5)	4.7 (0.7)***
7. Did you have the feeling that you could depend or rely on (therapist) when you had a problem?	4.3 (1.1)	4.8 (0.6)	4.7 (0.8)***
8. Do you feel that (therapist) knew what she/he was doing, that she/he was organized?	4.4 (1.0)	4.7 (0.6)	4.6 (0.8)***

[a] Number of cases for individual performance areas may vary by 15%.
[b] Worker performance was rated on a five-point frequency scale with the following scale anchors: 1, never; 5, always.
[c] Differences between the two states were analyzed using the t-test.
*$p \leq .05$.   **$p \leq .01$.   ***$p \leq .001$.

Over 16 categories of responses were identified, with great variation in the number of respondents for each category. Because of the small numbers of cases for many categories, these findings may be unstable and should be viewed with caution. The category mentioned by the highest percentage (9.9%) of respondents was the therapist's ability to establish a rapport or working relationship between the child and therapist. Developing communications skills (8.1%), problem-solving (8.1%), and morale building/emotional support (8.1%) were also identified by many primary caretakers (see Table 12.4).

How can IFPS Be Improved?

Each primary caretaker was also asked to list the aspects of the service that "did not help, or that you disliked about the counseling?" A wide variety of

Table 12.3.   Primary Caretaker Ratings of the Importance of Certain
Aspects of IFPS

Program components[a]	Utah (N = 101) M (SD)	Washington (N = 284) M (SD)	Total (N = 385) M (SD)
1. Was it important that the therapist came to your house for appointments?	4.4 (1.0)	4.7 (0.7)	4.6 (0.8)*
2. How important are the new skills or new ways of doing things that the therapist taught you?	3.9 (1.2)	4.4 (0.9)[b]	4.3 (1.0)*

[a] Program components were rated on a five-point scale with the following scale anchors: 1, not at all important; 5, very important.
[b] Number of valid cases for Washington sample for this question was 250.
*$p \leq .001$.

items were mentioned, with the response "nothing" mentioned by the highest percentage of respondents (59.5%). This finding lends support to the findings of generally high client satisfaction reported in the earlier sections. However, service refinements may be warranted, as one or more aspects of counseling were disliked by approximately 40% of the primary caretakers interviewed. The negative responses reported by a high percentage of primary caretakers were "the service was not long enough" (12.3%) and "parent disagreed with the worker's treatment techniques" (3.9%). With the exception of the criticism regarding length of service, it is surprising how few respondents identified service problems (see Table 12.5).

In order to serve families better in the future, primary and secondary caretakers, as well as IFPS therapists, were also asked what could be done to serve families better. These interviews were conducted at the time of the placement, and so responses are restricted to "failure" cases. This restriction and the small number of cases indicate that the findings should be viewed as preliminary. The most frequently reported response in each of the respondent groups was that "nothing" could be done better. The second most frequent response as for a longer service period. Primary and secondary caretakers identified the following improvements, listed in order of frequency of identification: greater therapists availability, more intensive therapy, more input from parents, more follow-up services, earlier intervention, and better prevention of runaway behavior.[3]

IFPS therapists identified "better screening" of families as the third highest response, followed by more follow-up services, being more available, provision of more intensive therapy, earlier intervention with families, and better prevention of runaway behavior. Thus even with relatively lower caseloads, both workers and parents felt that provision of more intensive

Table 12.4.   Aspects of IFPS Counseling That Were Reported by Primary
Caretakers as Most Helpful—Number and Percentage of
Respondents Reporting Items

Aspects of counseling	Utah (N = 99)		Washington (N = 234)		Total (N = 333)	
Therapist helped child to establish a rapport between therapist and child	16	(16.2)	17	(7.3)	33	(9.9)
Developing communication skills	9	(9.1)	18	(7.7)	27	(8.1)
Problem-solving	5	(5.1)	22	(9.4)	27	(8.1)
Morale building, emotional support, and showing a caring attitude	7	(7.1)	20	(8.5)	27	(8.1)
Use of behavioral charts and reward systems	5	(5.1)	20	(8.5)	25	(7.5)
Someone to talk to or express feelings to	6	(6.1)	16	(6.8)	22	(6.0)
Worker helped parent/family understand situation, self, and child	6	(6.1)	10	(4.3)	16	(4.8)
General parenting skills	3	(3.0)	12	(5.1)	15	(4.5)
Anger management and conflict resolution for parents or family	5	(5.1)	9	(3.8)	14	(4.2)
Therapist's availability and willingness to spend time with family	3	(3.0)	10	(4.3)	13	(3.9)
Therapist came to the home	3	(3.0)	10	(4.3)	13	(3.9)
Therapist listened	4	(4.0)	7	(3.0)	11	(3.3)
Mediation of family problems	3	(3.0)	8	(3.4)	11	(3.3)
Most or all aspects were helpful	1	(1.0)	7	(3.0)	8	(2.4)
Helped family get along better	4	(4.0)	3	(1.3)	7	(2.1)
Provision of concrete services	2	(2.0)	7	(3.0)	9	(2.7)

services earlier to families would have resulted in more effective services.
However, in all fairness to the IFPS therapists, it may be that these families
were referred to IFPS too late for the service to be useful.

Discussion

From the perspective of primary caretakers, the IFPS improved family
relationships, anger management, the child's behavior, and family communication skills. With the exception of some criticism regarding the length of
the intervention and types of treatment strategies used by the therapists, the
services were rated as very helpful. It may be that clients found the IFPS
program so responsive and convenient that they would have preferred con-

Table 12.5. Aspects of IFPS Reported by Primary Caretakers as Least Helpful—
Number and Percentage of Respondents Reporting Items

Aspects of counseling or service least helpful	Utah (N = 85)		Washington (N = 224)		Total (N = 309)	
Nothing	44	(51.8)	140	(62.5)	184	(59.5)
Service not long enough	8	(9.4)	30	(13.4)	38	(12.3)
Parent disagreed with or did not like therapist's treatment techniques (e.g., use of behavioral/reward systems with child)	2	(2.4)	10	(4.5)	12	(3.9)
Therapist was unable to improve or make a difference with family situation, especially the therapist's changing the child's behavior	4	(4.7)	5	(2.2)	9	(2.9)
Lack of confidence in the therapist's abilities or performance	4	(4.7)	3	(1.3)	7	(2.3)
Therapist did not spend enough time counseling the child	3	(3.5)	3	(1.3)	6	(1.9)
Parent felt too pressured or overwhelmed by the IFPS program and therapist	1	(1.2)	4	(1.8)	5	(1.6)

tinuing involvement with the IFPS therapist, even when the crisis had been resolved and more conventional services would be more appropriate. The services provided were even rated useful in the majority of cases when the child or children were placed, although this relationship was less strong in Utah. It could be, however, that parents were rationalizing a negative outcome. Nevertheless, it was surprising that so many primary caretakers stated that nothing else could have been done to prevent the child's placement.

Conclusion

This chapter presented the findings from interviews with primary caretakers of 396 of the families served by the IFPS units in Utah and Washington. In attempting to adhere to the recommendations of program evaluation experts, specific questions about consumer satisfaction with the therapist or aspects of the service were employed, along with items that rated family functioning in a number of discrete areas (see Chapter 8 for family functioning ratings). A variety of specific therapist behaviors and services were rated as helpful, many of which comprise the core of the IFPS programs in these and other states. In the next and final chapter of this report, we discuss the policy, service, and research implications of the eval-uation data in the context of recent developments in this field and other research studies.

Notes

1. For additional studies of consumer satisfaction in the social services, see Coul-ton & Solomon (1977), Ellsworth (1975), Hargreaves & Attkisson (1978), Magura & Moses (1984), Maluccio (1979a,b), Mayer and Timms (1970), Millar and Millar (1981), Perlman (1975), Rehr (1989), and Rehr & Berkman (1979).
2. See Fraser et al. (1989, Appendix I) for a copy of the Consumer Satisfaction Survey.
3. See Fraser et al. (1989, pp. 264–266) for more information.

Chapter 13

Implications for Practice, Policy, Research, and the Future

DAVID A. HAAPALA, PETER J. PECORA, and
MARK W. FRASER

This book has explored an intensive family therapy treatment model designed to help families in crisis. Earlier chapters have described the purpose and design of the FIT research project; discussed the characteristics of the clients, therapists, and the IFPS treatment model; reported on the apparent impact of these services in areas such as child compliance, parenting skills, and social support; and described out-of-home placement outcomes for target children who received IFPS treatment and for children from a matched case overflow comparison group who did not receive IFPS treatment.

The purpose of this chapter is to discuss the meaning of these research data. Of the hundreds of findings presented in the previous chapters, only a few of the project's results can be highlighted here. In this final chapter, we offer what we believe to be the most important and provocative results that we have discovered, provide some possible interpretations and implications of these results, and suggest some areas for further research.

Current Context for These Findings

Rapid IFPS Expansion

Here in North America, as well as abroad, local communities and states are increasingly setting aside money to finance the start-up and expansion of family-based, placement prevention services. IFPS, a distinct and specialized form of FBS, appears to be experiencing a surge of growth. At press time, 11 states alone had already begun approximately 125 new public or private IFPS programs.[1] About 400 social workers, counselors, and family therapists will staff these programs. On an annual basis, they will serve at least 7200 children targeted for immediate out-of-home placements from child welfare, child mental health, juvenile justice, and other programs.

University Faculty Expressing Greater Interest in FBS

With support from the Edna McConnell Clark Foundation, university professors in social work, psychology, counseling, child development, and other disciplines have begun periodic meetings to learn more about IFPS programs. These meetings involve discussions concerning the merits of various family-based programs, evaluations of current IFPS research, and ideas for teaching about these programs.[2] The National Association for Family-Based Services recently sponsored a national meeting with broad representation from various disciplines in the social and behavioral sciences. The meeting encouraged university professors to exchange teaching materials, expand their classroom treatment of FBS, and share with their students the growing need for professionally trained workers in the field. A few university programs have even developed or are developing special tracks for students interested in specializing in FBS. With the demands for qualified personnel to staff these programs around the country, additional pressures will be exerted on both undergraduate and graduate programs to prepare students for family-based work.

Can FBS and IFPS Handle This Kind of Growth and Scrutiny?

This kind of expansion has many benefits, but risks also lurk in rapid growth. From where will programs obtain competent, well-trained staff prepared to provide these services? Already one major report from California cited problems of finding qualified therapists as a major barrier to the implementation of IFPS (Yuan et al., 1990). Very few universities are able to offer enough relevant graduate education for the supervisors and therapists of FBS and IFPS because faculty know little about these models of service. Where can all the necessary start-up field training and consultation be found? Existing organizations that currently specialize in this type of training may find that demands outstrip their resources.

We are fearful that as a wave of enthusiasm and program expansion washes over practitioners, administrators, policymakers, professors, and others, little effort may be spent carefully considering the evidence base (as limited as it may be) for determining the types of family-based programs to be funded; the selection, training, and supervision of program staff; the target populations to be served; and the proper fit between stage of program development and type of evaluation design. These choices are crucial and often the impacts of ill-informed decisions are long-lasting. Superficial comparisons among very different program models in terms of "service units" and "treatment success," for example, may result in the selection of service models not equipped to serve targeted client populations appropriately. We also fear that "common knowledge" rather than empirical research may guide some policy decisions and prevent the expansion of more innovative and effective programs. Without continuing research and empirically informed decision-making, it is possible that research on poorly conceived and implemented family-based programs may result in the labeling of all family-based programs as "services that don't work." We hope that the findings from the FIT research project contribute to the knowledge base regarding effective FBS, while pointing the way toward future questions that must be answered in order to help families in crisis.

Understanding the Context for the FIT Study

As we have stated before, this study was designed in 1984 in response to a federal request for proposals (RFP) that sought research studies designed to identify families and children who benefit and fail to benefit from FBS. Because of funding, political, and logistical constraints, we were not able to employ an experimental design. The placement prevention findings therefore should be viewed with caution as these data, in and of themselves, do not provide sufficient evidence to claim that IFPS are more effective than conventional child welfare services. No true control groups or large comparison groups were used.

However, we do have considerable confidence that many families made significant improvements in functioning because the research data were gathered from multiple sources, using multiple measures at client intake, service termination, and 12-month follow-up. Both workers and family members reported consonant changes. Also, comparison of IFPS children to a small but carefully designed comparison group indicated that placement rates were significantly lower for treated children and their families. Nevertheless, the study findings and measures should be viewed within the context of what family-based programs and public policymakers were concerned with in 1985 and 1986, as well as what was the state of the art in FBS and IFPS evaluation at that time.

It is fortunate that some of the more recent studies in California (Mc-Croskey & Nelson, 1989; Yuan et al., 1990), New Jersey (Feldman, 1990), and Illinois (Rzepnicki, Schuerman, & Littell, 1991) have been able to learn from and improve upon the research studies conducted by Hennepin County, the Iowa National Resource Center on Family-Based Services, and the FIT study. There continues to exist, however, a need to conduct control group and other types of studies with varying intake criteria and definitions of treatment success.

Practice Implications

Keeping Families Together

We learned in Chapter 9 that the IFPS therapists studied in this research project were able to achieve success in placement prevention at case termination with 92.9% of the children who were targeted for out-of-home placement. In addition, 67% of the children at risk of placement were still at home 12 months after IFPS intake. In contrast, only 14.8% of the children at risk of placement in a small referred-but-not-served comparison group in Utah achieved treatment success (i.e., 85% of these children were placed during or after receiving more traditional child welfare or mental health services). These findings are consistent with previous quasi-experimental research that suggests that IFPS, based upon the Homebuilders model, prevent out-of-home placements.

Improvements in Parent and Child Functioning

Critics have charged that Homebuilders and IFPS may do little actually to change the negative interaction patterns among family members. It is one thing to avoid out-of-home placements, skeptics say, but it is quite another to influence parent and child functioning. Based upon results gathered from the FIT project, parent and child behaviors appear to be altered by participation in this treatment program. When primary caretakers rated problem severity in 28 specific areas of child, household, parent, and family functioning after the provision of IFPS, there were, on average, positive improvements on 26 of the 28 items. Likewise, IFPS therapists' pre- and posttreatment ratings of parent and child functioning on the 25 Family Risk Scales showed that there were significant improvements on 22 items. The scores related to social support indicated that there were significant pre- and postservice reductions in aversiveness for primary and secondary caretakers. Primary caretakers had less aversive relations with their spouses and more empathic friendships and less aversive relations with extended network and family members. Secondary caretakers also had less aversive relations with their spouses. Thus, based on parent self-reports and therapist ratings, IFPS appear to have promoted behavioral changes in parents and their children.[3]

As a whole, the findings provide important building blocks related to the IFPS knowledge base. Not only do IFPS appear to prevent out-of-home placements, but they produce significant improvements in family and individual functioning. Although the attitudes of social services and judicial personnel contribute to placement rates, it may be that changes in the skills, knowledge, and attitudes of both parents and children account, in a causal sense, for the low rates of child placement observed in this and other IFPS studies. Our design does not permit us to draw such a causal conclusion, but the evidence relating IFPS and improved child and family functioning is strong.

Concrete Services: Building the Capacity of Families

The IFPS therapists who participated in the FIT research study were involved in providing concrete services such as transportation, food, and child care. They also encouraged and taught clients to obtain concrete ser-

vices. These concrete-service activities are as much a part of the Homebuilders approach to helping families as the counseling and behavior therapy
techniques.

In the FIT project, data were gathered from IFPS therapists in two categories for concrete services: "doing for" clients—the direct provision of a
service or commodity; and "enabling or supporting" clients to learn how to
secure a service. In both cases, these approaches involved proactive helping.
Therapists reported enabling and direct provision of concrete services separately. Both types of services were provided across a wide range of cases with
adequate to good goal achievement (see Chapter 11). As reported in Chapter
10, the direct provision of concrete services by IFPS therapists was not
significantly associated with placement prevention in the multivariate analysis. However, enabling services were found to be positively associated with
successful treatment outcomes. The findings imply that concrete services
delivered by a therapist may not contribute as much to treatment outcome as
helping families learn to obtain "hard" services on their own. Thus, when
the therapist took responsibilitiy to show family members how to obtain a
service, there was more likely to be a positive treatment outcome.[4]

These findings lend additional support to previous work (Fraser &
Haapala, 1988; Haapala, 1983; Horejsi, 1981) that concrete services build
the capacities of families to meet basic needs. In addition, the IFPS therapist
offering to engage families around concrete services communicates that the
therapist views all problems as worthy of attention. Families are not asked to
compartmentalize problems into "appropriate" and "inappropriate" for
treatment. The use of enabling concrete services allows the therapist to
make a meaningful and important contact with the family. Also, by attending
to concrete needs, the therapist breaks the stereotype of being a high-status
authority figure who demands that counseling deal only with personal feelings and the structure of relationships—not child care, cleaning house, or
finding food. By breaking that stereotype, the IFPS therapist has effectively
structured an environment in which, paradoxically, it is easier to tap into the
emotional and relationship problems among family members. Finally, the
enabling-services finding appears to support the teaching or educational
approach that is a core ingredient in the Homebuilders model. Teaching
skills—even in such areas as the use of public transit—appears to be correlated with children remaining at home.

Toward IFPS Theory: Breaking the Cycle of Coercion

The child-parent interaction patterns that emerged from the data are
remarkably similar to patterns of behavior described in dysfunctional families by coercion theorists. A relatively new perspective on the etiology of
family problems, coercion theory interprets child behavior as a function of

parental skills and knowledge, as well as child traits and environmental influences. An expansion of modern social learning theory which places emphasis on imitation, reinforcement, and cognition (see e.g., Bandura, 1985), coercion theory places emphasis on "the central role of the family and peer group in providing the positive and negative contingencies that maintain the performance of both prosocial and deviant child behaviors" (Larzelere & Patterson, 1990, p. 305). Coercion theory is focused on parent, child, and environmental factors that maintain behavior and that lead to "coercive" parent-child interactions, interactions based on the use of power or force to elicit a conforming response. For example, in response to a child's disruptive behavior at the dinner table, a parent might reach across the table and slap a child to produce fear-induced quiet and compliance. Through the use of force, the child is coerced into compliant behavior. By extension, coercion theory also applies to the use of society's mechanisms to control antisocial behavior and elicit prosocial behavior. It focuses on parent and child behaviors that tend to involve strong and coercive responses from school officials, CPS workers, law enforcement officers, and other social control agents.

The Coercive Cycle. Coercion theorists argue that parents with poor child management skills inappropriately reward their children's aggressive behavior and fail to reward their children's prosocial behaviors. By rewarding aggressive behavior (with attention and punishment), parents and children enter into an escalating cycle of aggression followed by physical punishment (an aversive response). Children learn to obtain attention by hitting or otherwise being noncompliant, and parents respond intermittently with physical punishment rather than with measured and consistent consequation. Over time, parent-child interaction is characterized by oppositional behavior from children and coercive responses from parents. It is a cyclic pattern with serious consequences.

The result of this coercive cycle is that children are taught to be noncompliant in the home and, when they enter school, are quickly identified as disruptive. Because their parents have been noncontingent in reinforcing prosocial behaviors, such children often have poor social skills, and as indicated in studies by Dishion (1990) and Ramsey, Patterson, and Walker (1990), they are likely to be rejected by peers and perform poorly in the classroom. Thus the coercion perspective delineates a degenerative scenario in which children are handicapped by their parents' poor parenting skills, and fail at a very early age to develop social skills and internal controls (e.g., ability to work on a task and avoid disturbing the work of others) that are required for success in school and the community.

The Importance of In-Home Child Management Training. The coercion model also suggests that improving parents' child management skills will lead to prosocial behavior and reductions in oppositional behavior (Kazdin, 1985; Patterson, 1985). Another implication is that parents who learn effective child management skills will be less likely to use physical punishment and other force-based forms of child management. Training in the use of contingencies, monitoring children's behaviors, solving family problems, and providing rewards for desirable behaviors has long been acknowledge to be an effective intervention (Patterson, 1985; Forgatch, in press). And recent data indicate that the earlier that parent training occurs, the stronger its effects are on children.

However, while parenting training is widely believed to be effective, its delivery has been problematic. Families at the highest levels of risk appear to be the most difficult to recruit to and retain in treatment (Fraser, Hawkins, & Howard, 1988). Many families lack reliable transportation and stable household routines. They routinely miss appointments. Many exist in the midst of environmental stressors that trigger coercive parent-child interactions and that impair a parent's capacity to be self-reflective in treatment. Families that live in neighborhoods with high crime, infant mortality, and welfare dependency rates have external stressors that complicate daily living, creating survival priorities that may be little known or understood by parents from middle-class suburbs. For these and other reasons, families from low-income areas may be less able than other families to generalize to the home parenting skills learned in the office. How can we deliver what is known to be an effective treatment strategy—training in child management—to these families?

Homebuilders and other IFPS programs appear to resolve some of these treatment challenges. This service strategy eliminates the problem of office-to-home generalization, for treatment takes place in the primary setting where it will have the most effect. Similarly, home-based treatment with a concrete service focus has the potential to address housing, food, health, income security, and employment factors that may limit a family's capacity to respond to treatment. At a minimum, it eliminates problems attendant to loading family members into an automobile (or public transit) and arriving on time at a therapist's office for an appointment. Comparison of the Utah and Washington findings suggests that programs that lack flexible hours and an orientation toward concrete services may be biased against the participation of many families, especially those in which fathers serve as primary caretakers. From other work, we have found that fathers, in general, participate in treatment at lower rates (see Lazar, Sagi, & Fraser, 1991), and in two-parent families, it is often the child management practices of fathers that warrant special attention. Moreover, it may be the aggressive use of concrete services and the willingness to arrange many after-hours, in-home appointments with families that resulted in higher rates of success among ethnic minorities in the Washington Homebuilders sites. For many high-risk families—that might not be capable of participating in traditional services—HBS and IFPS appear to be reasonable alternatives to office-based services for the delivery of parenting skills training and other critical types of treatment.

In the context of HBS and IFPS, coercion theory helps make sense of the FIT project findings. Patterson, DeBaryshe, and Ramsey (1989) have argued that parental child management skill mediates the effects of socioeconomic status (SES) in producing antisocial behavior. That is, when one controls for child management skills, the long-standing and much-debated relationship between SES and delinquency washes out (Larzelere & Patterson, 1990). While they acknowledge that child attributes and environmental stressors directly affect noncompliant behavior, Patterson and his colleagues argue that parents' child management skills are a major locus for intervention, regardless of a family's income level and educational background. Their theory and the data that support it provide important links between parent's child management practices, including child neglect and the use of physical punishment, and subsequent child behavior. Patterson and his associates have shown that poor parenting skills are highly predictive of children's early oppositional behavior in the home, and early oppositional behavior in the home is highly predictive of subsequent oppositional behavior in the school and community. Although parents of delinquent children appear to use physical punishment more often than parents of children who are not delinquent, the coercion perspective supports a view that it is the noncontingent use of reinforcement (rather than physical punishment) that poorly prepares children to distinguish right from wrong, that leads to noncompliant behavior in the home, and that leads to subsequent school failure and delinquency (for a review, see Howing, Wodarski, Kurtz, Gaudin, & Herbst, 1990). Tongue-in-cheek, they have called this the "early starter" model of delinquency.

Short-Circuiting "Early Starters."   Although there is variation, many IFPS families fall into this "early starter" group. Parents tend to use physical punishment frequently and are poorly skilled in the use of verbal discipline. Families exist among many environmental stressors. Their homes are often of questionable habitability and suitability. Many parents have few resources. Some have long-standing struggles with substance abuse. A substantial proportion of parents are isolated and experience symptoms of depression, fear, and anger; and many are under the close scrutiny of CPS workers and court officials. Many children are described by workers and parents alike as noncompliant and oppositional. Older children are frequently truant from school and in trouble in the community because of status offenses and delinquency. Parents and their children appear to be embedded in webs of coercive relationships that produce controlling responses from police, school, and other agencies. Moreover, there is some evidence that major interactions with extended family members, friends, and neighbors are aversive—oriented toward social control and coercion ("You better stop hitting that child!" "Can't you do something about that child?"). On balance, the evidence suggests that parents and children are engaged in coercive relationships and that the children seen by IFPS therapists may be "early starters."

If so, how do we short-circuit the early starters? How do we break the cycle of coercion? Coercion theory suggests that many family problems are brought on by poor parenting skills and that training parents in child management—as early as possible—will reap long-term social benefits. As discussed in Chapters 6 and 11, parent training is a central component of the IFPS intervention, and as indicated in Chapter 8, parents made significant improvements in parenting skill. As shown in Chapter 10, older children were less likely to benefit from treatment and this is consistent with Patterson's finding that the effectiveness of parent training is related to a child's age. The older the child, the smaller the treatment effect. Moreover, the findings indicate that children who were truant or drug-involved and who had more extensive social service involvement (including prior out-of-home placements) were less likely to succeed in treatment. This implies that, while age may be a correlate of service outcomes, other child-related factors contribute uniquely to family problems and make breaking the cycle of coercion more difficult.

The relatively low out-of-home placement rates and significant positive goal achievement scores observed in the FIT project suggest that brief and intensive in-home parenting training (with ancillary concrete services) may be a viable strategy for reaching families in crisis. Although one often thinks of IFPS as services designed to prevent foster care placements, it seems quite likely that, if coercion theory is correct, IFPS may have derivative effects in education, juvenile justice, and other fields. For many families, IFPS appear to break the cycle of coercion.

The "Homebasedness" of Service: Why Does It Matter?

Another important component of FBS and IFPS appears to be the amount of time that workers spend in client's homes or neighborhoods. In the FIT project, the preponderance of client contact time was spent in families' homes, and primary caretakers rated the in-home provision of the services as one of the most helpful program components. A variety of clinical services— including crisis intervention, individual counseling, and family therapy— were provided in the home setting. These clinical services were accompanied by *in vivo* teaching of practical skills such as anger management, parenting, and conflict resolution techniques. Despite arguments to the contrary (e.g., Showell & White, 1990), little rigorous research has been conducted that directly compares HBS and office-based service methods, using similar clients and objective outcome measures. In fact, many experienced family-centered therapists have emphasized the importance of working with families in their home environment because initial and ongoing assessments are more accurate, worker persistence can be demonstrated, healthy family boundaries are reinforced, and therapists can more easily assume a supportive position that reinforces the parents' control and ability to make choices (e.g., Kagan & Schlosberg, 1989, pp. 77–78; Wasik, Bryant, & Lyons, 1990).

Many family situations that are encountered in FBS involve parenting deficits ranging from communication and role-setting to discipline skills. However, many experienced family-focused practitioners and evaluators of skill-focused treatment programs believe that parenting skills are more easily demonstrated and generalized when they are taught in the home at the time that an actual child-parent incident arises (e.g., setting limits around use of toys or the television, managing child behavior at bedtime, handling children who are fighting). Furthermore, many of the most dysfunctional families who can benefit from FBS cannot or will not attend sessions held in an agency office.

From a research perspective, it is usually inappropriate to compare clients served in office-based programs to clients from home-based programs. Clients who attend office sessions are generally more motivated, have more resources in terms of transportation and child care, and may be more likely to succeed in avoiding child placement. Findings from studies without carefully selected control conditions may be misleading.

Relationship-Building and Teaching Skills

In this study, much of the IFPS therapists' time was spent initially in building support and listening to clients. In working with families in crisis, an interactive style of listening is used. It helps therapists gain more knowledge of the family situation and build a more empathetic relationship with the caretakers and children. A treatment partnership in which clients participate as colleagues of the therapist is strengthened further when therapists work first on the family priorities for service, and set small, realistic case objectives as part of the initial case plan.

IFPS therapists, because of the relatively large amounts of time spent with the families, can incorporate assessments of family roles, rules, rituals, communication patterns, use of power, cohesion, adaptability, and other critical areas of functioning (Hartman & Laird, 1983). Nonblaming assessments are also emphasized, where family problems are framed as skill deficits (things to be learned) rather than as deep-seated emotional disorders or character flaws. While severe parent or child mental illness, requiring supplemental or long-term treatment, is occasionally encountered, many clients appear to benefit from a supportive, social learning approach to treatment that helps them improve the situation to a point where out-of-home placement is not necessary. A brief, behaviorally oriented intervention appears to allow these families to continue with less intensive services. In fact, recent comparative studies of the treatment of acting-out behavior disorders in children have found that behavioral parent training had superior outcomes, compared to strategic and other types of family therapy (Gurman, Kniskern & Pinsof, 1986; Wells & Egan, 1984, as cited in Johnson, 1986).

Program Management: Overcoming Obstacles to Provide Quality Service

Keeping Families Together through Goal Setting and Goal Achievement

The multivariate analyses indicated that achieving service-related goals was significantly correlated with children remaining at home with their families. On balance, modest goal achievement decreased the probability of unsuccessful service outcomes by 64% and tended to nullify the negative effects of the other risk factors.

We suspect that the services provided by the IFPS therapists are key to successful outcomes. However, the most successful programs may have well-grounded supervisors and managers who can effectively transmit to therapists the basic and necessary skills of behavioral observation, specificity of treatment targets, prioritization of therapist activities, and effective goal setting. The practical application of these skills allows clinicians to use a common, verifiable language of treatment for clients and each other. When therapists and family members are clear on the goals of treatment and progress benchmarks, reaching those goals is more likely. Managers and supervisors must believe in this approach, understand its technology, and prioritize these activities highly to ensure the commitment and follow-through of line workers.

Such findings should have great value for the supervisors and administrators of programs trying to replicate the IFPS approach. Since administrators and supervisors, not therapists, tend to establish the organizational culture, we believe that it is important that administrators and supervisors consider the combination of skills and attitudes necessary to keep client goal attainment high. Every program wants a high rate of success—short term and long range. IFPS successes may be due, at least in part, to the management backing of the program administration in maintaining a goal-oriented, empirically based approach for programs and paperwork.

Management Supports: A Crucial Key to Staff Morale, Program Integrity, and Service Outcome

Effective and compassionate organizational supports can critically affect the delivery of family-focused services. To date the greatest efforts invested in studying family-centered services have addressed treatment outcomes, client characteristics, and therapist and service delivery dimensions. While little information was gathered in the FIT project to elucidate the administrative and supervisory aspects of the programs studied, the data available suggest that program management should be given more careful thought and consideration.

HBS and IFPS present unique problems for social service program supervisors and administrators. Because IFPS workers are serving families in client homes away from the office, work unstructured hours, and are on call to families 24 hours a day, seven days a week, many policies appropriate for office-based personnel are inappropriate for IFPS staff. Since the effective delivery of any service rests, in part, on workers' job satisfaction, how well HBS and IFPS supervisors and administrators understand the idiosyncrasies of IFPS is crucial.

The findings from Chapter 7 indicate that the Utah IFPS therapists received less support from district child welfare administrators, other supervisors, other child welfare program units, or therapists, compared to the IFPS workers in Washington State. Not only did the Utah therapists perceive themselves as less supported, but the Utah IFPS therapists reported a sense of greater pressure from central and district office administrators, and their supervisors.

A similar pattern emerged for job satisfaction and IFPS program morale. Again, the Utah workers tended to be less happy with their work compared to their peers in Washington. Therapists from Utah rated the overall morale of their IFPS programs as below average, while Washington therapists rated the morale in their IFPS program as high. Both job satisfaction and morale were significantly lower for the Utah therapists, especially for one IFPS site.

It is important to remember that staff morale in any program ebbs and flows, and perhaps being a part of a state public agency, as was the case in Utah, means that high staff morale levels are more difficult to maintain. Since the Washington IFPS therapists collectively had more than twice as many months of in-home experience than their Utah counterparts and worked within a smaller agency that had many more years of IFPS delivery experience, it may be reasonable to expect lower ratings of support, greater ratings of pressure, and decreased morale among Utah staff.

However, it is curious, given this context, that the combined Utah programs also showed lower overall placement prevention rates. Of far greater concern, we believe, are findings suggesting that during the early years of

IFPS implementation, Utah administrators did not fully support the IFPS model being utilized, nor back the program's philosophy. For example, the Utah therapists, in comparing their values with those of their agency, saw themselves as more in favor of 24-hour initial contact, more willing to work evenings and weekends, more willing to provide 24-hour service to families, more willing to work with "unmotivated" clients, more in favor of goal-oriented casework and planning, and more in favor of family self-determination.

We are disquieted by these findings because we see the potential for the loss of program integrity and "model drift." Model drift refers to the quiet, steady change in the philosophy, policies, and activities of a program. The clarity and commitment to the original program design and practice change. Unlike model refinement, in which changes in a program model are instituted as the result of planned experimentation or compelling practice experience, model drift seems to represent a favoring of the path of least resistance, or a lack of clarity about what is important to maintain in a program model. In a public *or* private IFPS program, strong, consistent, knowledgeable, and supportive leadership is necessary to prevent drift.

While all of us seek freedom of action and choice, ironically, the greatest sense of support, competence, and creative freedom may be derived from clear work-related guidelines and parameters for staff activity. Deal and Kennedy (1982), experts in organizational behavior, posit that effective organizations make clear their values, identify and praise exemplary individuals within the organization and support and encourage organizationally cherished rituals and ceremonies. According to this thesis, a strong and effective corporate culture contains a system of rules that spells out how people are to behave most of the time. By knowing what is expected of them, it is asserted that staff waste little time in deciding how to act. In turn, by behaving as is expected by the organization, staff are more likely to be praised and nurtured within an agency. Knowing what is expected and being supported provide the base from which workers can be truly creative.

It means a great deal to people to belong to a group—especially a group with a strong identity. Perhaps this is because so much about life is uncertain and confusing. A clearly articulated and strong culture makes it possible for employees to do their jobs and feel better about their work. When workers feel successful, they are more likely to work hard.

The jury is out when it comes to knowing whether one model of family-centered services is more effective than another. However, evidence from the FIT project suggests that agency managers must make a commitment to a well-articulated approach to providing services. This is critically important to the effectiveness and the longevity of any program. An allegiance to a model's values, principles, and activities by line staff alone is probably not enough. The larger organization's managers must also believe in and act within the framework of the parameters of the approach. Unlike some more conventional human service programs, HBS and IFPS programs require extra effort on the part of managers. Managers need to be available to respond to staff telephone calls at home, and they should take leadership in making personnel policies that are more supportive of home-based workers. Office-centered personnel policies make home-based work difficult. Administrative leadership may be critical in developing program supports that produce effective workers.

We urge agency managers to evaluate themselves and their organizations before they decide to try implementing IFPS. The knowledge, commitment, and leadership of program managers and supervisors appears to be related to staff satisfaction and staff morale. More work, we believe, needs to be devoted to understanding the relationship between staff and management, and the impact of management practices on service outcomes.

Public Policy: Serving the Highest Risk Children

Children and Families of Color: Promoting Culturally Competent Practice

One of the most provocative findings from the FIT research study was from the multivariate analysis described in Chapter 10. Children of color targeted for placement in Washington State had a significantly higher chance of remaining at home during and after Homebuilders treatment than their white, non-Hispanic counterparts. This finding is significant for public policy because it offers hope that there may be a useful service approach to combat and possibly reverse the disproportionate use of out-of-home placements for minority children of color (Stehno, 1982).

How can this finding be explained? We think that the values and practices that are part and parcel of the Homebuilders program account, in large part, for the successful service outcomes for minority children. Many of the attitudes and skills necessary for IFPS are consistent with what has recently been called the "culturally competent" delivery of human services:

> Cultural competence is a set of congruent behaviors, attitudes, and policies that come together in a system, agency, or among professionals and enable that system, agency, or those professionals to work effectively in cross-cultural situations. The word "culture" is used because it implies the integrated pattern of human behavior that includes thoughts, communications, actions, customs, beliefs, values, and institutions of a racial, ethnic, religious, or social group. The word competence is used because it implies having the capacity to function effectively. A culturally competent system of care acknowledges and incorporates—at all levels—the importance of culture, the assessment of cross-

cultural relations, vigilance towards the dynamics that result from cultural differences, the expansion of cultural knowledge, and the adaptation of services to meet culturally-unique needs. (Cross, Bazron, Dennis, & Isaacs, 1989, p. 13)

While the Homebuilders program is far from perfect as an exemplar of culturally competent practice, many of the program's characteristics are consonant with culturally competent principles. Gutiérrez (1990) recently described how some of these service components help empower women of color, a group of clients disproportionately represented in the child welfare client population. We offer similar ideas below.

Accessibility. The Homebuilders program offers services in clients' homes within 24 hours of program referral. Therapists are on call to families 24 hours a day during the service period, and meet at times and places convenient to the family. According to Flaskerud (1986) and Owan (1982) the most significant service delivery issue for children of color is accessibility. Homebuilders clients do not have to go anywhere—service comes to them (see Stroul, 1988).

Involvement of Social Support Networks. The Homebuilders model of IFPS strives to improve child and family functioning by encouraging interactions with the family's social supports—extended family and friends. The natural forms of support for minority populations include family, community, church, and indigenous healers. These supports are important for continued growth and development of family members (Flaskerud, 1986; Kenyatta, 1980; Red Horse, 1980).

Therapists Take a Practical Approach to Solving the Problems of Everyday Life. The Homebuilders program offers client families hands-on strategies to deal with difficulties in parent-child interactions, home management, and tangible needs. According to Lewis and Ho (1975) families of color frequently expect professional mental health and social service providers to be able to handle a wide range of problems confronting the family. The value, effectiveness, and commitment of a service provider are gauged by how well he or she can solve "real life" problems, such as finding good day-care resources or calming an angry four-year-old. If the worker is successful at that level, then the family is more likely to trust the worker's ability to handle more serious or complex issues.

Concrete Services. Homebuilders therapists provide both "soft services" such as counseling, as well as "hard services" such as food, clothing, and transportation. While many children of color need and benefit from therapeutic interventions, concrete or tangible services are necessary as well

(Cross et al., 1989). Some clients will first present a tangible service need to a therapist in order to assess the worker's commitment to helping (Lewis & Ho, 1975).

Social Rituals. Homebuilders therapists strive to learn about and, where appropriate, follow the rules of social convention used by families served by the program. Minority families frequently practice different rules of social decorum. Social service and mental health workers need to respect and participate in these forms of social etiquette if they are to develop effective working relationships with these clients (see, e.g., McRoy, Shorkey & Garcia, 1985).

If we assume that many of the children and families of color served by the Washington IFPS therapists had previously received social and mental health services that were not culturally responsive to their needs, then a context may have been created that made those clients *more* appreciative and responsive to the Homebuilders program. The white children and their families participated in the IFPS program and benefited from the service. However, we hypothesize that the children and families of color had better service outcomes because the level of "culturally relevant" service was higher than anticipated. Minority families may have taken greater advantage and received more benefit from the service.[5]

Replication: Can Other Jurisdictions Demonstrate Comparable Treatment Outcomes for Children of Color and Their Families?

Results from the FIT project for Washington State Homebuilders showed that minority children of color were significantly more likely to remain at home when compared to white, non-Hispanic children. Previous research has shown that minority children are more likely to be placed, and placed in the least desirable placements. If findings similar to Washington Homebuilders were replicated in the major urban cities, which are frequently home to significant numbers of families of color, then placement costs may go down sharply and more children of color could remain at home with their families. The sample of ethnic minority families served in the FIT study was too small to analyze adequately the data by specific ethnic groups. Future studies need sample sizes sufficiently large to focus on various ethnic groups—ideally with different levels of acculturation.

Taking in account the methodological limitations, the findings are promising. Homebuilders-oriented family treatment may offer a solution to a major public policy issue: decreasing the current rates of out-of-home placements for children of color. According to McAdoo (1982), demographic data suggest that many minority populations are younger and have higher birth rates than white, non-Hispanic populations in the United States. By the year 2000, the racial make-up of the United States will change dramatically, with minority children outnumbering white, non-Hispanic children in some states and comprising 40% of the total population in the service delivery system. If we do nothing to address the differential placement of minority children in out-of-home care, the ethical and financial cost to our social system will be unbearable. The timely provision of preventive services such as prenatal care, IFPS, and other family support services that make placement unnecessary is a logical alternative. IFPS offers an alternative that may be worth experimental action on a broader scale. If more children and families of color receive culturally responsive IFPS, we could see a general reduction in out-of-home placements for children, and, specifically, fewer minority children may need to be placed outside their homes.

Which Families Are Best Served by IFPS?

A number of the social and demographic characteristics of both parents and children were significantly correlated with out-of-home placement. Many of these variables are easily known to referring agents at the point of HBS or IFPS case referral (e.g., target child out of home at time of referral, age of child, suspected or confirmed drug or alcohol involvement of target child, out-of-home placement history for target child). Tempting as it is to use these characteristics to screen potential cases from IFPS, we do not recommend such action.

We discourage the use of these types of client characteristics to determine client eligibility for four reasons. First, research in the FBS field is still in its infancy. While some model programs have been in existence for over 15 years, many programs have been operating for less than five years. Such programs are formative and developing. Prematurely setting limits on what client populations these programs might serve may prevent funding agencies from maximizing potential benefits. We must continue to develop IFPS models to serve the most difficult, and often most costly, clients.

Second, the client characteristics associated with treatment failure are not perfectly correlated with failure. In fact, the success rate for some families with a high-risk profile is over 50%. Even if success rates for some subgroups are low, occasional success may be worth the human effort and dollar investment because we have few other choices.

Third, caution should be exercised when generalizing from this particular research project. The sample selected was from only two western states and limited to six sites within those states. The findings may not apply to other jurisdictions.

Fourth, as IFPS programs learn that some families are at greater risk for treatment failure, program modifications may be developed and implemented that decrease the odds that those families will fail in the future. Such efforts are currently underway for treating drug-affected families, for example.

We believe that it is time to evaluate rigorously the differential effectiveness of various IFPS and HBS programs and to refine treatment models rather than delimit treatment populations. If we collectively start limiting the kinds of clients who are eligible for this program because we are afraid that they will fail, then we may defeat one of the original purposes of this type of service: to serve the most difficult families who have children in danger of out-of-home placements.

Unless treatment programs continue to address high-risk children, they will have fewer reasons to exist. In this context, broader research and development efforts are needed to refine programs to work with families where children have extensive placement histories, are drug-involved or truant, and come from homes where parents have lost hope and believe placement to be the most desirable option.

Future Research

While the possibilities for research in this field are extensive, we suggest nine issues for future research. We believe that these issues should be prioritized highly on our collective research agendas.

The Use of Designs with Greater Control

Most recent studies in HBS and IFPS have utilized quasi-experimental designs. A few research projects have attempted randomly to assign cases to experimental and nonexperimental conditions and each has experienced serious difficulty in maintaining commitments to the procedure.

Some of the most problematic issues in carrying out these studies include lack of full participation and support from referring workers; insufficient case flow to assure adequate and comparably sized samples; program start-up problems (such as inexperienced program personnel, insufficient numbers of staff, staff turnover); excessive reliance on clinical staff to collect data; and insufficient funding for staff to monitor research activities, collect and properly analyze data, systematically follow clients after termination, and write up completed research projects.

The field needs many rigorous studies of IFPS (see also, Wells & Biegel, 1991; Yuan & Rivest, 1990). An exemplary study should have sufficient and competent staff to collect most data independently from clinical staff, manage and analyze data expertly, and write reports professionally. Such a study should use only mature programs with long histories of large numbers of appropriate referrals. Cases should be randomly assigned to treatment and other conditions after careful screening. Researchers should incorporate behavioral observation methods and, in selecting a sample, take into account base rate probabilities for various kinds of child placements—some of which may be quite low (Rzepnicki et al., 1991). In addition, all necessary data might be obtained to engage in a careful cost-benefit analysis.

Positive results from such studies might provide compelling evidence to convince funding sources, skeptics, and others that IFPS are effective. And such studies might be complemented by parallel studies using single-case and qualitative designs.

The Maintenance of Treatment Effects over Time

The FIT project results included significant and positive changes in reported parent and therapist ratings of child and family functioning and parent ratings of social support. Comparisons were made between service intake and termination. More information is needed to understand the stability of these findings after IFPS treatment has been completed and the intensive service is withdrawn from the families. Placement prevention rates did decline over time, but it would be important to distinguish, if possible, what contributed to child placement: a lack of IFPS "staying powering," differences in criteria for child removal among staff, or, more likely, a lack of necessary support services in the community. The field needs to identify community-based social services and other family supports that are necessary to help the most vulnerable families maintain the gains made in IFPS treatment. An alternative approach is to view IFPS treatment as a short-term crisis intervention and education service that also needs to be available to previously served families either as a brief "tune-up" (Bonita Lantz, personnel communication, February 1988) or as a full-length intervention.

What Is the Role of Effective Program Management upon IFPS?

The FIT project findings suggested that program integrity, successful treatment outcomes, therapist job satisfaction, and morale may be associated with clear and consistent administrative and supervisory support. As mentioned earlier in this chapter, ineffective programs and those experiencing model drift may be those with less supportive and knowledgeable managers. Little has been done to study IFPS program management carefully and systematically and this area needs further research.

A careful study of the relationship between management and the delivery of HBS and IFPS would be difficult and costly. It is not easy to investigate second-order impacts, management–line staff working relationships, perceived and attributed power, pressure, and support from all program staff. However, the findings from such a study might help us better train and select administrators in FBS programs.

How Effective Are HBS and IFPS Programs with Drug-Related Referrals?

Drug-involved children and parents who are referred to IFPS programs pose special problems. Children who were drug-involved had significantly higher service failure rates, and drug and alcohol involvement on the part of parents raises grave concerns about child safety in many homes. In some cities drug-addicted babies have flooded hospital nurseries because birth mothers have abandoned their infants. CPS workers have taken many babies away from drug-addicted parents. A few IFPS programs such as the Bronx Homebuilders demonstration project and the Families First initiative in Detroit have begun serving these families. Detailed information is needed to assess the effectiveness of these programs and ascertain what, if anything, might be added or withdrawn from program models to increase their effectiveness.

"Imminence" of Out-of-Home Placement: Does It Mean Anything Anymore?

Recent studies (Feldman, 1990; Mitchell, Tovar, & Knitzer, 1989; Yuan et al., 1990) suggest that the identification and referral of children at "imminent risk" for out-of-home care is a major trouble spot. If children are truly at risk, one would assume that a high percentage of comparison group cases would experience placement. However, these studies show high rates of placement avoidance. Perhaps because the prediction of placement is quite complex, securing a population of children at risk of imminent placement appears in recent studies to have been extremely difficult. Is "imminent risk" one of those colloquial terms that cannot be operationalized? Are we asking referring agencies and workers to do the impossible?

We think not. A high proportion of the comparison group cases in Utah were placed. This suggests that it is possible to identify high-risk families and children. Major work is needed to devise better screening methods and to train public agency workers and supervisors regarding the characteristics of target children. Control group studies, for example, might be undertaken only *after* a juvenile court judge has approved placement and a suitable foster family, group home, or psychiatric facility located. While we expect that the placement prevention rates of the treatment group would be lower than those reported in many studies, a significant difference between the groups might be hypothesized on the basis of the current research.

In addition, referring staff must feel comfortable in recommending difficult families for IFPS. If, for example, a worker believes that there is a chance that a child may be hurt, but that IFPS has a good chance of preventing maltreatment, should the worker refer? Most IFPS advocates would argue for referral, especially if local administrators and judges are willing to support difficult referral decisions. Unless referring agencies can refer families on the brink of placement, the full potential of these services cannot be realized, and the likelihood of placement cannot be used by therapists to create "teachable" moments. Taking advantage of the imminent placement crisis is an important dimension of IFPS, but it is not without risk.

Quality Assurance and IFPS Treatment

A new program developed by BSI involves an effort clearly to articulate and quantify the critical activities of IFPS staff that are presumed to be closely associated with treatment success. Unlike previous efforts to improve staff and program performance by simply providing training and consultation, the new quality review program uses behavioral observation data, client and other staff feedback, and MIS data to assess the process of service delivery and treatment outcome. A thorough evaluation of this innovation is necessary to determine its impact.

Qualitative Research and Ethnography

Most studies of FBS have been quantitative—the primary mechanisms for collecting information were based upon frequency counts. This approach is not considered appropriate when trying to gather rich, descriptive information about individual clients, families, or workers. Instead, qualitative methods such as participant observation, phenomenological inquiry, extended case histories, and open-ended interviews can be used to provide in-depth information about the families receiving services, the processes of helping, the conditions associated with change, and the techniques used by therapists.

The field needs more qualitative studies to describe, in detail, what staff do when they provide these services. Such studies may allow others to understand better what is entailed when providing and receiving these services. They may also be used to compare and contrast program models, if they are done carefully. In addition, some components of service that have not been previously well established might be further explained. How does a worker shift from empathetic listening to teaching a client to learn a new skill? How can a new therapist learn to identify "teachable moments"? What opportunities exist to change the focus of a client-therapist dialogue to discuss a treatment goal identified for improvement? A major contribution to the FBS field could be made by such studies and they are overdue.

Cost-Effectiveness

What are the cost differences between families receiving IFPS and similar families who receive an alternative service? The Homebuilders program has published a number of cost comparisons (Kinney et al., 1990, p. 55). But a rigorous experimental study with a benefit-cost component would give us further understanding of the fiscal investment that is necessary to avoid child placement. Such a study would need to grapple with the challenges associated with estimating costs, benefits, time horizons, and other benefit-cost variables.

Placement and Beyond

Lastly, we would like to share with you our growing doubts about the extensive (and, occasionally, exclusive) reliance of evaluators on placement as an outcome measure. There are many predictors of placement that are, themselves, related neither to successful IFPS treatment nor to family characteristics. System variables such as funding for foster care, state legislation regarding out-of-home placement, court attitudes toward family integrity versus child protection, and even recent media events related to child abuse may affect whether children in similar situations but in different states are placed. Because placement has many causes, it cannot be viewed as a simple linear function of service and client characteristics. Other environmental factors operate to affect placement rates.

FIT findings suggest that parents and children make behavioral and attitudinal changes in IFPS treatment and, reported elsewhere, that these changes distinguish successful from unsuccessful treatment (Fraser et al., 1989). In other fields, behavioral change and functioning are often used to measure the effectiveness of mental health, delinquency, and substance abuse prevention programs. There is no compelling reason why these criteria should not become central to FBS research. If the goal of HBS and IFPS programs is to prevent placement, then the FIT project has shown that this is associated with goal-driven services that appear to produce behavioral changes in children and their parents. Prevention of placement is an important public policy goal, but as the sole outcome for a single program or a large multisite study, it is conceptually flawed. It is time for the field to move beyond placement as the primary outcome criterion.

Conclusion

IFPS programs like Homebuilders represent a bold, new approach in family treatment. Focused on maintaining family integrity, these services have roots in social learning, systems, ecological, and Rogerian theories. IFPS are founded on a dramatically different perspective: clients are colleagues, treatment is located in the home, work starts within 24 hours of referral, families are helped with concrete needs, intensive and brief behaviorally oriented training is provided, and so on. This approach seems to break through the limitations of traditional family treatment and offers exciting new possibilities for working with troubled families.

Homebuilders and programs based on the Homebuilders model appear to help many children remain in their homes. Based upon our findings, parents and children showed significant improvements in functioning. Families that demonstrated even modest goal achievement during treatment were significantly more likely to avoid placement. On the basis of therapist ratings and parent self-reports, brief and intensive in-home treatment appeared to produce remarkable changes in families, including families with children of color.

In light of the limitations of the research design, the findings must be viewed with caution, but on balance they offer promise. Much work, however, remains to be done to realize this promise. We must learn, for example, how to ensure that only those families with children at risk of immediate out-of-home placement are referred to these programs. Several recent studies have experienced problems identifying families with children at risk of imminent placement. We must further examine the generalization of behavioral changes over time. For how long should we expect a brief intervention to prevent or delay placement? What kinds of behavioral changes are sustained over time? And from a management perspective, many factors remain scarcely researched. What role, for example, does a programmatically informed and supportive management team play in the delivery of effective IFPS? Finally, there are a host of questions related to the replicability of IFPS. How do we make certain that program attributes associated with goal achievement are replicated in new programs? To what degree should the model be changed to meet unique local conditions? To what degree should the model remain invariant across settings and cultures? These and other questions need to be addressed to expand our understanding of IFPS and to increase our confidence that these programs can be effective in preventing the placement of children in high-risk families.

Ultimately, the Homebuilders model and others like it must show that they are adaptable to other settings if they are to become a commonly accepted element of the continuum of human services for children and families. From this study, we have learned that even modest goal achievement reduces the risk of service failure for the highest risk families. Goal achievement, in turn, was related to three critical elements of service: the building of client-therapist relationships through interactive listening and client advocacy; the provision of concrete services to improve the habitability of the home and strengthen the client-therapist relationship; and the use of learning-focused training to improve family members' problem-solving, communications, and parenting skills. The use of these three strat-

David A. Haapala et al.

egies—each of which represents a long stream of research in social treatment—in the context of a crisis-oriented, home-based, intensive, and brief service model appears to produce encouraging outcomes. We are optimistic that future work will extend our confidence in this innovative treatment method. The expansion of IFPS programs such as Homebuilders offers bright, new hope for families in crisis.

Notes

1. More than 125 IFPS sites are developed or being developed across the country (sites): Alabama (5); Colorado (2); Connecticut (6); Kentucky (8); Michigan (22); Minnesota (7); New Jersey (10); New Mexico (11); New York (33); Tennessee (11); and Washington (11).

2. For information about one such program, see Tracy et al. (1991) and Whittaker et al. (1990) or contact Dr. Elizabeth Tracy at the Mandel School of Applied Social Sciences, Case Western Reserve University, Cleveland, OH 44106.

3. Data from pre-post test designs may be confounded by regression to the mean. Findings may be influenced by the tendency of extreme scores to move toward middle ground (i.e., regression toward the mean). This situation is usually accompanied by large standard deviations in the initial pre rating and substantially smaller standard deviations in the post rating. Extreme scores regress over time. For most of the problem-related measures in the FIT study, the standard deviations at posttest were somewhat smaller than the standard deviations at pretest. But the differences were not large. (See, for example, Table 8.5.)

4. It may be that the types of family situations requiring direct provision of concrete services are more difficult, accounting for the lower placement prevention rates for direct provision types of cases. But problem severity, family characteristics, and other factors were forced into the multivariate equations to help identify the differential effects of "doing for" versus "enabling" types of concrete-service provision.

5. The design of the FIT Project does not allow us to determine from a causal perspective that IFPS produced differing placement prevention rates for families of color. In fact, other nonservice related explanations of differential outcomes may exist. Reflecting systemic biases, for example, the finding might be explained by differential intake and placement decision-making regarding families of color. Placement may be viewed as a more viable option for families of color, even when child and parent difficulties in such families are not as severe as those observed in white, non-hispanic families. The Washington Homebuilders finding, suggesting that minorities did significantly better in treatment, could mask unmeasured pre-treatment case and intake decision-making differences that place less dysfunctional families of color in the "at risk" group. If so, observed placement findings could be favorable for families of color because these cases were actually "easier."

Appendix A
Description of 17 Preventive-Services Programs

The 17 programs reviewed by Jones (1985) represent a variety of service programs, and have been clustered according to three types:

1. Comprehensive Social Work Services (CSWS): The program includes counseling and social services provided directly and by referral through social work staff.
2. Counseling/Psychotherapy (C/P): The program emphasizes work with individuals and families to modify behavior through such techniques as psychotherapy, role modeling, training, and education. The provision of social services is not emphasized or provided directly, although families may be referred to other agencies to arrange for services. Diagnostic assessment (often through considerable home observation) is stressed.
3. Service Planning/Interagency Contracting (SP/IC): The agency plans and monitors the delivery of needed services by other agencies, rather than providing the services itself.

The first two types are related to the "family social casework" and "parent therapy" models of family intervention identified by White et al. (1973). The third type is a new designation. Examples of "parent education" and "parent training" models, as described by White and his colleagues and meeting the requirements for inclusion in this review, could not be found.

For this table, program intensity was classified according to three levels:

- High: Family members are seen for more than one hour a week.
- Medium: Family members are seen three or four times a month (about once a week).
- Low: Family members are seen every two weeks or less.

Program duration was categorized into three levels:

- Long: over a year
- Medium: six months to a year
- Brief: less than six months

It should be noted that the reported failures in the Philadelphia study are those cases in which foster care placement was *recommended* by the agency, not necessarily those in which it actually occurred. Other studies such as Sherman et al. (1973) and Jones et al. (1976) have shown that cases referred for placement often do not enter placement.

313

Study	Site	Source of Cases	Selection criteria
Bowen Family Center (Sullivan et al., 1977)	Voluntary agency especially created by the Juvenile Protective Association, Chicago	Agencies in community targeted by program	Substantial child neglect Serious limitations in family functioning
Own Home Study (Sherman et al., 1973)	Three public county departments in NY and PA and one voluntary child welfare agency in Boston	Regular intake	Judgment of social worker that preventive services were the service of choice
New York State Project (Jones et al., 1976)	Special units set up in two public county departments in NYS and seven voluntary child care agencies in NYC	Local DSS intake primarily; some from community outreach	Foster care likely within six months Case amenable to preventive services in judgment of agency
Youth Services' Family-Based Servie (Levine & McDaid, 1979)	Program set up by oluntary child care agency in Philadelphia	City public welfare agency	One or more children in placement or facing placement Agency and family believe positive changes can occur
Lower East Side Family Union (LESFU) (Beck, 1979; Dunu, 1979)	Specially created voluntary agency on lower east side of NYC	Families are referred by SSC, schools, police, community agencies, and other families	"High-risk" cases had one or more children at high risk of placement and family life had a highly uncertain quality
Homebuilders (Kinney, 1978; Haapala & Kinney, 1979)	Specially created voluntary agency in Tacoma, WA	Community agencies	Family is too dys-functional for tra-ditional social services Family and referring agency sign state-ment saying Homebuilders is last option before placement
In-Home Fam-ily Support Services (Stephens, 1979)	Program set up by voluntary child & family agency in Des Moines, IA	Community agencies or self-referral	Family not already receiving in-home services from an-other agency

Program type[b]	Intensity	Duration	Sample size	Percentage entering care	Control or comparison group
CSWS	High	Long	162 children	17% during active contact with agency	None
CSWS	Low	At least medium (8-1/2 months when study ended	147 children	13% during 12 months of study	None
CSWS	Medium to low	At least medium (8-1/2 months when study ended)	356 children (home at assignment)	7% in care at end of evaluation (8-1/2 months after assignment)	18% in care
CSWS	High	Medium (one year on aerage)	32 families	*Placement rec-ommended for 31% after 4 months of service	None
SP/IC	Varies	Unknown	193 "high-risk" fam-ilies served in 1977	6% required placement	None
C/P[l]	High	Brief (4–6 weeks)	207 families during first three years of program	14% in care within one year of intake	None
C/P	High (al-most 6 hours/ week)	Unknown	26 children at risk of placement served from 6/77 to 12/77	23% entered care during the 6-month period	None

(continued)

Study	Site	Source of Cases	Selection criteria
Parents and Children Together (PACT) (Callard and Morin, 1979)	Program set up by Human Development Division of Wayne State University, Detroit	Public foster care and protective-services department	A placement issue was involved Parents who did not express sufficient desire to keep children at home, were untreated substance abusers, chronically psychotic, potentially violent, severely mentally impaired, or serious abuses of their children were excluded from service
Bronx Project[c] (Halper and Jones, 1981)	Specially created unit in Bronx Field Office of Special Services for Children (SSC) in NYC	Protective/diagnostic units in Bronx Field Office	Case was new to SSC Met "at-risk" guidelines Primary caretakers who were drug addicts or psychotic were not accepted Children requiring specialized medical placements were not eligible
Hudson County Project[c] (Maghura and DeRubeis, 1980)	Specially created unit of a large public county department in NJ	Regular intake	Children likely to enter care in two years without service Excluded from service were families in crisis at time of referral, cases with foster care within the last three years, children prepared for residential treatment
Omaha Project[c] (Rosenberg et al., 1982)	Specially created unit at Meyer Children's Rehabilitation Institute, Omaha	County CPS	Children under age 7 Not under cost referral No children in care for three years prior to referral

Program type[b]	Intensity	Duration	Sample size	Percentage entering care	Control or comparison group
CSWS	High (1–6 hours/ week)	Medium (6 months on average	214 children at risk of placement who had had at least 2 months of service between 6/77 and 9/78	8% had entered placement by 9/78	None
CSWS	Medium (three contacts per month on average)	Long (14 months on average)	156 children	4% had entered placement by end of evaluation	17% had entered placement
CSWS	Low (average of two contacts per month)	Unknown	First 23 families served by project	17% had at least one child enter care at end of one year of project	13% of "known" control families experienced foster care and 11% of "blind" control families
CSWS	Unknown	Long (average of 12.8 months at end of project)	80 families	4% had a child enter care by end of evaluation	11% had a child enter care

(continued)

Study	Site	Source of Cases	Selection criteria
Richmond Project[c] (Ware et al., 1981)	Specially created unit in the Family Services Division of the Richmond, VA DPW	jADC and general relief applicants	Family applying for ADC or general relief No children in care for two years before referral
Intensive Crisis Counseling Programs (Carroccio, 1982)	Specially created service in two voluntary counseling and mental health agencies under contract with Florida Dept. of Health and Rehab. Services (HRS)	HRS's Single Intake and Protective Services	Danger or imminent removal of child from home
Home and Community Treatment (HCT)[d]	Mendota Mental Health Institute, Madison, WI	Community agencies, but all screened by county MHC	Screened by county Mental Health Center Other treatment attempted but failed Family judged sufficiently motivated to benefit from service
Family and Community Services (FCS)[d]	St. Aemillian Child Care Center, Milwaukee	Mental health clinic, county DSS, and others	Only intervention likely to produce change in the family
Family Training Program (FTP)[d]	Winnebago Mental Health Institute, Winnebago, WI	County DSS	Parents are willing to work with program Parents aren't severely mentally ill, alcoholic, or drug-addicted
Project OPT[d]	Special project set up by Wisconsin Dept. of Health and Social Services, Madison	County DSS	Family willing to sign a contract to permit initial data collection

[a] Source: M. A. Jones (1985), A second chance for families: Five years later—A follow-up of a program to prevent foster care. Washington, D.C.: Child Welfare League of America, pp. 27–34. Reprinted with permission of the Child Welfare League of America.
[b] Defined in text.

Program type[b]	Intensity	Duration	Sample size	Percentage entering care	Control or comparison group
CSWS	Low (at least two contacts a month)	Unknown	62 families	7 children placed by of project[e]	One child placed by end of project
C/P	High	Brief (maximum of 6 weeks)	196 children	3% removed by state by end of 6 weeks of service	None
C/P	High (average of 3.6 hours per week)	Medium (11 months on the average)	70 families from 1973 through early 1982	12% of families had one or more children enter care during or after intervention	None
C/P	High (average of 5.4 hours per week)	Medium (12 months on the average)	45 families from 1977 through 8/81	22% of families had one or more children enter care during or after intervention	None
C/P	Unknown	Medium (average of 10 months)	20 families from 1977 through 8/81	30% of families had one or more children enter care during or after intervention	None
C/P	High (average of 2.7 hours per week)	Brief (4 months on the average)	32 families from 1977 through 9/78 (duration of project)	13% of families had one or more children enter care during or after intervention	None

[c] One of the seven federally funded projects modeled after the New York State project.
[d] One of the four Wisconsin projects, similar in design, described by Cautley and Plane (1983).
[e] Percentages not computed because denominators were uncertain.

319

Appendix B
Clinical-Service Descriptions[a]

Clinical service therapist activities	Work primarily with	Primary focus
1. Use of reinforcement: Explain reinforcement theory; teach need for follow-through; identify/suggest concrete reinforcers with family members; teach/help family implement reinforcement schedules	Parents	Educational
2. Tracking behaviors: Show parents how to count frequencies of problem behavior, how to graph behavior, how to analyze trends; show children how to make out their own behavioral charts	Parents/children	Educational
3. Environmental controls: Make court referrals; work with community system to provide structure; reduce risk through removal of weapons, identifying safe "time-out" space	Parents	Application
4. Natural/logical consequences: Teach concept and skill; help parents identify consequences	Parents	Educational
5. Time out: Teach parent time out as a personal coping skill and also a behavioral consequence; prepare child for the consequence; model approach to help parent develop skill; teach what happens after time out	Parents	Educational
6. Active listening skill: Instruct on reflective listening techniques, using written materials, videos, role plays, modeling; assign homework; set up experimental period, etc.	Parents/children	Educational

(continued)

Clinical service therapist activities	Work primarily with	Primary focus
7. "I" statements: Give rationale, instruct on techniques; lead practice, role play; use teachable moments to model techniques; use homework, e.g., practice writing "I" statements when upset	Parents	Educational
8. No-lose problem-solving: Teach rationale and compare with other approaches; teach how to isolate problems and break them down into smaller manageable issues; help family practice on areas of conflict	Parents/children	Educational
9. Problem ownership: Teach concept of personal territory regarding problems, owner responsibility, how to respond acording to whose ownership	Parents	Educational
11. Anger management: Teach persons how to identify anger at earlier stages and interrupt anger chain; rehearse; teach de-escalation techniques (self and others)	Parents/children	Educational
12. Depression management: Inform about depression; identify possible reasons for its persistence; develop plan to reduce, also safety planning if client is suicidal; help family members identify what they can do to help	Parents/children	Application
13. Anxiety and confusion management: Get information on anxiety-producing situations for person; develop strategy with person, e.g., self-talk; coach client through anxious moments	Parents/children	Application

(continued)

Clinical service therapist activities	Work primarily with	Primary focus
14. Self-criticism reduction: Discuss why self-criticism is harmful; help person list unhelpful self-statements and replace with helpful; have client count negative self-statements; teach and help client rehearse positive "self-talk"; model positive messages	Parents/children	Education/application
15. Build self-esteem: Involve or refer person in esteem-building activities; try to reinforce strengths and positive aspects; teach client how to use positive self-talk; also addressed in almost any activity that helps family to function better	Parents/children	Educational/application
16. Handle frustration: With children, teach them how to handle no, directions, limitations, from parents; with parents, teach them what to do when their child is frustrated; also teaching "I" messages, positive self-talk, relaxation techniques	Parents/children	Educational
17. Impulse management: Identify with parents and child situations when one is likely to be impulsive (i.e., shoplifting); teach consequential decision-making; give homework on what one does or doesn't want to happen, make prevention plan	Parents	Educational/application
18. Use of crisis card: Make up a individualized crisis card with person, recognize emotions prior to escalation, identify calming activities	Parents/children	Application
19. RET concepts: Explain basic RET principles and theory; thoughts, not events, influence feelings; use RET primer	Parents	Educational

(continued)

Clinical service therapist activities	Work primarily with	Primary focus
20. RET techniques Identify and question/dispute person's irrational thoughts and beliefs; practice with client to help reduce unhelpful thoughts, identify cues that generate such thoughts, challenge these negative thoughts and make more realistic appraisals; give homework	Parents	Educational/application
21. Pleasant events: Help client identify how pleasant events occur; help them plan; make assignments or do with clients	Parents/children	Application
22. Relaxation: Use progressive relaxation/imagery instruction; show and then watch client self-instruct; may use tapes; also teach/employ breathing exercises, physical exercise	Parents	Educational/application
23. Track emotion frequency and/or intensity: Teach person to monitor own or family members' emotions or moods, to recognize emotion prior to escalation, to identify both frequency and intensity; often includes charting	Parents	Educational
25. Conversational or social skills: Teach specific skills to manage interpersonal situations, communication, etiquette, relationship dynamics; use videotapes, handouts, coaching sessions	Children	Educational
26. Problem-solving: Help family resolve parent/child issues; implement no-lose problem-solving, fair fighting, break problems down into manageable sizes, generate alternative solutions	Parents/children	Educational/application

(continued)

Clinical service therapist activities	Work primarily with	Primary focus
27. Negotiation skills: Teach ways to avoid conflict, power struggles; teach brainstorming techniques, how to evaluate/revise solutions	Parents/children	Educational
28. Give and accept feedback: Teach how to give feedback without blaming, scapegoating, or criticizing; teach importance of being able to learn from feedback/criticism; also model openness	Parents/children	Educational
29. Appropriate sexual behavior: Teach responsible sexuality; birth control information; use books, tapes, films; self-help groups for victims; for sexually abusive families teach personal boundaries, impulse control	Children	Educational
30. Accepting no from others: Teach social skills; children's story; assertiveness, negotiation skills	Children	Educational
31. Improve compliance: Help parents set up structure/behavioral management arrangements; charts, reinforcement, consequences	Parents	Educational/application
32. Territorial concepts: Teach assertiveness and territoriality; use books, tapes, practice sessions on problem areas	Parents	Educational
33. Fair fighting: Teach fair-fighting rules, negotiating, problem-solving techniques; practice sessions	Parents/children	Educational
34. General assertiveness concepts and skills: Teach saying no, not infringing on others' rights, expressing opinions, standing up for own rights	Parents/children	Educational

(continued)

Clinical service therapist activities	Work primarily with	Primary focus
36. How to use journal: How to keep journal; applications to improve self-talk, track personal or family member behavior, for ventilation/de-escalation	Parents/children	Educational
37. Listening to client: Use reflective, empathetic listening to assess problems, build relationships, de-escalate feelings	Parents/children	Application
38. Encouraging: Give reassurance; help client see more options; reinforce positive steps; challenge negative self-talk; model positive approach	Parents/children	Application
39. Monitoring clients: Make home visits, phone calls, collateral contacts; check school attendance/compliance	Parents/children	Application
40. Building hope: Model positive view; explore options; implement crisis card, positive self-statements	Parents/children	Application
41. Relationship building: Be available and helpful; follow through on appointments; provide concrete services (physical necessities); active listening, show concern and understanding; develop recreational/social activities for family	Parents/children	Application
42. Family council: Teach now to conduct, rules and procedures; help family set up and conduct	Parents/children	Educational
43. Clarify family roles: Assess member roles in family; help family set appropriate and clear expectations	Parents/children	Application
44. Process of change: Teach how behaviors are	Parents	Educational

(continued)

Clinical service therapist activities	*Work primarily with*	*Primary focus*
learned and are learnable; teach how change occurs (small steps); teach how to get change, reinforcement, shaping, progressive approximation; how to recognize progress		
45. Child development: Teaching parents to understand developmental stages, age-appropriate behaviors, changing needs of children, to have realistic expectations based on age, how to help a child learn self-dependence; use child development materials, handouts	Parents	Educational
46. Social skills: Teach skills to handle specific interpersonal situations, etiquette, relationship dynamics; use videotapes, handouts, role play, practice/coaching sessions	Children	Educational
47. Clarify or specify problem behaviors: Work from generalized labels of problematic behavior down to specifics; break into small, manageable goals; examine why this is a problem; determine problem ownership, family goals/values in relation to problem	Parents/children	Application
48. Defusing crisis: Structure situation, allow venting/sharing of feelings in safe environment, clarify problems, look at options, counter "awfulizing," use time out/separation of clients	Parents/children	Application
49. Reframing: Help family look at different	Parents/children	Application

(continued)

Clinical service therapist activities	Work primarily with	Primary focus
views of their situation/problems; help them relabel behaviors in more benign, nonthreatening description		
50. Setting treatment goals and objectives: Negotiate expectations, work for mutual agreement on goals, methods, measurement of success	Parents/children	Application
51. Providing reinforcers: Provide money, recreation, clothing, etc., as rewards for positive behavior	Parents/children	Application
52. Refer to other counseling: Provide information about resources and eligibility requirements/intake procedures; includes advice on how to access services and be good consumers; make take to appointment	Parents	Application
53. Make treatment plans: Negotiate mutual agreement on treatment methods to be used, how to measure success, consequences, timetables	Parents/children	Application
54. De-escalating Help family to structure activities and routine for those times when conflict/chaos predictably occur	Parents/children	Application
55. Values clarification: Discuss values/motivations of parent and child, help them identify differences and how these affect behavior; bridge age gap; use values clarification tools	Parents/children	Application
56. Offer support/understanding: Listening, empathetic response, ask for clarification, encouraging	Parents/children	Application

(continued)

Clinical service therapist activities	Work primarily with	Primary focus
57. Build structure/routine: Work with family on organization, chores, time limits, help them build charts/schedules, define consequences/rewards; reinforce parent follow-through	Parents/children	Application
58. Clarify family rules: Help family members to define, communicate, agree on rules, write down and post	Parents/children	Application
59. Track/chart behaviors: Create behavioral charts, record and follow behavioral contract	Parents/children	Application
60. Behavior rehearsal/role play: Practice for client on new skills, such as parenting, assertiveness, social skills, communications	Parents/children	Application
61. Provide literature: Give handouts on topics being discussed	Parents	Application
62. Provide paper/pencil tests Administer measures and exercises, i.e., Hudson scales, Magura, values clarification exercises	Parents/children	Application
63. Multiple-impact therapy: Conjoint family therapeutic technique to deal with extreme problems in family relationships	Parents/children	Application
66. Refer to other counseling: Suggest referral, provide information to client; make contact with provider, give information	Parents/children	Application
67. Refer to social service or informal helping network: Suggest referral, provide information to client; make contact, give information	Parents/children	Application

(continued)

Clinical service therapist activities	Work primarily with	Primary focus
68. Consult with other service: Meet in case coordination, provide and request/receive information and clients, negotiate in clients' behalf, give information about HBS	Other	Application
69. Advocacy with utilities: Negotiate to acquire, continue, or have service reinstated for client; work out repayment agreements	Other	Application
70. Advocacy with schools: Negotiate for special programs or allowances	Other	Application
71. Meet with other providers: Staff cases, share information, solve problems, get child into programs	Other	Application
72. Attend/testify at court: Make progress reports or recommendations; advocate for clients	Other	Application
73. Money management: Teach budgeting techniques and management of expenditures; help clients set up budgets; monitor budgets/expenditures	Parents	Educational/application
74. Time management: Teach and help persons implement techniques for organizing their time; prioritizing activities; scheduling time	Parents/children	Educational
75. Teach use of leisure: Develop lists of possibilities; help select and plan	Parents/children	Educational/application
76. Teach job hunting or interviewing skills: Teach now to interview for job, grooming, hygiene, attire	Parents/children	Educational/application
77. Academic skills, school performance:	Children	Educational

(continued)

Appendix B (Continued)

Clinical service therapist activities	Work primarily with	Primary focus
Tutor child, help build academic competency in a specific area, help complete assignments, improve skills; arrange for remedial education		
78. Develop informal supports: Teach now to make friends; give assignments; use social support network map, community interaction checklist; request help from relatives, neighbors, etc.	Parents	Educational/application
79. Recognize suicide potential: Do suicide risk assessment	Parents/children	Application
80. Skills for protecting children from sexual assault or abuse: Teach self-protection skills, dynamics and warning signs of possible sexual abuse; teach assertiveness, personal space and boundary issues, contingency plans	Parents/children	Educational

[a] This information is based on a study conducted by Robert Lewis. For more information see Lewis (1990).

References

Alexander, J. F., & Parsons, B. V. (1982). *Functional family therapy.* Monterey, CA: Brook/Cole.

Allison, P. D. (1984). *Event history analysis: Regression for longitudinal event data.* Quantitative applications in the social sciences series paper #46. Beverly Hills, CA: Sage.

American Chamber of Commerce Researchers Association (1989). *Cost of living index—Second quarter of 1989* 22(2), Louisville, KY: American Chamber of Commerce Researchers Association.

Anderson, D. F. (1983). Disentangling statistical artifacts from hard conclusions. *Journal of Policy Analysis and Management, 2*(2), 296–302.

Armstrong, K. A. (1982). Economic analysis of a child abuse and neglect treatment program. *Child Welfare, 62*(1), 3–13.

AuClaire, P., & Schwartz, I. M. (1986). *An evaluation of the effectiveness of intensive home-based services as an alternative to the placement for adolescents and their families.* Minneapolis, MN: Hennepin County Community Services Departmente, and the University of Minnesota, Hubert H. Humphrey Institute of Public Affairs.

Austin, M. J., Cox, G., Gottlieb, N., Hawkins, J. D., Kruzich, J. M., & Rauch, R. (1982). *Evaluating your agency's programs.* Newbury Park, CA: Sage Press.

Axinn, J., & Levin, H. (1982). *Social welfare—A history of the American response to need* (2nd ed.). New York: Harper and Row.

Baily, W. H. (1978). *A comparison of performance levels between BSW and BA social workers.* Unpublished doctoral dissertation, Catholic University of America, Washington, D.C., available through University Microfilms International.

Bandura, A. (1985). Models of causality and social learning theory. In M. J. Mahoney & A. Freeman (Eds.), *Cognition and psychotherapy.* New York: Plenum.

Barrera, M., Jr., & Ainlay, S. L. (1983). The structure of social support: A conceptual and empirical analysis. *Journal of Community Psychology, 11,* 133–143.

Barrera, M., Jr., Sandler, I. N., & Ramsay, T. B. (1981). Preliminary development of a scale of social support: Studies on college students. *American Journal of Community Psychology, 9,* 435–447.

Barth, R. P. (1990). Theories guiding home-based intensive family preservation services. In J. K. Whittaker, J. Kinney, E. M. Tracy, & C. Booth (Eds.), *Reaching high risk families: Intensive family preservation in human services.* Hawthorne, NY: Aldine de Gruyter.

Barth, R. P., & Berry, M. (1987). Outcomes of child welfare services under permanency planning. *Social Service Review, 61*(1), 71–90.

Beck, B. M. (1979). *The lower east side family union: A social invention.* New York: Foundation for Child Development.

Berk, R. A., & Rossi, P. H. (1990). *Thinking about program evaluation.* Newbury Park, CA: Sage.

Berkman, B. (1980). Psychosocial problems and outcomes: An external validity study. *Health and Social Work, 5,* 5–21.

Bernfeld, G., Cousin, M. L., Daniels, K., Hall, P., Knox, K., McNeil, H., & Morrison, W. (1990). *St. Lawrence Youth Association Community Support Services Annual Report* (November, 1990). Kingston, Ontario: St. Lawrence Youth Association.

Bernstein, B., Snider, D. A., & Meezan, W. (1975). *Foster care needs and alternatives to placement.* Albany, NY: State Board of Social Welfare.

Billingsley, A., & Giovannoni, J. M. (1972). *Children of the storm: Black children and American child welfare.* New York: Harcourt, Brace, Jovanovich.

Blossfeld, H., Hamerle, A., & Mayer, K. U. (1989). *Event history analysis.* Hillsdale, NJ: Lawrence Erlbaum Associates.

Booz-Allen and Hamilton, Inc. (1987). *The Maryland social services job analysis and personal qualifications study.* Baltimore, MD: Maryland Department of Human Resources.

Boyd-Franklin, N. (1989). *Black families in therapy: A multisystems approach.* New York: Guildford Publications.

Bremner, R. (Ed.) (1970–71). *Children and youth in America* (Vol. I, 1600–1865; Vol. II, 1865–1965). Cambridge, MA: Harvard University Press.

Bribitzer, M. P., & Verdieck, M. J. (1988). Home-based, family-centered intervention: Evaluation of a foster care prevention program. *Child Welfare, 67*(3), 255–266.

Bronfenbrenner, U. (1979). *The ecology of human development.* Cambridge, MA: Harvard University Press.

Brown, G. (Ed.) (1968). *The multi-problem dilemma.* Metuchen, NJ: Scarecrow Press.

Bryce, M. (1979). Home-based care: Development and rationale. In S. Maybanks & M. Bryce (Eds.), *Home-based services for children and families: Policy, practice, and research.* Springfield, IL: Charles C. Thomas.

Bryce, M., & Lloyd, J. C. (Eds.) (1981). *Treating families in the home: An alternative to placement.* Springfield, IL: Charles C. Thomas.

Bureau of Children's Services Advisory Committee (1982). *Task force report on staff qualifications and deployment.* Olympia, WA: Department of Health and Human Services, Bureau of Children's Services.

Burkett, S. R., & White, M. (1974). Hellfire and delinquency: Another look. *Journal for the Scientific Study of Religion, 13,* 455–462.

Burt, M. R., & Balyeat, R. (1974). A new system for improving the care of neglected and abused children. *Child Welfare, 53*(3), 167–197.

Butcher, J., & Koss, M. (1978). Research on brief and crisis-oriented psychotherapies. In S. Garfield & A. Bergin (Eds.), *Handbook of psychotherapy and behavior change.* New York: John Wiley & Sons.

Buxbaum, C. B. (1981). Cost-benefit analysis: The mystique versus the reality. *Social Service Review, 55*(3), 453–471.

Cabral, R. J., & Callard, E. D. (1982). A home-based program to serve high-risk families. *Journal of Home Economics, 74*(3), 14–19.

Callard, E. D., & Morin, P. (1979). *Parents and children together: An alternative to foster care.* Detroit, MI: Wayne State University, Department of Family and Consumer Studies.

Callister, J. P., Mitchell, L., & Tolley, G. (1986). Profiling family preservation efforts in Utah. *Children Today, 15*(6), 23–25, 36–37.

Carroccio, D. F. (1982). *Intensive crisis counseling programs.* Tallahassee, FL: Florida Department of Health and Rehabilitative Services, Office of the Inspector General, Office of Evaluation.

Cautley, P. W. (1979). *The Home and community treatment process: Helping families change.* Madison, WI: Mendota Mental Health Institute, Home and Community Treatment.

Cautley, P. W., & Plane, M. B. (1983). *Facilitating family change: A look at four groups providing intensive in-home services.* Unpublished manuscript, Wisconsin Department of Health and Social Services, Madison.

The Center for the Study of Social Policy. (1988). *State family preservation programs: A description of six states' progress in developing services to keep families together.* Working Paper FP-3. Washington, D.C.: The Center for the Study of Social Policy.

Chambers, C. A. (1963). *Seedtime of reform: American social service and social action, 1918–1933.* Minneapolis, MN: University of Minnesota Press.

Chen, H. T. (1990). *Theory-driven evaluation.* Newbury Park, CA: Sage.

Chestang, L. W. (1978). The delivery of child welfare services to minority group children and their families. In *Child welfare strategy in the coming years.* Washington, D.C.: U.S. Department of Health, Education, and Welfare, Administration for the Children, Youth and Families, Children's Bureau (OHDS 78-30158).

Child Welfare League of America (1989). *Standards for service to strengthen and preserve families with children.* Washington, D.C.: Child Welfare Leagues of America.

Churchill, S. R., Carlson, B., & Nybell, L. (1979). *No child is unadoptable: A reader on adoption of children with special needs.* Beverly Hills, CA: Sage.

Cohen, S., & Wills, T. A. (1985). Stress, social support, and the buffering hypothesis. *Psychological Bulletin, 98,* 310–357.

Compher, J. V. (1983). Home services to families to prevent child placement. *Social Work, 28*(5), 360–364.

Cook, T. D., & Campbell, D. T. (1979). *Quasi-experimentation: Design and analysis issues for field settings.* Chicago: Rand McNally.

Coulton, C. J., & Solomon, P. L. (1977). Measuring outcome of intervention. *Social Work Research & Abstracts, 13,* 3–9.

Cox, D. R. (1972). Regression models and life tables. *Journal of the Royal Statistical Society,* Series B, *34,* 187–202.

Cross, T. L., Bazron, B. J., Dennis, K. W., & Isaacs, M. R. (1989). *Towards a culturally competent system of care: A monograph on effective services for minority children who are severely emotionally disturbed.* Washington, D.C.: Georgetown University Child Development Center.

Crumpler, A., & Casper, M. (1986). Child protective services intensive services unit. *Frontline* 2(1), 4 (newsletter of the National Child Protective Workers Association).

Deal, T. E., & Kennedy, A. A. (1982). *Corporate cultures: The rites and rituals of corporate life.* Reading, MA: Addison-Wesley Publishing.

Dishion, T. J. (1990). The family ecology of boys' peer relations in middle childhood. *Child Development, 61*(3), 874–892.

Dumas, J. E. (1984). Interactional correlates of treatment outcome in behavioral parenting training. *Journal of Consulting and Clinical Psychology, 52*(6), 946–954.

Dumas, J. E., & Albin, J. B. (1986). Parent training outcome: Does active parental involvement matter? *Behavioral Research and Therapy, 24*(2), 227–230.

Dumas, J. E., & Wahler, R. G. (1983). Predictors of treatment outcome in parenting training: Mother insularity and socioeconomic disadvantage. *Behavioral Assessment, 5*, 301–313.

Dunu, M. (1979). The Lower East Side Family Union: Assuring community services for minority families. In S. Maybanks & M. Bryce (Eds.), *Home-based services for children and families: Policy, practice and research* (pp. 211–224). Springfield, IL: Charles C. Thomas.

Edna McConnell Clark Foundation (1985). *Keeping families together: The case for family preservation.* New York: Edna McConnell Clark Foundation.

Ellingson, L. (1990). *Reducing out of home placements through family-based services.* Unpublished manuscript, Beltrami County Department of Human Services, Minnesota (mimeograph).

Ellsworth, R. B. (1975). Consumer feedback in measuring the effectiveness of mental health programs. In M. Guttentag & E. L. Struening (Eds.), *Handbook of Evaluation Research* (Vol. 2). Newbury Park, CA: Sage.

Emlen, A., Lahti, J., Downs, G., McKay, A., & Downs, S. (1978). *Overcoming barriers to planning for children in foster care.* Washington, D.C.: U.S. Department of Health and Human Services, U.S. Children's Bureau (OHDS 78-30138).

Fanshel, D., & Shinn, E. B. (1978). *Children in foster care: A longitudinal investigation.* New York: Columbia University Press.

Fanshel, D., Finch, S. J., & Grundy, J. F. (1989a). Modes of exit from foster family care and adjustment of time of departures of children with unstable life histories. *Child Welfare, 68*(4), 391–402.

Fanshel, D., Finch, S. J., & Grundy, J. F. (1989b). Foster children in life-course perspective: The Casey Family Program experience. *Child Welfare, 68*(5), 467–478.

Feldman, L. (1991). Target population definition. In Y. T. Yuan & M. Rivest (Eds.), *Evaluation resources for family preservation services.* Newbury Park, CA: Sage.

Feldman, L. (1990). *Evaluating the impact of family preservation services in New Jersey.* Trenton, NJ: New Jersey Division of Youth and Family Services, Bureau of Research, Evaluation, and Quality Assurance.

Festinger, T. (1983). *No one ever asked us . . . a postscript to foster care.* New York: Columbia University Press.

Fixen, D. L., Blase, K. A., Olivier, K., Lander, L., Clark, C., & Adams, C. (1988). *Annual report: Alberta family support services*. Calgary, Alberta, Canada: Hull Community Services.

Flaskerud, J. H. (1986). Diagnostic and treatment differences among five ethnic groups. *Psychological Reports, 58*, 219–235.

Forgatch, M. S. (in press). The clinical science vortex: Developing a theory for antisocial behavior. In D. Pepler and K. Rubin (Eds.), *The development and treatment of childhood aggression*. Hillsdale, NJ: Lawrence Erlbaum Associates.

Frankel, H. (1988). Family-centered, home-based services in child protection: A review of the research. *Social Services Review, 62*, 137–157.

Fraser, M. W., & Haapala, D. A. (1988). Home-based family treatment: A quantitative-qualitative assessment. *Journal of Applied Social Sciences, 12*(1), 1–23.

Fraser, M. W., Hawkins, J. D., & Howard, M. (1988). Parent training for delinquency prevention. *Child and Youth Services, 11*(1), 93–125.

Fraser, M. W., Pecora, P. J., & Haapala, D. A. (1989). *Families in crisis: Findings from the Family-Based Intensive Treatment Project—Technical report*. Salt Lake City, UT: University of Utah, Graduate School of Social Work, Social Research Institute; and Federal Way, WA: Behavioral Sciences Institute.

Fraser, M., McDade, K., Haapala, D., & Pecora, P. (1990). Assessing the risks of treatment failure in intensive family preservation services. In A. Algarin, R. M. Friedman, A. J. Duchnowski, K. M. Kutash, S. E. Silver, & M. K. Johnson (Eds.), *Children's mental health services and policy: Building a research base*. Tampa, FL: University of South Florida, Florida Mental Health Institute.

Fraser, M. W., Pecora, P. J., Popuang, C., & Haapala, D. A. (1992). Event history analysis: A proportional hazards perspective on modeling outcomes in intensive family preservation services. *Journal of Social Service Research, 16*(1/2).

Garbarino, J., Sebes, J., & Schellenbach, C. (1984). Families at risk for destructive parent-child relations in adolescence. *Child Development, 55*, 174–183.

Geismar, L. (1979). Home-based care to children: Harmonizing the approaches of research and practice. In S. Maybanks & M. Bryce (Eds.), *Home-based services for children and families* (pp. 325–332). Springfield, IL: Charles C. Thomas.

Geismar, L., & Ayers, B. (1958). *Families in trouble*. St. Paul, MN: Family-Centered Project.

Geismar, L., & Krisberg, J. (1966). The family life improvement project: An experiment in preventive intervention. *Social Casework, 47*(6), 563–570.

General Accounting Office (1990). *Home visiting: A promising early intervention strategy for at-risk families* (Report No. H60/HRD-90-83). Gaithersburg, MD: General Accounting Office.

Gerber, L., Brenner, S., & Litwin, D. (1986). A survey of patient and family satisfaction with social work services. *Social Work in Health Care, 11*, 13–23.

Gershenson, C. P. (1990). Observations on family preservation services evaluations. *Frontline Views, 1* (November), 6–7. Washington, D.C.: The Center for the Study of Social Policy.

Gibbs, J. T., Huang, L. N., & Associates (1989). *Children of color: Psychological interventions with minority youth*. San Francisco, CA: Jossey-Bass.

Giblin, P. T., & Callard, E. D. (1980). Issues in evaluation of action research: A social service model. *Social Work Research and Abstracts, 16*(4), 3–12.

Giordano, P. C. (1977). The client's perspective in agency evaluation. *Social Work*, 22(1), 34–39.

Goldstein, H. (1981). Home-based services and the worker. In M. Bryce & J. C. Lloyd (Eds.), *Treating families in the home: An alternative to placement*. Springfield, IL: Charles C. Thomas.

Gottlieb, N. (1987). Dilemmas and strategies in research on women. In D. S. Burden & N. Gottlieb (Eds.), *The woman client: Providing human services in a changing world*. New York: Travistock Publications.

Gottlieb, N., & Bombyk, M. (1987). Strategies for strengthening feminist research. *Affilia*, 2(2), 23–35.

Green, J. W. (1982). *Cultural awareness in the human services*. Englewood Cliffs, NJ: Prentice-Hall.

Grohoski, L. (1990). *Family-based services in Minnesota: A statewide view and case study*. Unpublished manuscript, Minnesota Department of Human Services, Research and Planning Unit, Community Social Services, St. Paul (mimeograph).

Gruber, A. R. (1973). *Foster home care in Massachusetts: A study of children—Their biological and foster parents*. Boston: Governor's Commission on Adoption and Foster Care.

Gurman, A. S., Kniskern, D. P., & Pinsof, W. (1986). Research on the process and outcome of marital and family therapy. In S. Garfield & A. Bergin (Eds.), *Handbook of psychology and behavior change* (3rd ed.). New York: John Wiley and Sons.

Gutek, B. A. (1978). Client satisfaction. *Journal of Social Issues*, 34(4), 44–56.

Gutiérrez, L. M. (1990). Working with women of color: An empowerment perspective. *Social Work*, 35(2), 149–153.

Haapala, D. A. (1983). Perceived helpfulness, attributed critical incident responsibility, and a discrimination of home-based family therapy treatment outcomes: Homebuilders model. Report prepared for the Department of Health and Human Services, Administration for Children, Youth and Families (Grant #90-CW-626 OHDS). Federal Way, WA: Behavioral Sciences Institute.

Haapala, D. A., & Fraser, M. W. (1987). *Keeping families together: The Homebuilders model revisited*. Federal Way, WA: Behavioral Sciences Institute.

Haapala, D. A., & Kinney, J. M. (1979). Homebuilders's approach to the training of in-home therapists. In S. Maybanks & M. Bryce (Eds.), *Home-based services for children and families* (pp. 248–259). Springfield, IL: Charles C. Thomas.

Haapala, D. A., & Kinney, J. M. (1988). Avoiding out-of-home placement of high-risk status offenders through the use of intensive home-based family preservation services. *Criminal Justice and Behavior*, 15(3), 334–348.

Haapala, D. A., Kinney, J., & McDade, K. (1988a). *Referring families to intensive home-based family preservation services: A guide book* (draft). Federal Way, WA: Behavioral Sciences Institute.

Haapala, D. A., McDade, K., & Johnston, B. (1988b). *Preventing the dissolution of special needs adoption families through the use of intensive home-based family preservation services: The Homebuilders model* (clinical services final report from the Homebuilders Adoption Services Continuum Project). Federal Way, WA: Behavioral Sciences Institute.

Halper, G., & Jones, M. A. (1981). *Serving families at risk of dissolution: Public preventive services in New York City.* New York: Human Resources Administration.

Halpern, R. (1990). Parent support and education programs. *Children and Youth Services Review, 12,* 285–308.

Hargreaves, W. A., & Attkisson, C. C. (1978). Evaluating program outcomes. In C. C. Attkisson, W. A. Hargreaves, M. J. Horowitz, & J. E. Sorensen (Eds.), *Evaluation of human service programs.* New York: Academic Press.

Hartman, A., & Laird, J. (1983). *Family-centered social work practice.* New York: Free Press.

Haugard, J., Hokanson, B., & National Resource Center on Family-Based Services (1983). *Measuring the cost-effectiveness of family-based services and out-of-home care.* Oakdale, IA: University of Iowa, School of Social Work, National Clearinghouse for Family-Centered Programs.

Hayes, J. R., & Joseph, J. A. (1985). *Home-based family centered project evaluation.* Columbus, OH: Metropolitan Human Services Commission.

Hennepin County Community Services Department (1980). *Family study project: Demonstration and research in intensive services to families.* Minneapolis, MN: Hennepin County Community Services Department.

Heying, K. R. (1985). Family-based, in-home services for the severely emotionally disturbed child. *Child Welfare, 64*(5), 519–527.

Higgins, P. C., & Albrecht, G. L. (1977). Hellfire and delinquency: Revisited. *Social Forces, 55,* 952–958.

Hinckley, E. C., & Ellis, W. F. (1985). An effective alternative to residential placement: Home-based services. *Journal of Clinical Child Psychology, 14*(3), 209–213.

Hindelang, M. J., Hirschi, T., & Weis, J. G. (1981). *Measuring delinquency.* Beverly Hills, CA: Sage Press.

Hirsch, J. S., Gailey, J., & Schmerl, E. (1976). A child welfare agency's program of service to children in their own homes. *Child Welfare, 55*(3), 193–204.

Hodges, V. G., Guterman, N. B., Blythe, B. J., & Bronson, D. E. (1989). Intensive aftercare services for children. *Social Casework, 70*(7), 397–404.

Holder, W., & Corey, M. (1986). *Child protective services risk management: A decisionmaking handbook.* Charlotte, NC: ACTION for Child Protection.

Holliday, M., & Cronin, R. (1990). Families first: A significant step toward family preservation. *Families in Society: The Journal of Contemporary Human Services, 71*(5), 303–306.

Horejsi, C. R. (1981). The St. Paul family-centered project revisited: Exploring an old gold mine. In M. Bryce & J. C. Floyd (Eds.), *Treating families in the home: An alternative to placement.* Springfield, IL: Charles C. Thomas Press.

Horejsi, C. R. (1982). *Values and attitudes in child welfare: A training manual.* Missoula, MN: University of Montana, Department of Social Work.

Howing, P. T., Wodarski, J. S., Kurtz, P. D., Gaudin, J. M., & Herbst, E. N. (1990). Child abuse and delinquency: The empirical and theoretical links. *Social Work, 35*(3), 244–242.

Hutchinson, J. R., & Nelson, K. E. (1985). How public agencies can provide family-centered services. *Social Casework, 66*(6), 367–371.

Janchill, M. P. (1975). *Criteria for foster placement and alternatives to foster care.* Albany, NY: Board of Social Welfare.

Janchill, M. P. (1981). *Guidelines for decision-making in child welfare: Case assessment, service planning, and appropriateness in service selection.* Albany, NY: The Human Services Workshops.

Jensen, G. F., & Rojek, D. G. (1980). *Delinquency.* Lexington, MA: D. C. Heath.

Johnson, H. C. (1986). Emerging concerns in family therapy. *Social Work, 31*(4), 299–306.

Jones, M. A. (1985). *A second chance for families: Five years later.* New York: Child Welfare League of America.

Jones, M. A., Neuman, R., & Shyne, A. W. (1976). *A second chance for families: Evaluation of a program to reduce foster care.* New York: Child Welfare League of America.

Kagan, R., & Schlosberg, S. (1989). *Families in perpetual crisis.* New York: W. W. Norton.

Kammerman, S. B., & Kahn, A. J. (1989). *Social services for children, youth and families in the United States.* Greenwich, CT: The Annie E. Casey Foundation.

Kaplan, L. (1986). *Working with multiproblem families.* Lexington, MA: Lexington Books.

Katz, D., Gutek, B. A., Kahn, R. L., & Barton, E. (1975). *Bureaucratic encounters: A pilot study in the evaluation of government agencies.* Ann Arbor, MI: Institute for Social Research.

Kazdin, A. E. (1985). *Treatment of antisocial behavior in children and adolescents.* Homewood, IL: Dorsey Press.

Kenyatta, M. I. (1980). The impact of racism on the family as a support system. *Catalyst, 2,* 37–44.

Kinney, J. (1978). Homebuilders: An in-home crisis intervention program. *Children Today, 7*(1), 15–17, 35.

Kinney, J., & Haapala, D. (1984). *First year Homebuilders mental health project report.* Federal Way, WA: Behavioral Sciences Institute. (mimeograph).

Kinney, J. M., Haapala, D. A., & Booth, C. (1991). *Keeping families together:* The Homebuilders model. Hawthorne, NY: Aldine de Gruyter.

Kinney, J. M., Madsen, B., Fleming, T., & Haapala, D. A. (1977). Homebuilders: Keeping families together. *Journal of Consulting and Clinical Psychology, 45*(4), 667–673.

Knitzer, J., Allen, M. L., & McGowan, B. (1978). *Children without homes: An examination of public responsibility to children in out-of-home care.* Washington, D.C.: Children's Defense Fund.

Kohlert, N. M., & Pecora, P. J. (1989). Worker perceptions of FPS components, support and job satisfaction. In M. W. Fraser, P. J. Pecora, & D. A. Haapala (Eds.), *Families in crisis: Findings from the Family-Based Intensive Treatment Project.* Salt Lake City, UT: University of Utah, Graduate School of Social Work, Social Research Institute; and Federal Way, WA: Behavioral Sciences Institute.

Kugajevsky, V. (1979). Foster grandparents program. In J. G. Abert (Ed.), *Program evaluation at HEW: Research versus reality* (Vol. 3, pp. 123–179). New York: Marcel Dekker.

Kuhn, T. S. (1970). *The structure of scientific revolutions.* Chicago, IL: University of Chicago Press.

Lantz, B. K. (1985). Keeping troubled teens at home. *Children Today, 14*(3), 9–12.

Larzelere, R. E., & Patterson, G. R. (1990). Parental management: Mediator of the effect of socioeconomic status on early delinquency. *Criminology, 28*(2), 301–323.

Lawder, E. A., Poulin, J. E., & Andrews, R. G. (1984). *Helping the multi-problem family: A study of services to children in their own homes (SCOH)*. Philadelphia, PA: Children's Aid Society of Pennsylvania.

Lazar, A., Sagi, A., & Fraser, M. (1991). Involving fathers in social services. *Children and Youth Services Review, 13*(4), 287–300.

Leeds, S. J. (1984). *Evaluation of Nebraska's intensive services project*. Unpublished manuscript, University of Iowa, National Resource Center on Family-Based Services, Iowa City.

Leiby, J. (1978). *A history of social welfare in the United States*. New York: Columbia University Press.

Levin, H. M. (1983). *Cost-effectiveness: A primer*. Newbury Park, CA: Sage.

Levin, H. M. (1985). *Cost-effectiveness: New perspectives in evaluation* (Vol. 4). Beverly Hills, CA: Sage.

Levine, C. (Ed.) (1988). *Programs to strengthen families: A resource guide* (rev. ed.). Chicago: Family Resource Coalition.

Levine, R. A. (1964). Treatment in the home. *Social Work, 9*(1), 19–28.

Levine, T., & McDaid, E. (1979). Services to children in their own homes: A family-based approach. In S. Maybanks & M. Bryce (Eds.), *Home-based services for children and families: Policy, practice, and research* (pp. 260–271). Springfield, IL: Charles C. Thomas.

Lewis, R. E. (1989). The characteristics of home-based services. In M. W. Fraser, P. J. Pecora, & D. A. Haapala (Eds.), *Families in crisis: Findings from the family-based intensive treatment project* (pp. 107–150). Salt Lake City, UT: University of Utah, Graduate School of Social Work, Social Research Institute; and Federal Way, WA: Behavioral Sciences Institute.

Lewis, R. E. (1990). *Service-related correlates of treatment success in intensive family preservation services for child welfare*. Unpublished doctoral dissertation, University of Utah, Salt Lake City.

Lewis, R. E., & Fraser, M. (1987). Blending informal and formal helping networks in foster care. *Children and Youth Services Review, 9*, 153–169.

Lewis, R. G., & Ho, M. K. (1975). Social work with Native Americans. *Social Work, 20*, 379–382.

Lieberman, A. A., Hornby, H., & Russell, M. (1988). Analyzing the educational backgrounds and work experiences of child welfare personnel: A national study. *Social Work, 33*(6), 485–489.

Lloyd, J. C., Bryce, M. E., & Schultze, L. (1980). *Placement prevention and family reunification: A practitioner's handbook for the home-based family-centered program*. Iowa City, IA: University of Iowa, School of Social Work, National Resource Center on Family-Based Services.

Loeber, R., & Stouthamer-Loeber, M. (1986). Family factors as correlates and predictors of juvenile conduct problems and delinquency. In M. Tonry & M. Morris (Eds.), *Crime and justice* (pp. 29–149). Chicago, IL: University of Chicago Press.

Maas, H., & Engler, R. (1959). *Children in need of parents*. New York: Columbia University Press.

Magazino, C. J. (1983). Services to children and families at risk of separation. In B. G.

McGowan & W. Meezan (Eds.), *Child welfare: Current dilemmas, future directions* (pp. 211–254). Itasca, IL: F. E. Peacock.

Magura, S. (1981). Are services to prevent foster care effective? *Children and Youth Services Review, 3*(3), 193–212.

Magura, S., & De Rubeis, R. (1980). *The effectiveness of preventive services for families with abused, neglected and disturbed children: Second year evaluation of Hudson County Project.* Trenton, NJ: Division of Youth and Family Services, Bureau of Research.

Magura, S., & Moses, B. S. (1984). Clients as evaluators in child protective services. *Child Welfare, 63*(2), 99–112.

Magura, S., & Moses, B. S. (1986). *Outcome measures for child welfare services: Theory and applications.* Washington, D.C.: Child Welfare League of America.

Magura, S., Moses, B. S., & Jones, M. A. (1987). *Assessing risk and measuring change in families: The family risk scales.* Washington, D.C.: Child Welfare League of America.

Maluccio, A. N. (1979a). *Learning from clients.* New York: Free Press.

Maluccio, A. N. (1979b). Perspectives of social workers and clients on treatment outcome. *Social Casework, 60*(7), 394–401.

Maluccio, A. N., & Fein, E. (1987). Effects of permanency planning on foster children: A response. *Social Work, 32*(6), 546–548.

Maluccio, A. N., Fein, E., & Olmstead, K. (1986). *Permanency planning for children—Concepts and methods.* New York: Tavistock Publications and Methuen.

Maximus, Inc. (1985). *Child welfare statistical fact book.* Washington, D.C.: U.S. Department of Health and Human Services, Office of Human Development Services, Administration for Children, Youth and Families, Office of Planning and Management.

Maybanks, S., & Bryce, M. (Eds.) (1979). *Home-Based Services for children and families: Policy, practice, and research.* Springfield, IL: Charles C. Thomas.

Mayer, J. E., & Timms, N. (1970). *The client speaks.* New York: Atherton.

McAdoo, H. (1982). Demographic trends for people of color. *Social Work, 27,* 15–23.

McCroskey, J., & Nelson, J. (1989). Practice-based research in a family-support program: The family connection project example. *Child Welfare, 68*(6), 573–587.

McRoy, R. G., Shorkey, C. L., & Garcia, E. (1985). Alcohol use and abuse among Mexican Americans. In E. Freeman (Ed.), *Social work practice with clients who have alcohol problems.* Springfield, IL: Charles C. Thomas.

Milardo, R. M. (1983). Social networks and pair relationships: A review of substantive and measurement issues. *Sociology and Social Research, 68*(1), 1–18.

Millar, R., & Millar, A. (Eds.) (1981). *Developing client outcome monitoring systems: A guide for state and local social service agencies.* Washington, D.C.: Urban Institute Press.

Miller, L., & Pruger, R. (1978). Evaluation in care programs: With illustrations from homemaker-chore in California. *Administration in Social Work, 2*(4), 469–478.

Mitchell, C., Tovar, P., & Knitzer, J. (1989). *The Bronx Homebuilders program: An evaluation of the first 45 families.* New York: Bank Street College of Education.

Mnookin, R. H. (1973). Foster care: In whose best interest? *Harvard Educational Review, 43*(4), 599–638.

Moch, M. (1975). *Quality of service management and instrumentation* (contract No. 600-75-0141). Washington, D.C.: Social Security Administration.

Morisey, P. G. (1990). Black children in foster care. In S. M. L. Logan, E. M. Freeman, & R. G. McRoy (Eds.), *Social work practice with Black families*. New York: Longman.

National Association of Social Workers (1980). *Summary of Walter Hampton Baily's DSW dissertation: A comparison of performance levels between BSW and BA social workers*. Washington, D.C.: National Association of Social Workers.

National Center for Comprehensive Emergency Services to Children (1978). *Comprehensive emergency services: Training guide* (2nd ed.).

National Resource Center on Family-Based Services (1988a). *Annotated directory of selected family-based programs*. Iowa City, IA: University of Iowa—Oakdale Campus, School of Social Work.

National Resource Center on Family-Based Services (1988b). Factors contributing to success and failure in family-based services. *Prevention Report*, Spring/ Summer, 1–2.

Nelson, J. P. (1984). *An experimental evaluation of a home-based family-centered program model in a public child protection agency*. Unpublished doctoral thesis, University of Minnesota, School of Social Work, Minneapolis.

Nelson, K., Emlen, A., Landsman, M., & Hutchinson, J. (1988). *Family based services: Factors contributing to success and failure in family based child welfare services: Final report* (OHDS Grant #90-CW-0732). Iowa City, IA: National Resource Center on Family Based Services, School of Social Work, University of Iowa.

Olivier, K., Dawood, G., Geake, G., Oostenbrink, A., Unrau, Y., Blase, K., & Fixen, D. (1990). *Alberta Family Support Services Annual Report* (November 1990). Calgary, Alberta: Hull Community Services.

Olsen, L., & Holmes, W. (1982). Educating child welfare workers: The effects of professional training on service delivery. *Journal of Education for Social Work*, *18*(1), 94–102.

Olson, D. H. (1986). Circumplex model VII: Validation studies and FACES III. *Family Process*, *25*, 337–351.

Olson, D. H., & Killorin, E. (1985). *Chemically dependent families and the circumplex model*. St. Paul, MN: Family Social Science, University of Minnesota.

Olson, D. H., McCubbin, H. I., Barnes, H., Larsen, A., Muxen, M., & Wilson, M. (1983). *Families: What makes them work*. Beverly Hills: Sage.

Olson, D. H., Portner, J., & Lavee, Y. (1985). *FACES III*. St. Paul, MN: Family Social Science, University of Minnesota.

Olson, D. H., Russell, C. S., & Sprenkle, D. H. (Eds.) (1989). *Circumplex model: Systematic assessment and treatment of families*. New York: Haworth Press.

Orr, L. L., & Bell, S. H. (1987). *Valuing the labor market benefits of job training and employment programs: Procedures and findings from the AFDC homemaker-home health aide demonstrations*. Washington, D.C.: ABT Associates Inc.

Overton, A. (1953). Serving families who don't want help. *Social Casework*, *34*, 304–309.

Owan, T. C. (1982). Neighborhood-based mental health: An approach to overcome inequities in mental health services delivery to racial and ethnic minorities. In D. E. Biegel and A. J. Naparstek (Eds.), *Community support systems and mental health: Practice, policy, and research* (pp. 282–300). New York: Springer.

Patterson, G. R. (1985). Beyond technology: The next stage in developing an empirical base for parent training. In L. L'Abate (Ed.), *Handbook of family psychology and therapy* (Vol. 2). Homewood, IL: Dorsey Press.

Patterson, G. R., DeBaryshe, B. D., & Ramsey, E. (1989). A development perspective on antisocial behavior. *American Psychologist 44*, 329–335.

Pecora, P. J. (1991). Investigating the allegations of child maltreatment: The strengths and limitations of current risk assessment systems. In M. Robin (Ed.) *Assessing reports of child maltreatment: The problem of false allegations.* (Special issue of *Child and Youth Services Review*).

Pecora, P. J. (1990a). Designing and managing family preservation services: Implications for human services administration curricula. In J. K. Whittaker, J. Kinney, E. M. Tracy, & C. Booth (Eds.), *Reaching high-risk families: Intensive family preservation in human services.* Hawthorne, NY: Aldine de Gruyter.

Pecora, P. J. (1990b). Using risk assessment technology and other screening methods for determining the need for child placement in family-based services. A summary of a presentation for the Fourth Annual Empowering Families Conference, National Association of Family-Based Services, Detroit, Michigan (November 5, 1990).

Pecora, P. J., Delewski, C. H., Booth, C., Haapala, D. A., & Kinney, J. (1985). Home-based family-centered services: The impact of training on worker attitudes. *Child Welfare, 64*(5), 529–540.

Pecora, P. J., Briar, K., & Zlotnik, J. L. (1989). *Addressing the personnel crisis in child welfare: A social work response.* Silver Spring, MD: National Association of Social Workers.

Pecora, P. J., Kinney, J. M., Mitchell, L., & Tolley, G. (1990a). Selecting an agency auspice for family preservation services. *Social Service Review, 64*(2), 288–307.

Pecora, P. J., Haapala, D. A., & Fraser, M. W. (1991a). *Comparing family preservation services with other family-based service programs.* In E. M. Tracy, D. A. Haapala, J. M. Kinney, & P. J. Pecora (Eds.), *Intensive family preservation services: An instructional source book.* Cleveland, OH: Case Western Reserve University, Mandel School of Applied Social Sciences.

Pecora, P. J., Fraser, M. W., & Haapala, D. A. (in press). Intensive family preservation services: An update from the FIT project. *Child Welfare.*

Pecora, P. J., Fraser, M. W., & Haapala, D. A. (1991b). Intensive, home-based family preservation services: Client outcomes and issues for program design. In K. Wells & D. Biegel (Eds.), *Family preservation services: Research and evaluation.* Newbury Park, CA: Sage Press.

Perlman, R. (1975). *Consumers and social services.* New York: John Wiley & Sons.

Phillips, M. H., Shyne, A. W., & Haring, B. L. (1971). *Factors associated with placement decisions in child welfare.* New York: Child Welfare League of America.

Pine, B. A. (1986). Child welfare reform and the political process. *Social Service Review, 60*(3), 339–359.

Polansky, N. A., Chalmers, M. A., Buttenweiser, E., & Williams, D. P. (1981). *Damaged parents: An anatomy of neglect.* Chicago, IL: University of Chicago Press.

Pray, J. E. (1991). Respecting the uniqueness of the individual: Social work practice within a reflective model. *Social Work, 36*(1), 80–85.

Rabin, C., Rosenbaum, H., & Sens, M. (1982). Home-based marital therapy for multiproblem families. *Journal of Marital and Family Therapy, 8*(4), 451–461.

Ramsey, E., Patterson, G. R., & Walker, H. M. (1990). Generalization of the antisocial trait from home to school settings. *Journal of Applied Developmental Psychology, 11*(2), 209–223.

Rapp, C. A., & Poertner, J. (1987). Moving clients center stage through the use of client outcomes. In R. J. Patti, J. Poertner, and C. A. Rapp (Eds.), *Managing for services effectiveness in social welfare organizations.* (Special issue of *Administration in Social Work, 11*(3–4), 23–38).

Red Horse, J. G. (1980). American Indian elders: Unifiers of Indian families. *Social Casework, 61,* 490–493.

Rehr, H. (Ed.) (1989). *Using client satisfaction as an indication of effectiveness: A brief review.* In B. S. Vourlekis, & C. G. Leukefeld (Eds.), *Making our case—A resource of selected materials for social workers in health care.* Silver Spring, MD: National Association of Social Workers.

Rehr, H., & Berkman, B. (1979). Patient care evaluation. In H. Rehr (Ed.), *Professional accountability for social work practice* (pp. 92–110). New York: Prodist.

Reid, W. J., Kagan, R. M., & Schlosberg, S. B. (1988). Prevention of placement: Critical factors in program success. *Child Welfare, 67*(1), 23–36.

Rodick, J. D., Henggelaer, S. W., & Hanson, C. L. (1986). An evaluation of the family adaptability and cohesion evaluation scales and the circumplex model. *Journal of Abnormal Child Psychology, 14,* 77–87.

Rosenberg, S. A., McTate, G. A., & Robinson, C. C. (1982). *Intensive services to families-at-risk project.* Unpublished manuscript, Nebraska Department of Public Welfare, & University of Nebraska Medical Center, Omaha.

Rosenthal, J. A., & Glass, G. V. (1986). Impacts of alternatives to out-of-home placement: A quasi-experimental study. *Children and Youth Services Review, 8,* 305–321.

Rossi, P. H., & Freeman, H. E. (1989). *Evaluation: A systematic approach* (4th ed.). Newbury Park, CA: Sage.

Rzepnicki, T. L. (1987). Recidivism of foster children returned to their own homes: A review and new directions for research. *Social Service Review, 61*(1), 56–70.

Rzepnicki, T. L., Shuerman, J. R., & Littell, J. H., (1991). Issues in evaluating intensive family preservation services. In E. M. Tracy, D. A. Haapala, J. M. Kinney, & P. J. Pecora, (Eds.). *Intensive family preservation services: An instructional sourcebook.* Cleveland, OH: Case Western Reserve University, Mandel School of Applied Social Sciences.

Schram, D. D., McKelvy, J. G., Schneider, A. L., & Griswold, D. B. (1981). *Preliminary findings: Assessment of the juvenile justice code.* Urban Policy research and Institute of Policy Analysis (National Institute of Juvenile Justice and Delinquency Prevention, Grant No. 79-JN-AX-0028). No address.

Schwartz, L. M., & AuClaire, P., (1991). Intensive home-based service as an alternative to out-of-home placement. The Hennepin County experience. In D. E. Biegal and K. Wells (Eds.), *Family preservation services: Research and evaluation.* Newbury Park, CA: Sage.

Schweinhart, L. J., Weikart, D. P., & Larner, M. B. (1986). Consequences of three preschool curriculum models through age 15. *Early Childhood Research Quarterly, 1,* 15–45.

Seaberg, J. R. (1988). Child well-being scales: A critique. *Social Work Research and Abstracts, 24*(3), 9–15.

Seaberg, J. R. (1990). Child well-being: A feasible concept? *Social Work, 35*(3), 267–272.

Seltzer, M. M., & Bloksberg, L. M. (1987). Permanency planning and its effects on foster children: A review of the literature. *Social Work, 32*(1), 65–68.

Settles, B. H., Culley, J. D., & Van Name, J. B. (1976). *How to measure the cost of foster family care.* Washington, D.C.: U.S. Department of Health, Education, and Welfare, Office of Human Development Services (DHEW Publication No. 78-30126).

Shapiro, D. (1976). *Agencies and foster children.* New York: Columbia University Press.

Sherman, E. A., Phillips, M. H., Haring, B. A., & Shyne, A. W. (1973). *Service to children in their own homes: Its nature and outcome.* New York: Child Welfare League of America.

Sherraden, M. W. (1986). Benefit-cost analysis as a net present value problem. *Administration in Social Work, 10*(3), 85–97.

Showell, W., & White, J. (1990). In-home and office intensive family services. *Prevention Report,* (Spring), 6, 10. Oakdale, IA: The University of Iowa, School of Social Work, National Resource Center on Family Based Services.

Shyne, A. (1976). Evaluation in child welfare. *Child Welfare, 55*(1), 5–18.

Shyne, A. W., Sherman, E. A., & Phillips, M. H. (1972). Filling a gap in child welfare research: Services to children in their own homes. *Child Welfare, 51*(9), 562–573.

Slonim-Nevo, V., & Clark, V. A. (1989). An illustration of survival analysis: Factors affecting contraceptive discontinuation among American teenagers. *Social Work Research and Abstracts, 25*(2), 7–14.

Smith, L. L. (1986). A crisis intervention model. *Emotional First Aid, 3*(1), 9–17.

Solomon, B. B. (1985). Assessment, service & black families. In S. S. Gray, A. Hartman, & E. S. Saalberg (Eds.), *Empowering the black family: A roundtable discussion with Ann Hartman, James Leigh, Jacquelynn Moffett, Elaine Pinderhughes, Barbara Solomon, and Carol Stack,* (pp. 9–20). Ann Arbor, MI: The University of Michigan, School of Social Work, National Child Welfare Training Center.

Spaid, W. M. (1988). *An assessment of family variables as they relate to child placement outcomes in family-based services.* Unpublished doctoral dissertation, University of Utah, Graduate School of Social Work, Salt Lake City.

Stack, C. (1974). *All our kin: Strategies for survival in a black community.* New York: Harper & Row.

Stehno, S. H. (1982). Differential treatment of minority children in service systems. *Social Work, 27,* 39–46.

Stein, T. J. (1985). Projects to prevent out-of-home placement. *Children and Youth Services Review, 7*(2/3), 109–122.

Stein, T. J., & Rzepnicki, T. L. (1983). *Decisionmaking at child welfare intake: A handbook for practitioners.* Washington, D.C.: Child Welfare League of America.

Stein, T. J., & Rzepnicki, T. L. (1984). *Decisionmaking in child welfare services: Intake and planning*. Boston: Kluwer-Nijhoff.

Stephens, D. (1979). In-home family support services: An ecological systems approach. In S. Maybanks & M. Bryce (Eds.), *Home-based services for children and families: Policy, practice, and research*. Springfield, IL: Charles C. Thomas.

Stroul, B. (1988). *Series on community-based services for children and adolescents who are severely emotionally disturbed. Home-based services* (Vol. I). Washington, D.C.: Georgetown University Child Development Center.

Sudman, S., & Bradburn, N. M. (1974). *Response effects in surveys: A review and synthesis*. Chicago, IL: Aldine.

Sue, S. (1977). Community mental health services to minority groups: Some optimism, some pessimism. *American Psychologist, 32*, 616–624.

Sullivan, M., Spasser, M., & Penner, G. L. (1977). *Bowen Center project for abused and neglected children: Report of a demonstration in protective services*. Washington, D.C.: U.S. Department of Health, Education, and Welfare.

Szykula, S. A., & Fleischman, M. J. (1985). Reducing out-of-home placements of abused children: Two controlled field studies. *Child Abuse and Neglect, 9*(2), 277–283.

Tardy, C. (1985). Social support measurement. *American Journal of Community Psychology, 13*(2), 187–202.

Tatara, T., Morgan, H., & Portner, H. (1986). SCAN: Providing preventive services in an urban setting. *Children Today, 15*(6), 17–22.

Tavantzis, T. N., Tavantzis, M., Brown, L. G., & Rohrbaugh, M. (1985). Home-based structural family therapy for delinquents at risk of placement. In M. P. Mirkin & S. L. Koman (Eds.), *Handbook of Adolescents and Family Therapy* (pp. 69–88). New York: Gardner Press.

Teare, R. J. (1987). *Validating social work credentials for human service jobs: Report of a demonstration*. Silver Spring, MD: National Association of Social Workers.

Tracy, E. M. (1990). Identifying social support resources of at-risk families. *Social Work, 35*(3), 252–258.

Tracy, E. M. (1991). Defining the target population for intensive family preservation services: Some conceptual issues. In K. Wells & D. E. Biegel (Eds.), *Family preservation services: Research and evaluation*. Newbury Park, CA: Sage.

Tracy, E., Haapala, D. A., Kinney, J. M., & Pecora, P. J. (Eds.). (1991). *Intensive family preservation services: An instructional sourcebook*. Cleveland, OH: Case Western Reserve University, Mandel School of Applied Social Science.

Tracy, E. M., & Whittaker, J. K. (1987). The evidence base for social support interventions in child and family practice: Emerging issues for research and practice. *Child and Youth Services Review, 9*, 249–270.

Van Meter, M. J. S. (1986). An alternative to foster care for victims of child abuse/neglect: A university-based program. *Child Abuse and Neglect, 10*(1), 79–84.

Videka-Sherman, L. (1985). *Harriet M. Bartlett practice effectiveness project*. Silver Springs, MD: National Association of Social Workers.

Wahler, R. G. (1980). The insular mother: Her problems in parent-child treatment. *Journal of Applied Behavioral Analysis, 13*, 207–219.

Wahler, R. G., & Dumas, J. E. (1989). Attentional problems in dysfunctional mother-child interactions: An interbehavioral model. *Psychological Bulletin, 105*(1), 116–130.

Wahler, R. G., & Afton, A. D. (1980). Attentional processes in insular and non-insular families, *Child Behavior Therapy*, *13*, 207–219.

Wahler, R. G., Leske, G., & Rogers, E. S. (1979). The insular family: A deviance support system for oppositional children. In L. A. Hammerlynck (Ed.), *Behavioral systems for the developmentally disabled: School and family environments* (pp. 102–127). New York: Brunner/Mazel.

Wald, M. S., & Woolverton, M. (1990). Risk assessment: The emperor's new clothes? *Child Welfare*, *69*(6), 483–511.

Wald, M. S. (1988). Family preservation: Are we moving too fast? *Public Welfare*, *46* (3), 33–38, 46.

Wald, M. S., Carlsmith, J. M., & Leiderman, P. H. (1988). *Protecting abused and neglected children*. Stanford, CA: Stanford University Press.

Ware, T., et al. (1981). *Intensive supportive services to minimize foster care placements: Final report*. Richmond, VA: Commonwealth of Virginia, Department of Welfare.

Wasik, B. H., Bryant, D. M., & Lyons, C. M. (1990). *Home visiting: Procedures for helping families*. Newbury Park, CA: Sage.

Wells, K., & Biegel, D. E. (Eds.) (1991). *Family preservation services: Research and Evaluation*. Newbury Park, CA: Sage Publications.

Wells, K. C., & Egan, J. (1984). Behavioral and structural family therapy for oppositional behavior disorder: A comparative treatment outcome study. Paper presented at the Annual Meeting of the American Academy of Child Psychiatry, Toronto, Canada.

White, K. R. (1988). Cost analyses in family support programs. In H. B. Weiss & F. C. Jacobs (Eds.), *Evaluating family programs* (pp. 429–443). New York: Aldine de Gruyter.

White, S. H., et al. (1973). *Federal programs for young children: Review and recommendations* (three vols.). Washington, D.C.: U.S. Department of Health, Education and Welfare.

Whittaker, J. K., & Garbarino, J. A. (1985). *Social support networks*. Hawthorne, NY: Aldine de Gruyter.

Whittaker, J. K., & Maluccio, A. N. (1988). Understanding families in trouble in foster and residential care. In F. Cox, C. Chilman, & E. Nunnally (Eds.), *Families in trouble* (Vol. 5: Variant family forms). Newbury Park, CA: Sage.

Whittaker, J. K., Kinney, J. M., Tracy, E. M., & Booth, C. (1990). *Reaching high-risk families: Intensive family preservation in the human services*. Hawthorne, NY: Aldine de Gruyter.

Whittaker, J. K., Tracy, E. M., & Marckworth, M. (1989). *Family support project: Identifying informal support resources for high risk families*. Seattle, WA: Federal Way, WA: Behavioral Sciences Institute.

Willems, D. M., & DeRubeis, R. (1981). *The effectiveness of intensive preventive services for families with abused, neglected or disturbed children*. Trenton, NJ: Bureau of Research, New Jersey Division of Youth and Family Services.

Wood, K. M., & Geismar, L. L. (1989). *Families at risk: Treating the multiproblem family*. New York: Human Sciences Press.

Wood, S., Barton, K., & Schroeder, C. (1988). In-home treatment of abusive families: Cost and replacement at one year. *Psychotherapy*, *25*(3), 409–414.

Wooden, K. (1976). *Weeping in the playtime of others.* New York: McGraw-Hill.
Yale Bush Center in Child Development and Social Policy, and Family Resource Coalition (1983). *Programs to strengthen families: A resource guide.* Chicago, IL: The Family Resource Coalition.
Young, D. W., & Allen, B. (1977). Benefit-cost analysis in the social services: The example of adoption reimbursement. *Social Service Review, 51*(2), 249–264.
Yuan, Y. T., & Rivest, M. (Eds.) (1990). *Evaluation resources for family preservation services.* Newbury Park, CA: Sage.
Yuan, Y. T., McDonald, W. R., Alderson, J., & Struckman-Johnson, D. (1988). *Evaluation of AB1562 demonstration projects: Year two interim report.* Sacramento, CA: Walter R. McDonald & Associates.
Yuan, Y. T., McDonald, W. R., Wheeler, C. E., Struckman-Johnson, D., & Rivest, M. (1990). *Evaluation of AB1562 in-home care demonstration projects* (Vol. 1: Final report). Sacramento, CA: Walter R. McDonald & Associates.

Index